WITHDRAWN

DATE DUE

PRINTED IN U.S.A.

Mountains on the Market

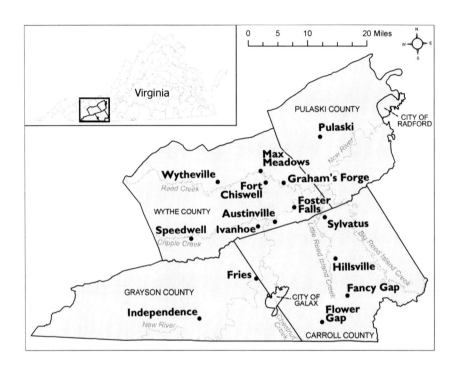

Mountains on the Market

Industry, the Environment, and the South

Randal L. Hall

UNIVERSITY PRESS OF KENTUCKY

Scholarly publisher for the Commonwealth,
serving Bellarmine University, Berea College, Centre
College of Kentucky, Eastern Kentucky University,
The Filson Historical Society, Georgetown College,
Kentucky Historical Society, Kentucky State University,
Morehead State University, Murray State University,
Northern Kentucky University, Transylvania University,
University of Kentucky, University of Louisville,
and Western Kentucky University.
All rights reserved.

Editorial and Sales Offices: The University Press of Kentucky
663 South Limestone Street, Lexington, Kentucky 40508-4008
www.kentuckypress.com

Frontispiece: Upper New River valley, Virginia
(GIS/Data Center, Fondren Library, Rice University)

16 15 14 13 12   1 2 3 4 5

Library of Congress Cataloging-in-Publication Data

Hall, Randal L., 1971–
Mountains on the market : industry, the environment, and the South / Randal L. Hall.
    p. cm. — (New directions in Southern history)
Includes bibliographical references and index.
ISBN 978-0-8131-3624-0 (hbk. : alk. paper) — ISBN 978-0-8131-3649-3 (pdf) —
    ISBN 978-0-8131-4046-9 (epub)
1. Industrialization—New River Valley (N.C.-W. Va.)—History.
2. Natural resources—New River Valley (N.C.-W. Va.)—History.
3. New River Valley (N.C.-W. Va.)—Economic conditions.
4. New River Valley (N.C.-W. Va.)—Commerce—History. I. Title.
    √ HC107.A127.H35 2012
    330.9754'7—dc23
                        2012008339

This book is printed on acid-free paper meeting
the requirements of the American National Standard
for Permanence in Paper for Printed Library Materials.

Manufactured in the United States of America.

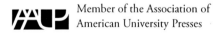

Member of the Association of
American University Presses

To Jim Barefield, for commending to me verbs,
Henry Adams, and a sense of the ridiculous

Contents

Illustrations follow page 140

Introduction

Here again, the very earth cries out beseechingly, for a way to market.
—S. F. C., "A Ramble in Southwestern Virginia" (1849)

Thomas Jefferson bears much responsibility for the longtime idealism about agrarian life in the United States, but he also revealed a deep faith in the power of industry and commerce. "All the world is becoming commercial," he informed George Washington in March 1784. "Our citizens have had too full a taste of the comforts furnished by the arts & manufactures to be debarred the use of them."[1]

Representing Virginia in Congress, Jefferson was negotiating his home state's cession of its western territories to the young United States. He had definite ideas about where Virginia's western boundary should fall—the state should extend "to the meridian of the mouth of the great Kanhaway" River. He listed several reasons. First he put forth, "That within that are our lead mines." Next he explained, "This river rising in N. Carola traverses our whole latitude and offers to every part of it a channel for navigation & commerce to the Western Country." But the river would make deep demands on state resources: "It is a channel which can not be opened but at immense expense and with every facility which an absolute power over both shores will give."[2]

Jefferson had identified two issues—mineral resources and infrastructure needs—that preoccupied market-oriented residents of western Virginia's mountains for the subsequent two centuries. The lead mines he mentioned abut the Blue Ridge Mountains along the New River, the name given the upper reaches of the Kanawha. The New River rises as two forks in Ashe County, North Carolina, along that state's northern border. The branches combine and flow toward the northwest, eventually uniting with the Gauley River to form what we now know as the Kanawha. The New River's path through mineral-rich Virginia lands presented not only a great opportunity for commerce, but also a great challenge because of the area's isolation and the need to transport bulky minerals to more densely populated areas.

Industry grew slowly in early Virginia. The Northeast and then areas of the Midwest pushed the United States to the forefront of industrialized nations in the early nineteenth century, but the South lagged somewhat behind. The region developed industrial capacity ahead of most nations, but several factors explain the southern states' poor showing relative to the parts of the United States that surged to world industrial leadership. Slave owners operating profitable plantations shaped much of the southern economy and regional politics; they benefited by buying manufactured items made elsewhere while keeping their focus on commercial crops. Their concentrated wealth and slaves' lack of purchasing power stunted home markets, and the growing of lucrative staple crops dispersed the population because comparatively poor soils mandated large amounts of land for each plantation. The region thus did not have the large cities and broad consumer demand that catalyzed industry in the Northeast and Midwest. Canals and railroads often lost money because they had to meander far to reach nodes of customers. And the Appalachian Mountains ranked as the spot perhaps least hospitable to early industrialization owing to the inherent difficulty of transportation across the rugged terrain.

Despite these obstacles, entrepreneurs in the South developed a variety of industries. Railroads coursed through several parts of the region by the end of the 1850s, and the manufacturing of textiles and cotton gins as well as the mining and processing of iron and copper ore, coal, and phosphates commenced before the Civil War. And as Jefferson had expected, extractive industries took hold even along the New River in the Appalachian Mountains.

The lead mines lay in present-day Wythe County, Virginia. Wythe County (formed in 1790), Grayson County (taken from Wythe in 1793), and Carroll County (carved largely from Grayson in 1842) make up a substantial section of Virginia's Blue Ridge Plateau and New River valley near the border with North Carolina. Lead was identified there in the 1750s, and miners worked the deposits by about 1761. In *Notes on the State of Virginia*, Jefferson also pointed out a second valuable mineral in this same highland spot: "we are told of iron mines . . . on Chestnut creek, a branch of the Great Kanhaway, near where it crosses the Carolina line."[3] By the 1780s, charcoal furnaces and forges were producing iron in the area, with a predominantly enslaved workforce, and over time iron challenged lead for precedence. In the 1850s, a third mineral garnered national attention: Carroll County played host to a boom in copper mining and smelting. Following the Civil War, zinc rose in importance as well, and industrial plants in neighboring Pulaski County (cut from Wythe and Montgomery counties in 1839) began to process both zinc and iron ore.

This book delves into the exploitation of natural resources along the upper New River over a 250-year period. Entrepreneurs and both local and northern corporations looked to extract and refine the valuable ores waiting beneath this predominantly agrarian landscape.[4] Jefferson's remarks reveal that the state and federal governments, in particular the military, also tracked and pushed the development of mining there. As governor of Virginia in 1780, Jefferson himself dispatched troops to guard the lead mines against a rumored Loyalist uprising during the Revolutionary War, and military needs likewise dictated the mines' fate during the Civil War. Government geologists continued to map and observe the area into the Cold War era. Natural resources became national resources. Entrepreneurs often drew on the state and national governments' expertise—for instance, by relying on the findings of the antebellum state geological survey and, following the Civil War, by using the U.S. Army Corps of Engineers to improve commercial navigation on the river. Other geologists acted as paid, private consultants to mining firms. Advocates of industrialization, hoping to boost the region's economy and image after the Civil War, had much to say about the area's prospects. Networks of geologists passed along scientific data, and families and clusters of local investors refined and bequeathed knowledge of the mining business. The expansion of railroads brought the area further into the industrial mainstream. As the nineteenth century neared its end, the New River flowed past enterprises ever more thoroughly incorporated into the national economic web.

In short, from the colonial period through the twentieth century, capitalists—backed by the power of the state and boosted periodically by wartime needs—engaged in a search for profits among the ancient rocks of the Blue Ridge. The story along the New River captures America's history in microcosm. Leading white people displaced the Native Americans through war and diplomacy, won and kept political control, made the fewest concessions required to hold back the unrest of workers both slave and free, utilized land and resources individually and corporately, and did so ever more efficiently by applying science and technology with little regard for the environment. And as the twentieth century waned, many types of industry moved elsewhere, leaving land and labor alike to adjust to a consumer-driven service economy.

These businesses existed in a largely rural setting, and, except in a few instances, they did not occupy the forefront of industrial innovation or prove crucial to the national economy. But the value of studying industrial development along the New River lies in understanding, for a comparatively isolated spot, the continuity of entrepreneurial values across regions and time, the coexistence of agriculture and industry, the flexibility of slave and free workforces, the growth over time of business and industrial expertise within families and small-scale networks, the persistent importance of scientific geological investigation, and the ways that improved transportation gave remote industrialists a chance to join more fully the broader American economy. Investigating industry and internal improvements uncovers an economic and social web that included attorneys, engineers, mine owners, merchants, government employees, and managers. They worked hard as leaders of this region, aiming for their own profit as they simultaneously developed businesses, roads, and other institutions important to the community.

As economic historians have pointed out, intense exploitation of the sheer abundance of nature's materials, some formed over eons, helped bring the United States to global leadership.[5] That exploitation, however, left lasting scars on the landscape. Geological time met the rather more urgent drive for profit.

Explaining the Hinterland

The 250-year analytical arc presented in this book has potential importance to professional historians even though any such long-term analysis, told with context and specificity, tends to bring into question the very idea of southern history. Historians have in two ways undermined easy claims of southern distinctiveness. First, a growing number of studies have fleshed out the variety of economic, social, and political institutions and viewpoints below the Mason-Dixon Line, resulting in a quite diverse lineup showcasing subregional particularity. Works by David Brown and Victoria Bynum on antebellum southern dissenters and by David Stricklin on twentieth-century Baptist radicals come to mind as recent notable examples.[6] Second and tugging in the opposite direction, much new work links the South to unifying national and global processes, laying out how southerners fit broader patterns. On this line of thought, one can look first to scholars who situate the southern mainland colonies and the antebellum South in the Atlantic world and then, for more recent times, to Matthew D. Lassiter and Joseph Crespino's edited collection *The Myth of Southern Exceptionalism.*[7] The local and the global stretch the regional into an ever-wispier midpoint of a strand of taffy. In this book, I take part in both intellectual movements—I write as both a splitter and a lumper, if you will—yet without surrendering the idea of the South that clings together in the sticky middle.

This book ties Virginia to capitalist development and environmental exploitation from colonial times to the present.[8] From radically different starting points, Peter A. Coclanis, Walter Johnson, Lorena S. Walsh, and William Scarborough have concluded that profit seeking and market relations in fact largely shaped the South from the beginning of the settler colonies there.[9] And where an older generation of historians used antebellum southern industrial activity primarily to talk about the limits and possibilities of slavery and slave life, a new generation of scholars such as Bess Beatty, Aaron W. Marrs, Laura Croghan Kamoie, and Tom Downey has put together a fuller analysis of early southern industry and infrastructure. Without ignoring the importance of slavery, they explore southerners' willingness to support even the most cutting-edge pursuits anywhere profits seemed feasible.[10]

Perhaps influenced by the intensity of market forces in our own time, this book joins that latter group, and the findings tear at once widely assumed distinctions between South and North. Historians wielding a capitalist South have less of a claim to a uniquely southern history but in turn can contribute to a more robust understanding of wider developments. I use the capitalists of the New River valley to underscore the diversity even within a single "southern" state, but I also want to emphasize that planter and industrialist, mine worker and railroad investor, North and South, shared the evolving capitalist framework with other parts of the world. Here, we will gaze at broad vistas while digging deep into details of earth and enterprise. Taken to extremes, of course, community and individual specificity joined with global context might disrupt all ideas of the "South," turning that descriptor into a purely geographic rather than analytical term.[11] Southern history written in this way teeters just this side of dissolution and fragmentation; it threatens, on the one hand, to fly apart into general American history or transnational history if the context grows any larger and, on the other hand, to whittle itself into individual fragmentation if the details go any deeper, chipping away any hope that the historian can discern patterns among the shavings.

A humbled yet richer version of southern history results. More attuned to local specifics and simultaneously to national and international outlines, this southern history eschews sweeping generalizations in favor of seeking out the shades and subtleties that mark the region as distinct, even as it makes up a few strokes of a more encompassing history. Toward that end, I work not only to strengthen our understanding of the southern economy but also to add a sharper awareness of entrepreneurs' implicit environmental attitudes, the environmental limitations, and changes over time, thus building on pioneering works in the burgeoning field of environmental history.[12]

In chapters 1 and 2, the remoteness of the New River valley demonstrates the typical early republic and antebellum southern quandary of developing land that cannot support a dense population, a dilemma previously analyzed in two limpid books by John Majewski.[13] Whereas northern and upper mid-Atlantic coastal cities had richly endowed, accessible hinterlands, most southern cities did not. In the struggle of leading New River valley residents to assemble a labor force and to get goods to faraway markets, we see the consequences of the South's lack of major cities.

The first chapter, covering the eighteenth century, also highlights the role of the state in supporting the entrepreneurial work of elite men. It takes back to the late colonial era Scarborough's findings that in the antebellum period the richest men of the South invested widely beyond the plantation hedges. After the Peace of Paris, the investment patterns shifted slightly: local gentry joined elite eastern Virginians and well-connected northerners in pushing new ventures. Together, they developed communities and businesses that made these remote mountains look much like other contemporary regions of the inland United States.

In parsing the mix of coerced and free labor utilized by the New River industries in their early years, chapter 1 also builds on the findings of John Bezís-Selfa and Thomas M. Doerflinger, who studied areas farther north in Virginia, Maryland, and New Jersey. The mines and furnaces embodied a flexible, pragmatic capitalism in its infancy, nurtured by state entanglement in private initiative.[14] Another recent subcurrent in writings on the Revolutionary War and the early national era analyzes the conflict that tore at the colonies from within, forcing the gentry to battle back, yet to make some concessions in order to maintain control. Albert H. Tillson Jr. and Michael A. McDonnell, among others, have pushed this argument.[15] In the New River valley, such stark conflict embroiled the eclectic workforce assembled at the lead mines; well-connected wealthy men still controlled the mines after the revolution, but they had to tolerate and deal with their foes among the workers.

Workers along the New River likewise reflected local specifics and wider trends. Drawing a detailed picture of one small place has its limitations because eighteenth- and nineteenth-century workers left few records. The records that do survive, though, reveal consistent, low-level conflict that employers and slave owners had to manage. By all indications, they managed quite well. A generation of scholars who have witnessed capitalist development in Russia and China since 1989 have no trouble imagining that free markets and repression went hand in hand in the early American republic. I can only hint at the workers' perspective, and their picture thus must remain fuzzy until the narrative reaches the twentieth century, with its more copious record keeping. The earlier exchanges that I can document, though, add to Seth Rockman's findings for Baltimore that the limited assertiveness of both slave and free workers took place within often suffocating constraints imposed by the early national and antebellum capitalists in the upper South.[16] Racism, ethnic differences, and skill level divided the workers in the New River valley, adding to their inability to challenge their industrial taskmasters.

Chapter 2 traces economic development along the New River during the first half of the nineteenth century. Business historians have identified those decades as the dynamic time when a corporate capitalist order began to mature. Family businesses evolved into more complex corporations, and the rich resources of the United States allowed a wide variety of people to become entrepreneurs in spite of periodic economic downturns. Because of an understandable focus on plantations and slavery, southern historians until recently have neglected to take an appropriately detailed look at how southerners encouraged and sometimes impeded corporate development. Sean Patrick Adams's work, though, has argued that eastern Virginia planters did grow to accept corporate structures and a role for the state, but, owing to their urge to protect profitable investments in slaves and plantations, they fashioned the laws in ways rather less conducive to rapid growth than in Pennsylvania.[17] In this chapter, the struggles among the families owning the lead mines give ground-level insight into how corporate forms could benefit southern industry. These Virginians had little difficulty gaining corporate charters from the legislature whenever they felt the situation warranted it, raising some question as to how widely scholars can apply Adams's point that the state's corporate laws hindered development.

In addition to complicating existing debates, studying the New River valley opens up new lines of inquiry. For instance, antebellum engineers and scientists have garnered only the most sporadic investigation by southern historians, yet these emerging professionals contributed in vital ways to economic growth and the internal improvements movement that reshaped residents' interactions with the mountain landscape. Chapter 2 captures their role in the infrastructural projects advanced by lawyers, merchants, land speculators, and mine owners. John Lauritz Larson, in the most important recent analysis of the internal improvement movement in the early republic, constructs a thesis-driven brief for central planning that foreshadows the Civil War and the Gilded Age. He emphasizes southern intransigence as blocking national initiatives, and my findings here indeed echo his conclusion that state and local interests and private initiative took precedence. However, beginning in the 1840s, the resulting railroad and turnpikes in the New River valley functioned more effectively than Larson's thesis intimates they should have. The enthusiasm that mine and furnace owners and their likeminded investors in Wythe and Carroll counties had for these projects, as well as the way these men worked with and within state and local governments to get resources instead, backs up John Majewski's conclusions that southern supporters of market development, with the aid of government and in spite of local fights for economic advantage, made considerable progress toward their goals before the Civil War.[18] They overcame many of the limitations imposed by their mountain environment.

With a detailed look at a copper-mining boom, chapter 2 also demonstrates the ease with which antebellum capital near and far scurried to seemingly profitable opportunities. The dispersed mix of politicians, doctors, lawyers, experienced mine owners, merchants, and others who poured money into this endeavor shows just the sort of outlook that the Confederate economy more effectively relied on. As hope for compromise on slavery disappeared, most white New River valley residents rallied to the cause of the Confederacy. Historians such as Majewski and Chad Morgan have explained how the Confederacy turned to and essentially took control of the industrial capacity already developed in places such as Wythe County.[19]

At long last, too, historians have begun to use time frames that span the Civil War, which has far too often served as a convenient but artificial divide. When studying the economic realm, reaching across those war-worn years makes a difference. Scholars such as Jonathan Daniel Wells, Peter S. Carmichael, and Bruce W. Eelman have argued that boosterist rhetoric and openness to industry in the South predated the conflict, as did the growth of demographic categories such as teachers, merchants, and journalists. On these interpretations, we agree. But whereas Wells posits growing southern middle-class cohesion and self-identification during the 1850s, I have found little such identity among that group along the New River. The area's 1851 slave outburst, discussed in chapter 3, brought most whites together across classes as the state stumbled toward secession, a process similar to the dynamics that William A. Link has shown molding opinion in the bulk of Virginia in the final antebellum decade.[20]

The prewar southern openness to economic diversification means that ideas of a "New South," long ago made popular among scholars by C. Vann Woodward, should keep on dissipating in favor of more complex interpretations: the enduring postwar power of many of the same individuals and families who had underwritten the New River valley's antebellum spurt of development supports this view. During the war, some of the New River valley's industrialists continued to prosper, and, emerging from the conflict, the region's leaders welcomed outside capital just as they and their fathers had before the war. The centralization of capital markets in northeastern cities made national investment in southern opportunities more efficient and frequent. Even before the war, free workers toiled alongside slaves, and after Appomattox, with exclusively wage labor at work, the sharpest distinction between North and South faded.[21]

Chapters 4 and 5, on the late nineteenth and twentieth centuries, unearth a different kind of southernness. The region might seemingly have disappeared into a national mainstream as local entrepreneurs reached out and welcomed full-scale Wall Street finance, which thereafter controlled industrial development in the New River valley. But explaining the terms on which the southerners took part in the evolving national economy requires a complex balancing act. Woodward's image of the South of the time as having a "colonial" economy—in which the terms of transactions benefited southerners minimally—overstates the case a bit, but perhaps not by too much. Extractive industries in particular lend themselves to such an interpretation, as lumber and lightly processed lead and zinc, for instance, were ripped from the land and put on northbound rails to become more profitable final products. Yet the presence of southerners among the investors and leaders of the companies even after the surge of outside capital undermines too hasty generalizations, as does the production along the New River of somewhat more advanced products such as sulfuric acid and textiles. Similarly, abandoned textile mills now seem a particularly southern result of chasing smokestacks and branch plants, yet recent work reminds historians that the free flow of capital caused the same problem in late-nineteenth- and early-twentieth-century New England and will surely go on producing similar results as comparative advantage ebbs and flows in other parts of the world labor market.[22] That the South's abundant labor and low wages allowed its late-nineteenth-century industry to expand in the way it did reflects changing market conditions, not a tectonic shift in regional values.

Few scholars have taken seriously companies' early-twentieth-century attempts to use welfare capitalism to bond employees to the workplace: academics have too readily dismissed welfare capitalism as only an empty ploy to stymie unionization. In certain settings, though, the ploy had some positive effects, and in chapter 5 I explore workers' responses to such efforts. Most studies of post–New Deal unions likewise tell of brief triumph followed by declension, implicitly dismissing labor unions' relatively peaceful years of the 1950s and 1960s as a time in which workers gained little. However, I join historians such as Jennifer Klein in taking seriously the gains in employee benefits that marked the period.[23] The overall productivity growth in the U.S. economy lifted living standards, even for nonunionized workers deep in the mountains. These standards may have trailed the affluence in many parts of the developed world, but the postwar era left both good and bad in its wake.

The concluding chapter also completes a cycle of sorts with the story of deindustrialization along the New River in the face of globalization, a topic more often studied in northern cities. In the Virginia towns of Ivanhoe and Fries and Galax and Austinville, we find the Americans for whom globalization has to a considerable extent meant loss. Michael Dennis, Timothy J. Minchin, and a few others have touched on deindustrialization in the South, but it deserves more analysis; it may apply to more southern sites over time (or may not, given rising real costs in developing nations).[24] The rise of service industries and Virginians' subsequent turn to cultural resources to spur tourism again puts them in company with some other parts of the developed world, even though the revamped economy can hardly take a more southern form than relying on Appalachian scenery and hill-billy music to attract paying visitors.[25] Cool air and pleasing vistas underlie nature as a new kind of resource.

The new tourism in many regions of the United States could not have taken place without a rejuvenation of the landscape enabled by the wrenching decline of older types of agriculture and industry. From their earliest arrival in the region, white people embraced images of inexhaustibility when discussing resources along the New River (and on much of the continent, for that matter), with severe damage to the land being the predictable result. Yet centuries of environmental degradation may have now reversed course, though often in carefully managed parks, national forests, and industrial forests. Thomas D. Clark helped pioneer this line of investigation decades ago, but historians have only inched toward adequately exploring it.[26]

In this book, I engage these intellectual debates, large and small, by crafting an analytical narrative. Historians have moved beyond asking *whether* a market economy took root in the South to showing *how* people in the region, from colonial times forward, shaped their lives in response to their environmental setting and a mix of global, national, regional, and local opportunities and changes. Geology made possible certain activities along the New River that other southerners could not achieve, but, conversely, the climate of the Appalachians also blocked the growing of the staple crops that marked other large southern subregions, and the topography slowed transportation improvements. Enterprising southerners, however, shared—with each other and with other Americans—an ability to muster capital from a variety of investors; a keen awareness of how international and national events affected their local ventures; an amoral willingness to assemble and manage a labor force using all available means; an eagerness, fostered by steady improvements in communication, to adopt new technologies when appropriate, whatever the damage to the environment; and the power to change their business course when profits dried up, whatever the damage to communities. Laying out the story over two and a half centuries captures the price Americans have paid for the country's economic strength.

Like other rural areas, North and South, East and West, the upper New River valley from the beginning of European settlement has served in large measure as a hinterland in a complicated capitalist hierarchy. The wielders of capital lived in England and Tidewater Virginia at first, but then later in Philadelphia and New York and wherever corporations' stockholders happened to scatter. Historians have worked out with some clarity the processes by which the resources of places such as the Blue Ridge fueled industrial growth and drove American urbanization and economic expansion.[27] But the prospect from the hinterland too often comes across as hazy. This book brings that picture into microscopic focus by dissecting economic and environmental change in one small place. The movement of life here, as in the interior of a cell, shows larger impulses at work.

Chapter 1

Industrial Inroads and Pragmatic Patriots

The Blue Ridge chain provided both a natural and a political barrier for colonial Virginians, but entrepreneurs increasingly breached that wall in the mid-eighteenth century. At the end of the 1750s, leading Virginians saw the potential of the lead deposits on the New River, and they purposefully combined political connections, British mining skills, and slave labor to bring industry into the highlands. Their drive for profit vaulted them over the rocky impediments. During and after the American Revolution, the search for efficient labor and management carried on with a new urgency and enough success to ensure a long-term future for mining and refining on the New River.

The white settlers who came to the Blue Ridge from eastern Virginia brought with them the hierarchies, labor systems, and economic and political assumptions familiar to Tidewater residents. Society along the New River sprang to life as a distant but integrated limb of the British Empire. The lead mines, like many capitalist undertakings, struggled to turn a profit, but investors nevertheless lined up to try their hand. The vigorous economic expansion of the early republic channeled new businessmen and workers into the New River valley, keeping the industrial communities awash in democratizing national currents. But entrepreneurs new and old kept the Blue Ridge economy moored to old faiths about power and the primacy of profit. Economic hierarchy had not vanished with independence, nor had the view, prevalent from whites' arrival, that natural resources existed for the purpose of exploitation regardless of damage to the land.

Founding Virginia's Industry

In the autumn of 1762, John Bartram, an aging Philadelphia naturalist, rambled north from the decade-old Moravian settlements in North Carolina's Piedmont backcountry. Bartram had wandered through many of the colonies, and his collecting of specimens helped his British patrons understand North America's resources. He climbed the Blue Ridge at Flower Gap. That road, near the present border of Carroll and Grayson counties, served as a principal passage into the mountains, where Bartram hoped to find flora new to science.

Accompanying four hunters heading his way, Bartram found those mountains "really very high." The group "followed A run through two of ye ridges but ye third ridge was very high & so steep that ye wagoners when on ye top cuts down A great saplin & fastens ye smaller end to ye tail of ye wagon to hinder it from running too fast down. . . . [M]any hundreds of loads of wood is piled on ye sides of ye road toward ye bottom on each side of ye ridge & great fires is made to consume it out of ye way." Unaware of the even more extensive environmental destruction to come, Bartram observed that this profligate use of timber "scrats ye mountains back & sides finely." Once atop the Blue Ridge, Bartram saw "much middling good land & fine savannas & plentiful streams on these mountains but it's so could & wet & ye snow frequently two foot deep in winter . . . that it must be uncomfortable liveing." Moving across the plateau and descending to the lead mine at the New River took two days: "it rained ye first day but then it cleared up: we set out after Killing A dear & breakfasting on it then rode A good pace till toward night. [O]ne of ye hunters killed 2 dear part of which we ate & left ye rest. [N]ext morning we set out & cleared ye mountain about noon thence had 4 or 5 miles to ye mine."[1] Like these hunters, Indians had long killed deer for commercial exchange, but the industrial work Bartram saw at the mine exploited nature for profit in a much more systematic, intensive way.

A Virginian named John Chiswell had surely encountered the same harsh conditions when traveling in the region in the 1750s, but on one of his treks Chiswell apparently first recognized the mineral wealth there. John Chiswell's father, Charles (born circa 1677), reportedly immigrated to Virginia from Scotland. In the early eighteenth century, he served as clerk of the General Court, and through friendships with such men as Lieutenant Governor Alexander Spotswood, Charles Chiswell became a successful merchant, extensive landowner, and an agent in the slave trade. In the 1720s, on vast acreage granted him in Hanover County, he began mining iron ore and producing pig iron, a business that his friend Spotswood had also entered. Old acquaintance William Byrd of Westover (1674–1744) visited both operations in 1732 and described the elder Chiswell as "a sensible, well-bred man, and very frank in communicating his knowledge in the Mystery of making iron, wherein he has had long Experience." Charles Chiswell acquainted his son with these industrial skills, and when Charles died in 1737, John gained considerable wealth.[2]

The son maintained his father's eminence and carried it westward. John Chiswell established himself as a successful planter and merchant, and he served in the Virginia House of Burgesses in the 1740s and 1750s, representing Hanover County and then Williamsburg, where he moved around 1751. He then reached into the mountains. Since well before the start of the white influx into mid-eighteenth-century southwestern Virginia, the area had lacked a settled Indian presence, though Shawnees, Cherokees, and others crisscrossed the mountains as they hunted and fought. Land speculators such as James Patton, who lived near Staunton in Virginia's Shenandoah Valley, and his brother-in-law John Preston began to file claims along the upper New River and its tributaries in the 1740s, and a few settlers followed, particularly after the Iroquois confederacy, in the 1744 Treaty of Lancaster, agreed with Pennsylvania, Maryland, and Virginia officials to relinquish the Indians' claims to land west of the Blue Ridge. Nonetheless, the region's poorly defined status in the middle of various Indian claims made it home to both conflict and diplomacy in the two decades before the American Revolution. On the frontier of Virginia in 1754, settlers' clashes with Indians intensified. The legislature called on John Chiswell and a small group of other men to raise and distribute relief funds to Euro-American residents there.[3]

Lieutenant Governor Robert Dinwiddie wrote in 1755, "There are also Tin, Lead, and Antimony in several Places near the Great Mount's, and, I doubt not, other rich Minerals; but [for] the want of Persons of Knowledge, and [of] Monied Men, these Discoveries must be Dormant for some Time." Chiswell soon rose to the challenge of developing the resources of upland Virginia. Like many of his contemporaries, he saw the potential for profit in the western lands and wrangled extensive land grants. At some point in his travels, probably in 1759, he found or found out about deposits of lead ore near the banks of the New River in what then was called Augusta County. A British traveler in Virginia in 1759 reported that Chiswell planned "to try for lead upon some hunting grounds belonging to the Indians, towards New River, and the Green Briar; where, it is said, there is fine ore, and in great plenty, lying above ground."[4] Chiswell's ties to prominent

Virginia leaders helped him take advantage of the natural bounty. On May 6, 1760, the governor and the Council of Virginia granted Chiswell a thousand acres "lying on both Sides of the New River, beginning on the South Side, at Humberstone Lyons's lower Corner, and running down the said River." They simultaneously granted John Robinson an adjoining thousand acres "running down the said River."[5]

Settlement had barely begun to reach the upper New River, and Indians still made the white investors uncertain about security. Throughout the winter of 1760–1761, the troops of Colonel William Byrd III (1728–1777) camped only a few miles from the lead veins. Byrd was building a road and a string of forts through southwestern Virginia to facilitate British control of the upper Cherokee towns during the French and Indian War. He fortified a blockhouse at his winter quarters, and by early 1761 Virginians labeled it "Fort Chiswell," presumably named by Byrd to honor his friend. Only a few years later it became a crucial intersection on the Wilderness Road to Kentucky. In July 1761, Byrd referred to the fort as "this our most advanced post" and had 651 troops gathered there preparing to move farther west. Supplies came from the Moravian settlements in the North Carolina backcountry: the Wachovia church leaders recorded in 1761, "We furnished much meal to the troops on New River; 500 men on horseback took it from our mill across the Blue Mountains." That same year, Lieutenant Governor Francis Fauquier appointed Chiswell and Dr. Thomas Walker, a prominent land speculator who operated the Loyal Land Company, to act as Virginia's commissioners to the Cherokees, "to purchase the Prisoners brought in by the Cherokee Indians." Chiswell and Walker journeyed to meet representatives of the Cherokees at Fort Chiswell.[6]

With three powerful partners—Fauquier, Byrd, and Robinson—Chiswell subsequently formed the "Lead Mining Company" to exploit the lead ore. Robinson, Chiswell's son-in-law, served as the Virginia treasurer and Speaker of the House; and Byrd had inherited his family's longtime economic and political power (in July 1757, he had 605 slaves scattered across four estates). Important planters all, they looked to expand the range of their constant pursuit of profit. Fauquier joined them but soon withdrew. Mining began in 1761, but not until February 1762 did Chiswell, Byrd, and Robinson resolve a conflicting land claim with Walker's Loyal Land Company and thus gain unchallenged title to the ample site straddling the New River.[7]

The men who formed the lead company tapped into two long-standing currents of Virginia government. First, like their fathers' generation at the pinnacle of Virginia society, they expected government to serve their personal economic goals. Their forebears had shaped the colony's land policies, tobacco-inspection laws, and slave regulations to suit private needs. The younger men's expectation of secure land titles and military protection of the area simply adapted that tradition to a backcountry industrial endeavor. These men continued another tradition as well: the quest for wealth. They saw the iron industry already producing handsome returns in both domestic and international markets for some investors in Virginia and Maryland; lead, they believed, had the same potential. From the first settlement, Virginia planters had sought financial gain, and they fashioned their crop mix and ancillary investments accordingly, with the physical work always performed by bound laborers.[8] Exploiting the lead deposits simply added a new layer to long-running economic practice. These men did not need Adam Smith's *The Wealth of Nations* for guidance. They and their ancestors had already laid out a pattern that would long endure—raw capitalism, tight-knit economic leadership, and close ties to the government.

In a summary of Virginia's resources, Fauquier described the riskiness of the investment: "There have been Mines both of Copper and Lead discover'd but neither of them work'd, excepting one Mine very rich in Lead lying on a branch of new River in the road to the upper Cherokee Nation. The proprietors of this are now beginning to work it, of which number I was one my self but quitted it on a Doubt whether Lead would bear the Expence of so long a Land Carriage as is necessary to bring it to market."[9] But Chiswell, even more fervent than his energetic peers among Virginia's elite, took the initiative in making the new enterprise pay. Looking for expertise, he went to Bristol, England, in 1762 to have the ore assayed, to buy equipment, and to make arrangements with the merchant house of Joseph Farell and William Jones, the city's leading tobacco importers. While there, Chiswell secured the services of experienced smelter William Herbert and other skilled Welsh workmen, who agreed to bring their expertise from that advanced mining region to the Virginia backcountry. Herbert arrived in June 1763, and by the fall that year wagonloads of lead traveled to the Moravian settlements in North Carolina, probably via Flower Gap, to be exchanged for provisions such as flour. Chiswell and Herbert soon had a furnace in operation to smelt the ore, and in 1764 the company drove black slaves to the mines. For security, the proprietors stored their lead at nearby Fort Chiswell.[10]

The intricate world of transatlantic commerce and credit had brought Herbert and the other specialists to the lead mines. In a lawsuit years later,

Herbert explained that Chiswell had solicited him in Bristol to serve "as a manager or conductor of his . . . works for smelting and refining of ores and metals . . . to which art or mystery your orator had been regularly brought up, and then and long before had exercised" in Great Britain. For decades to come, much of the mining expertise of North America came via a similar path. On April 20, 1763, Herbert agreed to "immediately proceed to the lead mines" with his wife and maidservant; he contracted for an annual salary of £130 for at least seven years, a house "fit for his station," and twenty acres free of rent, as well as the right for three years to choose to return to Bristol at Chiswell's expense. Herbert, "being unacquainted with the sd. John Chiswell and his circumstances," insisted that Chiswell's merchant contacts in Bristol, Joseph Farell and William Jones, guarantee the contract in the event Chiswell defaulted; Herbert knew that Farell and Jones had sufficient property in Virginia to fulfill the agreement. Kinsmen David Herbert the elder and David Herbert the younger negotiated lower salaries (£40 and £50 per year, respectively) but similar guarantees.[11]

Imperial politics, like imperial debts, eddied and flowed around the mines. Both the fort and the mines rested just beyond the Proclamation Line of 1763 and thus lay west of the ground that the British wanted Virginians to develop. Yet the undertaking had already begun to flourish. In fact, British Indian agent John Stuart saw fit to include the lead mines on a 1764 map of the South, even though organized white settlement remained sparse. On Stuart's map, the mines and Dunkard's Bottom—a community established in 1745 a few miles farther downriver—anchored a wide, mostly blank expanse of southwestern Virginia.[12]

William Herbert wrote Byrd in March 1764 to let him know that "the Negros came all safe & well" and to promise to send frequent updates about the mining endeavor. He assured Byrd that he had "seen most mines of note in His Majestys Uropean dominions" and that "there is all the prospect that we can expect" promising that the new mine "will be a good workes in depth." Progress had slowed during the severe winter, though, with the furnace shut down for most of the season. Moreover, "All the people that lives heearabout are laving thayer places" because of the British proclamation. Herbert reported nonetheless that he had had success "in preswading our people to stay" and that he would work hard "to prevent our leaving the mine."[13]

As Herbert expected, the new lead business withstood the king's decree. In 1765, Cherokee leader Attakullakulla (Little Carpenter) left a party of

Cherokees at the mines while he journeyed to Richmond to parley with the governor and the Virginia Council; Chiswell accompanied the native diplomat on the return trip to help protect him from white settlers. On other occasions, John Stuart and Cherokee leaders scheduled meetings to take place at the mines.[14] In October 1768, Stuart negotiated the Treaty of Hard Labor with the Cherokees, gaining additional land concessions from the native inhabitants. Stuart and the Cherokees marked the lead mines as a pivot point on a line that delineated anew an official border with the Indian nations. The colonists immediately violated the treaty.[15]

The lead mines might have grown unchecked but for a series of disasters that the owners brought on themselves. John Robinson's death in 1766 brought to light that as Virginia's treasurer he had failed to destroy redeemed currency notes. In a daring act of capital formation, he had instead distributed the notes as loans to privileged Virginians and their businesses, including more than £8,000 to the mining partnership. His portion of the mines, along with the rest of his estate, had to go toward repaying his debt to the government. The situation thus bound the mining company in a long-term Dickensian legal saga, managed by Edmund Pendleton. To make matters worse, on June 3, 1766, the excitable Chiswell killed a man in a tavern in Cumberland County. The county court indicted Chiswell and, following the usual process, sent him to Williamsburg for trial. The justices in Williamsburg approved his bailment after he was transferred to the capital. Chiswell's release sparked an outcry, and he turned into a symbol of the abuse of power by wealthy, well-connected Virginians. He died, likely by suicide, in Williamsburg on October 15, 1766, before his trial. In 1768, for £2,010, Byrd, the only surviving original partner, bought from Robinson's estate the thirty-six slaves working as miners. But Byrd, a heavy gambler, had already started his own accelerating decline toward insolvency, ending in suicide on January 1, 1777.[16]

Sparse records survive for the late 1760s and early 1770s. The lead mining apparently halted for a time after Chiswell died, but it then resumed, though with little vigor or growth. In 1772, Byrd attested that in June 1767 the company dismissed William Herbert for misusing company funds and for spending too much of his time purchasing and trading deerskins and merchandise in his own commercial endeavors. The surviving partners briefly used John Buchanan, a land speculator and friend of Thomas Walker, to market the lead still produced, but John Esdale succeeded Buchanan in that capacity by February 1768.[17] In February 1776, Edmund

Pendleton wrote that the mines had "produced no proffit For ten years past" and that he had thus "estimated them very low."[18] Their fruitfulness, however, became obvious when revolution rose to the top of the docket.

Working for Revolution

War, as it often does for entrepreneurs, brought relief. In spite of periodic ongoing violence between whites and Indians, settlers had flooded into southwestern Virginia after the end of the French and Indian War in 1763. William Preston, a surveyor, land speculator, planter, county official, delegate to the House of Burgesses, and militia leader, ranks high on the list of those who profited most. He had a good start on prosperity because his well-connected uncle, James Patton, and his father, John Preston, had filed some of the first land claims along the upper New River. To aid further development, in 1772 legislators created Fincastle County from massive Augusta County, and Fort Chiswell became Fincastle's seat. William Preston, perhaps the region's leading citizen, was named Fincastle's sheriff and surveyor, among other offices. On January 20, 1775, after the Continental Congress requested that citizens establish committees of safety throughout the colonies, Preston was elected to Fincastle's fifteen-member committee; in November, he took over as its chairman. The legislature eliminated Fincastle County in 1776, and the lead mines region fell into the newly created Montgomery County. Preston remained a major power broker in the new county, serving as county surveyor, county militia leader, and justice of the peace.[19]

From the 1740s, settlers in the valley of Virginia created a society reminiscent of the older communities farther east. Successful newer immigrants such as Patton and the Prestons, backed by the Tidewater elite, brought to the backcountry the same sense of financial striving and social hierarchy that came naturally to men such as Byrd, Robinson, and Chiswell.[20] Virginia leaders, in creating the new county governments and backing their militias, recognized the region's potential importance and the need to foster development there. To the mine owners' benefit, Preston acted as a powerful magistrate keeping order in the New River valley.

Preston, the Fincastle committee, and subsequent Montgomery County leaders indeed had vital work to do, for Virginia and the other colonies recognized that the lead mines would have to provide much of the ammunition for the developing war. In July 1775, the Virginia Convention passed the following resolution: "That the committee for the county of Fincastle shall and may contract with the proprietors of certain lead mines in that county for such quantities of lead as may from time to time be judged necessary, and delivered at such places as shall be directed by the Committee of Safety, and in case of refusal of such proprietors, the said committee of Fincastle shall and may agree with the said proprietor for the use of the said mines, and employ proper persons, and furnish necessary materials, for the making of lead at the charge of this colony."[21]

Slaves, criminals, and angry Welshmen dug lead for the American Revolution. William Byrd and other stakeholders in the company rented the mines to Virginia and worked with Harry Innes, agent of the Virginia Committee of Safety, to assemble an efficient workforce. James Callaway was appointed manager of the mines by February 1776 because his predecessor had failed to deliver enough lead. Callaway oversaw some enslaved workers who had tried to run away to the British forces of Lord Dunmore (John Murray). Some of the slaves had been scheduled for transport to the West Indies, and others Virginia had purchased outright to work in pits described as up to seventy feet deep. The skilled Welsh immigrants continued to work in the mining and smelting as well, and several white criminals soon joined them after receiving a pardon from the governor in exchange for agreeing to work three years in the mines. Production took off in 1776—the *Virginia Gazette* noted in August, "From undoubted authority, we can assure the publick that 15,000 wt. of pure lead have been got from our mines in the back country; which, after being cast into bullets, we hope will be unerringly directed against our enemies."[22]

The lead supply and the lead mines came to the attention of the Continental Congress in Philadelphia. On July 16, 1776, barely two weeks after drafting a more important document, Jefferson sent a letter on behalf of the Virginia delegation to Governor Patrick Henry. "We take the liberty of recommending the lead mines to you as an object of vast importance," Jefferson asserted. "We think it impossible they can be worked to too great an extent. Considered as perhaps the sole means of supporting the American cause, they are inestimable. As an article of commerce to our colony, too, they will be valuable; & even the waggonage, if done either by the colony or individuals belonging to it, will carry to it no trifling sum of money."[23] Leaders of the new state of Virginia had already anticipated the military's needs. On July 13, they had ordered Peter Terrel to hire four guards and move nineteen slaves from the "Public Jail" to the distant mines. The Virginia Council estimated that the annual value of each man's work varied from £8 to £15, and council members recorded the names and owners of these men destined to work for liberty's arsenal: Joachim and Joe, owned by Edmund Bailey; Luke, property of William Bailey; Peter, property of Thomas Jacobs; Charles, property of George Wythe; Jamie, Reubin, and Ned, property of Mr. Bowdoin; Juba, property of William Maury; Peter, property of Mrs. Reade; Gilbert, property of Mrs. Roan; James, Fielding, David, and Hercules, property of Baleigh Dolman; Bristol, property of William Montague; Aaron, property of Thomas Parramore; and James and Prince, property of William B. Brown.[24] On October 11, 1776, the council approved more than £20 of expenses incurred by Harry Innes while escorting slaves to the lead mines, perhaps the group named here.[25] But sending the slaves did not suffice. On receiving Jefferson's letter, John Page, president of the Virginia Council, and the other council members "sent off an express to the lead-mines, ordering a large number of hands to be immediately hired, to assist those already employed there."[26]

A fledgling country at war needed gunpowder as well as bullets. Bedford County planter Charles Lynch used state slaves also to work a saltpeter deposit on the New River, downstream from the lead mines. He reported to Virginia's congressional delegation in November 1775, "I have purchas'd a place on New River Where a small river cal'd Reed Iseland emtys in about Eight Miles below the Led mines. The Mineral lies on the south West side of Reed Iseland river facing the North East." Lynch had already begun manufacturing gunpowder, likely in Bedford County, beginning early that same year, and he was making fifty pounds per day by summer. But he needed additional sources of saltpeter. In February 1776, the state loaned Lynch £100, administered by Harry Innes, to help him develop both the Wythe County deposit and his manufactory.[27] In May 1776, Lynch reported difficulty finding labor and asked "to hire hands of the Publick at a Moderate Price if they have Any to Dispose of, for carrying on the business, paying Such hire in gun powder." The state convention obliged immediately, resolving "that the Slaves now Prisoners in the publick Gaol be delivered to the said Charles Lynch," along with a £50 loan and authority to borrow up to £500 as needed.[28] In April 1778, however, the state transferred those hands to the lead mines, a move that, along "with the incursions of indians," left Lynch unable "to make any considerable Quantity of Salt Petre or Powder."[29] The search for lead fared better.

Callaway's work at the lead mines initially satisfied state leaders. In October 1776, he had ten tons ready for shipment to the Continental army;

the Virginia officials granted his request for a salary increase to £150 per year plus expenses in June 1777. In October, they provided Innes £450 to use toward mining expenses, including buying a wagon and team. On December 5, 1777, though, the council named Charles Lynch to succeed Callaway as manager, and Lynch pushed production as hard as possible and oversaw rebuilding of the furnace in 1778. The supply seemed adequate until in early 1781 the vein of lead waned. "It is impossible to give you an Idea of the Distress we are in for want of Lead," Thomas Jefferson wrote in April 1781, with the battle of Yorktown still months away. Desperate efforts to find more ore brought results by May, though, and production kept going through the end of the war.[30]

As masters learned of the disposition of their runaway property—taken from the jails to the mines—they often petitioned the legislature for the slaves' return. The legislators sometimes obliged, but at other times they kept the slaves and offered payment of rent instead. In December 1778, the legislature rejected Charles Sayer's request to have his slave Africa come home.[31] In May 1780, though, the legislators agreed to send Juba and Gilbert back to their owners.[32] Bristol, a slave of William Montague of Lancaster County, had attempted to defect to Dunmore and the British by boat but ended up at the mines. In June 1779, the legislature demonstrated the soaring inflation of wartime Virginia when it approved compensation to Montague for the use of Bristol of £8 per annum for 1776, £10 for 1777, £20 for 1778, and £60 for 1779, with the slave to be returned to his master at the end of that year. Lynch needed all the hands he could obtain to keep the complicated operation going, and the legislature made every effort to supply them. Prices rose further as the war dragged on.[33]

Some slaves were asked to sacrifice even more for the cause. For instance, Tom, a slave of Joseph Selden's, tried to reach the British in 1775 and ended up at the lead mines. However, a petition for compensation filed years later explained Tom's fate: "Your Petitioner further Sheweth that the said Negro Fellow being valued was among other Negroes sent to the West Indies in the year 1776 to be sold in order to procure a Supply of Powder and Ammunition for the use of the State." The ship to the islands was seized and condemned, however, so Tom's sale availed nothing for his breakaway home colony.[34]

The initial wave of jailed slaves did not long provide an adequate number of workers. In August 1777, the Board of War implored the Virginia Council to do all in its power to produce lead. The state's leaders cooperated: "The Council do advise the Governor to employ Mr Duncan Rose [a Petersburg merchant working as a state agent] to purchase, upon the best Terms he can, twelve Negro Men Slaves for the purpose of working the said Chiswells mines to the greatest advantage."[35] In October, Governor Patrick Henry assured the Board of War that it could expect "Considerable Supplies" of lead.[36] His optimism perhaps relied on the state's slave purchases: John Fox sold Ned, a former sailor, and Ralph, a sawyer and ship carpenter, to the state for £400 in warrants on October 25, 1777. On November 5, £150 went to Benjamin Powell for Robin and £130 to Douglas Willet for Ned after the Court of Admiralty ordered the men sold following their capture from the enemy. Three days later John Crammond received a warrant for £124 in return for his slave Aberdeen. Virginia gave a warrant of £150 to William Robinson "for the use of John Hancock" in return for Caesar. The state was still buying slaves as late as November 11, 1778, when Elizabeth Reade received warrants of £300 for Peter, a slave already rented from her and working at the mines.[37] In September 1779, the Commissary of Stores furnished clothing for thirty male and five female slaves at the mines.[38]

The workforce also included another set of unwilling men: white criminals. Wartime exigency created at the mines perhaps the most diverse group of workers in the backcountry, a tangle of the most desperate parts of society. Virginia leaders wrested industrial labor from unlikely sources, expanding on the prewar mix of white and black. Even late in the war, the governor pardoned several men on condition that they labor for three years at the mines. Thomas Johnston (or Johnson) and William Smith (alias William Nugent), for instance, received their pardons in the spring of 1782 and had "thirty days allowed them to get to the mines," after which they could not stray more than three miles from them.[39] They may not have gone, however, or if they did, they did not stay long. Their names appear on a list of four such pardoned convicts in a letter to the governor in November. It apparently describes convicts gone missing from their work: they undermined the fight for political independence in search of their own. The tally pictures Smith as about twenty-seven years old and from the Pennsylvania backcountry. He had circulated counterfeit money. Johnston, "a noted Horse Thief," had migrated from near Frederick Town, Maryland. John Dean, convicted of robbery in York County despite his "weak, or injured Intellects," had probably joined his wife and family in Gloucester County. Twenty-five-year-old Ireland native Timothy Campbell, "last from Pennsylvania," had a good voice but when drunk acted "audaciously impudent." The last report of Campbell found him boarding a vessel for the West Indies.[40]

In an industrial setting so complicated, workers might well escape. In *Notes on the State of Virginia,* Thomas Jefferson left a detailed look at the state of the lead mines in about 1781:

> On the Great Kanhaway, opposite to the mouth of Cripple creek, and about twenty-five miles from our southern boundary, in the county of Montgomery, are mines of lead. The metal is mixed, sometimes with earth, and sometimes with rock, which requires the force of gunpowder to open it; and is accompanied with a portion of silver, too small to be worth separation under any process hitherto attempted there. The proportion yielded is from 50 to 80 lb. of pure metal from 100 lb. of washed ore. The most common is that of 60 to the 100 lb. The veins are at sometimes most flattering; at others they disappear suddenly and totally. They enter the side of the hill, and proceed horizontally. Two of them are wrought at present by the public, the best of which is 100 yards under the hill. These would employ about 50 labourers to advantage. We have not, however, more than 30 generally, and these cultivate their own corn. They have produced 60 tons of lead in the year; but the general quantity is from 20 to 25 tons. The present furnace is a mile from the ore-bank, and on the opposite side of the river. The ore is first waggoned to the river, a quarter of a mile, then laden on board of canoes and carried across the river, which is there about 200 yards wide, and then again taken into waggons and carried to the furnace. This mode was originally adopted, that they might avail themselves of a good situation on a creek, for a pounding mill: but it would be easy to have the furnace and pounding mill on the same side of the river, which would yield water, without any dam, by a canal of about half a mile in length. From the furnace the lead is transported 130 miles along a good road, leading through the peaks of Otter to Lynch's ferry [later, Lynchburg], or Winston's, on James river, from whence it is carried by water about the same distance to Westham [near Richmond].[41]

This sprawling complex, a worldly backwater swirling with activity and unfree laborers, presented quite a security challenge in a sparsely populated area.

Dissent at the Lead Mines

Throughout much of the Revolutionary War, reports—some well founded, others fantastical—of planned Indian and Loyalist attacks reached William Preston, and he scrambled to keep an adequate number of militiamen guarding the lead mines. In 1776, the governor authorized the erection, at state expense, of "a Stockade Fort" at the mines, including a guardhouse and a magazine. Concern intensified in the spring of 1779 with news of a plot. County militia major Walter Crockett sent fifty troops to aid the sheriff. James McGavock, a prominent Fort Chiswell merchant and landowner who had served on the Fincastle Committee of Safety, arrested nine suspected Loyalists, and several justices (in the absence of Preston, the senior justice) tried the suspects in May at Fort Chiswell but issued lenient judgments. Preston sought a moderate course, even trying to maintain a dialogue with known Loyalist leaders. Nevertheless, unrest persisted. In July 1779, spies reported seeing a gathering of a hundred Loyalists intent on mayhem, with a rumored four hundred more nearby, preparing to attack the mines. (In December 1779, Charles Lynch paid one Benjamin Price £15 "for Acting as Spy July Last.") In March 1780, Thomas Jefferson urged Preston to "take the most immediate measures for protecting the lead mines." Later in the year, more arrests followed revelations of a summertime plot for Loyalists to attack the mines and then march to Charlottesville to release British prisoners: Preston labeled the plot "A most horrid Conspiracy." The Patriot militia rounded up sixty Loyalists, and, with Preston in charge this time, the justices tried them in August, jailing some of the guilty, sentencing some to military service, and lashing others.[42]

With Loyalism widespread in the entire upper New River valley, areas quite close to the mines felt the most disunity: "up New River betwixt the River and the Flower Gap and also on the Two Reed Islands and Greasey Creek and Walkers Creek." This area stretches from the Blue Ridge escarpment to the New River and encompasses much of present Carroll County and the southern portion of Wythe County.[43] Thomas Jefferson saw it as "the most disaffected part of our State."[44] The Loyalists, generally not well off, had many reasons for their actions, ranging from local grievances against rich, heavy-handed leading men to ethnic tensions between German and Scotch-Irish settlers to more abstract loyalties to Great Britain.[45] Class and politics mingled. But whatever their motivations, the state's harsh response reflected the seriousness of the threat the Loyalists posed to those rebelling against the king. Mine superintendent and militia colonel Charles Lynch even punished some captured Loyalists without the benefit of a trial. In August 1780, he replied to William Preston's protests, "[P]erhaps Justice to This Country May require they shou'd be Made Exampels of."[46]

Loyalists hoped to attack the lead operations from the outside, but threats also popped up within. Some of the men who had felt Lynch's "Justice" worked the lead furnace. Loyalist discontent penetrated the mining community itself in the summer of 1780 as some of the Welsh immigrants working there—including John Jenkins, one of the "Principal Men" and Lynch's most highly compensated employee—swore an oath to the head of "the Insurgents in them Parts." The Welshmen also stood together, with the group vowing not to work unless all of them remained employed and Jenkins had charge. But Lynch, in his words, "was then so happy as to find out their schemes and frustrate them."[47] Jenkins, David Herbert, and Roger Oats confessed to Lynch their Loyalism and, according to Lynch, "have Given Me a good Deal of information on Others."[48] In turn, the Welsh crew saw Lynch as biased against them. Nancy Devereaux, whose husband, Charles Devereaux, Lynch was holding, wrote of "a missunderstanding between Colo. Lynch and the Welsh in General."[49]

Beyond their political leanings, the workers had practical reasons for their unrest. In April 1781, William Preston reported to Governor Thomas Jefferson "That the Workmen & Managers are in great distress for want of meat. . . . Such was their distress lately, that I was affraid the business would be retarded & therefore advised Col: Lynch's assistant to purchase a little bacon with lead for the present, until Colo. Lynch would return."[50] Workers had to parse their political options delicately: men at the margins, they had little information with which to chart a course out of their desperate conditions. Fighting off both the political and the material rumblings, Lynch used the bound laborers and managed to run the furnace for a time without the expertise of the Welsh, thus breaking their workplace resistance. Once "their infernal Scheme was quashed" by his peremptory justice, Lynch bragged, Jenkins "made some acknowledgements and promising all that I could ask, I took him into business again." Lynch refused to take back others among the strikers. Writing to state commercial agent and fellow industrialist David Ross, Lynch blamed these "Loosers by the Mistake" for stirring up rumors about mismanagement by Lynch and Captain Stephen Sanders, the assistant who helped manage the mines. According to Lynch, the disgruntled workers claimed falsely that "Sanders feeds them on bread and water half their time, and Drives hard." The desperate times may have drawn whites and blacks together in disobedience: according to Lynch, the malcontents included "mostly Torys and such as Sanders has given Lynch's Law too for Dealing with the Negroes etc."[51]

As Lynch hinted, the unwilling black laborers also worried state officials, and the militia was assigned there in part to guard against slave revolt. The initial force of jailed slaves brought to the mine came from various locations in eastern Virginia. John Hancock's slave Caesar had sustained wounds at the battle of Great Bridge in December 1775, and he was later sent to the mines. Ned, Reuben, and James of Northampton County went to the mines after having death sentences commuted. Stafford County slaves Charles, property of Robert Brent, and Kitt, property of George Brent, tried to escape bondage in March 1776 by hijacking a small schooner and forcing white boatmen to steer them to the British. The plot failed, but Charles's and Kitt's death sentences were commuted, and they were sentenced instead to dig for lead. Christopher Calvert's slave Davy joined them after being seized on suspicion of trying to escape to Dunmore near Williamsburg.[52]

Given that these slaves had already shown a deep desire for freedom, the mine operators had to maintain constant vigilance; the prospect of Welsh workers' joining forces with the slaves and convicts might have excited the managers' worst fears. At times, slaves fled the hard labor, as in 1778 when slave Charles "made an Elopement" from the mines and reached as far as Stafford County before capture. Perhaps the Welsh helped by turning a blind eye. George made it as far as Powhatan the same year; and in December 1778, John Hall received more than £11 for going to Bedford and to the Hollows in North Carolina to pick up two runaways. In 1779, a man named Luke, whom Duncan Rose had purchased on the state's behalf from John Kendal on the Eastern Shore, "ran away from the lead mines in *Fincastle county,* where he was employed in the country service." He was caught in Chesterfield County.[53] On at least one occasion, slaves may have attempted to sabotage the works, though white Loyalists or a combined group may have done the deed. In 1833, John Vest, asking the government for a Revolutionary War pension, recalled serving as a militiaman guarding the lead mines. The slaves "had to be closely watched," and "either the tories, Indians or negroes set fire to the furnace house and burnt four rafters on the roof before the fire could be extinguished." Vest added that later that "same night a ferry boat and a large canoe which was used in bringing the ore from the other side was loosed from the landing[,] set adrift and was no more found."[54]

Issues of Loyalism and slavery melded in one of the least likely stories unfolding at the mines. In October 1778, Margaret Goodrich asked the state to return six slaves being held at the lead mines. The Committee of Safety had sent them there after seizing, in 1776, the bulk of the estate of her husband, Loyalist merchant John Goodrich. State officials allotted Mrs. Goodrich £40 per year to rent slaves to cultivate the fields she had retained. Inflation had eroded that sum by 1778, though, and those hired slaves she could procure "frequently absconded from their duty," leaving her unable "to supply the wants of her family." She wanted Aberdeen, age twenty-one; Glasgow, age sixty-five; York, age sixty-five; Michael, age forty-five; Sarah, age fifty-five; and Phyllis, age sixty-five, to return home. The legislature refused.[55] Perhaps their age left these older slaves, both men and women, at the mercy of the state after most of the Goodrich workforce headed to the British lines; or, intriguingly, perhaps they stayed behind deliberately rather than leave all that they knew. For the cause of independence, though, women and older workers alike had to share the burden. From the viewpoint of the Patriots, desperate for laborers, anyone tainted with Loyalism earned no relief.

The young man Aberdeen's presence on the list of much older slaves stands out. In 1783, he petitioned the legislature for his freedom, and therein he explained his unusual path across Virginia's Revolutionary War landscape: "To the Honourable the Speaker of House of Delegates the Petition of Aberdeen rais'd by John Goodridge and waited on him untill his takeing the side of the British, Humbly sheweth, that your Petitioner at that time Left his P. Master & Deliver'd him self to James Hopper, Understanding his P. Master had order'd all his Servants to go on Board the fleet at Norfolk—in May 1776 was taken from Williamsburg by Colo. Lynch to the Led Mines, where he has labour'd Honestly Ever since—for which Service & the Leaving his P. Master & friends he grounds his hope, your Honourable House will give him his freedom."[56] One can only speculate whether Goodriches' older slaves who worked alongside Aberdeen at the lead mines had voluntarily failed to join Dunmore's fleet. Perhaps age, illness, or some other factor blocked their way. But Aberdeen's clear choice against fleeing to the British may have paid off for him.

The eventual close of fighting and the subsequent Peace of Paris brought reward to one of the two slaves named Aberdeen who persevered at the mines. The other Aberdeen, formerly owned by John Crammond and listed as age fifty in an early 1783 inventory, had reached more than twice the age of his fellow worker, then listed as age twenty-three. In October of that year, the legislature passed "an act directing the emancipation of certain slaves who have served as soldiers in this state, and the emancipation of the slave Aberdeen." He had "laboured a number of years in the public service at the lead mines, and for this meritorious services is entitled to freedom." The legislators, flush with independence, decided Aberdeen should be "hereby emancipated and declared free in as full and ample a manner as if he had been born free."[57]

The other state slaves won nothing from the American Revolution; their work did not make them free. The state still planned to get its lead supply from the mines; but with active conflict winding down, the legislature on December 10, 1782, authorized the governor and the Virginia Council to return the lead mines to their proprietors, to return hired slaves to their owners, and "to make any Contract they may think proper . . . with respect to the slaves the Property of the Public."[58] Thomas Madison acted on behalf of the proprietors in the subsequent negotiations. He wrote the governor on December 12, "I am willing to contract for any Quantity of lead on the most moderate Terms . . . but must request you to inform me whether you will let me have the Slaves that are publick Property and on what Terms, likewise what Quantity of Lead you will want & at what Time." The governor had to decide quickly because "some of the Gent. owners of the Slaves employed at the mines are now in Town & willing to treat with me for them."[59]

On January 27, 1783, Henry Young, the state quartermaster general, reported to Governor Benjamin Harrison that he had "contracted with the owners agreeable to your order."[60] Notwithstanding Charles Lynch's abuse of Loyalists, the state worked out a deal with him and Jacob Rubsamen, his partner, to provide the state with "fifty thousand pounds weight lead" in return for either specie or tobacco at the rate of six pence per pound of lead. For various state-owned supplies and tools (horses, kettles, a canoe, iron, and so on) at the mines, the pair had to pay £200. The German immigrant Rubsamen, who had reportedly worked in New Jersey's mining industry before the war, lived in Manchester, across the James River from Richmond, and during the war labored to make powder. He likely entered business relations with Lynch through that angle.[61]

Moses Austin and Enterprise in the New Nation

Ownership of the mines had partially changed hands during the revolution. For a time, one of the state officials charged with overseeing the lead supplies apparently owned at least part of William Byrd's former stake. (Byrd died at the beginning of 1777.) A 1781 petition to the legislature asked that land adjacent to the mines be reserved as a source of fuel for the furnace. The heavy exploitation during the war had left environmental scars other than the pits themselves: "the Wood has become scarce & is daily become more so." Local residents not connected to the mines would have needed the woods just as badly, for fuel and hunting, but the turn to the state to hold that resource for industrial use underscores the primacy of the well-connected lead-mining entrepreneurs in the area's economy. The petitioner, James Parberry, indicated that he had purchased half of Byrd's share in the mines from Patrick Henry, who had served as Virginia's governor from 1776 to 1778. Lynch, too, claimed that he owned at least a portion of Byrd's erstwhile stake.[62] But whatever the precise ownership list at the end of the war, the deal between the state and Lynch and Rubsamen meant that some agreement had been reached with the owners as well as with the commonwealth. The war over, the state had no desire to stand in the way of private business activity in an ever-more-vigorous marketplace. At the higher echelons of society, the American Revolution may have opened up the political and economic world a bit in the backcountry, as it did everywhere in the colonies, but the workers, black and white alike, felt little benefit.

As Henry Young prepared to sell the state property at the lead mines to Lynch and Rubsamen, he arranged for an inventory of the slaves and supplies. The report from January 1783 showed thirty adult African Americans present and most of the facilities in good order. The tally included four women among the adult slaves. One of them, thirty-year-old Phebe, had three children there. One slave named Jacob lingered near death, but the others enjoyed good health. The twenty-six men had an average age just short of thirty-three. To hire this experience-hardened workforce, Lynch and Rubsamen agreed to pay the state £348 per year. The inventory listed each slave's former owner, and Lynch and Rubsamen's agreement stipulated that they had to deliver up any slave who was "claimed," which implied that the commonwealth planned to sell or in some way return state-owned bondpeople to former owners.[63] Southern state governments, though, continued intermittently to purchase slaves and employ them on public-works projects until the Civil War.[64]

Following the return of peace in the 1780s, production continued without crippling interruption, as did the legal wrangling over ownership and debts. In February 1785, state officials moved most of the government-owned slaves from the mines to Point of Fork, leaving behind at minimum "one wench and three children [most likely Phebe and her children], the weather being too cold to move the children." Fielding, another slave, "deserted the mining" shortly before the journey began, thus at least temporarily avoiding the move by his well-timed escape.[65] But work carried on, perhaps at the hands of a few other state-owned slaves apparently held back by Lynch.[66]

In 1785, John Jenkins was leading the smelting despite his wartime flirtation with Loyalism. In 1787, Lynch still had operational control and was contending that he owned a one-third interest. The following year Edmund Pendleton and Peter Lyons, still struggling to settle John Robinson's estate, implored the governor and the Virginia Council for help, but even the attorneys did not know where the situation stood: "That after the Peace your Memorialists agreed to rent the Mines for two hundred pounds Specie a year to a Gentleman who they beleive [sic] was not able to work them to the extent the Public did, and when they presume Lead was not so valuable as in the time of the War, and submit to those circumstances, as a ground to claim an annual Rent, considerably beyond that sum: but beg leave to refer this Honorable Board to Charles Lynch Esquire, who can ascertain the commencement and end of the Public Service, as well as what will be reasonable Rent."[67] In 1790, Pendleton mentioned that the High Court of Chancery in 1789 had finally allowed £1,400 as rent for the mines during the war, and the justices' decree allotted an additional £700 to Lynch. Pendleton nonetheless demurred: "the Assembly has charged the Payment upon the Aggregate Fund, which is unproductive and the Warrants thereon sell at a loss of 6s in the pound, which is too great to bear, and we must wait 'til they can furnish a better."[68] The wait lasted past Pendleton's life. At one point, five suits regarding the mines rested in the Superior Court of Chancery in the capital. Not until 1822 did the state settle the Robinson estate's claims and the wartime rental agreement.[69] By then, however, the situation on the ground had changed several times.

New entrepreneurs entered the scene, adding fresh business knowledge to that already accumulated by the Virginians. In May 1789, brothers Moses and Stephen Austin, natives of Connecticut and merchants in Philadelphia and Richmond, signed a ten-year lease. Moses, who would later plan the Anglo-American settling of Texas, agreed to live on-site to oversee the mining and smelting.[70] In the new republic, the once easy, sometimes corrupt relationship between the state and men such as John Robinson had partially given way under the scrutiny of a more combative, less deferential political system. At the same time, the young nation's growing economic integration allowed private individuals to pull together the resources needed for an undertaking so large as a lead mine.

The Austins had already mastered chasing economic opportunity and tugging on personal ties to do it. Moses, born in 1765 in Connecticut, had joined his older brother Stephen in the merchant trade in Philadelphia in 1783. The next year Stephen and their partner Manning Merrill sent Moses to open a branch of the operation in Richmond, where he learned of the lead mine. In the late 1780s, as the state and the heirs of the owners tangled over the mine's finances, that operation declined, and tons of already-smelted lead sat unsold. When Moses convinced Stephen to sink his Philadelphia capital into leasing and reviving the mine, Virginia officials also loaned them twenty tons of unused lead to sell for initial operating funds. By November, Moses had ten men raising ore, and he and Stephen had started a business making shot in Richmond. Stephen recruited skilled miners in Philadelphia and sent them south, while Moses worked the political process in Richmond to obtain a lucrative contract to put a lead roof on the state capitol.[71] Pennsylvania had already begun its ascent to the pinnacle of American industrial development, and many times in the coming century New River valley entrepreneurs would follow the Austins in turning to that state for expertise and capital.

Perhaps the high point of the Austins' business came in 1790 and 1791. In June 1790, Stephen and Moses complained to Governor Beverley Randolph of the need for a protective tariff on lead, which the tariff of 1789 exempted. The Austins' reasoning highlighted transportation, the problem that would long plague Blue Ridge industrialists: "The many difficulties we have to encounter from the long distance inland which is attended with a very expensive Transportation makes [sic] it necessary to ask the aid and assistance of the Publick who we flatter ourselves will view our exertions in the manufactory of so usefull and necessary an article in a favourable light." With Randolph's encouragement, the brothers visited the national capital, New York, to make their case directly to Secretary of State Jefferson and various other administrators and legislators. They arrived at a fortunate moment. National political leaders from James Madison to Alexander Hamilton alike realized that the new United States needed a stronger tariff both to raise money and to encourage domestic manufacturing. The Austins thus found sympathetic listeners. A helpful tariff, enacted in August

1790, established a duty of one cent per pound on "bar and other lead." In March 1791, the U.S. Congress extended the duty to include "all manufactures wholly of lead, or in which lead is the chief article." For the Austins, revenue seemed assured.[72]

In 1792, Gilbert Imlay, in describing North America to his European readers, wrote, "A lead mine has been worked many years with considerable profit, which lies in the county of Montgomery, upon the waters of the Great Kanhaway."[73] Moses Austin indeed tried doggedly to make the mines profitable. In their 1790 plea to Governor Randolph, the Austin brothers included a description of the mines prepared by three upstanding citizens of their area. The trio certified

> that there are between fifty and sixty men employed as miners, artificers and labourers; that there are seven pits sunk, of about seventy feet in depth, which are so productive, that from six to eight tons of ore may be raised in a day; that the appearances give confidence to conclude, that the bodies of ore that may be found in the hill is inexhaustible; that at present a very simple, but improved manner of beating and washing the ore are adopted; that there are in forwardness materials for erecting a new Furnace, which may be ready for use in less than two months, but that built by the late Colonel Chiswell is now so repaired that above one ton and an half of Lead may be smelted every day while it stands.[74]

Virginia's leaders believed the Austins could succeed, and their optimism broke open the legal deadlock that had long held the mines in its grip. On May 27, 1791, a land grant for fourteen hundred acres, including the mines, named Lynch the recipient "in trust for the Lead Mine Company." Lingering suits had yet to resolve the state's interest in the mines as part of settling John Robinson's estate, but through the High Court of Chancery the government of Virginia and the original mine owners' heirs had apparently agreed to put the mines under unified private control. (Surviving records do not allow for a clear, full understanding of the process.) For much of the 1780s, Thomas Walker of the Loyal Land Company had recorded transactions regarding shares held in the lead mines by him and other Virginia notables, including Richard Jones, William Jackson, Colonel Ludwell, Colonel John Baylor, and Colonel James Madison. Walker's record of the matter closed in 1790, but notations on the front of the record mentioned "the account settled by the Co. in April 1791." With the murky matter more or less cleared up, the chancery court agreed that the Austin brothers could buy the lead mines in February 1792 for £6,505. Charles Lynch, along with a businessman in Richmond and another in Philadelphia, backed the Austins' promise to pay.[75] The mix of southern and northern expertise and funding typified the young country's dynamic economic development in the 1790s. In turn, Virginia's politicians, in an environment trumpeting civic virtue, likely breathed a sigh of relief when they freed the state of an enterprise born from John Robinson's corruption.

Because of the mines' distance from backcountry Piedmont centers such as the Moravian town of Salem, North Carolina, the Austins created a functioning community of stores, businesses (even a hatter), and houses around the mines. They established a ferry across the New River, and they bought land in Lynchburg to smooth the transfer of lead from wagons to boats headed to Richmond. Legislators carved Wythe County from Montgomery County in 1790, and Wythe then spawned Grayson County in 1793. The whole section of the state had started filling in, but no spot faster than the mine area. The mining community gained a post office designation—Austinville—and on November 3, 1793, Moses Austin welcomed the birth of a son named Stephen F. Austin, who in Texas would later surpass even his father in knotting together broad expanses of the North American society and economy. In 1796, the governor appointed Moses a captain in the militia.[76] Three years later a visitor described the bustling community of Austinville: "The town lies on a pleasant level tract, surrounded by high rocks and mountains, and although it lies low it is very healthful, as is the entire region. It is on the beautiful, clear stream known as New River; is regularly laid out; and has a number of good buildings, especially the house of the owner, Mr. Austin. Most of the residents work in the mines, which are a mile away, rich in lead, and not over one hundred feet deep."[77]

Stephen the elder's profits from Philadelphia provided much of the funding for the growth, but to build the lead business so fast also required an outside infusion of cash. Stephen and Moses sold an eighth of the business in November 1792 to Thomas Ruston of Philadelphia, who engaged in financial speculation on a scale that dwarfed the Austins' gambles.[78] Ruston called on Moses to serve as his local contact in a successful plan to survey and patent, along with John D. Blanchard, 242,000 acres of land in Wythe and Grayson counties in December 1795, with Moses to receive a commission.[79] Moses and Stephen together took part in buying and selling tens of thousands of acres in the two counties in partnership with Blanchard and two other Pennsylvanians, Joseph Rickley and George Lauman.[80] Though motivated by profit, the Austins' buying and developing of land facilitated further settlement of the community, though at the expense of accepting a significant degree of control from Philadelphia.

Profits failed to follow the growth of Austinville, however, and the Austins and their partners tumbled into financial disarray and fell out with each other over responsibility for the debts. Their workers did not properly roof the Virginia capitol, and in 1794 the state tried to collect the bond on the twenty tons of lead lent to the Austins in 1789. In 1794, the elder Stephen, reminiscent of John Chiswell some three decades earlier, traveled to England seeking—in vain, as it turned out—a buyer for the mines. In June 1797, legislators, perhaps hoping to bolster imported supplies of a product vital for security, ended the tariff on lead and lead products, lowering the prices that the Austins could demand.[81] In the frenetic atmosphere of the 1790s, bold but risky investments of this sort often failed without stigma, making the Austins typical of many energetic entrepreneurs throughout the nation. Their business in turmoil, Moses turned his attention to a new lead-mining venture in Spain's Upper Louisiana, in what would become Missouri, and Stephen desperately tried to avoid bankruptcy. In 1798, Moses Austin and his immediate family decamped for the West, leaving a son of another Austin brother running the floundering Austinville operation. Stephen angrily wrote, "[E]very shilling that can now be Scraped up from the wreck of the affairs which M A left behind will not pay me ten shilling on the pound of the just balance due me from him." James Newell, a local official and farmer, operated the mines on the Austins' behalf from around 1801 to 1806, but because the Austins had not met their financial obligations, he ran into continual difficulty. In 1802, petitioned by two of the Austins' sureties, the chancery court once again ordered the sale of the business. After more delay, in 1806 the Austinville mines were indeed auctioned for £9,550 to three men: Maryland native and onetime shoemaker Daniel Sheffey, a Wythe County attorney, Virginia General Assembly member, and future four-term Federalist congressman; iron maker David Peirce, a Pennsylvania native; and Thomas Jackson, a British immigrant who had moved to Austinville from Philadelphia to aid the Austins with their lead smelting.[82] The unlikely trio, brought together at the geographical margins by their ambition, would try to coax consistent profitability from an enticing industrial enterprise that thus far had brought only sporadic gains to its many eager owners.

Regardless of ownership, one aspect of the mining operation stayed consistent: the use of slave labor. One cannot determine the relative numbers of white and enslaved workers, but slaves made up a substantial portion of the workforce, both at the mines and among the men and women who had no choice but to take their mining experience to Upper Louisiana with Moses Austin. During the dispute between Moses and Stephen, the brothers arranged for several inventories of their property at the Austinville mines. Twenty-six to twenty-eight slaves lived there in 1800 and 1801, at least some of whom had been purchased from a "Mr. Epps" (likely a member of the Eppes family) of Petersburg, Virginia, and brought to the mountains. A slave community was developing alongside the white community in Austinville, for at least three slave families included a man, a woman, and children, with James, Kesiah, and their five children composing the largest.[83]

Entering the nineteenth century, then, the lead mines community had grown into a worldly place, defying later images of the southern backcountry as isolated and backward. A series of energetic businessmen had directed workforces of bewildering complexity: Welsh and English immigrants, state slaves, privately owned slaves, convicts, men, women, children. Capital had flowed there from various regions of North America; knowledge and expertise sometimes came from even farther. Success hinged in part on tariff laws and competition from abroad; the product traveled hundreds of miles to serve urban customers. Further filling in this complex picture, iron joined lead in the economic framework of this mountain outpost. Both industries poured smoke into the Appalachian skies.

The Iron Industry

As Jefferson's *Notes on the State of Virginia* pointed out, iron making also had an early start in the region. The instability of this form of investment led to a dizzying array of early transactions. In 1779, Richardson Owen petitioned the state legislature to grant him land on lower Chestnut Creek, where he may have already begun constructing an iron furnace and bloomery forge. By the mid-1780s, the complex was called "Kincannon's Iron Works" in local records, and Andrew Kincannon and Daniel Carlan owned the operation. They subsequently sold it to Hugh Montgomery, who sold it to Joseph Jackson, who in 1803 pledged the business, with six hundred acres, as security to Irish immigrant Alexander Smyth, a politician and attorney who practiced in Wythe County. On September 27, 1814, Smyth sold "the Forge and bloomery at the Great falls on chesnut creek in Grayson County" as well as the land to Thomas Wistar and John Cooke of Philadelphia for $480. Upstream on Chestnut Creek but also in present Carroll County stood Blair and Dickey's Iron Works, a furnace and forge operated by Matthew Dickey and Thomas Blair. Blair, also a merchant, took full ownership of the renamed Blair's Forge in 1794, and he sold it and the small slave workforce there to his son, John, on June 30, 1804. County residents regarded Thomas Blair, a former resident of Pennsylvania and possibly a former Loyalist, as a leader for many years, and antebellum voters perennially chose John Blair as Grayson County's delegate to the state legislature. Thomas Blair and Dickey, along with William Bourne, had a hand as well in the Point Hope Furnace on Peach Bottom Creek to the west in present Grayson County. It was operating by the 1790s. Still in today's Carroll County, but well east of Chestnut Creek, the Rockcastle Forge sat near Little Reed Island Creek. It, too, opened in the eighteenth century, and after the property passed through several hands, David Peirce bought it in 1818. These mines, furnaces, and forges endured for significant lengths of time, but the ore in Carroll County, owing to its high sulfur content, did not prove ideal for making iron using the technology of the time.[84]

Industrial data circulated across long distances: oral tradition in the 1880s held that Thomas Blair learned about iron ore along Chestnut Creek from John Chiswell. A local man told visiting geologist William M. Fontaine,

> Col. Chiswell, one of the first to attempt to develop the minerals of the state, had noticed the large amounts of iron ore in this portion of Carroll [County], and brought them to the attention of Blair who was engaged in the manufacture of iron. Blair, immediately after the Revolutionary war, moved out to this country, then practically a wilderness. He of course carried with him workmen of all kinds, and all the appliances needed for the mining and smelting of the ore. Quite a colony was formed. He erected a dam on Chestnut creek, put up a furnace, built many houses, and cleared the land around. Some of the buildings were quite pretentious, especially for that period. When, however, the ore came to be tried, it is said, the difficulty reported to exist in all the other gossan deposits of the plateau, was encountered. It was said that the iron would

not weld. Blair then resorted to the ores of Wythe county as a source of supply. The remains of his dam and furnaces are still to be seen on Chestnut creek. The contrast shown by the fields that he brought under cultivation, with the virgin country, still to be found all around, is very interesting. These fields bare of stumps even, and worn out, remind one of districts in the eastern part of the state.

Fontaine and his informant had it right in regard to industrial destruction of the forests as well as the county's decline in the iron business. In 1850, three Carroll County forges produced a total of only seventy tons of bar iron, and they may well have used less-sulfurous ore from neighboring Wythe County.[85] While the iron lasted, though, Blair's businesses produced castings of various sorts for the area market, including twenty-gallon kettles, andirons, and skillets molded in 1797 at Point Hope Furnace by the "Furnace Keeper," Daniel Jones, whose son Samuel served as a furnace filler.[86]

Industrial enterprises dictated much of the region's civic as well as economic development. The founding of Austinville provides only one example out of several. For instance, businessmen's political power meant that the road system of future Carroll County first developed to funnel supplies to the lead mines and then to carry lead to eastern Virginia and Piedmont North Carolina. The Flower Gap road that John Bartram had used to go from North Carolina to the lead mines soon evolved into a federal postal route. When Grayson County was formed in 1793, the county court included Matthew Dickey and others involved in the iron industry. Not coincidentally, the court soon ordered "that a road be opened from Blair and Dickey's furnace to the county line, From the Furnace to the ground where the Courthouse is to be erected, thence to the Forge," and mandated that an election for overseer of the poor take place at the forge. The need for an overseer of the poor underscores the complexity of the local society that was growing up around these extractive outposts. At the top of that structure, local leaders could seamlessly weld business and politics.[87]

And as evangelical religion exploded in the South in the early nineteenth century, traveling preachers used the mining communities as reference points for their spreading of the Gospel. Eager young ministers surveyed the sins of the backcountry and identified the industrial sites as vital nodes amid the scattered farms. Dirty miners rather than the self-sufficient farmers idealized in later nostalgia about the mountains attracted the clergymen's attention, indicative of the furnace communities' importance in local development. A young Barton W. Stone, on his way west from North Carolina in May 1796, stopped for several weeks in Wythe and Montgomery counties, finding the area "entirely destitute of preaching." He spoke "at Colonel Austin's, the proprietor of the lead mines on New River," among other spots. Joseph Thomas, a North Carolina native who spent part of his childhood with his brother on Chestnut Creek in Grayson County, found Christian inspiration in the Reverend Lorenzo Dow's 1804 visit to the lead mines and the surrounding area. Thomas himself came back to the county in 1808 as a teenage minister: "At the iron works, the upper and lower forge, in other places around where I attended, and at Grayson Court-House, I saw my labor was not in vain in the Lord." In August 1815, he returned: "I went into Grayson County, and on the 27th. at B's [presumably Blair's] iron works, at 7 o'clock I preached to a large assembly. The time, the place, and the people felt awful as the spirit of the Lord moved upon us. It was a weeping, crying, praying and enquiring time among sinners. This was a morning of richest glory and happiness to my soul, as I could scarcely contain the joy of the heavenly visions which bursted forth to my view."[88] Nonetheless, the democratic effects of evangelical religion did not upset the economic arrangements shaping the furnace communities.

Despite Carroll County's initial failure as an iron center, a better use for its unusual ore deposits would later emerge. In the meantime, iron making accelerated and endured in neighboring Wythe County, challenging even the lead mines as the foremost shaper of that county's industrial development. In 1786, Patrick Henry, Walter Crockett, James McCorkle, James McGavock, and Thomas Madison agreed to start an iron furnace on John Stephens's "Land lying on Reed Creek at the Mouth of Tates Run."[89] The 1790s saw several iron-making businesses take shape. A primitive bloomery forge was started on Francis Mill Creek, near Cripple Creek, in 1792. Near Speedwell, also on Cripple Creek, a better furnace operated by the mid-1790s.[90]

Works for iron also began to pop up in the 1790s farther east in Wythe County. John Bartram, after crossing Flower Gap in 1762, had likely descended from the Blue Ridge plateau by going down Poplar Camp Mountain. In 1798, three partners agreed to start a furnace near the base of that mountain; travelers in 1799 recorded their view of the spot: "By a mill-pond, along which there was a poorly kept road, laid with saplings, there stood several saw-mills, an inn, and a forge is to be built." Partners in the forge included Thomas Blair, who had been operating his iron enterprise a few miles away on the plateau, and two other Grayson County men, who in 1802 sold their interests to the sons of William Herbert, the onetime head of operations at Chiswell's lead mines. The Herberts in turn sold out in 1808 to David Peirce, who by then owned part of the lead mines. Poplar Camp Furnace operated for some two decades.[91] By the time it shut down, competing furnaces dotted the valley, and iron making in the county kept on throughout the antebellum period and beyond.

Francis Preston, a congressman from 1793 to 1796 and son of the powerful William Preston, owned the business in Speedwell. He described the ironworks in some detail soon after its founding. In doing so, he made clear the ties between his business, the neighborhood's natural resources, the surrounding area's market economy, competing iron furnaces in western Piedmont Virginia and eastern Tennessee, and industrial expertise north of the Mason-Dixon Line. He bragged, "The furnace has been built within three years and all the other buildings consisting of dwelling houses, kitchens store house and large convenient stables were commenced within the same time and are now finishing and in good order. The furnace runs from 12 to 15 tons per week, the Castings smooth and of a Superior quality." Building of the forge, too, had nearly wrapped up: "It is said to be the best built forge in Virginia, it being out of Choice timber cut in proper Season and executed under the direction of a first rate forge Carpenter from Pen[n]-sylvania it has now three fires and calculated for another, two hammers, it is 45 feet wide and fifty five long, well covered with joint shingles &c." Francis Preston anticipated no trouble selling the iron; demand far outstripped supply, with local consumers having to go as far as Tennessee and Rocky Mount, Virginia, to fill their needs. He claimed already to have inquiries from his own prospective customers as far away as Tennessee.[92] (See appendix A for Preston's lengthy description of what one might well describe as his iron-making factory.)

Nonetheless, in contrast to the lead industry's reach from Austinville to Richmond and Baltimore, the market for iron centered in the locales near the furnace. Eastern Virginians and Marylanders could purchase iron from suppliers much closer than distant Wythe County; furnace owners in other regions worked the widespread iron ore with methods—and on a scale—similar to those used by their New River valley peers. As a result, the capital invested in the lead mines always dwarfed the investment in any single iron furnace. Like the investors in lead, though, the early New River iron makers turned to Pennsylvania and elsewhere for knowledge and expertise.

As with the lead mines, slaves and free whites worked together in the iron business almost from its inception. The valley's necessary tradition of a diverse labor force moved from one extractive industry to another. Slaves labored alongside whites at the Blairs' works, and a man named Bird, labeled a "free Negroe" in the Blairs' ledger, boarded and likely worked there, too.[93] And on Christmas 1795, Francis Preston admitted, "as to hiring negroes I am more than ever engaged in it as Servants here cannot be procured by any means."[94] Seven years later, securing labor remained a challenge. Francis's brother John wrote in 1802, "Brother William informs me that you complained of a scarcity of hands to carry on your iron works & would be willing perhaps to hire some; Should this be the case and we can agree I would hire seven of my best negroe men to you for a year & also the waggon and team you had last summer; The horses are in good order again & every thing about the gears will be well repaired. The men that I would hire are, Billy Pointer, Will Braxton, Butcher Ned, Henry, Daniel Farrow, Hanibal, & Tom—with the last mentioned, China must be hired, as she is his wife, the others have not wives."[95] White men, too, toiled at the ironworks. Robertson Gannaway, a carpenter (and later minister), recalled: "[I]n the winter of 1801, I came to Cripple Creek. . . . I wrought at my trade, at an Iron Works, called Speedwell, on Cripple Creek and a more wicked and blasphemous company I have never fallen into, in all my travels."[96] Preston and other iron makers could not afford choosiness as they pulled together the laborers they needed. Gannaway's depiction of a rough and rowdy crowd had merit.

Under various owners, the Speedwell iron furnace operated until the 1830s and was rebuilt after the Civil War. In approximately 1807, though, Francis Preston relinquished the ironworks in order to concentrate on developing a saltworks, which likewise utilized slave labor. His wife, the daughter of Patrick Henry's sister, had inherited the salt business, situated farther west at Saltville in the Holston River basin in neighboring Washington County.[97] The saltworks, another extractive industry, shaped the area around it in much the way the lead and iron operations did in Wythe County. This industry also played a vital role later in the Civil War and endured into the twentieth century.

Francis Preston, born in 1765, felt the shifting winds of the postrevolutionary republic. His education at the College of William and Mary and his service as a state legislator led to his election to the third U.S. Congress, which opened in March 1793; the House of Representatives seated him in spite of alleged voter intimidation in his behalf. Times had changed since his father's connections in Williamsburg had led to the family's nearly unfettered power in the mountains. In 1795, Francis Preston's longtime acquaintance Alexander Smyth, also born in 1765 and already experienced as a state legislator in the combative postwar political atmosphere, upbraided Preston in a public letter. Smyth accused Preston of having a hundred times the property of his average constituent, of showing sympathy toward supporters of monarchy, of encouraging confrontation with Great Britain so that the price of salt would rise, and of voting in favor of revenue laws that aided U.S. manufacturers. Preston won reelection in 1795, but two years later he lost his bid for a third term.[98] Smyth's allegations that Preston lacked a democratic touch had merit. Preston's son William (b. 1794) later described growing up in Saltville with tutors and servants. William recalled, in terms that reflected a refined education, that his mother's "wealth and her *manière à due* in some sort segregated her family from the poorer and plainer community in which she lived, and thus in my earlier childhood my associates were almost entirely domestic."[99]

Despite a disastrous tenure as a general in the War of 1812, Smyth went on to serve six terms of his own in Congress. Preston later served extensively in the Virginia General Assembly, and his family members held many high offices. Preston and Smyth battled in the political arena while sharing the same basic economic values: both practiced law and to different extents invested in industrial enterprises; Smyth had even managed the saltworks for a time in the 1780s, before Preston owned it.[100] This elite economic consensus foreshadowed the New River valley's nineteenth century. Although the extremely enterprising could still find opportunity in the Blue Ridge minerals and in the valley of Virginia more broadly, a small but slowly evolving group of men kept economic and political control tightly linked and closely held. When the Virginia legislature added a new county in 1832, formed from Wythe and Washington counties, the town of Saltville, so important to Preston, lay partly in the new county—known as Smyth County in honor of the recently deceased General Alexander Smyth.

Chapter 2

Turnpikes to Ore and More

Prosperous northeastern cities and their fertile hinterlands led the young United States into a new industrial age in the first half of the nineteenth century, but the comparatively rural white people in the South continued to prosper in older ways. Because the lack of cities limited consumer markets in the region, the extractive industries, including those in the New River valley, rarely grew into more complex manufacturers and processors. A modest great divergence started.[1] Slavery remained at the heart of the South's economic and political system, and copper and lead, for instance, often went north for use in workshops and factories. In many ways, however, southern extractive industries kept on flourishing within the market-based norms that guided the entire country through its industrial evolution.

In the early nineteenth century, both the lead mines and the budding iron makers along New River had to overcome the same challenges of transportation, business organization, and market conditions that vexed their peers elsewhere. And as occurred in the rest of the nation, conditions had improved by midcentury for those mountain businessmen as well as for entrepreneurs in a new Blue Ridge industry, copper mining and smelting. Turnpikes and railroads eased transportation problems; private and public geological investigations identified promising spots for extractive capitalism; investors eagerly—sometimes too eagerly—put money into new ventures; and free laborers, too, fought for better returns on their skills and hard work. As in the rest of the United States, the routine use of incorporation changed the form of business for some New River valley firms, whereas families kept control of others. Southern capitalists in the nineteenth century continued to find a ready place in the American economic mosaic in spite of regional divergence on slavery.

Landscapes of Change

At the turn of the century, the rigor of the trip through Flower Gap had moderated little since the time of John Bartram's 1762 travels. In 1808, the Reverend Joseph Thomas saw an awe-inspiring landscape dotted with human activity as he trudged northward to the same spot: "I then went on and crossed the Blue Ridge at Flour Gap. Here I had the most extensive and delightful prospect of creation I ever had before. From thence I could see the distant hills and little mountains thrown, as it were by a careless hand, yet in beauteous order, over distant lands below." More settlers had arrived, but their modest changes to the landscape did not diminish its power in Thomas's imagination: "Numerous farms with many a rural scene rose into review, watered by parling rills, while distant Yadkin rolled along. Yonder stands dread Arrarat, forty miles distant, rising like an awful pyramid crowned as with a turret on the lofty mountain's top. The contemplations of the mighty former of all, that arose from the sight, were profitable to me as I was led to adore the great Creator, as wise, good and powerful without any parallel, and to view myself as a base particle, insignificant as nothing. I was then in Grayson County, Virginia."[2]

More than three decades later, in June 1841, Brother Van Vleck, a Moravian missionary visiting the area from Salem, North Carolina, described the area at the summit of Flower Gap with language that likewise looked to the romantic sublime. Even atop the mountain, though, the community had developed considerably in the intervening years: "The Mountain Ridge is from 10 to 20 miles wide, sloping gradually towards the north, the water courses flowing in that direction into New River. Many farms are scattered along the top of the mountain, which is undulating, and produces good pasturage. The woods were embellished by the flowering laurel, now in richest bloom, and by the still more splendid honeysuckle of these regions, the blossoms of which decked the copses on both sides of the road, and along the clear, cool mountain-streams, dashing over their rocky beds." The arduous path down the mountain still made him catch his breath, however: "With our faces now again towards home, we descended the Flower Gap, justly so called from the laurels and honeysuckles, crowning its brow, and walked down the steep, rough road, leading our horses,—with deep, precipitous vallies on both sides of us,—the mountain torrent rushing through the abyss below."[3]

In 1857, Hardin Taliaferro, an Alabama Baptist minister and a native of Surry County, North Carolina, made his attempt to sum up the dramatic landscape and the human marks on it. Taliaferro recalled hunting deer around Flower Gap, and he described the view from Fisher's Peak, just west of Flower Gap: "From the top of Fisher's Peak one has an unsurpassed view, east, west, north, and south, of mountain piled upon mountain, lifting their heads high in the immense blue horizon far as the eye can take in an object, strengthened and assisted by the clear and pure atmosphere of that elevated region. If heathen mythology were true, this might have been the place where giants piled mountain upon mountain to scale the walls of heaven. Then 'knobs' of lesser size more modestly lift up their heads to aid and swell the grand variety, while hills and ridges assist the spectator to gradually descend to small valleys, river and creek bottoms, where now and then may be seen small farms, cabins, and houses. But the view is indescribably grand."[4]

These vivid accounts help situate the New River valley's lead, iron, and copper mines, a few miles away from Flower Gap, properly within their rural setting. In the Northeast's burgeoning cities, though, such tableaux led readers to forget that even in the midst of farms and the sublime, southern industrialists were chasing profit with all-American vigor and that civic boosters were pushing for the turnpikes and railroads that by midcentury had begun to link all of the interior United States east of the Mississippi. Taliaferro described the area in a volume of exotic tales, published in 1859 under the pseudonym "Skitt," which contributed to outlandish ideas about the rural South. These stereotypes, in tension with positive Jeffersonian views of rural life, would only grow stronger into the twentieth century in spite of the upcountry South's robust mix of antebellum economic activity.[5] Local businessmen, though, paid little attention to reports of their ignorance.

Family Capitalism and Corporate Quickening at the Lead Mines

The operation of the lead mines grew more complex following the Austins' forfeiture and the 1806 sale of the enterprise to Daniel Sheffey, David Peirce, and Thomas Jackson. In 1807, James Mease, a Philadelphia physician, numismatist, and geological observer, published *A Geological Account of the United States*. He described the Austinville mines as being operated by the American Lead Mine Company, with "a number of the most experienced English workmen" tapping into "an inexhaustible quantity of ore." The shafts went deeper than before: "The present mode of digging the ore is to sink a shaft, beginning about two-thirds of the way up the mountain descending perpendicularly into the ground about 100 feet, at which depth the miners generally meet with water, which prevents them descending further, although they are yet above the level of the river more than 100 feet. The ore is often found at the top of the ground, but generally at about 50 feet from the surface, and continues to increase in quality and quantity as they descend." Mease noted the beginnings of a drainage tunnel: "To facilitate the obtaining of ore, a level has been commenced on the southwest side of the ore mountain at the foot, and extending so as to pass through the centre of the ore beds about 250 feet below the top of the works, which when completed will open a subterraneous passage, sufficient for a waggon, about half a mile through the main body of the ore mountain, and will answer the double purpose of supplying ore, and draining the water from all the works."[6]

In 1807 as well, Thomas Jackson completed construction of a 75-foot-tall shot tower on the banks of the New River, with a shaft in the tall riverside bluff that allowed molten lead to fall 150 feet into cold river water, forming excellent shot. Technology had grown more sophisticated in the five decades since John Chiswell had arrived on the scene.[7] For the first time, sustained growth in productivity had begun in the Blue Ridge as well as in the rest of the United States and Great Britain.

Business conditions varied, but a growing nation needed lead. Jackson testified that once the War of 1812 commenced, "navigation from New Orleans to the Atlantic ports of the United States was interrupted, and the necessities of the nation demanded lead." He gladly provided that lead for his "adopted country."[8] By 1810, Fort Chiswell merchant James McGavock had begun arranging for the hauling of lead pigs, each weighing around 130 pounds, to Baltimore commission merchant Henry Thompson. Wagoners had up to thirty days to complete the journey.[9] Jackson and Peirce, sometimes working together and sometimes competing, continued for many years to market much of their lead through Thompson, as did their successors in the 1830s. By the 1830s, Thompson, in turn, sold much of the lead to just two companies, the Baltimore Shot Tower Company and the Phoenix Shot Tower Company. The lead mines also took advantage of the developing backcountry economy, as Peirce and Jackson sold pig lead through Henderson & Beaty of Abingdon, Virginia. Despite the mine owners' careful relationships with good merchant houses, however, the lead business could not stand aloof from economic buffeting, including the financial panic of 1837. Henry Thompson pointed out in August 1837, "[O]ur Factories have not been doing any business for some time past and the sale of Lead very dull." A few months later he repeated his downbeat outlook: "[T]he price has declined greatly. . . . Our Shot Companies being now well supplied, we have not much prospect of making further sales to any extent for some time."[10]

Though Peirce and Jackson and their successors pocketed considerable profits much of the time, the work provided less reason for cheerfulness to the "eight healthy, likely, sound, Negro men" whom David Peirce hired from their Pittsylvania County owner in 1814. Ambrose, Major, Shadrick, Ned, Robin, Thom, West, and Jack could not "work under ground in the mines," per the contract, and Graham agreed to pay $800 and "return the slaves sound and well." These men joined a procession of now anonymous slaves who worked the mines. Free blacks also contributed by the 1830s. A list of the county's free blacks in 1838 places six men as miners at "L. mine."[11] Jackson and Peirce, in using black labor, fit the norm for both industrialists and large farmers in Wythe County: 1,618 slaves and 125 free blacks numbered among the county's 9,375 residents in 1840.[12]

The mine owners sometimes treated slaves harshly. At some point before 1814, Peirce and Jackson joined in the purchase of Jack, a "likely" bondman from the town of Staunton, much farther north in the valley of Virginia. Jack, it turned out, often ran away, and he had "Fits." He worked initially for Peirce at the Poplar Camp iron furnace, but absconded to Germantown, North Carolina, because, according to Jackson, Peirce whipped Jack "with a thorn brush." Jackson went for the slave, who tried to flee again on the way back to the Virginia mountains. He thereafter served Jackson but continued to rebel. On one occasion, Jackson picked up Jack from an acquaintance who was holding the runaway. Jackson flailed Jack with a thick switch, at which Jack protested, "Master you hurt me." According to the witness, Jackson "answered that it was his intention to hurt him." Once, retrieving Jack from the county seat, the mine owner "drove him before him" for more than a dozen miles on the way to Austinville. Outside in the rain all night, Jack caught an illness and died, leading to a lawsuit between Jackson and Peirce.[13]

Even though the partners mired themselves in legal procedures, they consistently operated the mines, often manning competing tunnels and furnaces on the property. Financial disagreements led to Sheffey's selling out to Peirce and Jackson at the end of 1812, leaving Peirce owning 13/24 and Jackson 11/24 of the property. In April 1815, tax assessors valued the lead mines, two furnaces, and other improvements, including more than twenty houses, presumably for miners, at $60,000. Jackson and Peirce fought vigorous legal battles for this property and raced each other to raise ore from the most promising spots. With the fight unresolved, Jackson died in 1824, and Peirce followed in October 1833. The heirs—including Peirce's talented son-in-law David Graham and members of the Raper family, who descended from Jackson's sister—likewise failed to cooperate with one another. In October 1827, for $14,000, one segment of Jackson's heirs, sons of his brother John, sold their substantial interest (11/48) to the wealthy James White (1770–1838) of Abingdon, Virginia, whose extensive holdings included investments in the saltworks in Saltville, Virginia, and other saltworks in Kentucky and whose wife had ties to the Preston family, long prominent in both politics and industry in Virginia.[14]

In the midst of the shifting alliances, Daniel Sheffey's regional eminence helped give the mines a small place in the development of early professional scientific investigation in the United States. Unlike gentlemen amateurs such as James Mease, Samuel L. Mitchill had a university appointment in New York. He also served in Congress with Sheffey, who shared with Mitchill a box of lead samples. Mitchill then wrote about the specimens in an 1818 book on mineralogy, and in 1820 he discussed them with Parker Cleaveland, a mineralogist at Bowdoin College. Cleaveland put the information into an 1822 edition of his influential book on geology. The ore at Austinville, he wrote, "is sometimes massive and coherent, and sometimes disseminated and friable, and is usually yellowish, reddish, or blackish. Galena and other ores of lead occur in this mine; but the Carbonate of lead, at present, predominates in the proportion of 5 to 1 over all the others." The varieties of ore came together in a productive way: Cleaveland reported that in 1812 "about 450 tons of lead were obtained."[15] Both scientific inquiry and better business methods would continue to improve Americans' efficiency in excavating natural phenomena.

For much of the 1830s, three and sometimes four competing companies mined lead simultaneously, but in 1838 the principals consolidated their concerns as the Wythe Lead Mines Company. As in other regions of the United States, the business owners began leaning toward more rational organization of their family firms. For ten years, relative peace then endured. The mine owners' consolidation agreement expired in 1848. Even though the owners had failed to profit during part of the 1840s, most of them reached a new agreement to operate together as the Union Lead Mine Company, but Alexander N. Chaffin and David Peirce's son Alexander began their own operation, with two furnaces and a competing store supplying the miners' needs. Bitter conflict sundered family relationships and led to vindictive property destruction, but then Alexander Peirce sold out to the other heirs in May 1855. Being "desirous of obtaining an act of incorporation with a view to carry on more successfully and profitably the manufacture of lead," the owners, Chaffin included, wasted no time in shutting off the possibility that dissident family members would again undermine the whole business. On February 18, 1856, the Virginia General Assembly agreed to incorporate the Austinville Lead Mining Company, with a capital stock of $300,000. Under a competent superintendent named William Kohler, the mining work thrived through the rest of the 1850s. In 1860, the Virginia legislature, with stiff urging from David Graham, gave the firm a new corporate charter as the Union Lead Mine Company, with capital listed at $400,000.[16]

The 1838 agreement that started the path toward incorporation may have occurred because of a lawsuit brought during the previous two years. The deaths of Thomas Jackson and David Peirce had left the ownership in many hands, revealing the weakness of an unincorporated business. Each cotenant legally could do as he or she wished as long as any profits from the mining were shared. In 1838, three competing operations were digging and smelting ore. Although any profits from the ore had to be divided, the three mercantile establishments associated with the competing businesses generated profits for the individual proprietors, with no portion going to the mining property's cotenants. In 1836, David Peirce's widow and some of her children and their spouses sued Jackson's successors and some of the other Peirce family members. The plaintiffs, without success, asked the county court (and then the appeals court in 1837) to mandate "a joint operation conducted by a disinterested and competent agent for the benefit of all." Without relief, the complainants would have to open their own competing operation, thus "embracing in self defence, this system of legalised plunder."[17]

Laborers along New River benefited to an extent from the managerial chaos of family capitalism. Mentioning "one hundred hands engaged about the mines 80 of them in regular employment," the Peirce suit claimed "[t]hat the wages of labor at the lead mines are high—have increased much lately, and are greatly [increased] by competition among the several tenants in possession." James Bell, who had worked at the mines off and on for thirty years, often as a manager, alleged that just thirty hands had been able to make 200 tons of lead before Peirce died. Because the new operators gained much of their profits from their stores, they had little incentive to keep wages low. They needed consumer demand. They ensured it by a system that foreshadowed widespread practice in later company towns: "[T]he laborers employed at the lead mines, though they usually contract to receive part of the whole of their wages in cash, yet in fact they generally receive only little money, but are paid by their employers in merchandize and provisions at retail prices, and those prices high." The defendants denied gouging workers and offered a liberal explanation for this system: "The competition between those who are now working their different interests, necessarily raises the price of labor. . . . Your respondents believe that any attempt on their part to reduce the price of labor or a refusal to pay the rates now given would be attended with the immediate cessation of all their operations, as workmen could not be employed for less." In spite of the exploitative mercantile policies, wages had purportedly increased 100 to 120 percent.[18]

Workers articulated their demands. Complainant John Jackson explained, "Alexander Peirce as he understands is selling bacon at sixteen and two third cents per pound and that apple brandy is selling at seventy five cents per gallon. . . . When the price of bacon was raised to a shilling by Peirce some of his hands left there but afterwards came back. Witness does not know that their wages were increased but has understood they were." One laborer corroborated the statement in April 1836. He earned $20 per month, $2 higher than ever before. He received half in cash, and the $2 raise had been enacted the previous autumn. He elaborated, "That some of the hands left then ['last fall'] on account (as they alleged) that the price of bacon was raised[,] and all the hands have returned and commenced work again." A former mine employee testified, however, that other workers received less: "hands generally receive from $12.00 to $17.00 per month—the common hands being hired at about $12.00 per month, and some small boys for five or six dollars, board being included in all cases." And mine manager and England native John Hodgson explained why wages would not likely rise far. He agreed with his questioner's contention that "there is an agreement by the managers at the lead mines that neither party is to hire a hand in the employment of the other, thereby preventing competition."[19] These wage rates compared unfavorably with a national average daily wage for unskilled laborers of eighty-one cents in 1836, though the New River employers came closer to the average rate of seventy cents per day in the South Atlantic states.[20] The Virginia workers fought for a better share of industrial profits at a time when their counterparts in northern cities likewise asserted their rights more vigorously.[21]

Despite their attempts at savvy bargaining following the bacon incident, the workers gained little respect. They had to work hard. Andrew Porter, a local constable and part-time mine employee, had little regard for his fellow workers: "[A]ffiant thinks that a majority of the miners are improvident men; and that they are worth no more at the end of the year than they were at the beginning." William A. Smith, a former store clerk at the lead mines, likewise testified in the 1836 Peirce suit in regard to the miners "[t]hat they were generally in arrear at the end of the year and that generally they are paid but little cash and as little as possible and only a sufficiency to induce them to stay."[22]

Mining and smelting lead spewed contaminants into the environment. The workers of the time knew the environmental hazards but had to take on the work anyway. A clerk shuddered at what the miners endured: "I believe the working under ground to be dangerous, and the work at the mines unhealthy." The list of hands at the mines included slaves, likely a sore point for the free white employees. Andrew Kincannon testified that in 1835 he hired four of his bondmen to the mines at the rate of $12.50 each per month, with the mines providing board, clothes, and taxes. Kincannon preferred, however, to rent slaves to farms: "I think there is more damage to a negroes health in working at the lead mines."[23] Perhaps such stipulations even meant that white workers had to do the most dangerous chores.

The duplication of facilities and energy may indeed have proved inefficient, as the 1830s lawsuit alleged. James R. Miller and Alexander Peirce attested in April 1836 that during the previous year "about four hundred Tons of lead were manufactured." The plaintiff's petition to the court explained how the miners had achieved those figures by adopting a short-term strategy. They had cut "more of the good timber such as ought to be saved for [the] time being . . . than in any ten years previous," using it only for cord wood rather than timbering for shafts. Timber had "been used more profusely for 2 or 3 years past than at any former period." The defendants, though, countered with John Hodgson's belief that "the lead mines take more timber" than in the past for "timbering up the ground where the work is done."[24]

Another, more serious allegation of deficient long-term practice went unanswered: "The mines and excavations are now sunk at random upon no enlarged and general plan, and the entire expence and labor bestowed upon a shaft is lost so soon as the vein discovered is exhausted, or the mines reach water. It has been found that the ore increases in quantity and richness as the depth increases but the miners have hitherto abandoned their shafts whenever they have reached water, which is pretty uniformly found at a certain depth. Thus the mines have heretofore been only worked at what are, in mining, inconsiderable depths, no means having been resorted to by running a level from the lower ground adjacent or by the use of steam power on the surface to prevent the influx of water."[25] Miners could change the landscape only so fast; drainage trouble complicated the mining there for many more decades.

Concerns about declining timber stocks soon became less pressing, though. On September 2, 1839, for $1,712.00, the company, with its constant need for wood to fire its furnaces, bought from the state a two-thirds interest in 242,000 acres originally granted in 1795 to Thomas Ruston and John D. Blanchard with Moses Austin's assistance. Ruston's son and two daughters, who apparently became owners of the land (or, at the least, Ruston's half of it) soon after it was surveyed, had failed to pay taxes and to properly register half the original grant with the county commissioner, thus forfeiting the land back to the state. In 1837 and 1838, Virginia legislators, looking both to raise funds and to develop the state's western sections, established procedures to reclaim and auction such land. Francis Allison Sr., a well-to-do resident of Pulaski County, procured the other third interest, joining Robert Raper and David Graham, who represented the lead mine company, in the purchase. Allison subsequently sold his third to William Y. C. White, another of the mining company stockholders. The Ruston Survey, situated mostly in Grayson County but with small portions in Pulaski and Wythe counties, adjoined the mine property and covered most of what in 1842 became Carroll County. Various parts of the tract already had claimants.

The influential men of Carroll County did not react passively to this industrial land grab. A technical irregularity in the deed, dated November 19, 1840, and recorded December 23, 1840, left the land sale open to challenge, and Fielden L. Hale, a litigious land speculator, merchant, and later mine owner in his own right, led the opposition. Hale contested the deed in 1842, and the litigation multiplied into dozens of lawsuits. Hale not only pointed out the irregular deed but also claimed that the original sale had not been properly advertised; in 1853, he finally seemed to secure in the county court the right to his own competing land grant within the Ruston Survey. However, the Virginia Supreme Court of Appeals gave Allison, Raper, and Graham the right to request a new deed. Complex court battles involving the Ruston Survey thus dragged on for several more years, and in Wythe County's court in 1857 Allison, Raper, Graham, and their partners won their deed to the massive tract.[26]

Other opponents contested the windfall, though. Joseph Jackson Jr., a Richmond attorney, raised claims on behalf of the heirs of John D. Blanchard, who had originally owned part of the 1795 grant; Jackson also bought from them a share of their rights. According to mine superintendent William Kohler, the mine owners granted Jackson and Blanchard's heirs two-sevenths interest in the land to end the matter. Hale and his Carroll County counterparts also maintained their attacks. Not until after the Civil War did the controversies close. In February 1866, Graham, Raper, and White settled with Fielden Hale. Hale exchanged his claims to eleven thousand acres of land in Carroll, plus $8,000, for a clear hold on more than eighteen thousand acres of onetime Ruston land in the same county. This case served as a model, and the Ruston landowners settled other cases along similar lines. According to Kohler, the land transactions then finally turned a profit. In the long run, convenient access to timber certainly aided the tunneling and smelting work at the mines. For Hale as well as for the Wythe investors, the land not likely to contain ore or timber necessary for industry could be divided into small farms and sold. Carroll County's agricultural development could thus move forward with more clarity once the industrialists had secured their hold on the most valuable resources.[27]

Despite periods of internecine conflict and legal entanglements, investors still made money at the mines. Although Austinville no longer played a major national role in the U.S. lead industry as it had at the turn of the century, industrializing America required ever more lead for pipes, pewter, paint, ammunition, and many other applications in growing cities. Court records show that from February 1848 to February 17, 1857, profit from the various lead-mining operations around Austinville totaled $102,578.03.[28] In 1850, Alexander Peirce produced 150 tons of lead with 40 workers, and the Union Lead Mine Company, with 60 men and 2 women laboring, smelted 250 tons of lead. An additional 4 men and 4 women used the nearby shot tower to make 40 tons of shot on behalf of the same company;

the somewhat lighter physical demands of that process may explain the women's greater presence on the manufacturing side of the lead business.[29] In 1860, the firm made 400 tons of lead pigs and 100 tons of shot with 125 workers.[30]

During the antebellum era, the Austinville lead mines declined from ranking as one of only a handful of lead-producing establishments in the nation to carrying on as a profitable but less important business. In 1810, the U.S. census reported lead mining and manufacturing operations in Pennsylvania, Massachusetts, and the new Louisiana Territory. Pennsylvania had the dominant lead-processing industry, with Virginia listed as the only other major contributor of the raw material. But the Louisiana Territory was already beginning to show its vast potential. Tench Coxe wrote, "Manufacturing all we produce of lead, we have been obliged to import a large balance of that useful metal for our workmen, after using all our own. Lead, which is convertible into various pigments, is a raw material of several useful manufactures in its separate state, or mixed with other metals. *The rapid advance of lead manufactures, on the purchase of Louisiana, proves that they not only steadily progress, but promptly extend on every new supply of the raw material.* Manufactures goad the whole landed interest to profitable exertion and production."[31] In 1840, Virginia (with 878,648 pounds) trailed by wide margins the Wisconsin Territory (15,129,350 pounds), Illinois (8,755,000 pounds), and Missouri (5,295,455 pounds) in the amount of lead produced.[32]

Antebellum technology along the New River looked much the same as earlier because a steady supply of water made the adoption of up-to-date steam power less than urgent. But the scale of work grew: men dug deeper and farther. For Virginia's geological survey, William Barton Rogers, a second-generation college professor in the state, reported on the work in 1836: "There are six openings at present wrought, each having drifts below the surface at various depths from 30 to 120 feet. These are all comprised within a space of less than 150 yards square. To the S. W. are numerous pits from which ore was extracted in former years. The entire distance through which the lead has been traced and wrought in this vicinity is about half a mile." Like Jefferson before him, Rogers had ideas for how to improve the mining: "At present a wasteful method of excavation is threatening serious injury to the interests of future mining operations in this region, and if persevered in, will destroy the usefulness of many portions of the veins now worked by rendering them almost inaccessible or incapable of being farther wrought." Moreover, "[i]n the operation of washing at what are called the Buddles . . . there is evidently a larger proportion of useful material carried off than ought to be allowed to escape." Mining obviously brought profits, however, in addition to the water pollution. Rogers marveled, "The fact that by far the larger portion of the lead which these mines furnish is carried in wagons to Baltimore, is a striking proof of the lucrative nature of the manufacture, and strongly indicates the benefit which in reference to this product, the public may be expected to reap from the extensive works of improvement which have been so wisely projected in this portion of the state."[33] State funding for science embodied a wider acceptance of systematically investigating the natural world for the purpose of development. Professional scientific literature such as Rogers's survey would soon proliferate, benefiting Virginia's mine owners by fostering the spread of up-to-date information.[34]

With more unity among the lead mines' owners, by the 1840s the methods used in Wythe County had begun to improve. More than a decade after Rogers's visit, a company employee who had observed the techniques used at a silver and lead mine in North Carolina proved that Rogers had rightly pegged the lead-ore washing operation as inefficient. This man helped his employers to discover that several decades of waste products in Austinville could be smelted at considerable profit. The company also found better ways to ventilate the shafts, which allowed for more extensive mining during the summer months, when dangerous air quality had plagued operations. And in 1851, completion of a long-awaited 241-foot vertical shaft, which connected to a horizontal shaft driven in from farther down the steep slopes, alleviated the problem even more. That deep shaft also then allowed for the profitable manufacture of shot within the mine, relieving the company of having to rent the nearby shot tower from Thomas Jackson's descendants. The cost of manufacturing shot thus fell by nearly two-thirds. The year 1851 also marked the final usefulness of one vein of ore that had been worked since 1839: miners had followed the vein for 1,527 feet.[35]

A traveler in 1855 nonetheless looked down, in that way visitors have, on the operation's technological state: "It is strange that the ore is raised chiefly *by hand*. A like primitive system prevails at the works, where a great many processes easily adapted to machine[r]y, are still laboriously performed by hand. The sweeps at the buddles or vats, for washing, are worked by hand; and it is strange enough to see men and little boys, each holding on to the end of a sweep, jumping up and down rapidly and stiff, like beings possessed! A cam wheel would do the thing so easy!"[36] Ignorance might explain the methods used, but the relative price of labor more likely dictated the mix of technology and human effort.

David Graham and New River Iron

Iron deposits in Wythe County likewise attracted visitors. Geologist William Barton Rogers outlined the New River iron area in 1837: "I would particularly bring to notice the very extensive range of deposits which, commencing at Mack's run [at the edge of present-day Pulaski County] and pursuing a course parallel to the Poplar Camp and Iron mountains, within from two to four miles of their base, continues to the southern boundary of the state. In this region, from two to three miles in width, this ore is found in the flanks of the calcareous ridges in massive beds, frequently enclosed by walls of limestone, and usually of a quality admirably adapted to the uses of the furnace." He turned to superlatives to explain the commercial potential of nature and to complain that such exploitation had not already progressed further. He wrote, "There is, perhaps, no other portion of the great limestone valley, either in Pennsylvania or Virginia, so bountifully supplied with this material in so available a shape, and none in which this valuable resource has been more indolently improved."[37] Even though the ever-critical Rogers disparaged their work, iron makers along the New River and Cripple Creek, a major tributary in western Wythe County, had amassed generations of local knowledge by the time he visited.

Iron making, drawing on dispersed ore deposits, necessarily involved a greater number of entrepreneurs than did the lead mines. For instance, around 1807 the Wythe (or Little Wythe) Furnace on Francis Mill Creek grew out of the earlier bloomery forge on the site. It passed through the hands of several owners, including David Peirce, and by the 1850s had been renamed the Porter Furnace. The Raven Cliff Furnace on Cripple Creek started operation around 1810, and the Barren Springs Furnace went into blast on the New River in about 1854. The Eagle (or Grey Eagle) Furnace on Cripple Creek started production in 1863.[38] Unlike the lead mines, though, these early ironworks did not grow so large or complex as to require incorporation.

David Graham stands out as the leading iron maker of the antebellum New River–Cripple Creek region. Family capitalism proceeded more peacefully in the iron industry than at the lead mines. In 1859, David Graham owned Graham's Forge on Reed Creek a short distance north of the New River; a rolling mill in the same complex; and the Barren Springs Furnace on the river's south bank. The rolling mill, a relatively small one, had "1 heating furnace, 1 train of rolls and 5 nail machines, driven by water power, and made in twenty-one weeks of 1856 161 tons of merchant bars, plate iron and nails." The forge, reportedly constructed in 1800 and rebuilt in 1856, featured "4 refinery fires and 1 hammer worked by water, and in 1856 made 161 tons of blooms and 23 tons of bars." Graham had earlier operated two separate facilities with the name "Paramount (or Parry Mount) Furnace" and possibly others. During the 1850s, he also supplied two other local businesses, Wilkinson's Forge and Peirce's Forge.[39]

Graham's rise to prominence had begun on April 25, 1826, when as a young man in his twenties he took over the lease on an older iron-making operation, which he later bought. Around the turn of the century, Andrew and James Crockett had begun Cedar Run Furnace on Reed Creek. In 1804, they attracted the attention of the state legislature by damming the creek, thus interfering with traditional riparian rights, but they reached a compromise, for that furnace eventually served as Graham's starting point. With his business under way, Graham rebuilt a forge there in September 1828 and added the rolling mill the same year. He solidified his standing in 1835 by marrying the daughter of recently deceased David Peirce, from whom they inherited a substantial interest in the lead mines.[40] Success nonetheless did not come easily. In 1865, Graham recalled, "[F]or many years I was hard pressed for money. . . . Mr. Fulton [perhaps Andrew S. Fulton] had invariably aided me whenever I called on him, frequently borrowing money for me on his own credit and otherwise aiding me in raising money."[41]

In 1810, the federal census reported that two active furnaces in Wythe County produced 140 tons of metal and that two forges produced 266 tons. In 1840, the county turned out 504 tons of cast iron and 180 tons of bar iron.[42] Output increased again by 1850. Edmund W. Lockett's twelve hands produced 75 tons of iron; Samuel E. Porter's twenty-five hands turned out 150 tons of iron and castings; and William Wilkerson used twenty-five laborers to create 200 tons of iron and castings. David Graham overshadowed them with sixty hands turning out 450 tons of pig iron, thirty workers making 80 tons of castings, thirty-one employees making 170 tons of bar iron, and ten workers making 80 tons of nails.[43] A decade later, on the eve of war, Graham's Barren Springs Furnace produced 350 tons of pig iron and 50 tons of castings with twenty-five workers. His forge nearby made 100 tons of bar iron and 20 tons of nails with twenty-five workers. David Huddle's competing forge made about 52.5 tons of iron, and Alexander Peirce's crafted another 50 tons.[44]

In spite of these busy furnaces and forges, agriculture long predominated in the counties of the upper New River valley. For example, in 1850 Wythe County included 9,618 white residents, 221 free colored residents, and 2,185 enslaved residents. Its 668 farms had a value, including both land and implements, of $2,180,709. In contrast, its manufacturing establishments employed 322 persons and represented a capital investment of $207,510, with production valued at $145,525. Homemade manufactures totaled another $28,804.[45]

Graham's businesses nonetheless provided good returns and required a mix of workers. Precisely how many slaves worked for him has gone unrecorded, but they made up a large contingent of the workforce. Moreover, free blacks provided some labor. Joseph J. Graham, acting as commissioner of revenue, counted the free blacks in Wythe County in 1838. The tally included Jas. Hill, Joshua Hill, and Lazarus Hill, shown as being at "D. Graham's." Thomas Finley, Randal Finley, and their families also made the list. Joseph Graham labeled each of the Finleys a "hammerman." In an antebellum forge, operating the heavy water-driven machinery that pounded impurities out of pig iron required considerable skill and judgment, and the Finleys must have earned David Graham's trust. Free blacks had limited freedom in the South, but skills of this sort gave them somewhat greater opportunity and security.[46]

Despite relative isolation in the Blue Ridge, Graham, a sharp businessman, stayed abreast of industrial and political developments elsewhere. He followed the national controversy over banking and the money supply during the 1830s. He experimented with water and land routes to find the best path to distant markets, and the geographical extent of his sales showed his corresponding success. He supported his brother Calvin's medical education in Philadelphia, and in turn in 1833 Calvin explained the British development of new hot-blast furnace techniques, which he had learned from his chemistry professor. Calvin encouraged David as the latter then experimented with the new methods. Information moved quickly if it carried the likelihood of profit.[47] In an 1859 tally, the height of his Barren Springs Furnace—forty feet—ranked in the top quarter of charcoal furnaces built after 1840. Height served as a proxy for technological sophistication, marking Graham's endeavor as an ambitious one on par with some cutting-edge coal-burning furnaces.[48]

Graham showed resourcefulness in preparing and marketing his products. He not only sold pig iron, bar iron, and nails but also cast various items, including skillets, pots of many sizes, ovens, and egg boilers.[49] He sold bar iron and kettles to the Preston family and other firms making salt in the nearby Holston River valley, and he had deals with merchants as far away as Greensboro, North Carolina, and Greene County, Tennessee. Graham also operated ancillary businesses such as a store and shoe shop, which cut down on his own operating costs and allowed him to earn additional profits from his neighbors. He even made inquiries about the more complicated requirements of casting cook stoves and making iron for gun barrels.[50]

In the mid-1830s, looking for another way to expand his business interests, Graham joined several investors, including his brother-in-law Alexander Peirce and mine owner–attorney Samuel McCamant, to incorporate a resort called "Grayson Sulphur Springs" on the banks of the New River. Their advertisement boasted of the water's curative powers, the comfort of the cabins, and the opportunities for fishing and hunting. The proprietors claimed that "the accommodations will be found equal to any fashionable Watering-place in Virginia." Journalists agreed by 1850, when one pointed out, "The Grayson Sulphur Springs, in Carroll County, are of recent reputation and still rising in favour. They are supposed to be of much efficacy in rheumatism and dyspepsia. Rising on the west side of the blue Ridge, the site partakes of all the physical characteristics of Harper's Ferry. The scenery is bold and grand, marked by a peculiar wildness, and warmly exciting to the imaginative and romantic nature."[51] The investors' understanding of the regional and national economy, gained through their industrial experience, helped them see this remote site's potential to serve other elite southerners, who sojourned there from warmer areas. As long as profits beckoned, these businessmen could see their landscape as beautiful rather than solely as a source of minerals.

Turnpikes and the Railroad

The resort owners and other furnace proprietors welcomed the transportation improvements of the 1840s and 1850s, which finally applied balm to the sore transportation difficulties that Thomas Jefferson had diagnosed more than half a century earlier. Road construction and maintenance in Virginia, conducted principally at the county level, had long suffered from a degree of administrative chaos. Beginning in 1816, though, Virginia joined other states in supporting internal improvements. The new Board of Public Works provided limited state support to state-chartered, privately operated companies. In its first decades, the board sank most of the available funds into the James River and Kanawha Canal. Powerful Tidewater planters opposed providing much support for other developments in the mountains, but they at least tolerated the canal project as a political necessity. By the 1840s, the gradual growth of population and political power in the mountain counties forced the legislature to expand funding for building roads in the highlands. As a result, by the early 1850s engineers and laborers had finished several turnpikes, including the Southwestern Turnpike down the valley through Wytheville, somewhat like the Wilderness Road before it; the Tazewell Courthouse and Fancy Gap Turnpike; and the Floyd Court House and Hillsville Turnpike, which extended west beyond Hillsville into Grayson County. These turnpikes aided the miners and refiners along the upper New River as they moved their heavy goods. At different points, both Samuel McCamant and Alexander Peirce served on the board of directors of the Wytheville and Grayson Turnpike. Lobbying by local citizens, headed by lawyer and politician Andrew S. Fulton and physician James N. Kincannon, brought that road's route directly by the Grayson Sulphur Springs.[52]

By the 1850s, the state retained only a veneer of commitment to private ownership of roads. For example, the state and the three counties affected (Carroll, Wythe, and Tazewell) shared ownership of the Tazewell Courthouse and Fancy Gap Turnpike Company, and the region's residents cheered the changes. When one road opened through Carroll County toward the North Carolina line, local officials William H. Cook, John Early, and Ira B. Coltrane voiced their enthusiasm: "We have never known and rarely heard of any improvement that gives so much satisfaction to the public. A large stream of travel has already been turned through it, and all passengers are loud in their expressions of admiration of the road and thankfulness to the legislature. 'The Fancy Gap Road' is already known from Nashville to Charleston, S.C."[53] A stagecoach line soon used that route on its run from Salem, North Carolina, to Wytheville. One of its customers in 1860 reported crossing the Blue Ridge "at the *Fancy Gap*": "The road is graded, and the ascent was very gradual for five miles. The mountain scenery was, indeed, very interesting. We were in the valley of a beautiful mountain stream, which poured over its many falls, and we passed a mill on it at some distance before reaching the highest elevation, then followed the stream up to its source, which appeared to be at the summit. Here we came to a tavern, and stopped for breakfast."[54] The turnpike helped the scattered residents of Fancy Gap, situated at the mountaintop, to cohere as a community, for the locale gained a post office in May 1860.[55]

In July 1849, the board of directors of the Tazewell Courthouse and Fancy Gap Turnpike Company named as its first president Andrew S. Fulton—Wythe County attorney, state legislator, Whig congressman from December 1847 to March 1849, investor in mining lands, and later circuit court judge. William H. Cook, an attorney in Hillsville, served as secretary. At the same meeting, the board, for an annual salary of a thousand dollars, contracted with James Hays Piper, a brother of Fulton's in the Wytheville lodge of the Free and Accepted Masons, to take on the turnpike's engineering duties. In October the board reported, "Mr. Piper is now upon the line and is progressing as rapidly as he can."[56] Fulton, Cook, and their fellow directors chose wisely when selecting Piper to survey and lay out their turnpike. Their choice also lays bare the tightly woven net holding together the men who spurred development in the Blue Ridge.

As a college student around 1818, Piper had gained lifelong renown by climbing Natural Bridge, but the Rockbridge County native then had a distinguished career as an educator (including briefly the presidency of what became the University of Tennessee at Knoxville), an engineer, and a politician. In the late 1830s and early 1840s, under the direction of the state's principal engineer, Frenchman Claudius Crozet, Piper worked as the engineer for the lengthy Cumberland Gap and Price's Turnpike through far southwestern Virginia (Botetourt County to Lee County), and he did the survey for the town of Wytheville following its chartering in 1839. He represented Wythe, Grayson, Carroll, Smyth, and Tazewell counties from 1840 to 1846 in the state senate, where he served at least for a time on the Committee of Internal Improvement. In 1846, he became chief clerk and later acting commissioner of the federal government's General Land Office, but he left the post in November 1847. Returning to Wythe County, he lived on Cripple Creek near Speedwell, where his wife, the former Frances Stuart Smyth, daughter of General Alexander Smyth, had inherited the blast furnace and surrounding lands that had once belonged to Francis Preston. In June 1850, after completing his work with the Tazewell Courthouse and Fancy Gap road, Piper agreed to act as the Southwestern Turnpike's chief engineer and superintendent.[57]

For his final job, he accepted in May 1854 a post with the Wytheville and Grayson Turnpike, which would run near some of the industrial developments as well as the major towns: "from a point at or near Wytheville in Wythe county, by the Grayson Sulphur springs and the old courthouse of Grayson county, to the North Carolina line at or near Fisher's gap in Grayson county," with "a branch road from some suitable point of their said road in Wythe county to the lead mines in said county; and also a branch road from a point at or near the Grayson Sulphur springs to Hillsville in Carroll county, or in the direction of said town." Piper's eulogist reported, "It was while engaged in locating this road that by excessive fatigue and exposure, he contracted the disease which resulted in his death." The road descended the Blue Ridge escarpment just east of the old Flower Gap at what quickly received the name "Piper's Gap," a fitting tribute to a man who perhaps did most to put in place the region's infrastructure.[58]

Piper's turnpikes soon had mechanized competition. Representatives of Wythe and adjacent counties had begun pushing for railroad access as early as 1831, but it took some time for the legislature to hear their voices.[59] The Virginia General Assembly eventually realized the need to tamp down the divisions between the state's eastern and western sections; in 1848, it chartered the Lynchburg and Tennessee Railroad to run from Lynchburg to what became Bristol, Virginia/Tennessee, thereby connecting the mountains to existing rails that ended in the eastern port of Norfolk. The legislature renamed the railroad the "Virginia and Tennessee Railroad" and invested heavily alongside private backers from Lynchburg, Richmond, and, to a lesser extent, the mountain towns. The railroad engines reached Max Meadows in Wythe County in October 1854 and Wytheville on December 14, 1854. Henceforth, the mines along the upper New River could dispense with using wagons to make long-distance shipments of products. A short wagon trip to the nearest depot would suffice. Farther west, a spur line ran from the main railroad directly to the saltworks in Saltville, but the iron makers of Wythe County would have to wait decades before they enjoyed that ultimate convenience.[60]

Industrialists eager for profit looked to water as well as to road and rail. David Graham served as one of the state's representatives on the railroad's board of directors in the late 1850s.[61] (He also gained new business from the railroad, casting "Rail Road Chairs," the flanged plate fastened beneath adjacent pieces of rail, holding them together.[62]) However, Graham also looked for additional transportation relief in his immediate neighborhood. In March 1856, the General Assembly passed "An Act to Incorporate the New River Navigation Company." It allowed Graham and others to raise capital "for opening and improving the navigation of New river from the Central depot of the Virginia and Tennessee railroad to the Wythe lead mines in the county of Wythe."[63]

The railroad executives, of course, recognized the mineral industry's potential to produce freight. The railroad hired eminent Pennsylvania geologist J. Peter Lesley to describe and map the possibilities along the route in southwestern Virginia. Lesley had assisted with Pennsylvania's first geological survey, which had taken place between 1836 and 1842 under the direction of Henry Darwin Rogers, himself a veteran of his brother William Barton Rogers's geological survey of Virginia. The railroad proudly printed Lesley's findings in its 1854 annual report. In addition to examining the gypsum and salt deposits in the Holston River watershed, Lesley looked at the scattered but locally useful deposits of coal near the New River in Pulaski and Wythe counties. Small amounts had already been mined: "This coal has been taken to the Lead Works and found to answer well in the Scotch furnace. . . . [O]ne bushel of this coal made one-fifth more lead than twelve bushels of charcoal." The visiting scientist then met with David Graham to learn more about the iron deposits of the region, and he toured the lead mines with their superintendent, William Kohler. Lesley provided the railroad with optimistic conclusions. Regarding iron ore, he wrote, "I judge that very great quantities of it remain to be worked in Wythe county, and that other exhibitions of it will establish, elsewhere, iron works not very distant from the road." As for lead, "There is no good reason for not supposing the veins inexhaustible."[64] Roads and railroads themselves made a relatively small impact on the land, but the act of improving transportation allowed for far more efficient exploitation of the environmental resources. The two processes went hand in hand.

Carroll County's Copper Boom

In addition to David Graham and his ferruginous peers, other successful capitalists started sending minerals along the turnpikes and the new Virginia and Tennessee tracks. During the 1850s, a driven lot of entrepreneurs came to the fore in Carroll County. Even though the iron industry there had long faltered because the pig iron proved too brittle, geologists and investors had not forgotten the extensive bodies of gossan ores—the weathered, decomposed type prevalent in the county. It turned out that the gossan deposits coexisted with copper ore. In the late 1840s, a copper boom began at Ducktown in the mountains of southeastern Tennessee. Nearby in Georgia, miners had struck gold, and a prospector looking for more gold had instead discovered the rich copper ores in Tennessee. By the early 1850s, companies had begun scouting for other copper lodes.[65] A copper rush to the Michigan shores of Lake Superior had also begun in the 1840s, further attuning investors' ears to the red metal's siren call. Mid-nineteenth-century Americans needed copper to sheath ships, make brass, fashion engine parts, mint coins, add to paint, and manufacture wire.

In the spring of 1853, Jonathan Worth, a North Carolina state legislator and future governor, traveled to Carroll County to buy horses for his Tarheel State turpentine operations. While there, he "heard of and visited a vein of native copper ore near Hillsville." With two brothers, his son, and his son-in-law, Worth leased or optioned "about one mile of distinctly marked vein." He hoped "to realize something handsome" from his investment owing to "the extraordinary quantity of pure native copper in the surface rock, the distinctness and extent of its appearance on the surface[,] the elevated mountains in which it is found allowing of draining to a considerable depth by short tunnels, the extreme cheapness of labor and provisions, and the facilities of getting it to market[,] a rail road from Lynchburg being now finished within 50 miles and which when finished will come in 25 miles," along with "a good dirt turnpike leading from one mile of the mine to the Rail Road." For advice on how to develop the property, Worth wrote to southern confidants as well as to New York merchants with whom he had done business.[66] He eventually brought in two Carroll County partners, James Earley and Fielden Hale, and they did business as Worth, Earley and Company.[67]

Worth and his partners soon had a great deal of company: a number of Tennessee businessmen, many of them with mining experience, joined what mushroomed into a speculative frenzy. The Tennesseans bought and leased land and opened mines in Carroll County, sometimes at the very spots that had earlier supplied ore to the county's abortive effort to produce iron. The gossan lode, actually several related veins, ran across nearly the entire county along the major ridges that cut into the plateau to the south of where Poplar Camp Mountain descended to the banks of the New River.

One Tennessee investor recalled, "Nearly everybody was excited about copper. It was the topic discussed constantly in hotels, on railroad trains, and everywhere."[68]

Another of the outsiders described the boom in mid-1854: "I came to this place direct from Ducktown. . . . The excitement exceeds anything I have ever seen at Ducktown, and the whole country is now in the hands of East Tennesseans, who were the first [t]o discover and appropriate it. The sluggish aristocracy of Virginia are aroused just in time to be too late, and are now engaged in an illiberal crusade against Tennesseans. They swear we are meaner than *Yankees*. We hear it with a good deal of philosophy." Despite the local antipathy, he tingled at the area's prospects: "I have already looked over much of the country, and am satisfied that it holds extensive beds of copper. . . . The iron ore leads or veins are extensive, and I think will develop some of the largest and richest mines in the world."[69]

The investors—such as John L. Yarnell and his son-in-law Thomas H. Roddy, both physicians and businessmen in Hamilton County, Tennessee; George Bachman of Sullivan County, Tennessee; and John Rhea of Washington County, Tennessee—flooded into Carroll County and executed agreements in which local landowners received a payment up front and generally retained from one-third to one-half of the mineral rights. In return, the mining companies gained unfettered access to the land, its timber, and its water.[70] Abraham Jobe, a Tennessee doctor and industrialist, joined his brother John, then a resident of Catoosa County, Georgia, and others to form a copper company. Abraham looked back on what he called "the Great Copper Speculation": "There were 19 of us and the enterprise was a vast one. My brother was agent for the company with headquarters at Hillsville, Virginia. We bought large interests in Carroll, Floyd, Patrick, and Grayson Counties in Virginia, and also property in North Carolina."[71] In retrospect, relinquishing mineral rights later inflicted much pain on small farm proprietors in certain regions of Appalachia, but the copper investors of the 1850s found no shortage of landowners ready to take what seemed a good risk with their hilly land.

But not all the investors and miners came from Tennessee. Yarnell worked with certain heirs of Carroll County iron maker John Blair.[72] Alexander Peirce entered the copper business in Carroll when he sold his stake in the Austinville lead veins to his co-owners in May 1855 for $15,000. Peirce retained his interest in the lead company's massive holding of Ruston Survey lands, for much of that tract lay in the area of Carroll County supposed to contain copper.[73] Samuel McCamant, a Grayson County attorney, put the Peach Bottom Mine in Ashe County, North Carolina, into production of copper in 1858, but as early as 1854 he was already speculating in Carroll County copper property with Wythe countians James N. Kincannon, Alexander Peirce, Andrew S. Fulton, and Thomas Boyd.[74] Prosperous Tennesseans—agriculturalists, a doctor, politicians such as state legislator John G. Stuart and former governor Aaron V. Brown, and seasoned industrialists such as railroad promoter Vernon K. Stevenson—predominated in the Meigs County and Virginia Mining Company. However, Fielden Hale of Carroll County served as superintendent and owned a significant share of that endeavor, as did Savannah businessman Gazaway Bugg Lamar (whose brother Mirabeau Buonaparte Lamar stood alongside Stephen F. Austin in leading Texas to independence).[75] Stuart assembled some of the company's holdings by purchasing the extensive mining rights already put together by Worth, Earley & Company.[76] Outsiders and locals rushed together, with visions of riches coloring their hopeful views of the mountain landscape.

By March 1855, a number of copper mines were working at full swing; other companies had just gotten started, and the mines had boosted nearly all parts of the local economy and added new elements to local society. The *Hillsville Virginian* reported, "They are now shipping ore more or less from the following places: Paint Bank, Early's, Gov. Brown's, Rhea's, Dalton's, Kincannon's, and nine places belonging to the Delphian Copper-mine Company, the respective names of which we do not know. At how many places they have simply cut copper, we do not know. All we can say is that the lead is twenty-five or thirty miles long; and there is no place in it but what the indications warrant a good copper-mine." The writer explained how the surrounding areas took advantage of the industry's development: "Our country has already felt its beneficial influence. There has been no scarcity of money here as in other portions of the country; things command the highest price; and a ready market is found at every farmer's door. The price of hauling has advanced; the quantity of plank needed cannot be got, though a steam saw-mill close at hand has been running day and night." The boom created its own challenges, too: "The price for labor is greatly on the increase; there is a vast amount of work to be done and but few hands to be got at any price, in fact operations ceased in the fall for want of hands, and it has been but recently a good many Englishmen came in and a good many moved in from different sections of the country, that the operations were not almost stopped by those who were constantly leaving the mines."[77] In addition to free immigrants, slaves also eased the shortage of workers in the copper mines. The county's population of slaves increased from 154 in 1850 to 262 in 1860, with many of them digging in the new mines.[78]

In 1856, the mines gained more international notice. Mining engineer C. S. Richardson visited the copper vein. Writing from Southampton, Massachusetts, he sent a long, detailed description printed in the *Mining Journal, Railway and Commercial Gazette* in London, one of the many specialist publications that had begun circulating professional mining knowledge to the corners of the earth.[79]

Copper Mines and the Expert Imagination

The companies tried hard to develop their holdings. By employing consulting geologists, owners sought to confirm the richness of the ores. Such consulting grew into a big business for mid-nineteenth-century geologists because the reports they issued played a vital role in allowing mine owners to attract additional investment when necessary. Like Virginia, many states in the early nineteenth century began broad government-sponsored geological surveys to identify resources worthy of development, but private geologists still had to tease out the characteristics of specific lands. These geologists had particular importance in evaluating deposits of coal, iron ore, and copper ore. They evaluated the landscape with an unapologetically commercial outlook.[80]

Montroville Wilson Dickeson investigated Carroll County's copper veins and issued reports for three different mining companies. A Philadelphia physician and numismatist with broad intellectual interests, Dickeson earned most renown as a pioneering archaeologist who opened various Indian mounds in the lower Mississippi River valley in the 1840s. However, he also earned money before the Civil War by preparing consulting reports on cypress timber, marble deposits, and copper veins.[81]

Dickeson visited the copper-rich area soon after many of the mining companies began raising usable ore. Miners initially sorted the copper ore and boxed only the richer varieties for shipment to distant smelting operations, such as the Baltimore and Cuba Smelting and Mining Company in Baltimore, Maryland, which had formed in 1845 to process copper ore sent from Cuba and which also handled most of the Ducktown ore. Other shipments from Carroll County went as far as Boston and New York, according to Dickeson.[82] The boxes of ore, each weighing about 500 pounds, lumbered by wagon more than a dozen creaking miles along the turnpike to railroad depots in Wythe County. Between December 31, 1854, and June 30, 1855, the Carroll mining companies shipped 1,454,868 pounds of ore through Lynchburg alone. Dickeson arrived in August 1855 to investigate lands owned or controlled by the Dalton Copper Mining Company of Virginia, responsible for 30,126 of the pounds that traveled via Lynchburg earlier in the year.[83]

Dickeson had two local guides: experienced mine operators Alexander Peirce and Samuel McCamant. The Virginia General Assembly incorporated the Dalton Copper Mining Company in March 1856, with Peirce and McCamant on a list of stockholders that included former congressman Andrew S. Fulton, James N. Kincannon, and Thomas Boyd, as well as a number of other men who held shares in the Wythe lead mines.[84] The Pennsylvanian Dickeson set out to explore the nearly two thousand acres owned or leased by the company, land that had once belonged to Alexander Peirce's father, the iron and lead entrepreneur David Peirce, and a "Dr. Kincannon" (probably James Kincannon). The Dalton Mine on the former Peirce property had been worked since mid-June 1854. Dickeson noted that "at no time was [sic] there more hands employed than fifteen workman [sic], and yet ninety boxes of copper ore were sent to market the first year, the returns of which gave twenty-four per cent. of metal; and there were seventy boxes still remaining at the mine." Development had taken place above ground as well: "In regard to the improvements that have been made on this property, there are several small dwellings, a boarding house, a blacksmith shop, carpenter shop, and three fine ore sheds, besides several more in the process of erection." Moreover, Dickeson found, "[t]he lands are well stocked with a fine growth of timber, which will furnish ample quantities of material for all building purposes, or mining operations. The whole area of the land, with but few exceptions, could be turned into fine agricultural farms, and excellent pasturing grounds, producing all the supplies required at the mines, without interfering with the underground operations." And as his employers expected, Dickeson concluded that the company's property "embraces all the requisites for a permanent investment of capital."[85]

On the same trip in August 1855, Dickeson also toured the nearly ten thousand acres owned or controlled by the Tennessee and Virginia Mining Company. The company's holdings ran in long strips, meaning that the acreage encompassed several miles of frontage along the lodes of ore, and many mines had opened already. Dickeson began his examination at one of the busiest, the Cranberry Mine, "situated near the waters of big and little Reed Island Creek, twenty-two miles south-east of Wytheville," in the central portion of the vein. The Cranberry extended half a mile along the Early Lead, a vein named for former owner John Early, who had taken a prominent role in developing the adjacent Tazewell Courthouse and Fancy Gap Turnpike. Dickeson described the mine: "Two shafts had been sunk on the south end of the lead, below the summit of the bluffs, which proved the lode upwards of six hundred feet. From the side of the hill a horizontal gallery was driven, on a course of 45° East of North, and extended upwards of four hundred feet, giving an average width of seventeen feet of copper ore." By the time of his visit, he reported, "one hundred and ninety tons of copper ore had been raised and shipped for market—and upwards of twenty tons of assorted ore remained in the ore sheds, and around the openings large quantities of poor ore, that would pay well if smelting works were erected in the State at any point along the lead." At the Wild Cat Mine, on the western boundary of the Cranberry Mine, 90 tons of ore had been shipped and 20 tons sat under sheds, even though the operation had begun only in February 1855. Other of the Tennessee and Virginia Mining Company's mines had produced nearly as much, with promising prospects for growth.[86]

William J. March entered the mining fray in 1856. His Great Outburst Mining Company encompassed only ten acres on a high ridge along Chestnut Creek near the southwestern edge of the vein of ore (where Thomas Blair and John Blair had operated their iron forge decades earlier), but March made his enterprise one of the best, for the property contained the union of several veins. In 1857, he pointed out the challenges facing the copper mines: the difficulty of transportation still ranked high on the list. As Dickeson had earlier noted, the cost of shipping the ore to a smelter meant that only the top-quality ore was used. In describing the situation, March provided the finest surviving peek into the mind of the copper-mining capitalist in the Blue Ridge and the skills required of the workers:

> [T]he cost of transportation, and present prices of ore, prevents [sic] all ores under 11 per cent. from being sent to market; therefore no more poor ore is cut down in the mine than is absolutely necessary for working room. The top portion of the lode being always the best, it is first stripped of its covering gossan, then carefully cut down, until the miner finds that it is getting below the standard;

he then sends it out and cuts down as much poor ore as the size of his tunnel requires.

The miner has two methods of judging of the quality of the ores he is working upon. The first is by "striping," or glancing the face of the ore with a pick, when the quality of the ore is known by the depth of color, and brilliancy of the stripe made. The best quality ores, or 35 per cent. and upwards, gives [sic] a stripe exactly like polished brass, but it [sic] soon tarnishes, and becomes dark blue. The ores that are too soft and friable to stripe, the miner judges by the second method. He takes some of the ore, and with the pole of his pick pounds it into paste, then, after mixing some of the paste with a little spittle to dilute it further, he puts it on his fore finger and draws it through the flame of his candle; the depth of the green color of the flame then given tells him its richness in copper.

The ores of the first quality sent out are thrown upon the floor of an ore shed, where they are turned over; and any poor ore that has accidentally got into it, is picked out. It is then bucked to about the size of a walnut, and when tolerably dry, well mixed and sampled, is boxed up and sent off to market. All the poor ores, or "seconds," (as they are termed,) that come out, are thrown in a heap to themselves, and no further notice taken of them—the owner hoping that some day he may find a market for them, by some cheap process of reduction, or a smelting establishment erected in the country.

All who are familiar with copper mines are aware that the great bulk of the ores seldom exceed [sic] 8 per cent., particularly sulphurets near the surface. Is it not therefore surprising that in the absence of a regular furnace, or any other means of bringing poor ores up to the required standard, that the mines can support themselves? [Y]et they do, and even make a fair profit.[87]

If March's clear-eyed assessment of the mine owners' challenges, motivations, and rewards left any doubt about the virility of the rudimentary industrial capitalism being practiced amid the agricultural fields of the Blue Ridge, then the enthusiastic comments of another skilled observer, geologist Richard Owen Currey, surely dispelled those lingering reservations.

In September 1859, Currey examined mile by mile the copper mines along these veins of ore, including the major mines in Carroll County and the similar if less productive ones in neighboring Grayson and Floyd counties as well as in Ashe and Alleghany counties, North Carolina. Currey could present many credentials: a Nashville physician trained at the University of Pennsylvania, an erstwhile college professor, the founder of three scientific journals, and a geologist studying Alabama, Tennessee, and Virginia. When he made his 1859 tour, he found new mines still being opened, but he also visited ones such as the Cranberry, which had operated continuously since 1854 and had in five years shipped 700 tons of ore. His description of March's Great Outburst typifies Currey's careful, descriptive style: "It takes its name from the great upheaval of gossan found capping the summit of this high ridge, and from which to the waters of Chestnut Creek, flowing at its base, is a precipitous descent of 300 feet. On this almost abrupt bluff Mr. W. J. March has driven in four tunnels across the mineral lode, and then followed it, excavating ores of a superior quality, the total drivage of tunnels being 306 feet." March "began work on this property in 1856, and so far has shipped 300 tons of ore, ranging from 10 to 30 per cent."[88]

Another significant company worked just west of the Great Outburst. The "Cook & Wistar property" described by Currey included two tracts totaling 600 acres adjoining March's works, along with 450 acres farther east. On land bought by Thomas Wistar and John Cooke in 1814, this operation deserves attention not for its production, but for its ownership. Quakers Wistar and Cooke had lived in Philadelphia, and their investment in Carroll County recalls Moses and Stephen Austin's earlier reliance on Pennsylvania capital as well as Francis Preston's confidence in the expertise of a forge carpenter from there.[89] Pennsylvanians' skills and money had pushed industry in the southern Blue Ridge virtually from its beginning.

At the far northeastern portion of the gossan vein, the Betty Baker Mine, near present-day Sylvatus, also resounded with activity under the ownership of the Meigs County and Virginia Mining Company: "Since the first day of May last, 130 tons of 20 per cent. ore has been taken out and shipped to Baltimore. . . . Since 1854 there have been shipped from this mine 595 tons, mostly of the black ore, with an average of 16 per cent." Currey reported, "Here was done probably the first work in this mining region."[90] Dickeson had also prepared a detailed report on the Betty Baker Mine, singling it out as the pioneering operation. At the time of Dickeson's report in 1857, the miners even utilized a small railroad "for carrying the ores to the sheds" on the property. The mine also generated a significant amount of waste that workers cast aside in pursuit of copper. Dickeson urged caution: "When the arsenical iron and the poorer kind of ores are thrown out to the weather, combustion takes place in about three days, which evolves a sulphurous acid gas so copiously, as to render it almost impossible to pass within a few feet of the mass."[91] Later generations of miners and industrialists would make more constructive use of those sulfuric rocks—to produce sulfuric acid.

In the fall of 1859, Currey found excitement building among the area mine owners because the Baltimore and Cuba Company had decided to build a smelter alongside the turnpike leading from Hillsville to Wytheville. Just as the announcement of a textile mill's arrival in a southern town marked progress in later decades, the building of a smelter in this midcentury mining community smelled of present and future success. In March, the company had bought five acres near Hillsville and started construction. At last, the copper entrepreneurs could overcome the substantial cost of shipping quality ore as well as the prohibitive cost of shipping marginal ore. At the Cranberry Mine, for instance, "All the ores to be raised in future from these properties are to be reserved for the Baltimore and Cuba Smelting Furnace, now being erected near this mine." By the end of October 1859, the smelter was producing refined copper at rates that more than pleased the owners.[92] It relied on the most up-to-date process, patented in 1857, for making the most of poor-quality sulfurous ore.[93] Iron, lead, and copper seemed destined to anchor Blue Ridge industrialization as it hustled toward the future.

Chapter 3

Wheels and Rails in the New America

The entrepreneurs of the Blue Ridge trod a rugged business terrain. Like their counterparts in Pennsylvania and elsewhere, they contributed to the dizzying growth of American industry. Yet they also lived in and supported a society that countenanced slavery, and they defended it with hands-on brutality. The Civil War freed the slaves yet set back aspects of Blue Ridge industrialization. Nonetheless, at the war's conclusion, the entrepreneurial energies of native white residents, newly reliant on wage labor, mingled with a fresh, stronger influx of northern capital. Old patterns continued, but with new intensity. Geological study grew more precise, the investments larger, the web of infrastructure tighter, business networks more important, environmental destruction more substantial, and profits more attractive. The corporatization of America, powered by changes outside the South but welcomed by many within it, engulfed the Blue Ridge in full force.

The full price of slavery and the plantation system became clear only after the war. Like northern corporate pioneers, antebellum southern elites had shaped laws conducive to their economic interest. Even in the midst of political democratization after the American Revolution, businessmen above the Mason-Dixon Line maneuvered around all obstacles in the way of their profit-oriented corporations.[1] Southerners likewise turned to corporations when the occasion demanded, but in the region at large the predominance of plantations and the lack of major cities meant that the need for and experience with corporate business life remained relatively rare. Entering the post–Civil War period, the corporate form of business organization showed its true national potential, but the South had to take a junior role; white men's concentrations of capital in slaves had vanished. New York City's banks and financiers—with the aid of an excellent harbor, the Erie Canal, the demise of the Second Bank of the United States, the blossoming of the railroad industry, and Civil War profits—surpassed even their peers in Philadelphia. In the postwar era, the financial and corporate leaders of both cities—on Wall Street and Chestnut Street—continued to wield great influence in the South. Something new had sprouted in the form of large private corporations, but they grew most quickly under the northern sun because the South had focused on exploiting its comparative advantage in commercial agriculture. Thus, even along the New River, where industry had dug in from the beginning of European settlement, northern companies came to dominate.

Slave and Free

By 1859, America's mounting sectional tensions had brought some uncertainty to the businessmen working back and forth across the Mason-Dixon Line to develop the region's minerals. In fact, residents of the upper New River valley had long encountered the debate about free labor and slave labor that occupied all Americans caught up in the expansion of market relationships. The New River counties had a good view of part of that expansion as slaves from Virginia and Maryland moved southwestward down the mountain turnpikes. In the early 1840s, British geologist G. W. Featherstonhaugh saw slave traders preparing to force a group of slaves to cross the New River in, likely, Wythe or Pulaski County. He recalled, "Just as we reached New River, in the early grey of the morning, we came up with a singular spectacle, the most striking one of the kind I have ever witnessed. It was a camp of negro slave-drivers, just packing up to start; they had about three hundred slaves with them, who had bivouacked the preceding night *in chains* in the woods; these they were conducting to Natchez, upon the Mississippi River, to work upon the sugar plantations in Louisiana. . . . The female slaves were, some of them, sitting on logs of wood, whilst others were standing, and a great many little black children were warming themselves at the fires of the bivouac. In front of them all, and prepared for the march, stood, in double files, about two hundred male slaves, *manacled and chained to each other.* I had never seen so revolting a sight before!"[2] Most white New River residents did not share the revulsion.[3]

In his account books, David Graham and his managers marked down emotionless remnants of both the quotidian rhythms of a nineteenth-century iron-making enterprise and the extraordinary moments that changed black workers' lives. For instance, on August 20, 1828, a man "got crippled by waggon." On Monday, November 10, 1828, "Isaac black man of Sanders commenced by the year at $70.00 per year. . . . [A]lso his son Clayton at $18.00 per year." More prosaically, on the fourteenth of the month "John Smith commenced coaling."[4] Graham's "Slave Book (Furnace)" recorded twenty-one slaves at work in March 1830, for example, and twenty-seven in December. Graham had rented most of the workers, though he owned bondpeople as well.[5] These industrial hands worked steadily—Graham, as his needs dictated, shifted them from the furnaces to the forge or to other tasks such as cutting wood and making or hauling charcoal. Moreover, he hired skilled white workers when necessary, and white laborers made up substantial portions of the unskilled labor force at his furnace. Graham's day book records nineteen white men at work in March 1847; salaries varied, with George Gibson receiving $12 per month and paying his own board, but James Lewis earning $20 per month plus board.[6]

Managing this complex workforce vexed Graham at times: he used a mix of incentives and violence. Like other iron makers, he rewarded skilled black workers with pay for extra work. Albert earned fifty cents per occasion for working at night in the rolling mill in 1846 and 1847, and in 1848 Trial gained nearly $50 for extra work with "Pig metal."[7] Despite incentives for extra labor, slaves sometimes avoided work by fleeing for days. For a single example, "Church run away" on November 26, 1830, but "Church returned" on November 29.[8] In September 1829, the time book records, "Sam lost one day by whipping for playing Cards and fighting."[9] Like all slaveholders in late antebellum Virginia, Graham had to judge when individual acts of resistance threatened to turn into dangerous widespread rebellion, but he could not afford to react too harshly to such transgressions because he already had to travel great distances in order to hire enough bondmen.[10] The free white workers sometimes proved equally troublesome. In 1858, Graham reflected on his supervision of their labor: "It has been my fortune (or misfortune), for the last thirty odd years, to have the control of a large number of persons, (free men) and no one knows better than myself, the necessity of discipline and proper subordination, and no one will go farther than I would to sustain it."[11]

Blue Ridge Rebellion

The majority of white residents of Grayson, Wythe, and Carroll counties, whether successful businessmen such as Graham or laborers in a mine or a field, had no qualms about supporting slavery during the 1840s and 1850s. Like their Patriot forebears putting down Tory resistance, the antebellum Virginians did not hesitate to clamp down on anyone who differed. Throughout the state in the 1850s, whites watched their slaves for signs of unrest, and whites opposed to slavery sometimes received harsh treatment. The Blue Ridge felt the statewide unease.[12] Most of the area's slaves did not work in industry, but slaves did shoulder key parts of industrial work. The industrialists and professionals who backed internal improvements—men who often owned large farms as well—rallied behind slavery.[13]

In December 1848, on the Sunday before Christmas, Jarvis C. Bacon, a Wesleyan Methodist minister who had recently arrived in Grayson County, preached, "If I was to go to my neighbour's crib and steal his corn, you would call me a thief, but that it was worse to take a human being and keep him all his life, and give him nothing for his labour, except once in a while a whipping or a few stripes." Mine owner and attorney Samuel Mc-Camant and attorney and turnpike director William H. Cook presented the prosecutors' case against Bacon. The circuit court convicted the Ohioan abolitionist of violating a state law that barred anyone from claiming that slave owners did not have the right to own their bondpeople. Virginia's Supreme Court overturned the conviction, seeing a difference between moral suasion and legal arguments, but incensed local people nonetheless drove Bacon from the county.[14] Fledgling abolitionists in other southern locales met a similar fate.

Quieting Bacon did not end discussion of slavery, though. On August 11, 1851, Grayson resident John Clements gathered several of his neighbors to confront four unfamiliar slaves he had seen in a wooded hollow near the bank of the New River. Simon, Lewis, and Jack belonged to Grayson County farmers, and the owner of Henry, described by a witness as "the smallest boy," lived nearby in Ashe County, North Carolina. When challenged, Henry fled into the New River current and surrendered there in the waters he had hoped would float him north to freedom. The other three runaways did not give up so easily. One black man "made a lick" with a scythe blade; he struck down Samuel Bartlett and then seriously wounded Clements and Alfred Bartlett. Another slave stabbed Cyrus Wilcox in the neck with a knife; and the third dropped William B. Hale with a well-thrown rock. The county court convicted Simon, Lewis, and Jack of Samuel Bartlett's murder and hanged them on October 31. But at a mass meeting, Grayson residents widened the circle of blame. Thinking Jarvis

Bacon had instigated the slaves' revolt, the group offered $1,000 for Bacon's apprehension: "the eye of a just God" would see him as "the murderer as well of the said Samuel Bartlett."[15]

Unable to catch Bacon, the mob vented its anger on one of the minister's local supporters, a prosperous slave owner named John Cornutt. Even a slaveholder could not safely entertain thoughts that smacked of abolitionism. On September 13, the vigilance committee, reported to include two hundred people, lashed Cornutt to a tree and whipped him until he agreed to sell his land and slaves and leave his native state. Sympathetic whites in Carroll and Wythe counties met and passed resolutions praising the Grayson throng. The editor of the *Salem (N.C.) People's Press* also lauded the mob: "We warn the citizens of this and other counties to be vigilant lest others, equally obnoxious as the Ohio incendiaries, whom we have frequently felt bound to notice, may intrude themselves amongst us, and spread desolation and death in our midst. We hope that experience has taught us that a *summary process* is the only effective remedy to be resorted to in such cases." Wesleyan activists had a toehold in the North Carolina Piedmont as well, so the editor in Salem shared his Virginia neighbors' worries.[16] In acting as vigilantes, the Virginians took part in an American tradition that extended well beyond the southern states to the North and the West, but popular violence against abolitionists proved particularly attractive as a political weapon.[17]

When Cornutt, rather than leaving, tried to file a lawsuit in response to his torture, the leading men of the area revealed how far they would go to stamp out opposition. On March 22, 1852, a mass meeting occupied the Grayson courthouse. There to explain its purpose stood two local worthies, Samuel McCamant and William H. Cook. The assembly coolly decided to prolong the witch hunt, resolving "[t]hat the committees of Vigilance heretofore formed be recognized by the Chairman of this meeting, and their numbers increased to two hundred each, and the said Committees report to a general meeting to be held at the Court House, on the 4th Monday in June next, the number and names of all Abolitionists yet remaining in the county." Next, the group ordered "[t]hat notice be given by said committees to John Cornutt, and all others defiled with Abolitionism, that unless they give positive assurance to live with us as becomes citizens of a slaveholding community, they will be permitted to remain in this county no longer than may be necessary to sell their property and close their business." And in an even more radical move, on par with the extralegal violence at the lead mines during the Revolutionary War, the crowd decided "[t]hat the Clerks of our county and circuit courts shall not be permitted to issue any writ or writs from their respective offices upon any memorandum made or sent by any persons, for the commencement of any suit or suits against citizens of this county for any act done by them, having for its object the expulsion of Abolitionists from the county, or to prevent further dissemination of abolition doctrines among us; if issued, that the Sheriff of this county shall not execute any such process upon such citizens." Attorneys who tried to pursue such suits risked tar and feathers; taverners had to turn them away. Those gathered explained that the situation demanded "at our hands this public expression of our just indignation and of our fixed purpose to protect ourselves and property—peaceably if we can—forcibly if we must." Passions did not settle quickly. In May 1852, citizens endorsed McCamant to continue serving as the prosecuting attorney for the county.[18]

Slavery, extractive capitalism, politics, and the law came together in McCamant's career, but those issues soon tore apart the nation. In early 1861, as the secession agitation climaxed, McCamant was serving in the Virginia House of Delegates. On April 2, 1861, at the behest of John Early, McCamant shepherded to passage a bill to incorporate a copper smelter in Carroll County. Perhaps already the Baltimore and Cuba Company had left the area, leaving the opportunities for smelting in the hands of the newly formed Carroll Mining and Manufacturing Company, which brought together an unduly optimistic group of Baltimore industrialists and merchants, including Unionist Johns Hopkins.[19] Soon, no Carroll County smelter would have a purpose.

As the Virginia House of Delegates took care of its work, a separate convention sat in Richmond, pondering whether Virginia should secede from the nation it had fought to create some four score years earlier. Representing Carroll County, copper investor Fielden Hale voted in favor of secession both before and after (April 4 and 17) the Confederates fired on Fort Sumter to start the Civil War. Representatives from Wythe County and Pulaski County voted in the same way.[20] Across the state, most opposition to breaking up the Union came from areas with low numbers of slaves, but the upper New River valley's industrial and commercial development, aided by the railroad and turnpikes, helped align the counties there with eager secessionists in eastern Virginia.[21]

The secession convention had sat since February 13, 1861, so Virginians had time to consider the issues. On March 11, the people of Wythe

County assembled at the courthouse and called Judge Andrew Fulton to the chair. Even as a Whig congressman, he had worried that sectional tension over slavery might lead to war. In March 1848, as he reflected on the implications of acquiring territory from Mexico, he wrote, "[T]he future is pregnant with evil."[22] When Jarvis Bacon had badly needed legal counsel, Fulton had stepped up as a lonely moderate voice to represent the besieged cleric.[23] In March 1861, however, Fulton led the citizens of Wythe County in petitioning the convention to approve secession. He addressed the county gathering to loud applause and "concluded by announcing himself to be compelled to advocate the secession of Virginia from the Union." William Cook, who had helped lead the anti-abolitionist unrest in the area a decade earlier, also spoke "at some length" in support of secession.[24] Mass meetings in Pulaski County and Grayson County (presided over by James Dickey, aged son of pioneering iron maker Matthew Dickey) likewise prepared pro-secession missives for the convention.[25] They got their wish.

Wartime Work

As Civil War battles raged, the mountain industries changed with the times. Wartime business generally boomed, but the fear and tension that disturbed whites throughout the South reached the New River valley industrial zone. On May 26, 1861, David Graham's daughter Elizabeth (Bettie Ann) recorded in her diary one of the fiercest worries of white industrialists, for whom John Brown's interracial raid at Harpers Ferry still resonated with generations of fears about slave uprisings: "About dark we were much alarmed, by Wesley riding up to the gate and hollowing [sic] that a terrible insurrection had arisen on Cripple Creek of 300 men, white & black." In this case, it turned out, the messenger had alarmed the family unnecessarily.[26]

The copper boom lasted until the Civil War, but the conflict started to destroy the industry in Carroll, Grayson, and Floyd counties. The Confederate government's Nitre and Mining Bureau chose to rely principally on the Ducktown, Tennessee, region to supply the South's copper needs (perhaps most vitally for the manufacture of percussion caps), while holding the dwindling Carroll mines in reserve. In late 1863, Union incursions forced the suspension of production at Ducktown, and Colonel Isaac M. St. John sent John W. Goodwyn to Carroll County to restart production there. On October 4, 1864, Great Outburst miner W. J. March, then an infantry captain, was detailed to serve with the Nitre and Mining Bureau. Based out of Wytheville, March was assigned to oversee the copper mines. Time has blurred the extent of the renewed mining. After the war, geologist T. Sterry Hunt, at one point a colleague of Pennsylvania geologist J. Peter Lesley, explained that "the mines were worked for the account of the late Confederate government, and large quantities of ores were raised and sent, it is said, to Petersburgh to be smelted." Defeat soon made the work irrelevant in any case.[27] *New York Times* correspondent J. R. Hamilton, hypercritical of the South, visited the warworn area in late May 1867 and found "abandoned tunnels, caved-in shafts, desolated smelting works and dreary *débris* of various monumental follies."[28]

Unlike the copper mines and smelting works, the iron business roared: making war required making ordnance. At least four of the iron furnaces in Wythe County—Barren Springs, Raven Cliff, Wythe, and Graham's Cedar Run—made extensive wartime blasts. Grey Eagle Furnace began operation during the war as well. David Graham's son, David Peirce Graham (1838–1898), had joined the elderly ironmaster in the business, and as David Graham & Son, the company in 1861 and 1862 produced dozens of tons of pig iron for Joseph R. Anderson & Company, operator of the Tredegar works in Richmond.[29]

The Confederacy looked to the Tredegar complex as its main supplier of heavy weaponry. In early 1861, even before Virginia seceded from the United States, Joseph Anderson had contracted with furnace owners, including David Graham, to supply top-quality pig iron for manufacturing guns; later in the year Graham agreed to sell Anderson all the suitable iron his Wythe County furnaces could produce. Graham's initial shipments reached Richmond in May. Before the war, the Bellona Foundry had made at least one effective cannon using Graham's iron, leading Anderson to risk using the Wythe County metal. By November 1861, the Tredegar officials had learned that the change in supplier had not gone well. The company wrote Graham, "We regret to inform you that several of the guns manufactured from your metal have recently burst, the one at Columbus Kentucky with results that are distressing." A second letter soon let Graham know that "another large gun made from your metal burst at Port Royall in the hottest of the battle with the fleet."[30] The problems at Columbus particularly embarrassed Anderson. He had cast the Confederacy a massive rifled gun named in honor of General Leonidas Polk's wife. When the Lady Polk burst during a demonstration firing soon after the battle of Belmont, the explosion killed several soldiers. "[T]he stunning effect of the concussion" injured General Polk and tore his clothing "to pieces."[31]

Despite waning sales to Anderson thereafter, the Grahams thrived for the duration of the war. They diversified by also supplying mundane but important military needs, as when they sold horseshoes and nails to Jeb Stuart's brigade in April 1862. They subsequently sold both castings and pig iron to the Virginia and Tennessee Railroad, and they found deep profits in making salt kettles for use by the Saltville companies boiling that strategic commodity.[32] Representing the War Department's Nitre and Mining Bureau, which had done so much to centralize control of the Confederate states' industry, Colonel St. John in late 1863 pushed the iron company to keep the furnaces in operation. He reminded the senior Graham that to do so would "thereby be rendering an important public service." Graham obliged, and Cedar Run had twenty-three white workers and twenty-three slaves laboring in 1864.[33]

The lead miners also provided vital materiel to the Confederacy, and on that point Wythe County could make its deepest claim to importance to the Confederacy. In July 1861, a visitor reported that those miners were working seven days per week, day and night.[34] As in the Revolutionary War, the mines, directed by William Kohler, provided a great deal of the shot and the bullets for the rebels. Following the Civil War, a colonel in the Ordnance Department recalled, "Our lead was obtained chiefly, and in the last years of the war entirely, from the lead mines at Wytheville, Virginia. The mines were worked night and day, and the lead converted into bullets as fast as received." The 1860 census lists Robert Raper, one of the company's principal owners, as owning forty-one slaves, and David Graham owned twenty at the time, down from twenty-nine a decade earlier.[35] One cannot determine how many slaves worked the lead mines (or how many escaped to Union lines) because Raper and Graham had large agricultural landholdings as well, and Graham also had the iron furnaces and his forge. Moreover, Graham, at least, had long practiced hiring slaves. Notwithstanding imprecise records, however, unwilling slaves likely helped produce the Confederacy's lead, just as they had for the Patriots during the American Revolution nearly a century earlier. And like the revolutionaries and Tories of that time, both Confederates and loyal Americans recognized the mine's importance.

The state government, too, saw the region's significance to the war effort. The Virginia General Assembly in 1861 requested that the Board of Public Works determine the funding needed "to remove the obstructions to the navigation of New river by batteaux, and to improve the navigation of said stream by sluices, in such manner as will accommodate the transportation of military stores in batteaux." The bill soon passed by a vote of ninety-two to two with the support of local representatives such as Samuel McCamant.[36] In February 1862, the Board of Public Works agreed to pay the stockholders of the New River Navigation Company $1,385 for the company's rights, and in July the board sent engineer D. S. Walton and a crew to begin bettering navigation down the river from the Central Depot, where the railroad intersected the river at the downstream edge of Pulaski County. For $120, Walton purchased four kegs of powder from Stuart, Buchanan & Company in Saltville and set to work.[37]

In January 1864, a group of southwestern Virginia legislators petitioned Jefferson Davis to better protect the area: in addition to having "a large surplus of horses, cattle, hogs, grain, and hay," it produced "nearly all the iron, salt, and lead manufactured in the Confederate States." Union general George Stoneman picked up on the lead mine's significance, and a contingent of his troops accordingly burned the operation on December 17, 1864. At the time, Confederate general John C. Vaughn commanded about four hundred rebel troops at the mines, but he and his men "without firing a shot . . . retreated to the top of the mountain in Carroll County." A news report claimed that Vaughn, "believing exaggerated stories" of Stoneman's troop numbers, "retreated on the approach of a party that might have been an easy prey." On April 7, 1865, shortly before Robert E. Lee surrendered at Appomattox, Stoneman's men returned and again destroyed the partially rebuilt works, barely more than two weeks after they had resumed production.[38] Like all southerners flailing in their tumultuous postwar economy, industrialists on the New River would have to adjust to new conditions.

David Graham, for instance, survived the conflict, but some of his profits from it disappeared with the demise of the Confederacy and its currency. People in the area said Graham "was making a great deal of money out of the war." However, Graham wrote in September 1865, "I lost all I made for the government, probably over two hundred thousand dollars, all I saved was mainly for work done for the saltworks."[39]

Copper's Demise

Iron and copper in the New River valley met different fates after peace returned. The copper operations folded for several reasons. In 1873, T. Sterry Hunt reported that even before the war the richest ores had been exhausted and work had slowed because the remaining ores "were then rejected as not being rich enough for shipment." The antebellum smelting works "for some reason have been abandoned."[40] But not all the copper mines stayed closed at the war's end. In June 1866, the Hale Copper Mining Company, following the settlement earlier that year of the long-term litigation between Fielden L. Hale of Hillsville and the owners of the lead mining company of Wythe County, restarted mining on two thousand acres and then leased the adjacent Betty Baker property. Hale, who had represented Carroll County at Virginia's secession convention and whom Confederate deserters wounded near Hillsville in June 1863, had speculated on land with unclear titles, and the settlement finally allowed him to turn his considerable energies elsewhere.[41]

Hale moved to Cherokee County, Alabama, and in April 1867 he linked the copper company in Virginia to investors centered in New York City.[42] This group brought new life to the copper operation, just as northern investors poured money into many struggling southern businesses after the war. In November 1865, journalist Whitelaw Reid traveled by rail through Wythe County and southwest Virginia, and even so soon after the war's end he found economic activity on the rise: "The mineral wealth of this region is unimagined. Shrewd geologists were already traveling it in all directions; and with the next season we shall have the launch of company after company with 'magnificent mining prospects.'"[43]

To put up new smelting works several miles northeast of the antebellum ones, the new owners of the Hale Copper Mining Company hired mining engineer Frederic Anton Eilers (1839–1917), a German immigrant who later spent much of his distinguished career in the West and who was appointed a director of the lucrative American Smelting and Refining Company. Armed with an encouraging assessment by the engineering firm Adelbert & Raymond, his former employer, Eilers built the new Carroll County facility. He described it in late 1869: "The smelting works consist of five roast-sheds, twenty-five feet by fifty feet, for open heap-roasting; two stadels [staddles?] under cover, eight by six feet, for the roasting of concentrated mattes; a coal-house, capable of receiving ten thousand bushels of charcoal, and a very substantial building, sixty by fifty feet, which encloses the two blast furnaces, and a small engine and blast-house. . . . The blast is furnished by a McKenzie pressure blower, driven with a ten horsepower portable steam engine, built by the Washington Iron Works of Newburgh, New York."[44]

The company had prepared for the human as well as the technological aspects of the complex operation. Eilers continued, "Besides the smelting establishment, the company have erected a store, a large frame house for the Superintendent, a boarding-house, a large shaft-house, and covered, when over the deep shaft, twelve small houses for workmen, and the necessary stables and ore-sheds at the mouths of tunnels." Reopening the mines required fifty to sixty men, plus others to chop wood during the winter for charcoal. Then the demand for labor stabilized: "The working of the establishment, after the buildings were completed, required fourteen men in the furnace, who received from 75 cents to $1.25 per day, and about twenty-five to thirty miners, one-half of whom received $20 per month, the other half $26. One overseer at the mines and one at the smelting works received respectively $32.50 and $40 per month, and a mason $500 per annum. Besides the repairing of the furnaces, this man had also to cut the fire-proof rock in the quarry."[45]

At the end of 1869, the new facility still struggled. It had sold $17,000 of copper, "a small part of which was refined at the mines; the balance was sold to the Boston and the Taunton smelting works." Eilers complained that "thus far it has been impossible to raise as much ore" as the furnaces could handle, "partly because the mines were not sufficiently opened, partly on account of the scarcity of skilled miners." Moreover, "the mines contain what in other parts of the United States would be considered poor ores." Nevertheless, he outlined expansion plans.[46]

These plans did not work out, however. Eilers left his post at Betty Baker in 1869 to assist the U.S. commissioner of mining statistics in the West, the region with the brightest future for resource extraction.[47] On October 31, 1871, Fielden Hale, Garland Hale, and Ira B. Coltrane (a state legislator in the 1850s and the engineer who had helped lay out the antebellum turnpike down the mountain at Fancy Gap) sold the mineral rights to the Hale copper mine and the rights to Eilers's furnace to a Baltimorean named James E. Clayton, who at the same time bought from John Early, another local antebellum roads and mining promoter, his controlling interests in the Fairmont Mine, the Cranberry Mine, the Wild Cat Mine, the Ann Phipps Mine, and the prewar smelter alongside the turnpike between Hillsville and Wytheville (described as "the Mon[n]ier smelting works").[48] In 1873, though, T. Sterry Hunt stated flatly after visiting Carroll County, "Mr. A. Eilers established smelting works here, which were worked for some time with skill and success, but were suspended on account, it is said, of some financial difficulties, and have not been resumed."[49] Work by Clayton on Early's former properties seems to have ended abruptly as well, although throughout the 1870s Clayton, his brother Samuel, and later their partner James E. Tyson went on accumulating land in the mining regions of Carroll, perhaps looking to future development.[50]

A group of Pennsylvanians made one last attempt to mine copper in Carroll. In 1874, Pennock Huey, a former Quaker and Keystone State native who had served the Union with distinction during the Civil War, leased the mining property bought much earlier by Philadelphians Thomas Wistar and John Cooke alongside Chestnut Creek's Great Outburst gossan deposit. Huey (whose wife was part of the Wistar family) and other Pennsylvanians, joined by John T. Hamlett of Wytheville, incorporated the Wistar Copper Mining Company in 1875. James H. Gulick of Williamsport, a businessman and railroad developer, served as president, with Huey as treasurer. They seemingly had no luck raising capital, but in their effort to do so, they arranged for yet another mineralogist and chemist, an 1848 German immigrant named Frederick Augustus Genth (1820–1893), to traverse the Blue Ridge hills and valleys. To aid himself in evaluating the Wistar prospect, Genth, of the University of Pennsylvania, engaged Charles Rufus Boyd, a native of Wytheville and an engineer and mining consultant who had worked under Claudius Crozet and studied at the University of Virginia. (Boyd's father, a lawyer, had served in the Virginia legislature and on the antebellum Virginia Board of Public Works and had invested in the antebellum copper excitement; Boyd's brothers helped shape Louisiana State University.)[51] With this abortive Wistar effort, attempts to mine copper in Carroll County ground to a halt, though Boyd still cited the results of Genth's visit more than fifteen years later.[52] By then, the incredible copper mines of Lake Superior and the western states had erased most eastern copper mines from the national memory.

Renewed Life for Charcoal Iron

With reunification of the United States in 1865, the New River valley's iron and lead industries might well have followed its copper mining into oblivion. The ongoing development of the iron and steel industry in Pennsylvania and other northern states and around Birmingham, Alabama, could have meant the quick demise of New River–Cripple Creek iron. But it did not. Hot-blast, coke-burning furnaces came into standard use elsewhere; however, by a quirk of nature, charcoal-fired, cold-blast furnaces turned out iron with a peculiar hardness, durability, and affordability that could not be matched by newer technology until early-twentieth-century advances lowered the price of open-hearth steel. Car wheels for railroads and streetcar lines required iron with these characteristics. As a result, the iron industry along the upper New River watershed peaked between 1880 and 1900.[53]

Outsiders took a fresh look at the area soon after the war. In 1869, mining engineer Eilers reported to readers of a national trade journal, "None of the iron works built in this region are able to do justice to the enormous supply of ores. The principal hindrance in this direction is the present poverty of the South. Since, however, the attention of northern, and especially Pennsylvania, capitalists has been drawn to this neighborhood, the prospect for the conversion of these natural stores of raw material into merchantable forms, to be added to the wealth of the country, has grown much brighter." He described the "works of the Stratford Iron Company, lately built by Northern capitalists": "[S]ituated on Max creek, close to the foot of Poplar Camp mountain," the property had "very extensive deposits of limonite . . . , and the company has erected substantial works to beneficiate these ores." The furnace, the largest along the New River to that time, "has a diameter of fifteen feet at the bosh, and is over forty feet high. An engine, much too large for the present extent of the works, drives the cylinder-blast. The air is heated by passing through a system of iron pipes at the top. From these it passes into a large receiver, and finally, under heavy pressure, into the furnace. The steam necessary for the driving of the blast is generated by the waste gases from the tunnel-head." Despite the up-to-date structure, though, this engineer criticized the results: "The product of the furnace is said to be eight tons per day, which is not as much as it should be, considering the kind of ore used and the size of the furnace. The resulting iron is of very uneven quality, and mostly white, undoubtedly in consequence of the extremely bad and negligent roasting and sorting which the ores receive before smelting."[54] This initial foray into using advanced hot-blast furnaces had gone astray. Ongoing northern investment played its important role, but the New River valley, like a few other small iron-making districts in Michigan and elsewhere, would specialize in cold-blast charcoal furnaces for decades to come.[55]

In 1869, Eilers also sketched David Graham's longtime charcoal iron business: "Graham's works consist of two cold-blast furnaces, one near his house, on a small stream, which furnishes the power for his wooden cylinder-blast, the other on the southern bank of New river, some three miles from the former. A small establishment for the conversion of a portion of the pig-metal into wrought iron, a foundry and rolling-mill are situated on Reed creek." He explained that they did not produce large amounts of iron because "[t]he blast furnaces run alternately during the summer of every year." They produced "from three hundred to five hundred tons of superior iron. Some of this iron is shipped east, but a great part of it is converted during the winter into castings, wrought iron and nails for the use of the neighborhood." Graham's antebellum mansion stood nearby. Though the scale of the works and the extent of the market no longer matched those elsewhere in Reconstruction America, this visitor judged the quality affirmatively: "The wrought iron is far better than most of the northern iron, and is principally used for farming purposes. The supply of ore on the property will be, at the rate of present consumption, sufficient for hundreds of years." Furthermore, "extensive tracts of wood on the [Poplar Camp] mountain will furnish them a large amount of cheap fuel for many years to come."[56]

David Graham died in 1870, and the 1870 census of industry lists his company as the only producer of pig iron in Wythe County, netting 600 tons and employing thirty workers that year.[57] His family carried on among the New River–Cripple Creek region's leading iron makers, blurring distinctions between antebellum and postwar leadership. The firm came under the management of Major David Peirce Graham, who also inherited and expanded the family home, and John William Robinson (1837–1906), who in 1867 had married Major Graham's sister Bettie. His two other sisters and their husbands, J. Williamson McGavock and Harold Mathews, also inherited shares in the iron and lead businesses.

John William Robinson grew into a key figure in New River industry. A native of Bedford, Virginia, he arrived in Pulaski County in the 1850s to work at the new railroad depot in Dublin. In the late antebellum era, he joined the mercantile operation at Graham's Forge. During the war, he served briefly in the army but was ordered back to Wythe County to supervise iron production for the Grahams. After the war, he also formed his own wholesale house in Lynchburg as well as other retail operations, and beginning in 1869 he, along with M. B. Tate and James S. Crockett, began acquiring iron operations along Cripple Creek. In 1878, David Peirce Graham joined them in their endeavor, while Robinson continued to help manage the Graham properties.[58]

Railroads and Growth

Graham and Robinson lost their brief local monopoly after 1870 as a nationwide boom in the iron industry echoed in the area. The market for the New River iron soon reached far beyond Blue Ridge farms, for the high-quality metal attracted notice and investment. Wytheville engineer Charles Rufus Boyd enumerated the active charcoal-fired operations in Wythe County in 1881. The list of furnaces took in the old standards, some back in action after a period of dormancy—Raven Cliff Furnace (1810, rebuilt 1876), Cedar Run Furnace (1832), Barren Springs Furnace (1853, rebuilt 1873), Eagle Furnace (1863). The fresh additions included the Brown Hill Furnace (1870), the Walton Furnace (1872), the new Speedwell Furnace (1873), the new Wythe Furnace (1873), the Irondale (or Noble) Furnace (1880–1881), the Beverly Furnace (1880), the New River Iron Company's Foster Falls Furnace (1881), and the New River Mineral Company's new furnace being built two miles upstream from the lead mines, at what would become Ivanhoe.[59] (For more technical details on operating these furnaces, see appendix B.) In the early 1880s, an observer could already call New River–Cripple Creek "the famous car-wheel iron region of Southwestern Virginia."[60]

The magnitude of the nineteenth-century iron-making businesses along the New River came to pale in comparison with counterparts in more fully industrializing regions. Early in the century, Virginia had earned a place among the national leaders. In 1810, the state's furnaces ranked second to Pennsylvania and just ahead of New Jersey in tonnage of iron produced.[61] But the situation changed. In the year from June 1879 to May 1880, Wythe County had eight establishments in the census category of iron and steel manufacturing. Those eight businesses produced 4,851 tons of metal worth $133,325. On both counts, Wythe ranked fourth among counties in Virginia. The state as a whole had forty-four establishments producing 55,722 tons worth $2,585,999. Among all states, Virginia had the sixteenth-highest tonnage. By comparison, Pennsylvania's most productive county, Alleghany, alone produced 848,146 tons worth $46,078,375.[62]

Economic boosters in Virginia looked on Pennsylvania's development with envy and dreamed of uniting the iron ores of the upper New River with the coal and coke produced on the other side of the valley of Virginia, in the Flat Top region along both sides of the Virginia–West Virginia border.[63] In the 1870s and early 1880s, political representatives from communities along the New River garnered federal appropriations that allowed the Army Corps of Engineers to begin deepening channels in the river to improve its utility for commercial navigation. Opposition to the U.S. government, so prevalent in southern whites' Reconstruction-era rhetoric, did not hinder Virginians from taking advantage of federal expertise. The plans extended those formulated by the New River Navigation Company just before and during the Civil War. The engineers' report stated that "the object of the improvement, as expressed by the promoters of the scheme, is to connect the iron, lead, and zinc deposits of Wythe County and the copper of Carroll with the coal of the Kanawha fields." The plan for these connections never reached fruition; however, furnace owners did begin moving tons of pig iron down the river to its intersection with the main railroad line at the town of Radford (a community that began as an eighteenth-century river crossing near the present border of Pulaski and Montgomery counties). The iron makers used flat-bottomed keelboats between fifty and seventy feet long, from six to eight feet wide, and with a draft of two feet or less. Perhaps realizing the feasibility of that alternative, railroad investors in the 1880s negotiated the terrain—political, economic, and topographical—to create branch railroad lines that served the mineral companies' needs. The Army Corps of Engineers thus ended its hydrological work on the upper New River.[64]

The new railroad lines, built by the Norfolk and Western Railroad, stand out as key to the region's development in the late nineteenth century. The rails ran like tendrils along the New River, up Cripple Creek, up Little Reed Island Creek, and finally up Chestnut Creek. In 1883, long before all of the track had gone in, John W. Robinson explained the furnace owners' perspective:

> Unfortunately for these furnaces they are all on the easterly side of The Valley while the Norfolk & Western RR. is on the westerly, a detached mountain range, for most of the distance, rising between the furnaces and the railway. . . . In order that the high grade coke—equal to any made in the U.S.—that will be made in the Flat-top coal-field, may reach the abundant and superior ores that supply these furnaces, it will be necessary to construct what is known as the Cripple Creek branch of the Norfolk & Western (one on which some work has been done). We hope to see work resumed on that branch early this year so that this region, highly favored in

the character of its ores and limestones, may have a fair chance in the iron-making race. Give it cheap and good coke and railway transportation to market, and it will not need to ask favors of any; it can make a high grade car-wheel pig as cheap as the cheapest.[65]

The furnace operators had to lobby the railroad executives to convince them that the potential freight hauling justified the necessary investment, a calculation common to nineteenth-century railroad development around the world, from Brazil to the Philippines.[66]

In 1870, former Confederate general William Mahone, already a powerful politician, had consolidated three railroads, including the Virginia and Tennessee Railroad line, to form the Atlantic, Mississippi, and Ohio Railroad. When his railroad went bankrupt in 1881, the Philadelphia-based investment firm E. W. Clark and Company bought it and operated it as the Norfolk and Western Railroad under the leadership of Frederick J. Kimball. Acutely aware of the possibilities presented by the close proximity of iron and coal, these men began building branch lines into the coalfields and then up New River, cutting away from the railroad's antebellum main line in Pulaski County at Martin's Tank, which was chartered as the town of Pulaski in 1886. In 1881, crews started putting in the new tracks, but progress was periodically interrupted by business slowdowns and hard negotiations between Kimball and furnace owners (as well as potential owners) to ensure sufficient freight traffic. Kimball at first demanded at minimum 2 fifty-ton coke furnaces, and as late as 1885, with some work already complete, Kimball wrote Robinson, "If something could only be done to bring about the erection of a coke furnace on the line of our Cripple Creek Extension, we could find some way to build that line, which would be of very great advantage to you." In pushing Kimball to complete the work, John W. Robinson coordinated his appeals with those of Philadelphian Richard D. Wood, New York mining financier Joshua Hendricks, zinc investor Charles B. Squier, and others.[67]

The so-called Cripple Creek extension reached Ivanhoe on February 10, 1888; a spur line up Little Reed Island Creek crawled its way to the Betty Baker Mine by the end of 1890. The road extended up the New River, passing alongside the still-functioning Grayson Sulphur Springs resort and going as far as Bartlett's Falls, near where local whites had their deadly 1851 encounter with escaped slaves. Norfolk and Western built the road there to reach the new Washington Mills textile firm, which arose at a spot conducive to the mill's accompanying thirty-nine-foot-high dam. The mill and dam were built at the cost of $1.25 million by Winston-Salem, North Carolina, banker, entrepreneur, and Moravian scion Francis H. Fries and his business partner William C. Ruffin. In 1900, Fries and Ruffin had gained congressional approval to dam navigable waters; the mill opened in 1903, complete with extensive child labor; and the town of Fries grew around it, all part of the U.S. textile industry's massive shift southward toward cheaper labor. Another rail branch followed Cripple Creek to Speedwell, and the engineers spun the final piece of the web when the railroad moved up Chestnut Creek, reaching its terminus in 1904 at what became Galax. Appropriately, merchant John Blair Waugh, a descendant of the pioneer Blairs who had smelted iron on Chestnut Creek a century earlier, numbered among the investors who convinced the Norfolk and Western Railway to lay its line to that point.[68]

The final strands of the rail network required ongoing local pressure on Norfolk and Western. The threat of competition fortified the company's willingness to build the smaller lines in the late 1880s and 1890s. For example, in 1889 the New River Plateau Railway Company, incorporated by the Virginia General Assembly on March 2, 1888, planned and laid out the line to run up Chestnut Creek to Galax. The company won approval from the Carroll County Board of Supervisors to move a heavily traveled riverside road to a spot higher up the mountain slope that crowded the water's edge. John W. Robinson; Lee S. Calfee, a Pulaski County merchant; David W. Bolen, a Carroll County attorney and politician; and other local men had joined Evans R. Dick, a Philadelphia banker (who also owned the Norma Furnace on Cripple Creek), and other Philadelphia-based railroad men on the list of those incorporating the New River Plateau line. Norfolk and Western, however, took over the other rail company and completed the construction.[69]

Heading off another potential competitor required Norfolk and Western to agree to a larger business deal. In 1884, the Virginia General Assembly incorporated the Virginia and Kentucky Railroad, intended to connect the coalfields of Kentucky and West Virginia to the Atlantic Coast via such Southside Virginia cities as Danville. The legislators modified the incorporation act in 1887 and again in 1892. In 1890 and 1891, planning for the new line had become serious. From September to December 1890, engineers and surveyors tramped along the shores of Snake Creek, Big Reed Island Creek, Reed Creek (by Graham's Forge), and New River as they plotted a course through the mineral lands of Carroll and Wythe counties. Much of the company's expertise and drive in the early 1890s came from second-generation civil engineer Alfred Varley Sims (1864–1944), a Canadian-born striver who had studied at the University of Pennsylvania. The 1892 revision of the Virginia and Kentucky's charter christened it the Atlantic Coast and Northwestern Railroad Company and named Sims director, vice president, and general manager. Working with Sims, Charles Rufus Boyd, the ubiquitous Wytheville engineer and geologist, shouldered much of the task of evaluating mineral prospects along the route through Virginia. The railroad relied on Boyd's cartography to explain its goals: "By observing Boyd's Map of South-West Virginia it will be seen that our road crosses diametrically every mineral vein in this phenomenally rich section, and it is reasonable to expect that the local freight derived from bringing together these raw materials for the manufacture of Iron &c will be very great." Despite appeals for northern and English capital in 1892, declining business conditions led to failure. Sims's project was derailed for good by the Panic of 1893 and the completion of a competing railroad that ran from Roanoke through Southside Virginia to Winston-Salem and that Norfolk and Western soon controlled via lease and then purchase. No one again seriously challenged Norfolk and Western's railroad monopoly in the upper New River valley.[70]

In addition to profiting from minerals and textiles, the railroad investors knew they could anticipate business based on timber, both along the New River and Cripple Creek extension and on two railroad spurs that separately entered the western portion of Grayson County to exploit the timber resources. In 1882, engineer Boyd reported, "Timber is so abundant in nearly every part of the county that some easy means of getting it out would insure a bountiful supply of very cheap charcoal to the furnace men for years to come." In places, timber had survived in great quantity because it stood too distant from the ore beds to be used for making charcoal, but generations of charcoal production had damaged other spots. Boyd described Carroll County: "A great deal of the northern half of the county has been cut over, and the timber made into charcoal, to supply the iron furnaces and the lead mines in Wythe County; but there is enough remaining to supply a large demand for years to come." Wythe County had developed similarly: "Very few of the great timber boundaries, once so plentiful on the south side of the county, still remain intact. The great demand for charcoal for furnace purposes has thinned out the timber on that side of the county very much; but on the north side and in the middle section there are large boundaries of very good timber."[71]

Large corporations with both local and northern investors created major timber operations following the railroad's development. When Leonidas Chalmers Glenn, a geology professor at Vanderbilt University working for the U.S. Geological Survey, did fieldwork along Virginia's upper New River in 1904 and 1905, he witnessed the havoc wrought by the timber firms: "The most striking feature in the basin is the activity in lumbering which has resulted from the recent extension of a railway into it. Small portable sawmills have been located in even the most remote mountain coves, and lumber, tanbark, and crossties are hauled as much as 30 miles over mountain roads that are in many places execrable. Those who are engaged in the industry get for their product prices that amount only to low wages for themselves and their teams. They practically give their timber away, cut their roads to pieces in hauling it, and by its removal hasten the erosion of their steep mountain slopes and narrow flood-plain areas." Communities, in return, got industrial business development that used some forest products. By 1910, Galax boasted "of a large furniture factory, a spoke and handle factory, and a considerable tannery, besides two newspapers, a good bank, a wholesale grocery, and a number of retail stores."[72] Trees would eventually grow back and serve a different purpose, tourism, but the ecology of the forests changed irrevocably when the timber companies stripped away the old growth.

Virginia Iron in the National Economy

To foster more traffic for its road, Norfolk and Western encouraged businessmen to develop the many resources along these new lines. Throughout the 1870s and 1880s, the Virginia furnace owners could look to the booming iron district in Chattanooga and Birmingham for an example of what financiers could accomplish by bringing together iron, coal, and railroads. Norfolk and Western sent Pennsylvania geologists Andrew S. McCreath and E. V. d'Invilliers to prepare assessments of the active mines and potential lodes along its new routes, and their almost acre-by-acre look at the terrain highlights the tight links between capitalists and geologists that had been put in place when William Barton Rogers began his work on the state geological survey decades before the Civil War. McCreath and d'Invilliers, in fact, served on the second geological survey of Pennsylvania, begun in

1874 under the direction of J. Peter Lesley, who had earlier served under Rogers's brother Henry in the Keystone State. McCreath and d'Invilliers followed in the Virginia footsteps of William Rogers, Charles Boyd, Montroville Dickeson, Richard Currey, and other geologists who had previously parsed the area—the cumulative nature of science led to better understanding and exploitation of the natural resources.[73]

The local mine owners had no doubts about the importance of geological assessments to their business prospects. John W. Robinson took pains to answer McCreath's inquiries about local conditions, which went into the 1887 book *The New River–Cripple Creek Mineral Region of Virginia*. John C. Raper, business agent at the lead mines, considered opening a new shaft "in order to make a good showing to Prof. McCreath when he comes out again." J. H. Shuff, an iron maker at Speedwell, congratulated Robinson following the book's release: "Prof. McCreath has given you New River and Reed Island fellows *a big puff* in his report on iron ores of S.W. Va. I thought I had treated him (McC.) well when he was here, but he has not done so well for the ores on Cripple Creek" because, Shuff presumed, "the RR has not been finished to Speedwell."[74] Norfolk and Western liberally distributed the books and maps resulting from these geological assessments in its quest to attract the largest possible amount of investment and industry along its line.

Beginning in the late nineteenth century, the ownership of both the new and the old furnaces and smelters reflected a region pulled ever more strongly into national capital flows. As in the rest of the late-nineteenth-century South, industrial development in the upper New River valley involved both local entrepreneurs and wealthier northern companies and investors. John W. Robinson in particular expanded his involvement in partnerships. In 1882, David Peirce Graham and Robinson still operated the Cedar Run Furnace, though they had either shut down or scaled back their forge in 1881. In addition, however, Robinson partly owned and managed several other furnaces, including J. Williamson McGavock and Company's Barren Springs Furnace. Outsiders fully controlled other furnaces. The Lobdell Car Wheel Company of Wilmington, Delaware, had cultivated business relationships in the South as early as the 1830s; it owned or leased the Walton Furnace at Max Meadows and the Brown Hill Furnace (rebuilt in 1882). (See appendix C for a detailed description of Lobdell's manufacturing process for car wheels.) Managed by C. S. Van Liew, the Ivanhoe Furnace, the area's largest, went into blast in March 1882 on behalf of Joshua Hendricks and other investors, including Graham, Robinson, and the Lobdell Car Wheel Company. Northern investors also operated the Radford Furnace in Pulaski County, which made iron for Philadelphian Richard Wood's Car Wheel Iron Company. By 1894, Robinson and Baltimore iron merchant Richard Curzon Hoffman, a Maryland native who had fought for the Confederacy, shared management of the Reed Island Furnace. And even the locally owned furnaces most often marketed their product through Hoffman's firm, R. C. Hoffman and Company.[75]

Some Virginia politicians heartily encouraged such outside investment in the Old Dominion. For example, in 1878 future governor J. Hoge Tyler of Pulaski County introduced a bill in the state senate that would have awarded substantial tax breaks "to all persons who may invest capital brought from without the bounds of the State in mining and manufacturing industries within their bounds." He spoke to his fellow senators about "a wealthy gentleman of Pennsylvania" looking at the iron-making possibilities of Virginia. Tyler fantasized about the cheerful effects of having "on every mountain side in Virginia" an ironworks like the Cambria Iron Works of Johnstown, Pennsylvania. His complaints even echoed antebellum southern critics such as Hinton Rowan Helper. Tyler called "attention to the fact that every farmer in the State produces his crops with tools manufactured abroad," and, he continued, "[w]e wear shoes upon our feet, hats on our heads, and repose upon beds manufactured at the North."[76] He saw such a state of affairs as inexcusable, and the Pennsylvanians who made their way south with funds in hand found many likeminded Virginians along the New River.

The local men and the first wave of postwar outside investors grew so at ease with each other that both groups looked askance at a new wave of wealthy outsiders. In December 1882, Hoffman warned John Robinson of the need to move quickly on a possible deal. He explained, "Now in regard to McGavock's interest in Reed Island would say that if he wants to sell, we think the other partners should buy, we are opposed to letting any outsider in, and would prefer we should keep our interests equal as heretofore. Our interests are all alike whereas any outside party might not be free from other interests and we would have trouble." Philadelphian Richard Wood likewise wrote Robinson, worried and anxious for an update about a proposed hundred-ton coke furnace: "I have a letter from Witherow and Gordon in which they say 'some parties in this town (Pittsburg) are considering the question of joining your blast furnace enterprise in Virginia.'" C. S. Van

Liew of the Ivanhoe Furnace fretted that Kimball and his Norfolk and Western backers were trying to use delaying tactics "to discourage owners of valuable mine properties on the line of the new road, and finally compel them to sell, in other words 'freeze them out.'"[77]

Like the disgraced eighteenth-century treasurer John Robinson and the other original proprietors of the lead mines, David Peirce Graham and the latter-day John W. Robinson also manipulated the law and the state to their own advantage. For instance, Graham was named executor of the estate of William Peirce when Peirce died in 1875. Peirce's widow later successfully sued Graham for directing the estate to sell valuable mining land to Robinson and their other partners for far below its value.[78] Moreover, Robinson worked with officials to make sure that workers at his furnaces stayed in line. In the fall of 1882, he wrote to a federal Internal Revenue agent to complain about the sale of illegal whiskey to furnace workers and to share the moonshiners' usual schedule. Robinson's partner James S. Crockett soon reported the arrest of two "blockaders" but added, "I dont think it will do much good."[79]

The workers had their own grievances that fall as well, grumbling about poor food and too few blankets at the Beverly Furnace's boarding-house.[80] Workers, though, still sought opportunities to labor in the mineral industries. In 1885, W. R. Gallimore wrote from Carroll County to the Graham and Robinson firm, asking for employment: "I have had 35 years practicle ixperience in mining for the principal minerals adapted to our country, first in the Silver mines, then gold, Copper, Lead, Iron and Zinc."[81]

The fortunes of the charcoal iron makers, owners and laborers alike, fluctuated with the national economy, and furnaces went into blast or lay idle accordingly. M. B. Tate, one of John Robinson's business partners, wrote to him in 1877, "Everything as dead as can be and no money in the country." Iron brokers Edward Ely and E. P. Williams similarly reported from Philadelphia in October that year, "There is really no improvement yet in the iron trade, notwithstanding the sanguine expectations of some of the papers," although in November they requested Robinson to send a hundred tons. At other times, business boomed. For instance, in 1882 Charles H. Brown of the Knoxville Car Wheel Company informed Robinson that the Tennessee firm was increasing its capacity and might soon need more iron. But in December 1885 Robinson and Hoffman made the difficult decision to let some furnaces stand idle in 1886 because they could not "see any other way to avoid losing more money."[82] In 1896, Hoffman explained the power of a competitive national market: "We could very readily dispose of your entire stock of iron if we were prepared to meet the prices of the Georgia and Alabama Irons."[83]

The international market also loomed. William H. Wren wrote Robinson in early 1885 to express optimism that the fighting at Pandjeh in Central Asia might help iron makers: "If England and Russia go to war in earnest I feel that iron will be in demand at good prices." In contrast, Frederick Kimball wrote Robinson in February 1885 to explain the negative side (for Robinson) of international commerce: "As a matter of fact, foreign ores, that is ores from Spain, Africa and Cuba, can be delivered at Norfolk and transported over our line to Lynchburg and Roanoke as cheaply as ores could be handled and delivered to the same furnaces from the Cripple Creek region, so great is the present business depression." In 1896, another sales agent lamented to Robinson, "It is plain to us that American [iron] manufacturers have got to get an [sic] European market for s[o]me of their material or else curtail their production."[84]

The last cold-blast charcoal iron from the region apparently came from the Foster Falls Furnace in 1914.[85] The iron industry as a whole had changed dramatically in the preceding forty years. An observer in 1911 pointed out, "The production in one year from a single mine, in Minnesota, of 3,000,000 tons of iron-ore" matched almost "80 per cent. of the entire output of all domestic mines in 1871." He also described "the marvelous improvements made in the conversion of iron into steel."[86] By the time of the last run at Foster Falls, the charcoal iron industry had declined for more than a decade. A presentation at the 1913 meeting of the American Institute of Mining Engineers explained that charcoal iron, including high-quality, high-cost southern varieties, had made up about 50 percent of the iron used in car wheels into the 1890s. But then the downward slide started: "The use of the lower cost mixtures containing coke pig iron and scrap, hardened with steel scrap, and given a certain chilling quality by the addition of ferro-manganese, began about 1888; and as it was possible to produce chilled wheels that would give the same results under test as those made from charcoal iron mixtures, it is easy to see how and why the business fell more and more, from year to year, into the hands of wheel makers developing and carrying on such practice." Charcoal iron had no future: "By 1900 the manufacture of charcoal iron wheels practically terminated in this country."[87]

As the nineteenth century closed, the teetering New River charcoal furnaces such as Foster Falls were joined briefly by coke operations in

Wythe and Pulaski counties, as railroad executive Frederick Kimball had demanded. In May 1892, the Dora Furnace went into blast in Pulaski under the guidance of its president, John W. Robinson. Philadelphia investors built a furnace in Max Meadows in 1890–1891 and under Matthew H. Maury's management put it in blast in 1895. In 1887–1888, with the arrival of the railroad, the Ivanhoe Furnace was rebuilt as a coke-fired facility and first began work on January 2, 1889. Ivanhoe then closed iron making in Wythe County when the furnace—owned since the early 1890s by Robert A. Carter's Carter Iron and Steel Company of Pittsburgh and managed by Carter's son, Howard—drained its last blast in 1915.[88]

The up-to-date furnaces such as the one in Ivanhoe allowed some young people of the area to take inspiration from industrial life. Rufus Johnston Wysor, who became a steel industry executive, recalled growing up in rural Pulaski County: "Frequently, on warm summer evenings, we would sit out in the yard till after dark. In those days there were two active blast furnaces in operation in Pulaski, seven miles distant. We admired the periodic brilliance whenever the 'big bell' at the top of a furnace would be lowered to allow the accumulated charge of iron ore, coke and limestone to slide into the stack. The ignited gas from the furnace would flash up for a few brief moments." He found ways to visit the furnaces so as "to witness the fascinating operations." After graduating from nearby Virginia Polytechnic Institute, he worked as a chemist at Foster Falls Furnace before attaining eminence in Pittsburgh.[89]

Workers also moved among iron and the region's other industries, sometimes overcoming layoffs, sometimes pursuing better wages. A. L. Parrish, born in 1870, related his work history to an interviewer in 1940: "I was born on a large farm in Allega[sic] County North Carolina and I stayed there until I was thirteen years old. I left the farm then and went to Foster Fall, Virginia and worked in the ore mines for two years. I then left Foster Fall and went to Austinville, Virginia and worked in the zinc mines for six years. Then I went from there to Ducktown, Georgia [sic] and worked in the copper mines for one year. Then I went to Bertha, Virginia and worked in the ore mines again for two years. I was married in Austinsville [sic], Virginia June 6, 1894. After working at Bertha I quit the mines and went to Saltville, Virginia and worked in the Matheison [sic] Alkali Plant for three years. I worked in the soda ash department."[90] Just as workers could protest conditions at the iron mines and furnaces by leaving, furnace owners could raid other industrial operations when they needed additional employees.

The workforce at these furnaces still included both whites and blacks, and on occasion workers' simmering dissatisfaction boiled over. At the Max Meadows facility, "fillers," the laborers who moved the heavy raw materials into the furnace, "struck for higher wages" on April 13–14, 1896.[91] A newspaper in Wytheville described them as a "mob composed entirely of Negroes" who "proceeded to break up a lot of tools, took charge of the carriages, emptied them of their contents—limestone, coke and iron ore—piled them in a heap, and then put an armed guard in charge. One of their numbers then got some oil, poured it on the floor of the stock house, and pushed a basket full of burning coke over on the floor, igniting the oil." Superintendent Maury and other managers put out the fire, and production resumed at Max Meadows the following day. Local courts indicted ten "rioters," including George Miller, "who it is claimed fired the stock-house."[92] In industrial settings, black workers had to do the hardest, dirtiest jobs for the least pay, so these "rioters" likely had good cause.

The decline of the iron industry led black workers to leave Wythe and Pulaski counties, part of a broader exodus of African Americans from the South. In 1870, Wythe's 2,342 blacks made up 20 percent of the population. By 1890, 3,170 black people composed 18 percent of the total; in 1900, 2,783 blacks made up 14 percent of the county; but in 1920 the remaining 1,743 black people constituted less than 9 percent of the county's population. In Pulaski County, the number of black residents rose from 1,809 (28 percent) in 1870 to 3,237 (22 percent) by 1900 but fell to 2,425 (14 percent) in 1920. The number and percentage dropped further in both counties during the 1920s. For comparison, Virginia's overall black population fell less dramatically between 1900, when blacks made up 36 percent of state residents, and 1930, when they represented 27 percent.[93]

Throughout the turn-of-the-century South, violence toward black people reached epidemic proportions; white workers found at best a limited common cause with their black counterparts. In the New River valley, as elsewhere, white people deployed extralegal violence to maintain racial control. Thomas Goodson (b. 1885) of Ivanhoe recalled in a 1974 interview, "We lynched a man over here on the other side of Cripple Creek. Me and Old Man Henry Allen and about a hundred of us shot the guns at him, and we buried him right over here on the country road right down the other side of where Betty Haller lives. He was a colored man, and he had attacked a girl. She was about 25. I done forgot who she was. I shot one of the shots at him. Old Man Henry Allen give me his gun and told me to shoot him. He was hanging up on a big limb."[94] And even though the black population of Wythe County had declined by the 1920s, a mob brutally killed a black man named Raymond Bird—accused of attempting to assault a twelve-year-old white girl—in his jail cell in Wytheville on August 15, 1926. The killers then used a car to drag his body through the streets and country roads. Black residents insisted that Bird's consensual relationships with white women motivated the mob, but the murder of Bird undoubtedly reminded the county's black people of their tenuous position, particularly with their labor less in demand by the furnaces.[95] Lynch law's original eighteenth-century stomping ground had germinated new atrocities.

George Lafayette Carter

In the iron industry's final years along the New River, one of the area's own entrepreneurs brought corporate consolidation, typical of late-nineteenth-century capitalism, to full development in southwestern Virginia. George Lafayette Carter, born near Hillsville in 1857, learned business methods in Lee Johnson's general store at Hillsville. Carter began clerking at the lead-mining company in Austinville in about 1878, and he advanced to keeping the books and then serving as general manager of the mines. John W. Robinson and David Peirce Graham owned much of that business. Carter learned from these men, and they gave him considerable responsibility.[96]

Carter allied with George T. Mills, who had overseen construction of the railroad extension along New River. Along with other investors, they founded the Pulaski Development Company to build and manage the Dora Furnace in Pulaski. Graham and Robinson, along with James S. Crockett, consolidated into this new operation their charcoal furnaces, including Beverly, Cedar Run, Eagle, Foster Falls, Graham, Noble, Raven Cliff, Speedwell, and Wythe. After Mills left the business, Carter served as vice president under John W. Robinson, who had already done so much to advance the local industry's efficiency and outside ties. The energetic Carter succeeded Robinson as the region's exemplar of corporate ingenuity.[97]

But in his own speculative ventures and investments, Carter carried the process several steps further, leaving Robinson and Graham as simple stockholders in Carter's enterprise. In late 1897, Carter still served as vice president and general manager of the Dora Furnace Company, concerning himself with muddy conditions and whether he had "plenty of Shanty room for 60 or 70 men" rushing to prepare some much-needed ore.[98] By the end of the 1890s, he had stepped well beyond the New River–Cripple Creek area. With the backing of New York bankers such as Thomas Fortune Ryan, Carter brought together various furnaces, mines, coalfields, and railroad property in 1899 to form the Virginia Iron, Coal, and Coke Company, described on Wall Street as the "consolidation under one ownership and management of the iron industries of Southwest Virginia." In addition to running the former Graham and Robinson properties, Carter's company came to control the Betty Baker Mine and a significant part of the gossan vein in Carroll County. Maintaining his natal ties in the county, Carter made a summer showplace of his wife's family home in Hillsville, a structure first owned by antebellum politician and industrial leader Fielden L. Hale. Carter later developed the Carolina, Clinchfield, and Ohio Railroad and finally exploited extensive mining properties around Coalwood in McDowell County, West Virginia. This secretive man's investment decisions mattered throughout southwestern Virginia, eastern Tennessee, eastern Kentucky, and parts of West Virginia for several decades. His Dora Furnace smelted its last iron in about 1920. On September 21, 1936, hundreds of people gathered in Pulaski to watch twenty-five sticks of dynamite bring down the 185-foot stack. Carter died December 30 that year, hailed, like a high-country Ozymandias, as an empire builder.[99]

Chapter 4

Corporate Peaks in the Valley

In the twentieth century, on a scale larger than ever before, the Appalachian rocks yielded to the urge for profit, and new entrepreneurs started money flowing in new ways: hydroelectric power, sulfuric acid, and carbide. During the so-called American century, capitalism on New River rose and fell with the national tides at a time when U.S. businesses evolved into the world's dominant economy. With the creation of these more sophisticated operations, the New River economy took a step forward from the purely extractive industrial work that has led historians to label the South a colony of the North, but highly skilled, cutting-edge workplaces still rarely characterized the highlands. Regardless of whether the colonial label applies, the industrial changes sometimes had devastating environmental effects. The longtime rhetoric of inexhaustibility, backed by twentieth-century technology, led to several former New River industrial sites landing on the Superfund list of dangerously polluted areas compiled by the U.S. Environmental Protection Agency (EPA).

The power of the U.S. government grew alongside the nation's expanding economy in the twentieth century, with many attendant ironies. White southern leaders, usually known for preferring limited government, complained whenever national legislation threatened to undermine regional subjugation of blacks. They spoke up less systematically on economic matters, but the Appalachian Power Company, controlled by Chicagoans, did fight hard against government regulation of the firm's hydroelectric power projects. Yet both local workers and businesses and outside corporations alike welcomed federal military spending. Historians debate the effect of federal outlays on overall southern development, but direct federal spending as well as companies' reinvestment of wartime profits, a factor less studied, contributed heavily to industrial development along the New River.

Late in the century, the federal government's control of international trade policy did most to shape highland industry as easier international movement of capital and goods made labor-intensive industries look for cheaper alternatives to areas such as the New River valley.

The Chemical Industry

In the 1890s, the sometimes-booming iron business, the new ease of railroad access, and changes in the refining process brought even the mines in Carroll County back into play. No longer worked for copper, they instead produced iron ore, as they had in the eighteenth century. The copper, stated mining engineer Edgar C. Moxham, had been "pretty nearly exhausted by means of drifts in many places," but those drifts had "extensively exposed for miles" the underlying iron ore. In September 1889, Charles B. Squier in New York had "heard of the excitement about Carroll Co. ores." By February 1892, miners were digging at Betty Baker and the Great Outburst, and Moxham explained why:

> Little more than a year has elapsed since railroad connection was made with this lead, and it is now being worked at two points—its extremities. It has not yet been fully developed (except by the copper-miners' drifts above referred to), and the mines are producing only 800 to 1000 tons per day, but their importance is already realized by the furnaces. Every furnace within 250 miles, with but two exceptions, uses from 25 per cent. upwards of its mixture from this source. It is found to be an excellent ore to mix with the other ores of the district, particularly the hard brown ores of the Potsdam series ("mountain ores," high in phosphorus and manganese, but comparatively cheap in price), which could not otherwise be used to anything like the same extent. It is said to give strength to the iron, and to be easily reduced, assisting the working of the furnace, and promoting economy in fuel. Being porous in structure, it contains somewhat more moisture than the limonite- and mountain-ores, but it is not found to be high in silica, and such gangue as it carries, being mostly micaceous, is light in weight, and not costly to the furnace. It is reported that the gossan-ore assists in obtaining a uniformly large percentage of foundry-iron from the blast-furnace.[1]

Only the presence of the railroad let this particular iron ore be moved long distances and mixed with other ores in an appropriate blend.

Moxham also pointed out the high sulfur content of the ore, which contributed to more advanced chemical industries' taking hold in the region. For a time in the 1890s, the Southern Chemical Company in Winston used ore from Betty Baker to make sulfuric acid, again taking advantage of the railroad line to do business by using natural resources in previously infeasible ways.[2] Textile and banking executive Francis H. Fries of Salem had helped make this commerce possible. Norfolk and Western had planned for the New River–Cripple Creek extension to go past Galax, descend the Blue Ridge around Flower Gap, and pass through Winston and Salem. However, between 1887 and 1891, Fries, backed by tobacco magnate Richard Joshua Reynolds and other investors, headed construction of the 122.53-mile Roanoke and Southern Railway, which ran from Roanoke to Winston and Salem, going down the Blue Ridge at a less-rugged spot well northeast of the New River–Cripple Creek mining region. Using political connections, Fries, Reynolds, and the other directors of the company building the road procured hundreds of convict laborers from both Virginia and North Carolina prisons, and using these unfree workers, the directors completed the Roanoke and Southern in late 1891, which led one Moravian chronicler to call Winston, Salem, and nearby localities "our no longer isolated towns." The Roanoke and Southern's success killed prospects for the Virginia and Kentucky Railroad, then on the drawing board to serve some of the same markets. In 1892, Norfolk and Western leased the Roanoke and Southern, making obsolete the earlier plans for an extension beyond Galax. When the Roanoke and Southern encountered financial trouble in 1896, Norfolk and Western bought the company outright.[3] The new route allowed easy, if indirect, movement of sulfur-rich ore from Carroll County's Betty Baker Mine to North Carolina's growing industrial Piedmont.

Southern Chemical needed sulfuric acid to make fertilizer, a product much in demand. Following the Civil War, southern farmers' use of fertilizer spiked as sharecroppers and small farmers made intensive use of the land. Depletion of natural guano from South America led southern agriculturalists and hence much of the southern economy to rely on chemical fertilizers.[4] As early as 1873, geologist T. Sterry Hunt heralded the possibility of linking Carroll County's sulfur-laden gossan ore to the rich deposits of phosphate rock in and around Charleston, South Carolina. Making the rock useful as a fertilizer required treatment with sulfuric acid. Much of the initial development around Charleston involved hauling the phosphate to the North or overseas for processing. Hunt called for completing the entire production process in the South, pointing out a potentially more efficient approach. Sulfur-rich ore from various locations, including Canada and Sicily, went to northeastern cities such as New York and Philadelphia, "where it is made into sulphuric acid for the treatment of the mineral phosphates brought from Charleston, S.C., the manufactured superphosphate of lime being shipped southward to enrich the cotton lands of South Carolina and Georgia." However, a rail line of seventeen miles would connect Carroll County's old copper mines to the existing Norfolk and Western network. Hunt prophesied that someone would build it: "[T]hese sulphur ores will one day be brought in contact with the South Carolina phosphates."[5] Technology would save the South's much-abused agricultural land.

Francis Fries, seeing an opportunity made possible by his earlier railroad work, and three other men formed the Southern Chemical Company, managed by chemist Herbert Bemerton Battle. The plant opened in northern Winston in 1898 and drew its power from the state's first power-transmission station, built on the Yadkin River by the Fries Manufacturing and Power Company.[6] A New Jersey corporation called the Virginia-Carolina Chemical Company rose to dominance in the southern fertilizer market at the turn of the century. In the time since Hunt's declarations in the early 1870s, a great number of fertilizer manufacturers had opened in various areas of the South, and Virginia-Carolina Chemical gained control of most of the southern companies.[7] In 1901, it absorbed the Southern Chemical Company, but Southern Chemical had lost already its supply of ore from Betty Baker in 1900.[8]

Another large northern chemical firm surpassed the Winston concern in the use of Carroll County's ore. Early in the twentieth century, the General Chemical Company constructed a long-lived sulfuric acid plant in Pulaski. That plant began operation in 1904 and relied on ore from the old Great Outburst (later called "Monorat" and "Iron Ridge") portion of Carroll County's gossan vein rather than from the Betty Baker section, which the Virginia Iron, Coal, and Coke Company purchased. The Great Outburst Mine had not sat idle, though; its postwar history featured a typical mix of northern and southern entrepreneurial activity.

The New York and Virginia Mineral and Mining Company worked the Great Outburst deposit in a stripping operation in the early 1890s. That company grew out of the similarly named New York and Virginia Mineral

Company, headed by George W. Palmer, a Saltville, Virginia, industrialist with interests in various mineral operations in southwest Virginia. Palmer's company obtained the land in July 1889 from Baltimore capitalist brothers James E. and Samuel Clayton and their partner, James E. Tyson. After the Civil War, the Claytons had operated the Ore Knob copper mine in Ashe County, North Carolina, but during the 1870s they had also bought extensive holdings of what they hoped would be copper-mining land in Carroll County. Palmer then in June 1890 turned the land over to the New York and Virginia Mineral and Mining Company, a firm that had the involvement of native southerner and investment wizard Richard Thornton Wilson of Wall Street's R. T. Wilson and Company. (Palmer and Wilson worked together on other projects as well.)[9]

The New York and Virginia Mineral and Mining Company in turn gave way to the impressive new General Chemical Company. Headquartered in New York, General Chemical formed in 1899 when twelve small chemical companies in the Northeast, the Midwest, and Canada merged. In a history of its first two decades, the company reported that "sulphuric acid is at the base of almost all that constitutes this basic business." Explaining that product, the writer waxed almost poetic: "Sulphuric Acid is used directly in the production of the so-called volatile acids, such as nitric, hydrochloric and hydrofluoric acids; also acetic acid. It is directly used in refining petroleum; in storage batteries; in fertilizers, alum products, explosives and the refining of copper. The great iron industry, whose products in most cases undergo what is known as 'pickling,' largely depends upon it; for pickling is done with sulphuric acid. This acid is used either directly or indirectly in almost all articles of chemical manufacture. It is the true hand-maiden of the chemical industry."[10]

At its works in Ontario, General Chemical developed a new process for burning the unusual sulfur-laden pyrrhotite ore like that in Carroll County, and in 1903 builders began constructing the plant in Pulaski, the first of its kind in the United States. The owners of the Monorat deposit near Galax had approached the General Chemical Company to seek its help in making the mining there profitable, and the larger firm absorbed the extraction operation, creating a subsidiary called the Pulaski Mining Company. General Chemical's annual report at the close of 1902 boasted of the firm's having "secured important raw material supplies." Most of the gossan ore, from which the sulfur had largely leached, had already been stripped for its iron by the close of the 1890s, and underneath lay this ore rich in both iron and sulfur. After the Pulaski plant roasted the pyrrhotite for its sulfur, the ferrous by-product went to iron furnaces, nearby at first and later to steel centers such as Birmingham. The dual source of profit made the operation feasible. The company explained, "And as the acid and the iron cinder are now by-products of one another,—and both are of high grade,—the operation of the mine, before impossible, became possible because of the two products that resulted."[11]

The General Chemical Company grew rapidly and in turn had a significant effect on the growth of Pulaski. In addition to the acid plant, the company also placed its foundry operation there, crafting various items needed throughout the company's branch plants around eastern North America. The slow decline of iron furnaces along New River meant that skilled workers could readily be had for the foundry.[12]

As the United States prepared to enter the First World War, the presence of a plant turning out sulfuric acid, a critical ingredient for making explosives, led the federal government to consider locating a munitions plant near Pulaski. Government officials, however, found "that there were very few flat pieces on which we could build a plant of that type."[13] Despite missing out on having such a ready market in the neighborhood, the General Chemical Company worked frantically during the war to meet the demand for its acid. One historian noted, "Sulfuric acid was indeed the key chemical of the war period." The company profited accordingly. After the war, in fact, those high returns raised political eyebrows as the country opened investigations into war profiteering. As the economy adjusted to postwar conditions, the General Chemical Company in December 1920 joined four other large chemical concerns in the holding company Allied Chemical and Dye Corporation. Each of the Allied units maintained its separate identity, but a certain amount of coordination and cooperation raised the efficiency of them all.[14]

From 1905 until 1955, the miners at Monorat worked two open pits about two thousand feet apart on the same vein. In 1918–1919, the Virginia Mining Company, as the parent corporation then called the wholly owned subsidiary, removed approximately one hundred thousand cubic yards of overburden, and one pit had reached a depth of two hundred feet; in 1925, underground mining commenced, connecting the two pits, called the Huey and the Bombarger. By 1962, mining work took place on seven underground levels reaching seven hundred feet into the earth. A tunnel drained waste into Chestnut Creek. Underground mining ended March 3,

1962, by which point the company estimated it had removed some 5,807,000 tons of pyrrhotite ore. The mining soon restarted in a third pit, the Howard. In 1968, Allied Chemical sold the Pulaski plant to the Downtown East Corporation but leased it back and kept it working for another eight years. Allied Chemical used the Monorat ore and the Pulaski plant for sulfuric acid production almost continually until July 1976. In 1977 and 1978, Allied partially filled the Howard pit with earth, and in 1980 the Huey pit was allowed to flood.[15]

When the chemical plant in Pulaski closed, it left behind a site contaminated by lead and other metals that threatened Peak Creek, which feeds into the New River at nearby Claytor Lake. The buildings were demolished around 2002, with asbestos-laden material buried on site. The Honeywell Corporation, which had merged with Allied, worked with the EPA to remedy the problems after the onetime industrial highlight landed on the agency's Superfund list of contaminated sites.[16] Honeywell still owns the erstwhile mineral pits in Carroll County, however, and even without ongoing mining, these pits still pour about seven tons of sediment into Chestnut Creek each year. After those pits closed, researchers with the U.S. Geological Survey evaluated the gossan lead and pointed out massive quantities of ore still in place, even though this same vein was being worked when Jefferson wrote *Notes on the State of Virginia* in the 1780s. As industrial methods and economic needs change, Carroll County's ore may again attract digging by hungry companies.[17]

Lead, Zinc, and Wall Street

General Chemical's path through the twentieth century mirrored the experience of other industries in the region. Blue Ridge industry along the New River rose to its high-water mark at the oldest of the mining properties there, the lead mine complex in Austinville. Like the iron furnaces, the lead operation in Wythe County rebounded following the Civil War. Production resumed in October 1865 and accelerated with the arrival of the railroads. These mines would outlast the iron mines and furnaces. And the war itself had brought about the debut of a new industry in Austinville: zinc mining. Among wartime developments, the Confederacy's discovery of zinc would have the most lasting effect on industry in the New River valley.

Mining engineer Anton Eilers drafted a detailed description of the Austinville facilities of the Union Lead Mine Company in 1869 (see appendix D) and argued that in the decades since the visit of William Barton Rogers in the 1830s, the mines had made tremendous progress: "Originally discovered by a Mr. Chisel, they have passed for more than one hundred years through all those stages of eternally changing prosperity and apparently utter failure, to which the best mine can be brought by irregular mining, litigation, and indifferent management. Since the last twenty-five years, however, much of this has been done away with, mainly through the untiring energy and good judgment of Mr. William Kohler, the able superintendent. The mines have prospered, paying a heavy yearly dividend to the stockholders; and to-day they are in as good a condition, and offer as flattering prospects for the future, as they did before an ounce of mineral was removed from the deposits." The discovery of the zinc had made a good site even better. The ores "consist mainly of carbonates of lead, clustering around solid lumps of undecomposed galena, and carbonate and silicate of zinc. The latter have been, up to within a few years, thrown on the dump as useless 'rock'; but are now mined and sold to Northern zinc works."[18]

Numerous underground shafts and galleries gave access to the several layers of ore. And the owners made good profits, though the workers did not benefit so well. The engineer explained that "the works employ over one hundred men and boys at very low wages, from $6 to $26 per month, that the charcoal used costs only seven cents per bushel, and that the economical management of an able and competent superintendent has succeeded in securing regular yearly dividends of from $30,000 to $45,000."[19]

Jacob Rubsamen, Charles Lynch's partner in the late-eighteenth-century lead mines, had recognized the zinc there in the early 1780s, but no one gave it much notice until the Civil War.[20] Zinc had grown in importance during the nineteenth century because demand for brass (an alloy of copper and zinc) expanded, and the use of zinc to galvanize iron became common. Paint, cosmetics, and ceramics required zinc oxide. During the war, the Austinville mines shipped "several tons" of zinc oxide to the Confederacy's smelters in Petersburg. In 1870, the Union Lead Mine Company, according to the census, had thirty workers, including twelve children, working at the furnaces and fifty-five people, including eight young employees, toiling in the zinc and lead mines, forty of them below ground. In 1874, the Virginia legislature rechartered the company as the Wythe Lead and Zinc Mine Company, reflecting the firm's new reliance on both minerals. In 1884, a visitor reported, "They employ 150 miners, mostly white, and pay them from $1 to $1.25 per day."[21]

Still controlled by the heirs of David Peirce and Thomas Jackson, the Wythe Lead and Zinc Mine Company for a time sold most of its zinc to northern producers, mainly the Lehigh Zinc Works of Bethlehem, Pennsylvania, and the Mercer Zinc Works of Trenton, New Jersey, which soon opened its own mine in the area.[22] In May 1888, however, after the railroad extension made the use of coal feasible, Wythe Lead in Austinville broke ground for a small zinc smelter, with "only one block of two direct-fired furnaces of 140 retorts each, placed in 7 rows of 20 retorts." The Austinville furnace averaged 400 tons of output per year and operated until August 1898, when the company ended smelting and began selling its ore to the Bertha Zinc and Mineral Company in Pulaski.[23]

The Bertha Zinc Company (forerunner of the Bertha Zinc and Mineral Company) emerged as the Austinville property's principal regional competitor in zinc production during the late nineteenth century. In 1866, David Shriver Forney, an artist and amateur mineralogist from Pennsylvania, discovered a major deposit of zinc ore in Wythe County, on 742 acres along a mile and a half of the banks of the New River some eight miles northeast of Austinville at Bertha.[24] Mining did not commence at Bertha until 1879, however, when a small shipment to Providence, Rhode Island, was tested and proved unusually pure. In November 1879, Bertha Zinc Company began building a smelter downriver in Pulaski County at Martin's Tank, the stop on the Norfolk and Western main line subsequently known as "Pulaski," and the furnace was first fired in early 1880. L. S. Calfee, a merchant at Martin's, contracted to transport the ore fourteen miles by wagon from the mines to the smelter, a job that ended when the railroads reached the mines in 1885. Those works were enlarged in 1886 and 1887, and by 1893 the mine and smelter together employed approximately 750 men. Both blacks and whites worked at the smelter, which used two types of coal. So-called Altoona coal came via a small, narrow-gauge railway from coal mines that the Bertha Zinc Company had bought within Pulaski County, while most of the smelter's fuel came from the Pocahontas coalfields near West Virginia and arrived in Pulaski on the Norfolk and Western line.[25] (For a detailed description of both the mining and refining operations, see appendix E.) The mines in Austinville had evolved over more than a century, but changes to the landscape and technology, such as the improving transportation routes and the increasing use of coal, allowed the investors at Bertha to create almost instantly a competitive business doing large-scale mining.

The Bertha spelter (zinc cast in slabs) gained an international reputation for its purity. In 1887, for example, 200 tons of the metal went to Russia for use in cartridges. In 1893, an engineer reiterated that Bertha zinc's many uses included the making of both bullets and money: "The metal finds its market among the great manufacturers of the Eastern States, who use it for making fine sheet brass, cartridge metal, seamless tubes, bronze statuary, lithographic plates, etc., and it has also been largely used by some European governments for making cartridges, and also by the mints of the United States."[26]

The Bertha Zinc Company grew out of "New England 'push.'" The initial investors and officers included Oliver Edes, president; Jason W. Mixter, treasurer and general manager; Edwin L. Edes (Oliver's son), secretary; and Thomas Jones, superintendent of the works. Prominent in Plymouth, Massachusetts, Mixter and the Edeses had long flourished in industries such as nail and rivet making, including zinc shoe nails and tacks as well as zinc plates. This group looked south in the 1880s, not only forming the Bertha Zinc Company but also partnering with Tennessean T. E. Heald to develop zinc properties around Knoxville. Longtime Virginia industrialist George W. Palmer bought into the enterprise in early 1880.[27] Thomas Jones brought international technical expertise to this mix of Virginia and Massachusetts capital. Born in 1840 in Bristol, England, to a skilled machinist, Jones had worked at steel plants in Wales and Saxony, joined a chemical works in Providence, Rhode Island, and then ran a zinc plant outside that city before taking command of the Bertha smelting operation.[28]

Large-scale industrial workplaces had become the norm for more and more Americans, and workers asserted themselves more forcefully in the 1880s than they had in the uncertain economic climate just after the war. Reminiscent of John Chiswell's 1762 trip to Bristol, England, Jones turned to Swansea, Wales, for skilled men to serve as workers and foremen at the smelter, leading to complaints to the Treasury Department by "the labor organization at Pulaski City."[29] This short-lived group—the Knights of Labor District Assembly 215, which included a consumer cooperative—formed in late 1886 or 1887. It marked the first time that local laborers pushed their interests using unity and organization rather than ad hoc and usually individual protest.[30] The Knights of Labor assembly in nearby Saltville resorted to an unsuccessful strike against the industrialists there, but the Pulaski local members apparently limited themselves to less direct measures. In January 1889, Pulaski workers warned national Knights leader

Terence V. Powderly that Thomas Jones's employee Francis Thomas intended to bring in forty Welsh immigrants in violation of alien contract-labor laws. Though the complaints reached the Treasury Department, Jones nonetheless succeeded in deepening his pool of workers, for the federal investigator later found recent Welsh immigrants who still owed the company heavy debts for their passage. The 1900 manuscript census listed furnace workers who had arrived from Wales in 1889.[31] The union activity in Pulaski may have inspired worker unrest upriver at the iron mines that year: iron buyer Francis E. Weston commiserated with John W. Robinson, "I am sorry you are having trouble with your laborers, and cannot promise us any ore."[32] The Knights of Labor, though, did little to hinder the control of men such as Jones and his fellow corporate officers. The businessmen had some nearby examples of worker unrest and organization to keep them alert: coal miners along the Norfolk and Western line in West Virginia regularly challenged company prerogatives, sometimes with violence.[33] Nonetheless, not until the eve of World War II would unions gain better traction in the upper New River valley.

And like Moses Austin a century earlier, the talented group of men at Bertha Zinc Company followed political developments that affected their interests. In 1888, Thomas Jones, L. S. Calfee, and other Pulaski industrialists and businessmen petitioned their representatives and senators not to reduce tariff protection on ore: "[W]e believe there never was a time in the history of our State when the protection sought was so necessary and beneficial to the infant industries in iron, zinc, lead, and coal that have just been planted in our midst, and which have already yielded large benefits to our people and promise immensely more in the near future if the confidence of our own people and those investing with us should remain undisturbed."[34]

The Bertha Zinc Company first used open cuts and then a decade later developed shafts to pursue the zinc ore. Even limited mechanization enabled more rapid and more destructive alterations of the environment. William H. Case, superintendent of the mine, described the strip mining: "[I]n open-cut mining for zinc, the enclosing clay is first removed as 'deads' to spoil-banks, and the zinc ore-bodies are then dug and sent to the washer, the process becoming one of 'stripping.'" Steam derricks had eased some of the labor formerly done by hand, but chimneys of limestone jutting up amid the ore as well as rain and storms still made work in the open cuts difficult. In search of more efficiency, particularly after the cuts had gone quite deep, Case switched in the fall of 1889 to sinking vertical shafts to at least ninety feet below the surface and then developing lateral shafts to follow the ore, which required timbering zigzag drifts around the limestone obstructions using yet more of the declining local stocks of timber.[35]

Individual miners' skill and endurance mattered in each system. Case explained what happened at the ore face: "The clay that invariably exists as an immediate covering, or blanket, upon the ore-bodies, is extremely compact and unctuous. The line or plane of demarcation between this clay and the ore-body is not always visible, but usually there has been a movement of the yielding clay upon the firmer ore-body, resulting in a distinct parting or cleavage-plane, and when this is not readily seen, the miner's pick or shovel determines the distinction as unerringly by 'feel' or sound, singly or together, as it would the difference between clay and sand or gravel, when thrust into them." Digging the so-called pipe shafts—metal lined, circular, and going straight into the ground—required less a feel for the earth and more simple strength: "They are circular, and, as sunk at Bertha, have an average diameter of 3½ feet, which dimension bears a close relation to the horizontal extent of a miner's spinal column when in position for digging in one of these shafts. With a pick and shovel fitted with special short handles, and a bucket to suit, a miner, with his anatomy disposed in the shaft so that his legs form the vertical, and his spine the horizontal limb of a right-angled triangle, can, with his helper operating a primitive windlass at top, sink a shaft 3½ feet in diameter, at Bertha, to depths of 100 feet and more for 22 cents per linear foot."[36] Later, after the digging of horizontal shafts, large iron buckets, each holding thirteen hundred to fifteen hundred pounds, carried the ore to the surface using steam power. There the ore was dumped into tram cars holding about two tons and pulled by locomotive to the head of a "water carriage," where water and gravity carried the ore from a hilltop to the processing facilities alongside the New River and the railroad track to Pulaski.[37]

The polluted water, of course, ran into the river. Water-borne waste from the zinc processing exacerbated a problem already created by the iron mines. Late in the nineteenth century, the iron companies had adopted hydraulic mining technology, which western gold miners had perfected; the Virginians used a highly pressurized stream of water to strip away earth and waste from the iron ore they sought. The run-off poured into streams and then the river. Government scientists in 1909 reported that as a result the New River was "rarely, if ever, clear, being of a reddish-brown color due to the hydraulic mining of iron ore carried on in Virginia."[38] Aquatic life undoubtedly suffered the effects of the improved technology.

In 1898, miners exhausted the zinc ore at the Bertha mine, and the grounds were leased to the Pulaski Iron Company, which then mined iron ore there for its furnace in Pulaski. The Bertha smelter, however, operated until January 1911 because its operators arranged to use ore from Austinville's Wythe Lead and Zinc Company, which in turn shut its less-advanced main smelter.[39] By 1911, though, all the primary zinc and lead operations in southwestern Virginia had a single owner, the New Jersey Zinc Company.

George W. Palmer, formerly of Syracuse, New York, served as president of the Bertha Zinc Company in its last independent years, capping a career of successfully digging dollars from the Virginia soil. Palmer, whose native city had its own longtime salt industry, had moved with his wife to Saltville, Virginia, in 1858 to join the salt and gypsum industries there; he and other New York investors leased salt operations from the Preston family. Palmer moved into a house in Saltville formerly occupied by iron and salt industrialist Francis Preston. During the Civil War, out of touch with his many relatives still in Syracuse, Palmer worked with General Jeb Stuart's brother to consolidate control of the saltworks in the Holston River valley. After the war, Palmer remained a major part of the valley's dominant company, the Holston Salt and Plaster Company.[40] Branching out with the Bertha zinc operations, he cooperated with John W. Robinson to convince Norfolk and Western to complete its extension along New River so that zinc ore could reach the Pulaski smelter by railcar rather than by wagon.[41]

In the late 1880s and early 1890s, Palmer relinquished control of both his companies to New York financiers. In 1887, he began cooperating with John H. Inman to form a "Mineral Trust," and by 1890 R. T. Wilson and Company of New York served as "managing directors" of the Bertha mine and smelter. The change in control had occurred definitively by 1889, for in that year New York native George Meade Holstein, who was serving R. T. Wilson and Company in western mining and railroad companies, was named general manager of the Bertha Zinc Company. Control began to shift earlier, however, as Palmer and his partners sought funds that allowed them to expand the plant in 1886–1887. In February 1892, Palmer turned over the reins, and the Bertha Zinc Company became a New Jersey corporation called the "Bertha Zinc and Mineral Company." Palmer likewise allowed R. T. Wilson and Company and other northern investors to take over the Holston Salt and Plaster Company in 1892–1893 and to convert it into a long-lived chemical corporation, the Mathieson Alkali Works.[42]

Both Richard Thornton Wilson and John H. Inman came from the South. Wilson worked as a merchant in antebellum East Tennessee, and

Inman was born into a family of businesspeople and merchants there and in neighboring Georgia. After serving the Confederacy—Wilson in London as a commissary agent, Inman in Tennessee as a quartermaster—they went to New York City. Inman gained his start with relatives in cotton trading, while Wilson made himself into a wizard at playing the stock market. These men made immense fortunes on Wall Street and at times guided investors into business ventures such as mines, factories, and railroads in the South. Wilson and Inman, along with peers such as Virginia native Thomas Fortune Ryan, kept in touch with southern developments in part via membership in the New York Southern Society.[43]

The corporate outlook of the region's new zinc investors such as Wilson must have resonated with another New Yorker who had been mining zinc in the area for some time. Charles B. Squier, a native of Rahway, New Jersey, and a second-generation investor in zinc properties, constituted, with his father, William Crane Squier (d. 1906 at age ninety-four), part of the firm of Manning and Squier. The elder Squier had helped organize the Passaic Mining and Manufacturing Company (later the Passaic Zinc Company) in 1848, and Charles Squier acted as its secretary and treasurer late in the century. In 1882, Manning and Squier in its own right acquired from David Graham's heirs zinc-rich properties in Wythe County on Little Reed Island Creek at Barren Springs, adjacent to the Bertha mines. Throughout the 1880s, Charles Squier corresponded with John W. Robinson as they strategized about how to entice Norfolk and Western into completing the New River extension.[44]

The hybrid of northern and southern men and money bore its ripest fruit in the early twentieth century. In 1897 and after, the New Jersey Zinc Company merged with the Passaic Zinc Company, Manning and Squier, and other related companies such as the Lehigh Zinc and Iron Company and the Empire Zinc Company. The New Jersey Zinc Company had formed in northern New Jersey in 1848 and made a success of using zinc oxide to manufacture paints. In New Jersey Zinc's early years, Manning and Squier served as the company's agent for selling the paint. Not surprisingly, Charles B. Squier became secretary and treasurer of the New Jersey Zinc Company after the consolidation of the late 1890s. He could reach out to investors such as Richard Wilson as well as to Wythe businessmen. In 1902, the Bertha Zinc and Mineral Company, which had just acquired the Austinville mines, arranged to merge with New Jersey Zinc as its Bertha Mineral division. In August 1902, an old business associate summed things up in a letter to John W. Robinson: "You and your neighbors are evidently going to be very flush with money when the Lead Mines deal is closed." George L. Carter also wrote to Robinson, his onetime mentor, "Glad you all sold the Lead Mines—think it was a good sale and sold at an opportune time."[45] All zinc and lead producers along New River henceforth reported to a single faraway board of directors.

Power and Carbide

Outside investors formed two of the area's major industries from their inception. After the Ivanhoe iron furnace, just upstream from Austinville, closed in 1915, the surrounding town appeared set to wane. The owners sold the furnace and related properties in 1918 to resolve a legal dispute. The new owner, oil and natural gas pioneer Addison Browne Dally Jr. of Pittsburgh, reorganized the operation as the Ivanhoe Mining and Smelting Corporation. For decades, he planned to restart mining and smelting operations there; however, nothing of significance ever materialized. In 1917, however, Ivanhoe found salvation in a different power. The National Carbide Corporation built a carbide production plant there. Calcium carbide results from combining limestone and coke in extraordinarily hot electric furnaces (see appendix F). The location seemed perfect: the Norfolk and Western Railway delivered coke, and quarries around Ivanhoe provided limestone. The third necessary ingredient—electricity—also flowed plentifully, for in 1912, about two miles upstream on the New River in Carroll County, the Appalachian Power Company had erected two hydroelectric dams.[46]

The Appalachian Power Company, incorporated in Virginia in May 1911, placed its headquarters in Bluefield, West Virginia, but H. M. Byllesby and Company of Chicago had created the firm. Company founder and president Henry Marison Byllesby, a Pittsburgh native, had earlier worked for Westinghouse Electric Company, and his new company grew rapidly. It specialized in operating municipal power systems, mostly in the West and the Midwest. For his venture in the Appalachians, Byllesby bought six potential power sites along New River in Carroll and Pulaski counties as well as two possible reservoir sites farther upriver. He acquired rights to develop the power systems in a number of towns, including Saltville, Wytheville, and Pulaski, Virginia, as well as Bluefield, Pocahontas, Welch, and Keystone, West Virginia—all within about fifty miles of the two initial hydroelectric projects. Appalachian Power also sold wholesale electricity to utility

companies already in place in Radford and Roanoke. Coal-mining companies that had operated their own small-scale coal-fired steam generators
could purchase Byllesby's hydroelectric power and sell even more coal. The
company spurned federal claims that it needed federal approval of its dam
projects and faced no consequences. In 1912, as many as 1,250 men worked
on building the dams and on erecting transmission poles and aluminum
wires. Many of the forty-five-foot chestnut poles came from the cleared
rights-of-way, and workers planted them in holes that at times were blasted
from solid rock. Development No. 2 even swamped the old Grayson Sulphur Springs resort so loved by a previous generation of entrepreneurs.
Power began to flow from Development No. 4 on August 15, 1912, and
from Development No. 2 on October 15, 1912. In 1913, approximately 237
miles of lines carried electricity throughout the region.[47]

Byllesby and his partners understood their new surroundings. A 1913
brochure touting the company opened with a resounding paean to Appalachian industry: "The Appalachian Power Company serves not less than five
different kinds of markets for the consumption of its product: 1. The Pocahontas coal fields. 2. Lighting and power requirements in cities and towns
of a large and long settled mining, industrial, agricultural and stock raising
region, which includes great areas of standing hardwood timber. 3. Iron
and zinc mining and smelting districts. 4. Gypsum, salt and alkaline districts. 5. Various industrial operations throughout the transmission zone
such as limestone operations and mills and factories of various kinds."[48]
Industrial needs had driven creation of many of the hydroelectric projects
around the world. Byllesby and his associates played a role in a worldwide
business, bringing mainstream technology to the upper New River valley.[49]
Like mining engineers, geologists, and cotton manufacturers, the hydroelectric specialists belonged to a technological and business community
that worked and thought across national boundaries.[50] They commodified
the power of water and gravity and thus enabled more intensive use of
other natural resources such as zinc, timber, and salt.

Regional boosters heralded the new company: when Byllesby, his vice
president Arthur S. Huey, and other officials visited Bluefield to check on
progress in January 1912, the Chamber of Commerce there held a welcom-
ing reception. Byllesby in turn wooed Appalachian industrialists. In June
1912, he ran a special train from Bluefield to the dam sites on New River to
show off the projects. Specially printed menus for breakfast and lunch
greeted the hundred or so interested mine owners, and a souvenir booklet

summarized the development. Viele, Blackwell and Buck, a New York City engineering firm that had recently built two dams on the Hoosic (sometimes "Hoosac") River in New York, had charge of the construction. Harold Winthrop Buck, once the chief engineer at the Niagara Falls Power Station, and M. A. Viele joined the day trip showing off their handiwork. They also joined Appalachian Power's board of directors. Development No. 4 took the name "Buck," and Development No. 2 was called "Byllesby." Like Moses Austin and Francis Fries, this new group of industrialists made the communities of the New River corridor into their namesakes.[51]

With its initial investment paying off and the company expanding, Appalachian Power in July 1917 agreed to supply electricity to a new customer whose creation the power company had pushed: the National Carbide Corporation. Boston native Stuart M. Buck, an uncle of Harold Winthrop Buck, conducted major coal operations in the Pocahontas field. He and fellow coal entrepreneur John J. Lincoln, a Pennsylvanian who had also moved to West Virginia, served as president and vice president of the new carbide company, which initially placed its headquarters in Bramwell, West Virginia. The company devoted $350,000 to building in Ivanhoe a carbide plant capable of producing 15,000 tons annually. With their knowledge of coal and generous long-term rates from the power company, Buck and Lincoln soon had a profitable new business. They chose as general superintendent in Ivanhoe chemist Edward James Kearns, a native of Ireland who had prior carbide experience in Quebec.[52]

To build the plant itself, the National Carbide organizers lured Ivanhoe resident Charles Ross Huddle (1884–1970) from his job as superintendent of the nearly defunct Ivanhoe Furnace Company. Huddle brought National Carbide's plant construction near completion, but he then returned to working, for decades, as the on-site engineer and caretaker of Ivanhoe iron and zinc land. The Huddle family had provided at least three generations of leadership to local industry: Huddle's father, John Foster Huddle (1842–1909), the brother of antebellum Wythe County iron founder David Huddle, had been born in Pennsylvania, studied at Freiburg University, and worked in the iron industry in Virginia and North Carolina, including service as superintendent of the Cranberry Iron and Coal Company in Cranberry, North Carolina. Charles Ross Huddle's son, Charles Richard Huddle (1911–1986, known by his middle name), would later work for the carbide plant until its closure, when he had charge of the works. From its founding, the carbide plant determined much of Ivanhoe's fate.[53]

Stuart Buck died in Bramwell on July 16, 1921, but a few months earlier, on May 1, 1921, the Air Reduction Company (Airco) had taken charge
of the National Carbide Corporation.[54] Airco, incorporated in November
1915, grew out of a predecessor business operated by banker Robert C. Pryn
and Percy A. Rockefeller, a nephew of John D. Rockefeller. Airco first focused on the production of pure oxygen and then in 1917 added acetylene
plants—it thus turned out the two products needed in oxyacetylene cutting
and welding, a vital industrial process then only some two decades old.
Until 1921, Airco bought the calcium carbide it needed for making acetylene, but with the acquisition of the National Carbide Corporation, Airco
secured an independent supply.[55]

Wythe County limestone, West Virginia coke, and the copious hydroelectric power of the New River combined to feed the flames needed by
heavy industry, but carbide's glory years passed quickly. Shipbuilding and
other wartime requirements boosted demand beginning in the late 1930s.
Employment in Ivanhoe peaked at about 450, and in 1941 National Carbide added a massive new carbide and acetylene plant in Louisville, Kentucky. Airco, headquartered in New York City, let National Carbide keep
its original identity until 1960, when the ever-expanding parent company
combined National Carbide and two other subsidiaries into a new division
called the "Air Reduction Chemical and Carbide Company." Airco extended its reorganization in 1966: in December, it announced the closure of
its aging Ivanhoe plant. Richard Huddle moved to Louisville to head carbide production there.[56]

In 1968, Airco donated the Ivanhoe plant and 175 acres to the Wythe
County and Carroll County Industrial Development Authorities. In 1979,
Richard Huddle, who by then had returned and was working as an industrial development official, oversaw demolition of the decaying structure his
father had built. In the late 1980s, the site earned a spot on the EPA's Superfund list of contaminated sites due to polychlorinated biphenyls (PCBs) in
leaking old capacitors in a basement, and in 1989 Airco's successor company agreed to clean up the pollution. In 1989, only about nine hundred
people lived within a mile of the site, which dozed near the center of the
still-unincorporated community of Ivanhoe.[57]

The Lingering Federal Presence

Even when major customers included governments, private industry for the
most part shaped the economy of the New River valley. Firms such as Na-

tional Carbide came and went as profits dictated. However, the national government's presence grew larger in Americans' lives during the twentieth century, and southwestern Virginia felt the effects just like everywhere else. Even the power of the New River itself spurred controversy, and the federal government moved to center stage there.

From 1934 to 1939, the Appalachian Power Company constructed a major hydroelectric project, the Radford (now Claytor) Dam, at the downstream end of Pulaski County. However, the federal government, as it had in 1912 during the company's initial dam-building work, asserted that the project needed its approval, this time via the Federal Power Commission. The extent of the upper New River's navigability during the nineteenth century became a much-researched and much-contested component of the lengthy court case that followed; federal power extended only to navigable waters. The courts weighed the extent to which pig iron had moved by keelboats from the Wythe County furnaces downstream to the railroad. The mountains of evidence included myriad documents about the U.S. Army Corps of Engineers' sporadic efforts fifty years earlier to improve navigation on the river. In the end, the case turned on "conflicting contentions as to state and federal power," and the federal government's 1940 victory in the Supreme Court meant that industry along the upper New River played a part in the dramatic expansion of the American administrative state during this time, an issue that roiled political waters around the nation.[58] Contrary to widespread depictions of a particularly southern intransigence toward the federal government, this New Deal–era fight against federal intervention came via a Chicago-based corporation.

During World War I, the federal government had decided that rough terrain precluded building a munitions plant in Pulaski County, but as World War II approached, the topography did not prevent military officials from giving in to the lobbying of the Norfolk and Western Railway. The railroad's executives urged federal authorities to construct the Radford Ordnance Works on four thousand acres covering both banks of the New River near the city of Radford and the New River Ordnance Plant near Dublin in Pulaski County. Construction began at Radford on September 7, 1940, and as many as twenty-three thousand people, most working for the Mason and Hanger Company of New York, pushed the project at an exceptional pace. The influx strained the residential and civic capacity of the city far beyond normal limits, but many local people profited. Boardinghouses, restaurants, and stores boomed. Men not snatched away by the draft as well as women welcomed the employment: for example, special trains helped them commute daily from as far as Roanoke and Bluefield, West Virginia. Total cost reached about $51 million. Munitions production started on April 5, 1941. The two facilities later combined and in 1963 were renamed the "Radford Army Ammunition Plant" (known popularly as the "Radford Arsenal"). A 1942 report indicated that officials chose the site due to the "desirability of the properties . . . , adequate water supply, proximity to coal mines and chemical plant, double track line of the Norfolk and Western Railway, railroad yard facilities at Radford, Pulaski, Bluefield and Roanoke, protection afforded by mountains, favorable climatic conditions, [and] efficient Anglo-Saxon labor."[59]

Employment levels at the Radford plant have bobbed up and down as international conflicts and the military-industrial complex have demanded: "Production employment reached 9,200 in 1945, 8,600 at the height of the Korean War, 9,300 during the Vietnam War, and 4,728 during the Reagan arms build-up. During the interwar years employment fell: To as low as 150 after World War II, to 2,575 after the Korean War, 2,500 after the Vietnam War, and 1,250 by 1996." Despite the varying levels, the plant's continuing presence has helped absorb workers—some of whom commute quite long distances—who were displaced by the closing of other extractive industries such as General Chemical's mines.[60]

The area's mineral resources also felt the touch of the military-industrial complex. Following World War II, the Cold War chilled international relations, and Carroll County's old gossan vein, still tapped for sulfuric acid, got another close look. The U.S. Interior Department's Bureau of Mines sent investigators to the area during 1947 and 1948. They drilled twenty-five holes for a total of 9,173 feet to analyze the ores. In their report, they explained their work: "The Bureau of Mines, in its program of developing reserves of strategic minerals, began a drilling project on the Gossan lead to determine the extent, continuity, and copper, lead, and zinc content of the deposit. The Betty Baker segment and the Lineberry tract of the Chestnut Creek segment were chosen as the best-situated and most favorable areas for early development." The federal scientists found it easy to work with the landowners, for ownership had become extremely concentrated: "The known outcrop length of 16.7 miles of the Gossan Lead has been owned or controlled by the Virginia Iron, Coal & Coke Co. [George L. Carter's former company] and the General Chemical Division of the Allied Chemical and Dye Corp. for over 50 years."[61]

In the early 1950s, as "the rearmament program of the United States and its allies gain[ed] momentum," a worldwide shortage of sulfur reignited interest in the Betty Baker end of the gossan lead. In July 1951, the Virginia Iron, Coal and Coke Company agreed to sell 7,792 acres there to the Freeport Sulphur Company, a brimstone behemoth that operated primarily in Louisiana and Texas. The sulfur crunch eased before the new owner tapped the Carroll County rock, though it did explore the site. The company took advantage of a relatively new government resource to examine the economic potential of the ore. Freeport Sulphur, Norfolk and Western, and the General Chemical Company cooperated with the Virginia Engineering Experiment Station at the Virginia Polytechnic Institute to test ways to better refine the ore. A few decades earlier, engineers and consultants from Philadelphia or other northern cities would have done such work.[62] Federal and state engineers and those employed by state-funded universities continued to keep a close eye on Carroll County's potentially strategic deposits through the 1950s and 1960s, extending in new form the long tradition of both military and scientific interest in the region's resources.[63]

New Jersey Zinc Company in the Twentieth Century

Even as Ivanhoe's National Carbide plant sprouted, matured, died, and left its toxic detritus, and the arsenal workforce pulsed to rhythms of war, the New Jersey Zinc Company continued to dig into the seemingly inexhaustible Austinville-area zinc and lead deposits. For the first eight decades of the twentieth century, this operation anchored industrial life along the river. The plant became just one of several branches of its New York–based parent: workers in Austinville had no choice but to see themselves as peers of their counterparts in Pennsylvania, New Jersey, Illinois, Colorado, and New Mexico. For managers, a stint in Austinville sometimes opened the way to higher office elsewhere in the firm.

The parent corporation's depth of resources allowed the Austinville managers to attend to details that would have been ignored earlier. For instance, by 1917 Walter O. Borcherdt, the superintendent, had given considerable thought to improving both the quality of the water supply for workers underground and the latrines there. That year the company drove a shaft 220 feet upward from the main mine adit as part of building a new half-million gallon water reservoir. The reservoir also made possible a gravity-fed fire-protection system that was completed in December 1919, protecting workers and the facilities. Ten-inch cast-iron lines directed water from the reservoir to the various parts of the plant.[64]

The company's biggest investments at Austinville, however, came in the wake of each of the century's two world wars. Both conflicts led to high demand and robust profits. Each time New Jersey Zinc invested in its properties to keep its long-term outlook strong. From February to July 1920, for example, Austinville buzzed with activity as a field "on the high ground southeast of the plant" transformed from corn stubble, wheat, and hay to the location of 80 four-room cottages with running water on lots of 60-by-150 feet. The company added on to the store and the offices, and it extended the railroad siding to better accommodate loading and unloading. On a larger scale, a new roasting furnace and oxide bagging facility rose. By August, the foundation for a 350-foot stack had been laid. A "considerable increase" in the workforce came aboard to fill the new houses and take on the additional work.[65] By mid-October, in only sixty-two working days, the Alphons-Custodis Chimney Construction Company completed the stack. Local company officials bragged that the stack reached higher than any structure "south of [the] Washington Monument."[66] Even after a lightning strike later cut the chimney's height to 295 feet, it dominated views of the plant for as long as it operated.[67] The postwar economic downturn closed oxide production soon after the new stack topped out; however, in 1922 processing and bagging zinc oxide began again, with a new round of improvements in place by early 1923. Never-occupied houses filled with workers, and the company store expanded again.[68]

In the late 1920s, New Jersey Zinc upgraded its basic facilities far beyond the oxide furnace. A new shaft, headframe, and concentrating mill opened in late 1927. The company named the 750-foot vertical shaft in honor of the recently deceased Joseph A. Van Mater, a former manager of the Bertha division, and the steel headframe towered 115 feet above the opening. Six levels of mining activity fanned out beneath the surface, about 100 vertical feet apart, with battery-powered electric locomotives moving ore along the horizontal shafts. Crushing machines operated underground, and the fine ore was then dumped into a shaft that emptied into cars on the bottom-most level, where the cars moved the ore to the Van Mater shaft for removal to the surface. Once above ground, the ore emptied from the headframe into the new steel and concrete concentrating plant, which covered more than half an acre down the hillside, with skylights allowing for natural illumination. The plant could process approximately 1,000 tons of ore per day. The nearly pure zinc at the bottom was piped to an area near the railroad tracks for drying, storing, and loading for shipment north, and by-products went to tailings ponds. (For more details on the plant at this time, see appendix G.) One by-product, finely crushed limestone, turned into a major secondary income producer at the new plant, with some 6 million tons sold by 1956. Farmers from near and far came to buy lime to spread over and improve heavily worked acidic soils. Some limestone from Austinville's massive open mounds joined zinc ore on the outbound trains.[69]

After typical belt-tightening during poor economic times in the 1930s, the New Jersey Zinc Company benefited from World War II. Government officials kept a close watch on mineral operations around the country, including in the New River valley, and the nation's war needs sent demand surging. The war right away allowed the Austinville operation to sell large accumulated reserves of zinc and lead concentrates: "A substantial part of the concentrates shipped in 1941 came from mine stocks accumulated in previous years," the U.S. Bureau of Mines reported. Virginia companies shipped 3,390 tons of lead and 22,913 tons of zinc during that year, all but one railcar of it from Austinville.[70]

In 1948, the New Jersey Zinc Company celebrated its centennial. A triumphal official history summarized the importance of war: "The Company's service in our country's several wars has been marked always by intensified activity, expanded production, and a determination on the part of everyone in the organization to do his part toward the victory which ultimately came. Through the years, each war program has followed a similar pattern, differing only in the magnitude of war demand for essential zinc products without which victory could not have been achieved." During World War II, "mines and smelters operated at peak levels" in order to "meet the huge demands of war." Brass shell casings consumed "hundreds of thousands of tons" of zinc, with Austinville's mineral thus littering Europe and Asia. But zinc filled numerous other military needs, including die castings "for vital parts of such ordnance items as shell fuses, grenades, rocket-bombs and land mines." Airplane parts were cast in zinc dies; zinc pigments coated "ships, tanks, guns, planes, cantonments," and so on; and zinc oxide reinforced rubber in the tires and tubes and hoses of equipment for war.[71]

With peace secured in 1945, New Jersey Zinc looked to use its wartime profits and pent-up consumer demand to keep the good times going. In 1948, the company listed the many consumer items containing zinc: face powder, soap, adhesive tape, buttons, shoe polish, house paint, roofing, linoleum, plastics, and many other products. Die-cast zinc had made tremendous strides toward fully infiltrating Cold War American life: "[Zinc die castings] may be found in the home as parts of washing machines, refrigerators, lighting fixtures, radios, hardware, tools and kitchen electrical appliances; in public places as parts of vending machines; in the office as parts of typewriters and other business machines. And last, but not least, zinc die castings provide many parts of automobiles—as carburetors, fuel pumps, hardware, grilles and many other utilitarian and decorative applications."[72] Zinc, in short, fulfilled consumers' dreams.

To meet this demand as the decade closed, the company had committed to a number of expansion and renovation projects at its many plants, Austinville included. In 1948, a new concentrates drier appeared alongside the stack in place of the obsolete oxide furnace; new staff houses were being built and old ones renovated, replete with up-to-date details such as white asbestos siding; and office space expanded again. Work on rebuilding the flotation mill began in 1948 and finished in 1953 at a cost of $277,000 —"Practically all existing equipment was discarded," the company reported. Concentrated zinc and lead flowed about half a mile in gravity-fed pipelines from the mill to the new drier.[73] By 1949, New Jersey Zinc had installed a new treatment plant to turn the flow from New River into better drinking water and fire protection for both the mine and the company-owned town of Austinville; a new sewage-treatment facility came to fruition as well. A new tailings dam started to fill nearby Bunker Hill Hollow with mine waste.[74] A grinding mill finished in 1954 represented "the last major improvement at the Austinville plant under the Company program of modernization which began in 1948 after it was apparent that the Austinville operation had an extended life."[75]

Cold War government policies facilitated New Jersey Zinc's commitment to expansion. The company informed stockholders in the 1951 annual report, "To encourage increased production of metals needed for defense purposes and the construction of facilities for such production, Congress passed laws, late in 1950 and in 1951, providing for accelerated depreciation of the cost of needed facilities, and for the deduction from earnings as current expenses, the pre-production development cost of opening up new orebodies." Work in both Pennsylvania and Virginia helped the company take advantage of this tax break.[76]

New Jersey Zinc's willingness to invest in the Austinville plant also rested on new discoveries of ore. Deepening the Van Mater shaft (to 1,200 feet by 1956) gave miners access to new ore in the old region of the mine, and tunnels led to ore in the mine's new Flatwood section, more than a mile from the main shaft. At Flatwood, the company added a 650-foot-deep secondary shaft for ventilation, removal of waste rock, and employee access, though the Van Mater shaft still provided the outlet for the crushed ore. And despite a brief slowdown in the industry in the late 1940s, the company made a major commitment to the area by taking an option to buy the unused Ivanhoe iron furnace facilities and lands, which aging oil and gas pioneer Addison Browne Dally Jr. owned and long-suffering local engineer Charles Ross Huddle kept watch on. Three years of careful diamond drilling ensued. New Jersey Zinc exercised the option in July 1950 after its engineers confirmed that extensive zinc deposits lay beneath the pockmarked ground some two and a half miles from the Austinville headframe. Workers broke ground for a new shaft at Ivanhoe on December 3, 1951. Ivanhoe's 90-foot headframe went up in September and October 1953. Equipment such as "drills, mucking machines, mine cars, locomotives, substation equipment, pumps, etc." followed. The new corporate layout linked the fate of the two old mining towns Austinville and Ivanhoe.[77]

The mining business had grown considerably more complex since John Chiswell's workers began digging for lead in the 1760s. To most efficiently tap the zinc in Ivanhoe, which lay upstream from Austinville on the opposite side of the New River, the company began driving a tunnel—10½ feet wide, 9 feet high, 1,000 feet deep, and 13,325 feet long—to connect the two subterranean operations. As at Flatwood, the new Ivanhoe shaft would take a secondary position to the Van Mater shaft in Austinville. Electric locomotives would move the Ivanhoe ore through the underground tunnels and shafts to Austinville for crushing and processing. Work on the tunnel began in 1952 from the Austinville end. The Ivanhoe shaft reached the bottom-most cross-shaft level at about 1,000 feet below the New River in 1953, and tunneling soon started from that end as well. Each end of the tunnel progressed on a slight rise, allowing water to drain back to pumping stations at both Ivanhoe and Austinville. The company's 1955 annual report proclaimed that the tunneling had passed the halfway point. On February 19, 1957, workers broke through, connecting the two ends. In September, the locomotives began pulling ore from Ivanhoe to Austinville through the completed tunnel.[78]

About five hundred employees worked for New Jersey Zinc in Austinville in 1948.[79] In 1953, about three hundred people worked the mine's three daily shifts, producing 2,400 tons of zinc ore each day. By the late

1960s, that production figure had increased only slightly, to 2,600 tons per day.[80] In the intervening period, though, worldwide need for zinc and thus production beneath Austinville and Ivanhoe rose and fell periodically. In July 1958, low demand led to Ivanhoe's relegation to stand-by status and the curtailment of work at Austinville. Ivanhoe resumed work in September 1959, and by the end of 1959 the joint operations hummed along at near full capacity. In 1960 and 1961, the company looked to the future again by cutting an eleventh underground level to reach new ore, although water-control problems made for slow progress. The year 1964 brought announcements of "[e]xtensive mine development programs" at Austinville "in order to maintain our ore reserve."[81]

New Jersey Zinc's well-developed facilities and rosy outlook for the future led the conglomerate Gulf and Western to purchase the company in 1966, moving decision making for Austinville and Ivanhoe yet farther beyond local control. Strong business conditions endured for a time, but in late 1980 Gulf and Western, citing high costs, ore depletion, and the investment that mandatory air pollution controls would require, shuttered its longtime zinc smelter in Palmerton, Pennsylvania, foreshadowing the fate of its Virginia division.[82] A commodities analyst pointed out that the conglomerate had "been terribly disappointed in their investment in zinc."[83] In mid-1981, as part of a move away from capital-intensive industries, Gulf and Western sold the portions of New Jersey Zinc that a group of investors thought could turn a profit. The Austinville plant did not make the list, so a different fate awaited it.[84]

For twenty-three decades, the men and boys of Austinville, in all their variety, sank shafts ever deeper. In 1981, the digging stopped. The final train loaded with zinc pulled out on December 9, 1981, and New Jersey Zinc's mines and concentrating mill in Austinville and Ivanhoe closed up at the end of December 1981. The pumps shut off, and the shafts flooded, bringing to a conclusion more than two centuries of major mineral extraction along this portion of the New River. The massive chimney, erected with such optimism in the high-flying 1920s, toppled on December 16, 1981. Competition from imports, the rising cost of labor and adherence to environmental regulations, and low zinc prices had made this operation obsolete, the last step in this operation's 240-year life as part of a world economy.[85] A commodities analyst reported of zinc in 1984, "The U.S. relies on net imports for about 66 percent of apparent domestic consumption."[86]

Gulf and Western gave its fire truck to the community, sold the company houses to local people, turned the sewer and water facilities over to new civic entities, and sold the rest of the site—more than a thousand acres—to the James River Limestone Company. This Virginia firm's new subsidiary, the Austinville Limestone Company, took over selling New Jersey Zinc's agricultural limestone, approximately 6 million tons of which remained piled on fifty-two acres, left there as a by-product of lead and zinc processing. By October 1982, the new business owners had opened their marketing; by 1997, they had sold 1.5 million tons, but another thirty years of reserves lay in readiness. In 1996, James River Limestone sold the Austinville operation to a small private partnership that continues to sell the leftover bulk limestone. In 2007, however, the new partners debuted an open-pit limestone quarry. They crush and process the freshly cut rock into limestone pellets that nourish the lawns, gardens, and golf courses loved by Americans.[87]

Capitalism did not forget the old mine itself, though. In 2002, local residents had to fight off a proposal by Duke Energy to build a gas-fired power plant at Foster Falls and to cool the equipment by drawing seven million gallons of water per day from the old mine shafts, water so polluted that the EPA had decided against mandating cleanup only because the water was sealed safely underground.[88]

The demise of New Jersey Zinc in Austinville dealt a crippling blow to heavy industry along New River. On October 15, 1985, the last train left Galax. Norfolk and Western shut down all service on the North Carolina Extension, which for almost a century had served Fries, Galax, Ivanhoe, Austinville, and the many points between there and Pulaski County. The company took up all the rails and reused them to maintain tracks in Cincinnati and other more thriving areas.[89]

Chapter 5

Left Behind

For the eighteenth and nineteenth centuries, the lives of workers in the New River valley show through to us only in flashes, secondhand snippets here and there. During the twentieth century, however, workers witnessed major changes in industrial life, and better corporate record keeping, the onset of mass media, and working people's own attention to their past mean that we can trace recent history in greater detail. Beginning around 1900, some of the companies in the valley, operating on a larger scale than ever before, funded amenities that helped ameliorate workers' tough conditions, and state legislation finally hindered the use of child labor in the textile industry. The arrival of the labor-friendly New Deal policies of the late 1930s as well as the labor shortages of the war years that followed gave workers their most advantageous moments in the history of industrial work along the upper New River. By the end of the century, though, global economic change left workers looking for alternatives.[1]

As ever, people with resources marked boundaries on the world occupied by those without. Behind the material advances of midcentury swirled neoliberal globalization, which soon left workers treading water in an economic eddy and reflecting on industries gone by. Twentieth-century economic growth lifted living standards in the Blue Ridge as productivity increases, driven by technology and organized by capitalists, redounded to workers' benefit. The creation of government safety nets, minimum-wage laws, public schools, and support for the elderly added unprecedented layers of security and opportunity. But the decline of heavy industry left in its wake an unstable service economy, growing unemployment, and a damaged environment that can recover only slowly. In a departure from historic patterns, the productivity gains of recent decades have benefited almost solely the top wealth holders. Early in the twenty-first century, the residents of the New River valley, citizens and noncitizens alike, face inequality and renewed uncertainty, recurring hallmarks of the preceding two and a half centuries of capitalist evolution.

Corporate Welfare

To forestall worker unrest and ensure labor stability, companies in the early-twentieth-century United States provided various benefits for their employees. Sometimes the need for workers in remote spots necessitated company programs far more elaborate than, say, the boardinghouses made available by owners of nineteenth-century iron furnaces. Along the New River, industrial works affiliated with larger national corporations kept abreast of management trends. For instance, the General Chemical Company owned and maintained around its Monorat mines in Carroll County "a large proportion" of the employee housing and operated a schoolhouse and community center, and the company's acid plant in Pulaski built an employee clubhouse and sponsored a baseball team and an annual picnic with concerts and games.[2] And when Francis Fries began the Washington Mills textile endeavor in 1901, the company built about three hundred houses for workers, a company store, and a bank. The mill aided the county in constructing a local school and a lyceum, which in 1923 evolved into a branch of the Young Men's Christian Association. "When I grew up, the house was furnished by the mill, the doctor was furnished by the mill, the mill built the school. It provided maintenance on our homes," Jackie Roop Sharp explained in 1986. "The mill was daddy."[3]

In 1916, a New Jersey Zinc Company official explained why companies undertook "welfare work" among employees: "The directors have no more moral and legal right to direct part of the revenues of the corporation to the application of Christianity to their own employees than they have to employ them in maintaining a mission to Africa; unless, and here is the vital point, it is to the advantage, in the long run, of the stockholders to do so." Those advantages included "improving the physical condition of the worker so that he may do more and better work in a working day"; "making employment with that corporation desirable, so that it can maintain its working force at full strength in a rising labor market without increasing wages"; and "diminishing lost time and interruptions to operation from strikes."[4]

New Jersey Zinc—which, like Washington Mills, provided houses and later a rooming house for some workers—initiated such welfare programs in Austinville. For example, the superintendent, W. O. Borcherdt, headed up a rifle club that started in 1916 and a chapter of the Red Cross Auxiliary that formed the next year. The employees decided on a company amateur minstrel show as a way to raise money for the Red Cross. The company sponsored house- and garden-beautification contests, and in 1921 Borcherdt played the mother of the bride in a womanless wedding skit that helped raise funds for paying a county nurse. Movies and a "community radio apparatus" operated in the company clubhouse by 1923. The company sponsored visits by a dentist from Pulaski and a community Christmas tree with gifts for poor children. Of more importance, New Jersey Zinc in the 1920s also organized a mutual relief association to which employees could contribute for protection against illness, disability, and death—the beginning of the employee benefits regime that still ties workers to the workplace.[5] The companies continued many of these programs, including housing, for as long as the mining continued along the New River, and employees experienced real benefits from them in spite of the companies' profit-serving intentions.[6]

Unlike racially diverse company towns in the coal-mining areas of West Virginia, racial homogeneity in the carbide and zinc operations meant that white workers reaped nearly all the benefits of the companies' welfare efforts. White men predominated in industrial activity following the demise of the iron furnaces, which had employed significant numbers of black workers. Ivanhoe, with its furnace, had enough black residents to have a segregated school for them, built with the support of the Julius Rosenwald Foundation. Records of the twentieth-century New Jersey Zinc Company, in contrast, do not show black employees in Austinville. Some black people worked at National Carbide in Ivanhoe, particularly in the early years, but in February 1964 the company, which also provided extensive housing for white employees, reported to federal officials only 2 black people (and 1 woman) among the 107 people on the rolls.[7]

Some white men began work in Austinville in the nineteenth century and then spent many decades with New Jersey Zinc after it took control. Under a program begun in 1911, the company sometimes granted pensions to people who retired after lengthy service. The company magazine featured stories about these longtime workers. In 1919, it listed the four longest-serving employees in Austinville: William Jones Sr., since 1856; Thomas Hundley Sr., since 1862; Robert Alley Sr., since 1859; and William Mabe, since 1865. Alley's obituary in 1929 narrates his industrial odyssey, which, as for many others at the time, began at an early age: "Robert (Uncle Bob) Alley died October 23, 1929, at Austinville. He was born in the year 1850, making him in his seventy-ninth year. Mr. Alley had spent his entire life at Austinville and his only employment was at the Zinc Mines at Austinville. He was employed by the predecessor company in 1859 and was in continuous service till March, 1921, when he was retired on pension."[8] Mabe's son, John W. Mabe, joined his father at New Jersey Zinc in 1896 and, according to a 1919 profile, earned a supervisory role: "Until 1907, he worked in various capacities in connection with the milling and smelting operations of the old company, being at one time, foreman of the old soft ore mill, which was being used for the crushing of the oxidized ores of lead and zinc. In 1907, shortly after the construction of the present hard rock mill, he was made foreman of that operation and has occupied that position ever since."[9]

Workers took on many different duties during the course of their work lives. James N. Gallemore, profiled in 1919, "was first employed in June, 1890 with the Wythe Lead & Zinc Mine Company as a water carrier at the old soft ore concentrating mill. His next job was 'trunking' zinc ore at the jigs, and between the ages of 12 and 15, he worked underground at various jobs. He then worked at the lead furnaces until 1902, except for one year at the zinc furnace, and was connected with the oxide furnace work from the first experiments conducted by Mr. Stone, until 1907, when he became a member of the carpenter crew at the new concentrating mill, working at repair and construction work until May, 1912, when he became foreman of the mill carpenter crew, and has since been in charge of construction [a]nd repair at the mill." The company's needs took precedence in individual work assignments for Gallemore as for his peers.[10]

According to a September 1969 seniority list at Austinville, longevity remained the norm. The most senior man in the mine department, Buford Gravley, had started on October 19, 1925, and James J. Gravley followed on October 6, 1927. Thirty-six of the department's 178 employees had begun working there before 1940. In the plant department, the most senior person, John E. Dean, arrived in 1926, and 17 of the 72 men had joined the company before 1940.[11] When New Jersey Zinc shut down in Austinville, 85 of the 203 people terminated had worked long enough to qualify for at least a partial pension.[12] Similarly, in December 1965 the National Carbide plant in Ivanhoe had 33 workers who had toiled there for thirty years or more.[13]

In oral histories recorded in the late 1980s, Ivanhoe residents sometimes recalled fondly the welfare efforts the area companies had made. For instance, Bonnie Hodge Bowers remembered, "My father worked for 32 years at the National Carbide, and at Christmas time each child got what they called an Airco bag. They were some type of toy for each child in the bag. Different types of fruit were in the bag too." Geneva Pickett Simmons reminisced about the company baseball team: "They had a regular ball team," which often played teams representing industrial plants in other area towns such as Austinville and Pulaski. Other workers looked back on the housing, in particular, as a helpful aspect of the companies' presence.[14]

Unions in the New River Valley

Despite longtime service and company welfare outreach, workers naturally sought more compensation and rights whenever they could, as their counterparts had done via sporadic unrest since the American Revolution. In the 1930s the pro-labor policies of Franklin D. Roosevelt's administration allowed unions to form in some industries that had held them off. The American Federation of Labor (AFL) had long focused on organizing skilled craftsmen, but the new Congress of Industrial Organizations (CIO) sought to organize the unskilled or semiskilled masses of industrial workers. The AFL fought back against the CIO by also reaching out to workers in industries other than its established interests. The AFL created the so-called federal union, its label for an industrial union serving a single factory. Federal locals reported directly to the AFL national officers rather than to an industry- or craft-specific union. Federal unions opened the way for the renewed presence of organized labor in the New River valley for the first time since the brief presence of the Knights of Labor in late-nineteenth-century Pulaski.[15]

The onset of unionization along the New River coincided with a nationwide burst of growth among unions, which took place as defense spending began lifting the U.S. economy out of the renewed economic downturn of the late 1930s. On June 1, 1940, Federal Workers Union Local 22-257 executed for the first time a one-year labor agreement with the National Carbide Corporation. Workers with a year or more of service would thereafter receive a week of paid vacation each year, along with five holidays. The agreement also mandated a new seniority system for layoffs and rehiring, and the terms included a grievance committee.[16]

Workers wanted more when the agreement came up for renewal a year later. AFL organizer Tom Cairns described the negotiations leading to a new contract: "We had a pretty strong scrap with the company's representatives for several days, this last being the third meeting which we have had, and the employees of the company at one time during the sessions held a meeting and voted unanimously to stop work on July 2nd unless an agreement was reached. . . . The advance granted was five cents an hour, with other modifications in the agreement calling for the adjustment of disputes by arbitration." The Ivanhoe employees won higher pay and a right to arbitration, but they had hoped to strengthen the union itself by forcing the company to hire only union members. Cairns explained, "The men part of the time were a little restless, since this is the first time they have made a new agreement at the expiration of the first one year agreement. Therefore, they thought the company was not treating them as they should have done. But, as you know, we are not always able to get all the things we would like to have and I am convinced in my own mind that the next time we make an agreement we shall not only be able to secure better wages but get a closed shop with the check-off. This time we were not able to secure that part, which was the main bone of contention since the men are pretty well satisfied with the advance in wages, but we took the position that we could not afford to strike for a closed shop alone and I instructed the men to that effect."[17] War, of course, altered labor relations before new negotiations could test Cairns's optimism.

The carbide workers' subsequent eagerness to push for greater gains amid wartime labor shortages attracted the attention of CIO organizers, who for much of a decade scrapped with the AFL for the Ivanhoe carbide workers. The CIO's United Gas, Coke, and Chemical Workers of America won a National Labor Relations Board election at the plant on December 20, 1944, and negotiated a contract with National Carbide, signed on January 31, 1945. In 1949, however, the AFL's Federal 22-257 retook the workers' loyalty. The CIO's Operation Dixie, a drive to strengthen its presence in the southern states, failed to unseat the AFL in Ivanhoe in an election in January 1953, despite a determined effort. Worker ardor in Ivanhoe had moderated in the early Cold War era. The AFL by then included the International Chemical Workers Union, formed in 1944 from various federal unions and explicitly "opposed to radical tenets." Its Local 382 won the 1953 election among the 150 workers in Ivanhoe, and it continued to represent the employees who signed their final labor agreement on November 21, 1965.[18]

The rivalry between the unions played out in other area industries, too, but times looked good for industrial workers. Charles Ross Huddle wrote from Ivanhoe in 1943, "[I]t is possible for most any labor to go to the Radford Arsenal and get from 45.00 to 50.00 per week for doing very little work when compared with [what] a man farming is compelled to do if he raises any thing. Recently they have been taking men of 50 years and above."[19] In that environment, where military spending drove the regional economy, the CIO and AFL could do battle without endangering the overall progress of labor. For instance, the CIO's United Gas, Coke, and Chemical Workers represented employees at the Radford Arsenal, operated by the Hercules Powder Company, and the workers at the General Chemical Company acid plant in Pulaski relied on the International Chemical Workers Union as early as 1943. The CIO's United Steelworkers of America in 1947 tried to organize the sixty-five production and maintenance workers at General Chemical's foundry and machine shop, but the drive failed.[20]

The area's sharpest labor-management conflicts took place following World War II at the New Jersey Zinc Company. Union recognition occurred in two steps there. On August 9, 1940, the National Labor Relations Board certified the AFL's Federal Labor Union No. 22–363 as the agent of employees in the mining division, but despite AFL opposition the Bertha Mineral Employees' Association gained credentials on December 19, 1941, as the representative of the men working in the processing plant. Both resulting contracts gave workers vacations, a seniority system, and grievance procedures.[21] The initial agreements led to no lasting satisfaction, however, and despite pressure from government policies and the AFL, Federal 22-363 threatened a strike over wages in mid-1945, a time of rapid inflation. The head of the AFL wrote the local officers in a condescending tone, "The rules, laws and procedure of the American Federation of Labor require a federal labor union to notify the President of the American Federation of Labor when it plans to take a strike vote. . . . The National is engaged in a cruel war. Our relatives are fighting in the Armed Forces. They must be supplied with all the things they need in order to protect their lives and to make a war a success. The workers who provide these things for our Armed Forces certainly cannot engage in a strike now."[22]

Despite this rebuff, the Austinville workers stayed with the AFL after the war's close. The local again asked for and this time received strike authorization in 1946, part of a national wave of postwar labor unrest. Organizer Kenneth Scott explained the environment: "The record of this

Company . . . is very bad so far as true collective bargaining with its employees is concerned. The Company has been involved with the Union since its inception in numerous arbitration, con[c]iliation, strikes and dispute panel cases. Management fights over every word or point in either contract negotiation or settling of any grievance. Therefore, negotiations are always long drawn out beyond reason."[23] New Jersey Zinc deserved its antiunion reputation. Its subsidiary, Empire Zinc, gained wide attention for tough negotiating tactics at its Hanover mine in New Mexico. A strike there dragged on from October 1950 to January 1952, with a few instances of violence and abundant allegations of communism.[24]

Wage cuts at New Jersey Zinc in 1949 sparked disputes in Austinville that escalated in 1950 into a short labor stoppage and then resulted in a six-month-long strike in 1951. Union members sometimes could drive even the AFL national leadership to action despite its desperate desire to avoid being labeled leftist. Regional director Paul J. Smith reported that in 1949 the union decided against striking due to the low price of zinc and lead. With the nation on a wartime footing in 1951, prices rose, and the company had no excuse not to grant its first wage increase since 1948. Smith wrote, "[T]he Company is relying on the 'no strike' attitude of the American Federation of Labor to be able to force these employe[e]s to continue at work for the present miserably low wage rate."[25]

The workers went on strike on April 2, 1951, shutting down the Austinville plant. Some 359 men had joined the union at least a year earlier and thus qualified for financial support from the national union: $10 per week for ten weeks. Conflict dragged on "principally by reason of the arrogant and obstinate attitude of the plant manager who insisted on his own interpretations of any proposed contract, or any company rules that he desired to post on the bulletin board." The AFL extended some assistance even beyond the usual ten weeks because the company's attitude hardened immediately when the workers' weekly union benefits officially ended.[26] The strike ended around September 24, 1951, with wage increases of eighteen to twenty-two cents per hour and what the local leaders called a "victory over the Company in one of the longest strikes ever held in this part of the Country."[27]

The company had a different perspective. New Jersey Zinc could fight so hard in part because antilabor sentiments and laws spread after the war. In January 1947, at a special session of the General Assembly, Virginia's legislators hastily passed a so-called right-to-work law. New Jersey Zinc exploited the new political environment but also gave new benefits to workers to forestall unrest. The Employee Relations Department reported for 1950, "The labor contract was automatically renewed in the early part of the year, but the Union thereafter attempted to revive the inconclusive 1949 wage reopening discussions. The Company's pension and insurance program was installed in July. The difficulties over wages came to a head with a strike called on October 9 which lasted for 47 days until November 24, ending with no change in wages or employment conditions." The results pleased the company: "The detailed no-strike provisions of the contract did not work out entirely as contemplated. However through local counsel we availed ourselves of a Virginia statute which made possible the issuance of a court order which probably served to diminish the vitality of the strike. This was probably one of the first instances where the Company has been able to encourage a spontaneous back-to-work movement by the use of legal process."[28]

Belying union claims to have won a victory in the long 1951 strike, the company negotiators regarded those results as satisfactory, too. The 1950 strike had cut zinc production in the state of Virginia (almost exclusively from Austinville) by 6 percent compared with 1949, but the longer 1951 strike cut statewide output by 41 percent from the 1950 levels. Lead production fell 54 percent. Despite the lost revenues, the company regarded the price as acceptable: "Matters of wages were treated by the Union as secondary to other demands calculated to upset well established practices and to invade the Company's proper direction of the work force. For a long time there appeared to be no particular disposition on the part of the Union representatives to reach a settlement. At the termination of the strike a contract was written which was admittedly imperfect in some respects but on the whole satisfactory to the Company, and a substantial wage increase was granted which we had been willing to give for some time."[29]

The company had squelched more democratic workplace procedures, but it also had to continue giving more fringe benefits as well as higher wages to workers. Discussions of expanding the federal role in social welfare cropped up often in early postwar politics, and companies such as New Jersey Zinc acted to forestall government intrusion. The company's Employee Relations Department closed its summary of the strike with an intentionally nonchalant note: "Incidentally, we gave notice extending the insurance program to 1955."[30] New Jersey Zinc's annual report to shareholders in 1950 made the link more explicit: "Improvements and increased benefits in the Company's long-established pension system and new group insurance and sickness and accident benefits, authorized by stockholders at a special meeting, held on July 14, 1950, were provided during the year for those employees who qualified for such benefits. Other employees will be included when satisfactory agreements in this connection can be made with their union representatives." In 1956, the annual report even more clearly charted the trend: "The 1955 Pension Plan, approved by the stockholders on October 20, 1955, was a prominent factor in the success of our negotiations with the unions in 1955."[31]

The implicit compromise of worker quietude in return for corporate benefits and good wages, along with some new government benefits such as expanded Social Security, marked the apex of blue-collar opportunity during postwar industry's golden years from the 1950s to the early 1970s.[32] The workers used grievance procedures to keep pressure on their supervisors, while officials at New Jersey Zinc shared strategies about arbitration with their counterparts at the National Carbide plant nearby. But even after the workers at Austinville changed their loyalties to the CIO's United Steelworkers union in 1954, strikes and strong conflict happened rarely. The merger of the AFL and the CIO in 1955 reflected the rightward move of the CIO and the decline of variety within labor unions, notwithstanding a minor stoppage in 1957. Nonetheless, workers kept a sharp eye on their interests and took action when necessary. In 1960, New Jersey Zinc workers in Austinville, in concert with their peers at the company's plants in Pennsylvania, went on strike from August 6 to November 30. One newspaper summarized, "The chief issue in the strike was the union's rights in the company pension plan." The United Steelworkers stood as the workers' representative until the end of work in 1981.[33]

Geneva Waller of Ivanhoe, looking back in 1988, felt the union at New Jersey Zinc in Austinville had accomplished more than had its counterpart at the National Carbide plant, where her husband had worked: "Austinville paid better than Carbide. The men up at the Carbide didn't get too many raises. Down at Austinville they would strike every once in a while, and they kept giving them raises. By the time Austinville closed out, they were really paying the men good. Carbide had a union; they struck once or twice, but it wasn't all that good pay."[34] Nonetheless, the jobs in both Ivanhoe and Austinville delivered to the workers a significant measure of postwar America's prosperity and consumer buying power. What came next took some of that power away.

Textiles and Corporate Betrayal in Fries

Copper, iron, carbide, lead, and zinc had vanished from the New River's industrial landscape by the end of 1981, but textile weaving continued just upriver in Fries. Like Ivanhoe's carbide plant, the Fries textile mill came into being, grew, and died during the course of the twentieth century, though the lack of unions made the textile employees' experience a different one. In the U.S. South, textiles flourished for a time because nonunion labor there pushed aside pioneering firms with higher expenses in states such as Rhode Island and Massachusetts. Francis H. Fries and William C. Ruffin's Washington Mills had opened in 1903 in the company-built town alongside a dam, which drove the massive mill's water-powered machinery. Those devices later gave way to electrical machinery, with the dam feeding a hydroelectric generator that lighted the town as well. May 1903 saw the first bale of cloth shipped out on the Norfolk and Western.[35] The mill's ups and downs embodied twentieth-century workers' lives, limits, and ongoing hopes.

The town of Fries, incorporated in 1901 as the mill was going up, reached a population of 1,775 in 1910, making it the largest town in Grayson County. The town's growth reflected the mill's prosperity: it expanded in 1911–1912. After another mill expansion in 1919, Fries attained a population of around 2,000 in 1920 and some 2,100 by 1930. George Jennings, who had arrived in Fries in 1904, later recalled the town in its early years: "Plenty of times I would leave here on the train for Pulaski and there was barely standing room. Fries was kind of a boomtown then." In 1926, Washington Mills reported 1,700 looms in operation, with 700 employees and 75,744 ring spindles making fine sheetings, drills, and osnaburgs. The Great Depression cut workers' opportunities in the New River valley as it did elsewhere in the country, but by 1937 the mill had bounced back, reporting 70,356 ring spindles and employment of 1,000 that year. By 1940, Fries's population had fallen somewhat from its peak, but the onset of war brought the textile industry, like other industries, into full production. Three shifts kept the mill humming day and night, and the town and its boardinghouses filled with "people from everywhere," one resident remembered. Boom days continued after the war, with about 1,200 people working in the mill.[36]

Children made up much of the workforce that drove the mill's early prosperity. Although child laborers in smaller numbers had aided other in-

(*Right*) William Byrd III, scion of one of Virginia's most prominent families, joined fellow notables John Chiswell and John Robinson in forming the lead-mining company along the New River in 1760. From *Bulletin of the Virginia State Library* 13 (January–April 1920).

(*Below*) "A Map of the Indian Nations in the Southern Department, 1766" shows the lead mines surrounded largely by blank space, reflecting the company's drive to bring extractive industry to the western edge of British settlement. Courtesy Clements Library, University of Michigan.

As this account book from 1800 documents, much of the lead mined along the New River in the early nineteenth century was hauled to Baltimore for use in producing shot. From *Zinc* 15 (May 1930).

(*Left*) In the 1790s, Francis Preston, son of revolutionary-era official William Preston, operated a charcoal iron furnace and forge along Cripple Creek in Wythe County. He served as a congressman and later had a prominent role in the salt industry in the Holston River valley. From William C. Preston, *The Reminiscences of William C. Preston*, ed. Minnie Clare Yarborough (Chapel Hill: University of North Carolina Press, 1933). (*Right*) One of the New River valley's most successful entrepreneurs of the first half of the nineteenth century, David Graham operated iron furnaces as well as a foundry. From Anne Ingles, ed., *Journal of Bettie Ann Graham, October 18, 1860–June 21, 1862* (New York: n.p., 1978).

David Graham and other furnace owners often rented slaves from the Piedmont area of the state, but he and his peers sometimes faced a tight market because so many slaves were sold south. This coffle of slaves preparing to cross the New River was described by George William Featherstonhaugh in the early 1840s. From G. W. Featherstonhaugh, *Excursion Through the Slave States, from Washington on the Potomac to the Frontier of Mexico; with Sketches of Popular Manners and Geological Notices,* 2 vols. (London: John Murray, 1844).

"Dipping Out.—Ike." David Graham's workers molded many of the kettles used for boiling salt at the works in Saltville. As at the iron furnaces and forges, slaves did much of the labor in the antebellum salt industry. In this 1857 image, a slave in Saltville dips salt from a kettle and places it in a basket to drain and dry. From *Harper's New Monthly Magazine* (September 1857).

This 1859 sketch by Pennsylvania artist Lewis Miller depicts a Wythe County foundry, almost certainly the one owned by David Graham alongside Reed Creek. Courtesy Abby Aldrich Rockefeller Folk Art Museum, the Colonial Williamsburg Foundation, Williamsburg, Va.

Incorporated in 1835, the Grayson Sulphur Springs resort on the New River subsequently took advantage of the transportation improvements brought about by turnpikes and railroads. From Henry Howe, *Historical Collections of Virginia. . . .* (Charleston, S.C.: Babcock, 1845; reprint, Baltimore: Regional Publishing, 1969).

SCHEDULE OF TOLLS

For the Tazewell Court-house and Fancy Gap Turnpike for a Section of 15 Miles, as approved by the Board of Public Works on the 30th November, 1852.

For 20 Sheep or Hogs, - - - 12 1-2 Cents. *10*
" 20 Cattle, - - - - 25 " *20*
and so on in proportion for a less or greater number. *5*
" A Horse, Mare, Mule, or Gelding, 6 " *5*
" A two-wheeled Riding Carriage, 20 " *10*
" A four-wheeled do do 40 " *25*
" A Cart or Wagon, if the wheels are not more than four inches wide, 12 1-2 Cents for each animal drawing it. *10 25*

If the wheels are more than 4 and less than 7 inches wide, 6 cents for every such aminal, and if the wheels are 7 inches wide or more, 2 cents for every such animal. Intermediate distances will be charged at the same rate.

Adopted by the Board of Public Works and the Directors of the Tazewell Court-house and Fancy Gay Turnpike Company.
ROB'T GIBBONEY, President.

The Tazewell Courthouse and Fancy Gap Turnpike allowed New River industrialists easier access to markets in North Carolina and to the Virginia and Tennessee Railroad in Wythe County. Courtesy the Library of Virginia, Richmond.

Montroville Wilson Dickeson, a Philadelphia physician and polymath, analyzed copper-mining possibilities in Carroll County for potential investors. The endorsement of a scientific observer helped mining companies raise the capital they needed. From Montroville Wilson Dickeson, *The American Numismatic Manual,* 3rd ed. (Philadelphia: J. B. Lippincott, 1865).

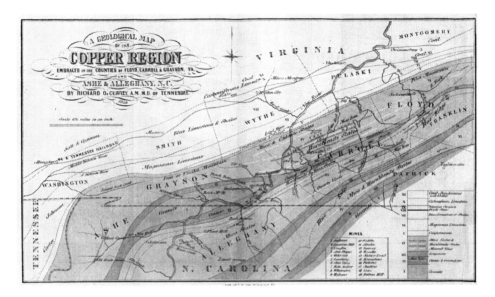

Richard Owen Currey, a geologist from Tennessee, charted Carroll County's copper mines in great detail in 1859. The map is from Currey's *A Geological Visit to the Virginia Copper Region* (Knoxville, Tenn.: Beckett, Haws, 1859).

Samuel McCamant, a mine owner, attorney, and public official, had a prominent role in squelching dissent on slavery in Carroll and Grayson counties. From Benjamin Floyd Nuckolls, *Pioneer Settlers of Grayson County, Virginia* (1914; reprint, Baltimore: Genealogical Publishing, 1975).

John W. Robinson, son-in-law of antebellum iron maker David Graham, contributed to the consolidation of the region's iron industry in the late 1800s. From Anne Ingles, ed., *Journal of Bettie Ann Graham, October 18, 1860–June 21, 1862* (New York: n.p., 1978).

This stock certificate from the 1880s captures northern financiers' growing interest in the minerals of the New River valley. The New River Mineral Company developed the furnace in Ivanhoe. From the author's collection.

Mining operations, beginning in the eighteenth century, had exhausted surrounding forests for charcoal and timbering. In the late nineteenth century, the arrival of railroads allowed remaining forests to be exploited for lumber to feed the needs of an urbanizing nation. In this early-twentieth-century image, oxen pull wagons of lumber into the town of Galax, perhaps for shipment or use in the local furniture factories. From *Golden Anniversary of Galax, Virginia, 1906–1956* (Galax, Va.: n.p., n.d.).

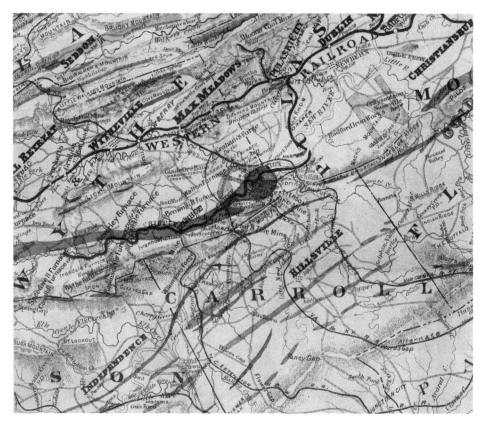

Geologist Charles Rufus Boyd charted the dense array of extractive industry in the region in this detail from his 1891 map "South West-Virginia and Contiguous Territory." From the author's collection.

The charcoal iron furnace at Foster Falls, shown in this pre-1912 photograph, operated from about 1881 to 1914. The photograph shows the typical placement of a furnace beside an embankment, allowing ore, limestone, and charcoal to be loaded from the top. The furnace has since been preserved as part of a state park. From George S. Jack and Edward Boyle Jacobs, *History of Roanoke County* (n.p.: n.p., 1912).

Beginning late in the nineteenth century, hydraulic mining accelerated the damage done to the Wythe County landscape by iron companies, just as the same method devastated large areas in the western states. From Thomas Leonard Watson et al., *Mineral Resources of Virginia* (Lynchburg, Va.: J. P. Bell, 1907).

"Near Cripple Creek, Virginia. View southwest in pit of Porter brown iron ore mine of Pulaski Iron Company from 85 feet above working level. Wythe County, Virginia. June 1, 1927." The open-pit mining of iron ore to feed the coke furnaces, first developed in the region in the 1880s, did substantial environmental damage, but many of these areas have been reforested and incorporated into parks and recreation areas. From the U.S. Geological Survey Photographic Library at http://libraryphoto.cr.usgs.gov.

This 1927 view of the coke-fired blast furnace of the Pulaski Iron Company highlights the tight relationship between industrial development and access to rail transportation in this rural setting. From the U.S. Geological Survey Photographic Library at http://libraryphoto .cr.usgs.gov.

(*Right*) Carroll County native George Lafayette Carter worked with northern financiers to consolidate most southwest Virginia iron furnaces into the Virginia Iron, Coal, and Coke Company. From Lyon G. Tyler, ed., *Men of Mark in Virginia: Ideals of American Life: A Collection of Biographies of the Leading Men in the State,* vol. 2 (Washington, D.C.: Men of Mark Publishing, 1906).

(*Below*) Zinc emerged as a major industry along the New River after the Civil War. The Bertha mine produced some of the very best spelter. From *Transactions of the American Institute of Mining Engineers* 22 (1894).

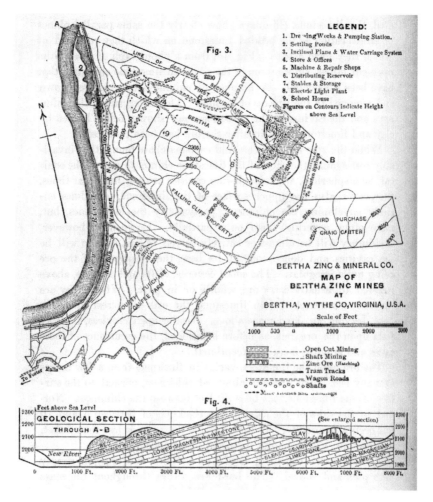

The General Chemical Company extracted ore from this Carroll County pit to produce sulfuric acid at a plant in Pulaski. From *The General Chemical Company after Twenty Years, 1899–1919 March 1st* (New York: General Chemical Company, 1919).

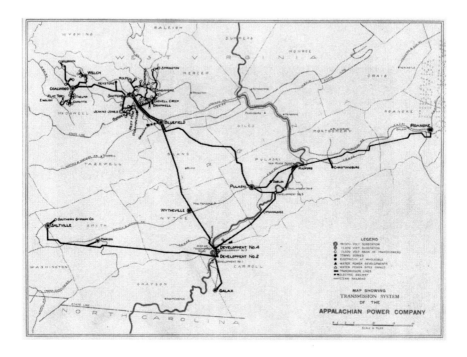

The Appalachian Power Company completed two hydroelectric dams on the New River in 1912 and began transmitting electricity to industrial customers in both Virginia and West Virginia. From *Hydroelectric Power in the South West Virginias* (Bluefield, W.Va.: Appalachian Power Co., 1913).

This Appalachian Power Company dam and the adjacent community were given the name "Byllesby" in honor of Chicagoan Henry Marison Byllesby, who headed the company. A number of communities ended up as namesakes of corporate leaders. From *Hydroelectric Power in the South West Virginias* (Bluefield, W.Va.: Appalachian Power Co., 1913).

The arrival of railroads aided agriculture as well as industry, as shown by this herd of sheep in early-twentieth-century Galax. Industry in the upper New River valley has always existed in the midst of a predominantly rural landscape. From *Golden Anniversary of Galax, Virginia, 1906–1956* (Galax, Va.: n.p., n.d.).

This lid from a tin of carbide captures the status of Ivanhoe's carbide plant as part of a subsidiary of New York–based Air Reduction Company. Less up-to-date than the plants in Keokuk, Iowa, and Louisville, Kentucky, the one in Ivanhoe was shut down in 1966. From the author's collection.

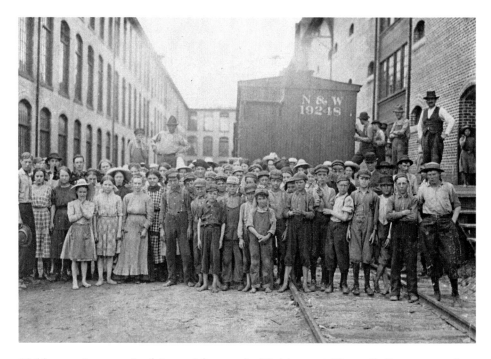

Children made up much of the workforce at the Washington Mills textile factory created on the New River by North Carolina industrialist Francis Henry Fries and others. This Lewis Hine photograph has the caption, "A part of the spinning force working in the Washington Cotton Mills, Fries, Va. Group posed by the overseer. All work. The overseer said, 'These boys are a bad lot.' All were alive to the need for being 14 years old when questioned." Library of Congress Prints and Photographs Division, LC-DIG-nclc-02073.

Washington Mills built the workers' housing for its mill in Fries, shown in this Lewis Hine photograph: "View of the Washington Cotton Mills, Fries, Va. Housing conditions are fairly good, but housekeeping not very good. Working conditions in the mill are very good. Good light, fresh air." Library of Congress Prints and Photographs Division, LC-DIG-nclc-01872.

Henry Whitter, a textile worker in Fries, recorded several hit songs as country music developed in the mid-1920s. His recording "New River Train" was released in 1924. From the author's collection.

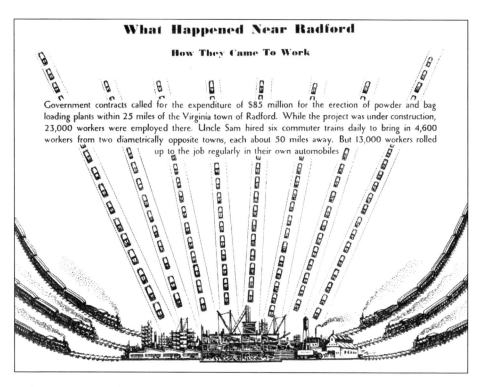

In the run-up to World War II, the construction of an army ammunition plant along the New River gave employment to local people and brought an influx of outsiders, who stretched the region's housing and transportation infrastructures to their limits. From *Automotive Industries*, October 1, 1941.

Following a period of high profits during World War II, the New Jersey Zinc Company upgraded its plant in Austinville. It operated there until 1981. From *Zinc* 26 (November 1948).

George T. Dickens cleans a chute in the concentrating mill of the New Jersey Zinc Company in Austinville. Workers in Austinville first unionized in 1940. From a company pamphlet titled *This Is Austinville* (Austinville, Va.: New Jersey Zinc, n.d.).

Similar to other surviving furnaces, the structure built by the Radford Iron Company in Pulaski County later became part of recreational acreage. In this case, the Boy Scouts' sixteen-thousand-acre Blue Ridge Scout Reservation borders it, and an image of the furnace serves as the reservation logo. Courtesy Dan Johnson, Blue Ridge Mountains Council.

Massachusetts native Thomas J. Wallner opened the Carroll Hosiery Mills in Hillsville in 1938, giving employment to the local men and women shown in this pre–World War II photograph. Apparel and textile plants took advantage of the region's nonunionized work-force during much of the twentieth century, but lower costs abroad have led most such plants to close. From the author's collection.

Tourism in the Blue Ridge Mountains benefited from construction of the federal highway system. Interstate 77, shown under construction over the New River in Wythe County in 1977, brings many visitors from states such as Ohio, North Carolina, and South Carolina. Courtesy Virginia Department of Transportation.

dustries, such as the lead and zinc mines, young people had much deeper and longer-lasting significance to textile mill owners such as Francis Fries. As part of a reform campaign, the National Child Labor Committee sent photographer Lewis Hine to photograph child workers; he visited Fries in 1911. His images capture many boys and girls clearly younger than the legal age of fourteen, though they all readily replied that they had reached that mark. The national group summarized, "In the Washington Cotton Mills, at Fries, Virginia, Mr. Hine counted six sweepers, sixteen doffers and twelve spinners, apparently from twelve to thirteen years of age." Local authorities could issue exemptions allowing people under fourteen to work if their parents had died or they had invalid parents, but the officials often collaborated with the mills in issuing permits for no reason. In 1909, for instance, fourteen of the thirty-nine exemptions granted by the mayor of Fries had no valid basis, according to the Virginia Department of Labor.[37]

Many years later Fries residents described child laborers as "so small when they first went to work in the mill that they pushed a box along to stand on so they could reach the frames they were working on." The very young did some of the less-skilled work: "Sweeping at the Mill was done by a group of eight and nine year old boys with a man who was the head sweeper. It was the head sweeper's job to take the boys through their sweeping duties twice each day. During the off-duty hours he would take them to an area above the mill to play until the next round of sweeping. Most of these little boys worked bare-footed in the summer months."[38] Shoeless boys playing by the river might evoke the carefree mischief of Tom Sawyer, but these youngsters had more in common with the hardscrabble life of an Oliver Twist.

By the 1920s, gradually tightening child labor laws had reduced the presence of children, but the textile mill owners in Fries, like their counterparts elsewhere in the South, nonetheless maintained tight control over their all-white nonunion workforce. Of the area industries, only the textile mill extensively employed women, whose lack of options made them more pliable and affordable than the workers at the extractive industries. With the decline of child labor, women became even more important in the mill's labor force.[39] Thelma Lou Delby in 1989 looked back on the conditions there: "The first job I ever had was at the cotton mill. I was about eighteen or nineteen. I think hourly wage was about $1.15 then [circa 1960]. Me and my sister Emma worked there; we got the job together. I went down to about 98 pounds. They didn't give you a dinner break, or any break, hardly.

. . . They had these batteries, they called it, that you filled; and we had to jump around. The battery was the machines that we had to load the thread in, just as fast as you could go. . . . That was a filthy place; they spit tobacco all over the walls and the floor. And the whole building shook. . . . They didn't even have a place for dinner. If you eat, you went in an old nasty bathroom. . . . The people looked dead and laid out, because there wasn't enough air in there. You had all this stuff blowing in the air. . . . And the heat—it was just unbearable."[40] The sisters toiled near the bottom of postwar America's nonagricultural wage ladder: in 1960, the minimum wage stood at $1.00; it rose to $1.15 in 1961.

In some ways, the 1970s brought even worse news for the workers. In that decade, Smith W. Bagley, a member of the most illustrious industrial family in Winston-Salem, North Carolina, helped trigger a long decline for the mill in Fries. From its beginning, Washington Mills had close ties to Winston-Salem via Francis Fries, and Bagley's grandfather, R. J. Reynolds, had founded the tobacco-manufacturing company that long held Winston-Salem in its grip. Beginning in 1969, Bagley and fellow North Carolinian James Ray Gilley, a Surry County native, put together a conglomerate that focused on food and textile manufacturing. Washington Mills fell into their grasp in January 1973, and the overall holding company soon took the name "Washington Group." It called the Fries unit "Washington Weaving."[41]

The Washington Group and its subsidiaries entered Chapter X bankruptcy protection on June 20, 1977, and in March 1979 a federal grand jury indicted Bagley, Gilley, and others on charges of stock manipulation. They had allegedly arranged, among other transgressions, for the sale at a loss of the diversified blue-chip stocks held in the company's profit-sharing, pension, and employee stock-purchase plans and pushed the subsequent investment of the money in Washington Group stock, artificially forcing up its value and allowing the conspirators to benefit financially. The company's bankruptcy damaged the employees' interests: many aging workers and former workers in Fries and elsewhere plunged into financial despair. The bankruptcy trustee called the abuse of the benefits plans "the single most callous act" he had discovered in his investigation. In August 1979, jurors acquitted Bagley—a prominent Democratic fund-raiser and Jimmy Carter's friend—of the criminal charges. Two federal prosecutors, U.S. Attorney Henry M. "Mickey" Michaux Jr. and Assistant U.S. Attorney Patricia W. Lemley, then took a rare step by accusing federal judge Robert R. Merhige Jr., who had political ties to the Reynolds family, of intentionally biasing the proceedings in favor of the defendants. In February 1980, Bagley settled, without either admitting or denying wrongdoing, a civil action brought on similar grounds in March 1979 by the Securities and Exchange Commission (SEC). Gilley, a 1950s basketball player at Wake Forest College, whose home overlooked the former R. J. Reynolds estate in Winston-Salem, likewise avoided criminal conviction and settled with the SEC.[42]

The company emerged from bankruptcy in 1982. By then, though, the residents of Fries looked back at the Washington Group only as a bad memory. The Washington Group and its recently appointed chief financial officer, K. Wayne Smith, had sold the still-profitable Fries plant to Riegel Textile Corporation on December 31, 1976, for $4.8 million, a price that, according to later bankruptcy investigators, undervalued the plant. They indicated that Washington Group leaders had made the sale to raise cash needed for a futile attempt to stave off the impending bankruptcy.[43]

The change of hands coincided with growing competition from international locations. Textiles declined quickly in Fries as liberal trade policies opened the U.S. textile market more fully to producers paying lower wages in developing nations. Soon after Riegel acquired the plant, it dropped the workforce to 800 people, 65 percent of them men, and the town itself declined to about 800 people. Riegel laid off large numbers of employees, cutting 700 jobs between 1983 and 1985, but it could not muster the investment needed to keep the equipment up to date. In 1985, Riegel became part of Mount Vernon Mills, a South Carolina textile company owned by the Oregon-based R. B. Pamplin Corporation. The Fries plant wove a type of flannel used in cotton work gloves, among other products. In 1967, the United States imported only about 700 pairs of the 27,700 dozen pairs of those gloves used in the country. In 1985, for the first time, more than half of this type of gloves was imported, and the overall number used had fallen. The Fries plant had no future owing to imports, its aging machinery, and its isolation. It stopped spinning yarn in September 1985 because its equipment did not meet new federal standards intended to prevent brown lung, a decision that led to additional layoffs. The surviving Fries workers continued to weave yarn spun elsewhere and trucked in.[44]

The plant tottered for a few more years. The U.S. military kept the end at bay for a while. William M. Barker, the plant manager in its final years, recalled, "We had a large government contract to produce nylon/cotton ripstop poplin. This fabric was printed at another location with a camouflage pattern. We all wondered why the camouflage was a desert (sand browns) pattern because all the hot spots then seemed to be in the jungle." "Little did we know," he continued, "we were weaving the fabric that would be used for the fatigue uniforms for the Desert Storm war."[45] In 1987, conservative Christian philanthropist Robert Boisseau Pamplin Sr., a native Virginian, sold the mill's dam and 5.3-megawatt power plant to Aquenergy Systems of Greenville, South Carolina, later a subsidiary of Enel, an Italian multinational energy giant. Finally, at the end of 1988, Pamplin closed the Fries weaving plant. Its never-unionized workforce had dwindled to around 164 workers in a hamlet of 750, a figure that slipped to 690 in 1990.[46]

A company attorney summarized the problem: "The investment it would have taken to have gotten Fries up to snuff couldn't be justified based on what the plant was making and the profits it was making." Protecting workers' lungs cost too much in an age of copious international trade. The 240,000-square-foot mill, with an additional 100,000 square feet in adjacent space, sat empty. In December 1988, Mount Vernon Mills deeded the buildings and more than fourteen acres of land to the town of Fries. As had happened in Austinville and Ivanhoe, the age of major industry ended in Fries.[47]

Laid-off workers and those forced into early retirement found the changes unsettling, to say the least. Jackie Roop Sharp remarked, "I saw those people every day for 20 years. I miss them."[48] The town as a whole faced the future with equal uncertainty and nostalgia for better times. When it received the massive Washington Mills structure from departing Mount Vernon, residents and officials pinned their hopes on acquiring new tenants for it. A survey preliminary to renting out the building uncovered dangerous substances (PCBs and asbestos), however, which hampered the effort and attracted the attention of the EPA. In 1992, town officials summarized the structure's importance and Fries's struggle: "After the property had been conveyed to the Town, regional agencies, civic groups, town officials, and private citizens began the process of marketing the vacant industrial facility to prospective tenants. . . . [T]he Town has made every effort to secure a tenant for the facility as the very future of the Town is contained within the walls of this building."[49] As early as 1986, though, local officials allowed themselves to see the future. "This area is so inaccessible," the assistant town manager said. "What industry wants to come here? Nobody's going to build a Texas Instruments [plant] here next week."[50] Fries's location, chosen as the best spot for a dam to power the textile mill, hampered its future.[51]

Despite trying hard, the town still failed to find a tenant, so, using a federal grant, officials eventually chose to demolish the hulking ghost looming over the riverbank. With industrial hopes dashed, the town turned toward an alternative that had been bandied about even as the plant closed. The local Civic League at the time pointed out, "Fries' music events could grow" and draw "dollar-carrying tourists for an annual singing and spending spree." "That's all I can think of," a member of the league sighed. "I'm not a city planner, but people who do have those credentials seem to think that is the way to go."[52]

The future apparently lay in tourism—the service industry—but the future arrives slowly. In February 2009, the town of Fries, in cooperation with a regional entity called the "Blue Ridge Crossroads Economic Development Authority," made a request for proposals to redevelop the Washington Mills site. Town planners announced their receptiveness to anyone willing to redevelop 13.3 riverside acres into a hotel and restaurant with retail and outdoor recreation facilities. The land and the plan had gained EPA clearance, and various state grants and tax credits stood ready to aid anyone who could spark the new postindustrial economy in Fries.[53]

Selling Mountain Culture

Residents of the upper New River counties had varied reactions to the changes of the twentieth century. Some responses took extreme forms. Floyd Allen (1856–1913), a Carroll County merchant and farmer, had a long-standing reputation for using force to get his way, whether in political tussles in behalf of Democrats or in business disputes with his brothers, one of whom he engaged in a gun battle in 1899. In the 1880s, he fought against a railroad proposed for the county. After the turn of the century, the local Republican Party began winning the county-level offices, and the state's 1902 constitutional revision modified the court system to cut down on local cronyism. Allen continued to trip on the line between order and disorder. He served as a constable at times, and in 1911 he was asked to help keep the peace at the New River site where workers were building the Appalachian Power Company's dams. But he also went on challenging the primacy of the law. On March 14, 1912, Allen was convicted in Carroll County's courtroom of interfering with police officers who had arrested his nephews. He refused to accept the verdict, however, and he and several members of his family drew pistols and killed the judge, the sheriff, the prosecuting attorney, a juror, and a witness. Allen and one of his sons died in the electric chair, several family members served long prison terms, and their exploits were recorded in folk songs still played today.[54]

Despite arriving by train at Galax or Betty Baker and passing factories and mines owned in part by East Coast financiers, northern journalists who covered these events nonetheless labeled the New River valley a savage cultural anachronism. The *Baltimore Sun* reacted to the killings with particular vehemence: "There are but two remedies for such a situation as this, and they are education and extermination. With many of the individuals, the latter is the only remedy. Men and races alike, when they defy civilization, must die. The mountaineers of Virginia and Kentucky and North Carolina, like the red Indians and the South African Boers, must learn this lesson."[55] Most people of the area neither responded to twentieth-century life with the violence of a Floyd Allen nor accepted the degrading stereotypes that still evoked the outrageous characters of Hardin Taliaferro's antebellum tall tales. In fact, some enterprising Blue Ridge natives exploited those same stereotypes, paving the way toward a new kind of industry, one based on rural culture. Fries's town planners hoped to rekindle that particular tradition after their textile mill died.

In the 1920s, a group of industrial workers from Grayson and Carroll counties, among them Henry Whitter (1892–1941), Kelly Harrell (1889–1942), and Ernest V. "Pop" Stoneman (1893–1968), took advantage of their citizenship in two worlds: knowing industrial life and commerce while living in what others saw as the backwoods remnants of the Elizabethan age. These men helped create commercial country music. In the spring of 1923, Henry Whitter took a break from his textile factory job in Fries and went to New York. He apparently arrived uninvited at the offices of Okeh Records and convinced the company to record his singing and guitar and harmonica playing. The company shelved the records until a few months later, when producer Ralph Peer's recordings of an Atlanta millhand and musician named Fiddlin' John Carson began selling vigorously. Okeh had a formal session with Whitter in December 1923 and quickly released his record with "Lonesome Road Blues" and "The Wreck on the Southern Old 97." Sales took off. In July 1924, Whitter returned to New York with two friends, including Fries storekeeper John Rector, to make additional recordings as the Virginia Breakdowners. That same summer, Ernest Stoneman, a native of Carroll County (near the Monorat mines) and a carpenter and millhand who had worked in both capacities at the Fries plant, heard Whitter's record. Stoneman decided he could play and sing just as skillfully. He rode the train to New York, auditioned in September, and with "The Sinking of the *Titanic*" had a hit for Okeh, the first of many strong-selling albums by Stoneman in the 1920s. In January 1925, Grayson County gave country music two more additions: another Fries textile worker, a singer named Kelly Harrell, recorded with Okeh; and John Rector and other local residents drove to New York to make recordings. At the end of the latter group's session with Okeh, the leader, Al Hopkins, did not have a ready answer when asked for the band's name. Much later, a band member recalled that Hopkins, with irony, replied, "We're nothing but a bunch of hillbillies from North Carolina and Virginia," and that Peer seized on the remark. As the Hill Billies, the group gave the new genre of commercial entertainment its label: hillbilly music.[56]

These musicians' supposed authenticity as isolated mountaineers appealed to urban record buyers who enjoyed the image of a simpler life in the Appalachians, but the men themselves knew better. Even the title of one of Henry Whitter's early records, "The New River Train," alludes to the rural industrial scene they knew back home.[57]

The popularity of these early stars waned in the late 1930s and the 1940s; Harrell returned to working in a textile mill during the Depression. Ernest Stoneman and his family, however, lived long enough to resurge as part of the folk music revival of the late 1950s and the 1960s. John Avery Lomax and Fletcher Collins Jr. collected songs in the area in the early 1940s and placed them with John and Alan Lomax's Archive of American Folk Song at the Library of Congress. In the late 1950s and the 1960s, young liberals who were looking for authentic traditional music flooded back into the area, as did Alan Lomax. Alan Jabbour, later one of Lomax's successors as head of the American Folklife Center, collected songs in Carroll County, and Eric Davidson and Paul Newman recorded numerous local players in Carroll and Grayson beginning in 1958. In the 1970s, British collector Michael Yates made extensive recordings, which the British Museum now houses. But all these folks carefully overlooked or downplayed the industrial enterprises that had graced this rural region since the 1760s. For instance, Davidson and Newman explain in their notes to the 1962 album *Traditional Music from Grayson and Carroll Counties,* "[L]ife in Grayson and Carroll Counties was almost exclusively agricultural in 1900." The "traditional anti-urban, anti-government, anti-wealth viewpoints exist today in the form of general anti-modern sentiment."[58]

These conceptions had the happy side effect of helping to attract tourists, an economic necessity once extractive and manufacturing industries began abandoning the upper New River area in the 1970s and 1980s. In Galax, one event had endured the waxing and waning of the popularity of hillbilly music and stood ready to anchor newly buoyant tourism. The annual fiddler's convention, sponsored by the Galax Moose Lodge No. 733, debuted in 1935. Its reputation blossomed: in 1938, folklorist John Lomax attended and made recordings for the Library of Congress. Held each August in the downtown Felts Park, the convention now features a weeklong series of musical performances and competitions, broadcast live on a radio station that reaches much of western Virginia and Piedmont North Carolina. Contestants and audience members flock to Galax from many states and other nations.[59]

Globalization at Work

Though somewhat less drained than Fries, Galax needs the boost that its musical festival provides. In addition to furniture-related industries that began shortly after 1900 to take advantage of abundant timber and the railroad's arrival, Galax drew further on the rural surroundings—dairy farms, in this instance—via a condensation plant opened by Carnation Milk in 1937. In 1950, the plant employed 150 people. Its arrival spurred among area agriculturalists a greater focus on dairy farming, a disciplined form of agriculture closely akin to industrial work. In that spirit, Carnation encouraged farmers to use artificial insemination to improve their herds. Galax also boasted its own textile plants by then. The Galax Knitting Company started its machinery in 1924; and as the Great Depression appeared to ease, the Galax Weaving Company, a subsidiary of the giant Burlington Industries, opened in 1937 and gave work to more than 300 people. The latter produced textiles used by furniture manufacturers. The Hanes apparel company of Winston-Salem, North Carolina, opened a branch plant in Galax in 1955 and six years later expanded into a much larger new plant after the Carroll-Grayson Development Corporation raised $1.3 million of the $2.15 million price tag.[60] Chasing factories worked for a time.

In 1972, John H. Zammito, a young economist surveying the South's ongoing industrial growth, explained why the region boasted more rural manufacturing than the rest of the nation: "Rural industrialization results from the simple fact that the pools of labor available in the 'backwoods,' though unskilled, are relatively cheap and have few significant alternative sources of income or employment." National and large regional companies, Zammito wrote, took note of other factors as well: "The profitability of a Southern location for national firms is linked to the supply of cheap labor, combined with the advantages of lower taxes, cheaper power rates, less labor organization, and the declining importance of transport costs in final product costs due to improvements in national transportation." These economic disparities within the United States fueled growth in places such as Galax. By the early twenty-first century, though, dairy, textiles, apparel, and furniture alike had dwindled on the Blue Ridge plateau; the differential in labor costs between the United States and other nations enticed companies elsewhere, a shift aided by international transportation improvements. In Galax now, heritage tourism draws on the tradition of commercial exploitation established by singers such as Henry Whitter and Ernest Stoneman; it holds promise in the absence of more stable lucrative alternatives.[61]

Nearby Hillsville followed a similar pattern. Local leaders there, like their counterparts in Galax and much of the South, raised capital to lure a manufacturer, and in 1938 the town gained a plant, the Carroll Hosiery Mills, with Massachusetts native Thomas J. Wallner as president and his brother Waldemar Wallner as treasurer. Like the textile mills in Fries and elsewhere after the demise of child labor, the hosiery plant relied heavily on women: in one early composite photograph, 93 women appear among the 180 nonsupervisory workers visible. The plant employed about 200 people in 1945. In 1958, an official of the American Federation of Hosiery Workers testified before a Senate subcommittee investigating problems facing the textile industry. The union representative directed the senators' attention to a pamphlet that singled out Carroll Hosiery as an exemplar of southern antiunionism. The Phoenix Hosiery Company of Milwaukee had bought both the Carroll Hosiery facility and the Philcord Corporation in Monroe, North Carolina. When the Monroe workers tried to unionize, according to this pamphlet, "The company responded by closing down its Philcord plant and moving the operation into its unorganized Carroll Mills at Hillsville, Va." In the meantime, Phoenix Hosiery had "all but shut down" its unionized northern locations. Carroll Hosiery, too, later shut down, as did much other manufacturing in the county, including the Hanes plant.[62]

One Carroll County woman's work history tells the rise and fall of the local apparel industry, which included several plants at its peak. Starting at the federal minimum wage of a dollar per hour, she worked at the Hanes plant in Galax from 1959 to 1962, hemming baby gowns for use by the post–World War II baby boom generation. She left manufacturing in 1962 to have children and help operate a family farm, but she returned to factory work when small-scale agriculture came apart at the end of the 1980s. She recounted, "I went to Mayville in 1989," putting pockets on uniforms "till 1995, when it went out of business. And I went down to Bassett-Walker and worked till 1998, and it went out of business. Went to Hillsville Apparel and worked till I guess it was 2000. I got laid off, but it finally went out of business too about six months later. Then I started at Kentucky Derby [Hosiery] . . . and went till 2003, and then I retired." At the close of her career, she passed the days turning inside out socks for a little more than $6.00 per hour.[63]

Unlike Galax and Fries, Hillsville lacks a historical rationale for using a music festival to attract tourists in recompense for the decline of manufacturing. It instead pulls in tens of thousands of visitors for its annual four-day Labor Day Gun Show and Flea Market, initiated in 1967 by the local Veterans of Foreign Wars post. Lemonade stands and yard sales substitute for low-tech industrial jobs.

With the winding down of major industries in Ivanhoe, Austinville, and Fries, those towns lost population, and the residents who hung on had fewer and fewer options for employment. Charles Huddle described Ivanhoe in June 1967, "Ivanhoe is about 99.9% static since the Carbide Plant closed. . . . There is not very much going on in Ivanhoe, several of the older people and some not so old have departed this life, and quite a number are just living to save the funeral expense."[64]

Notwithstanding Huddle's dry assessment, hopes for new industry lingered for quite some time among some residents, including his son, Richard, who worked to promote development. Before the railroad pulled up its tracks in 1985, Wythe and Carroll counties cooperated to advertise the 175-acre Ivanhoe Industrial Park as having "abundant" transportation options, with "direct service to the park" by Norfolk and Western.[65] Even by 1979, though, the place had wasted away to "a shadow of its former self," in the words of a newspaper columnist. The initial yearning for new heavy industries drained away.[66] Richard Huddle's son David, a writer and college professor, recalled, "The Ivanhoe of my childhood was one of the most marginalized pieces of landscape I've ever known. . . . At a certain point, poverty gets mean and ugly. There's a look and a smell to a house where people have lived without money for many years."[67]

In Ivanhoe, a remarkable oral-history project, begun in 1987, captured the pain of deindustrialization as well as the resilience of these small towns as life's rhythm along the New River returned to a slower beat.[68] Along with others in the community, Ivanhoe resident Maxine Waller, who had many family ties to the industries along the New River, formed the Ivanhoe Civic League in 1986. The organizers were spurred by the announcement in September that county authorities planned to sell the acreage that they had been marketing as an industrial park. Local government was giving up on developing Ivanhoe's economy. With Waller as the vocal leader, members of the Civic League earned admiration from community activists around the country. It lobbied both county and state leaders, temporarily blocked the sale of the land, launched cleanup efforts in the town, brought in college students as volunteers to repair houses, held a community reunion, began adult-education programs, and sponsored festivals and a play on local history. The Civic League members could not, however, reverse neoliberal economic globalization: they did not attract lasting industrial investment to their town.[69]

Waller and the Civic League gradually shifted from pursuing industry to pushing for the betterment of Ivanhoe through cultural revival. The Ivanhoe History Project grew out of this new approach. A group of ten to fifteen members of the Civic League collected and transcribed fifty-three oral histories. With involvement from outside activists such as sociologist Helen M. Lewis, the group published two books in 1990, one a history of the community and the other made up of oral-history transcripts. In the latter, the men and women of Ivanhoe unfold their memories of community life, talking about families, schools, churches, gardens, Western movies at the Ivanhoe theater, vicious fights, heavy bouts of drinking, local prostitution, their sense of being looked down on by the residents of Wytheville, and, again and again, laboring in the factories and mines.[70]

Workers, of necessity, responded pragmatically to the loss of industry; they had to find work if they could not retire. Buck Ingo recalled, "When the Carbide closed, people didn't know what to do. It had been going so long, since 1918. There weren't many people that moved away; a lot of them went to Radford [Arsenal]." Geneva Waller, too, delivered a matter-of-fact assessment of the closings: "Ivanhoe just happened to have old industry, and it played out, just like Austinville." She explained that when the carbide plant closed, many residents did in fact move, but "some of the men didn't leave; they went to other places and got work. Just as quick as they could, they took their retirement." New Jersey Zinc "hired a lot of them; they took all of them they could take. When the Austinville company closed out, all those men had to go somewhere and hunt work." Even after finding new work, though, some workers found the adjustment difficult. When Joanne Dotson's father lost his job at the carbide plant, he "went downhill from that time."[71]

Ivanhoe residents looked back on industrial work that crossed generations and companies. Geneva Waller recalled, "Before they built the Carbide, my father helped build the dams up at Byllesby, and then they built the Carbide and he worked at the Carbide. When he was a young man they had some mines over back from the schoolhouse. All back in there they mined, and they mined by hand. They dug out iron ore. He worked in that before the Carbide was built. That was all the work there was here then. . . . Granddaddy Wright when he was young worked at the mines, too, down at the furnace." Eula Jefferson's father and sister worked at the Fries textile mill, and her husband also labored there after National Carbide closed down. Elizabeth Koger, wife of a sharecropper, lived in Ivanhoe, and one of her brothers worked at the carbide plant. Her own industrial work took a different form, however: "Back in 1945 when the Second World War was on I went to Dublin and worked at Hercules. I sewed bags to put in the guns for the war. . . . They would fill the bags with gunpowder." Donald Blair worked throughout the area. He started with Radford Arsenal but got fired for accidently carrying matches into the plant. Then, in his wife's words, "He went to work at the cotton mill. He worked at the cotton mill four years. He got on with New Jersey Zinc and worked sixteen years, until they closed. Then he got back on at the cotton mill and worked up there two and a half years, and now he's at a furniture plant in Galax. He went from nine dollars and something an hour [at New Jersey Zinc] to $3.70 an hour." John Walke summarized, "You got tired working at one company, you moved out to another one."[72]

Herman Coolidge Winesett—a retired industrial worker and janitor, a renowned fiddle player, and a veteran of World War II—took part in some of the much-talked-about Ivanhoe Civic League activities. Later, his misfortune wrote the headline for what the twentieth century left behind in Ivanhoe. On August 12, 2000, his outhouse floor collapsed, depositing the partially paralyzed old man amid the nail-studded broken boards, white rats, and muck in the toilet hole. He waited and yelled. Some seventy-eight hours passed before mail carrier Jimmy Jackson, who noticed the envelopes piling up in the box, searched Winesett out. Maxine Waller by then worked for the Roanoke-based Southeast Rural Community Assistance Project. She acted as Winesett's advocate: the group tore down his old home and built a new one in its place, complete with an indoor toilet.[73]

New Paths

In the new century, the upper New River valley contends with new landscapes, both economic and environmental. The industrial activity that has survived globalization thus far tends to include relatively small plants taking advantage not of the region's natural resources, but of its cheap labor. Fewer and fewer executives can resist the lure of even lower costs in Central and South America, Africa, and Asia. Leaders of one of the final two significant facilities manufacturing furniture in Galax announced in March 2008 that it would stop production. The company turned away from abundant local timber in favor of importing and distributing home furnishings made in China.[74] Apparel companies likewise have shuttered their once plentiful sewing operations. For instance, in early 2009 Kentucky Derby Hosiery—owned by the Canadian company Gildan and making socks for retailers such as Wal-Mart—closed its plant in Hillsville in favor of Honduras.[75]

As costs have risen in countries such as China, some companies have boosted manufacturing in the low-wage southern region of the United States, but for now the trend has had little effect in the New River valley. Residents can still stretch their dollars, though, by shopping at the Wal-Mart store in Galax; consumers abandoned Hillsville's locally owned Ben Franklin five-and-dime when Sam Walton's behemoth branch opened for business on March 31, 1987.[76] There they buy goods made by the cheaper labor in faraway places. Lifelong Virginians now share the discount store's crowded aisles with recent immigrants from Mexico and, to a lesser degree, Central America.[77]

The region's present extractive industry, though small, makes a vivid mark. In 1857, Montroville Dickeson had described an old use of the ore at the Betty Baker Mine: "The action of the air upon this outcrop, causes it to decompose into a pulverulent mass, forming a beautiful red pigment, which is sought after by the housewives to color their woolen fabrics. . . . I believe that it would as a pigment, form an article of commerce that would be very profitable to the company." These properties of the ore did not go unnoticed by later entrepreneurs. Headquartered in Hiwassee in Pulaski County, the Hoover Color Corporation conducts the area's only substantial mining operation other than the Austinville limestone works. Hoover, whose pre-decessor company arrived there in the mid-1930s, produces coloring agents from iron oxide and limonite mined in open pits in Hiwassee and near Cripple Creek in Wythe County. The company provides many pigments for the Crayola crayons enjoyed by children in many countries.[78]

The region contributes more to the world than the childhood palette, however. The Radford Army Ammunition Plant soldiers on without sating America's military appetite. The U.S. government owns the facility but contracts operations to London-based BAE Systems, which in 2011 took over the lucrative deal from ATK Energetic Systems, a Honeywell Corporation spinoff that had acquired the old Hercules Powder Company. A 2009 report from the National Defense University points out Radford's strategic importance: "In the final accounting, it is not the tank, mortar, rifle, or pistol that is lethal, but the projectile delivered from the weapon. And as different as projectiles are, they are all linked by a single strategic commodity—propellant. All military propellants are a nitrocellulose-based chemical compound and today RAAP is the sole producer of nitrocellulose propellant."[79] Building the nation did not happen by global consensus. In the twenty-first century, as in the eighteenth, nineteenth, and twentieth, the products of New River industrial workers resound across the battlefields of a violent world.

The presence of industry—arriving at the heels of the first white settlers—had always reminded Blue Ridge residents that they fit within a larger context. Furnaces, smelters, turnpikes, and trains kept even the poorest farmers aware of broader trends, and industries succeeded in spite of daunting transportation challenges. But now, in a notable twist, the easy connections between this mountainous region and the major population centers of the East Coast dictate development on the Blue Ridge plateau.

Those connections have enabled immigration to pick up momentum in the Blue Ridge as in other southern settings. In 2009, Hispanics made up an estimated 15.4 percent of Galax's residents, though illegal immigration makes exact figures hard to come by. Many of the new arrivals work in the manufacturing plants that survive or in service jobs. Some labor on nearby Christmas tree farms, cultivating and shaping a crop of a peculiarly regimented nature, one that sends sediment, pesticides, and herbicides into New River but adds cheer to the holiday up and down the East Coast. The high elevations enable sought-after Fraser firs to flourish.[80]

Other Mexican immigrants have chosen a darker path, pulling the area into a form of international commerce most residents do not welcome. In

2008, the U.S. Department of Justice listed Galax as one of two Virginia cities known to host a Mexican drug-trafficking cartel, the Federation in its case. Because the United States has regulated the ingredients for methamphetamine, Mexican smugglers have begun to meet the demand by bringing meth from Mexico. "I think we're in a methamphetamine epidemic here," a Galax law enforcement officer explained in 2009. "This is a distribution point."[81]

Federal thoroughfares rather than state turnpikes and private railroads set the latest economic pattern. Interstate Highway 77, opened in the 1970s, runs just east of the old Flower Gap road and just west of where the Tazewell Courthouse and Fancy Gap Turnpike (the basis for present U.S. Highway 52) mounted the Blue Ridge escarpment.[82] Interstate 81 charges down the valley of Virginia, past Fort Chiswell and through Wytheville, shuttling heavy trucks near the Wilderness Road route that once led hopeful migrants past the lead mines and toward new lives beyond the Cumberland Gap. Like the Mexican drug couriers, a few major companies—such as beverage maker Gatorade (in Wythe County) and Volvo Trucks (in Pulaski County)—maintain plants in the New River valley at least in part for shipping convenience.[83]

Though places such as Fries and Ivanhoe still struggle, the tourist industry has burgeoned in parts of the area. Sightseers lazily flow along once-burdensome terrain. The National Park Service's Blue Ridge Parkway capped the mountain range beginning in the 1930s; it displaced the privately administered Georgia-to-Maine Appalachian Trail from its original route, which ran along the crest of the mountains through Fancy Gap and then to Galax and along the railroad tracks by Byllesby Dam on the New River.[84] The Primland luxury resort has co-opted several surviving miles of the original route near Meadows of Dan.

Throughout the first half of the twentieth century, mining and timber companies jettisoned cut-over or tapped-out lands to federal and state governments, which had conveniently begun to take an interest in conservation. The government bought back what the Crown and the Commonwealth had bartered or taken from the Indian nations and put in private hands. Sometimes following the old Indian paths from Shawnee country, the interstates funnel urban vacationers from places such as Ohio and Pennsylvania to scenic spots in the Jefferson National Forest and the Mount Rogers National Recreation Area, which encompass large areas of the old mining and timber company lands in Carroll, Wythe, and Grayson counties.[85]

Beginning in the 1760s, industrialists damaged the trees, the land, and the water of the New River valley: forests came down, open-pit mining left jagged scars, chemicals and waste spewed into the streams and the river. But in the late 1960s, with industrial activity slowing and tourism growing weightier on the economic scale, a portion of the local people joined outside environmentalists—including R. Philip Hanes, an heir to Winston-Salem's Hanes textile and apparel wealth—to stop another large-scale design for progress. The Appalachian Power Company planned to drown thousands of acres in Grayson County and neighboring Ashe and Alleghany counties in North Carolina with two more large dams on the New River upstream from Fries. After years of intricate legal and political wrangling, the U.S. Congress blocked the project in 1976. Lawmakers designated approximately 26.5 miles of the waterway a national scenic river, thus protecting it from development for the foreseeable future.[86] Rising environmental awareness around the nation in the early 1970s helped preserve the New River landscape.

Nature has made something of a comeback. With the river fairly safe behind federal legislative barriers, the EPA then spurred cleanup of some of the harshest chemical residues on the former industrial sites. Plants and animals have reclaimed the scarred mountainsides. Along a revised route, the Appalachian Trail, now federally supported, brings hikers into Wythe County after they make their way through the verdant Grayson County landscape near Mount Rogers, Virginia's highest point and the namesake of nineteenth-century geologist William Barton Rogers. Hikers and hunters do not find deer as readily as John Bartram and his companions did in 1762, but they see them often. These deer descend from ones that Virginia wildlife officials brought from other states in the 1930s and 1940s to re-populate the recovering forests.[87] In a profitable state-managed encounter, hunting and fishing bring local people and visiting urbanites alike into contact with nature.

Amid the natural beauty, cultural organizations and individual promoters work to shape popular understandings of both the region's environment and its history. The National Park Service and the National Council for the Traditional Arts together operate the Blue Ridge Music Center on the Blue Ridge Parkway, near Piper's Gap. The present owner of the mansion built by iron maker David Graham hosts GrahamFest, an open-air music festival on Labor Day weekend.[88] Old blast furnaces loom with little fanfare on Cripple Creek in the Mount Rogers National Recreation Area but with more context at a state park at Foster Falls. The furnace once owned by the Car Wheel Iron Company of Philadelphia rests now at the entrance to sixteen thousand acres of former industrial land owned by the Blue Ridge Mountains Council of the Boy Scouts of America. In 2004, Grayson County bought for public recreational use Peach Bottom Falls, the site of Blair and Dickey's eighteenth-century Point Hope Furnace.[89]

Only memories of industry disturb the route of the railroad that once coursed alongside the New River and its tributaries. The old roadbed evolved into a hiking corridor, the New River Trail State Park. Its deliberately gentle ups and downs graph the rise and decline of industry in the Blue Ridge. Birds cry out to break the mellow silence, but no locomotives rumble by. Once in a while a jogger pounds his way down the trail. Otherwise, for the moment, nothing's running but the river.[90] Red-tinted mine waste no longer clouds its water for the canoeists gliding by.

Assuming that I have correctly mapped the past, the unmarked remnants of John Bartram's Flower Gap road wend through the Hawks State Forest and the Stewarts Creek Wildlife Management Area. Through thick woods, soothed by the sound of Turkey Creek, one can hike the old road up a sharp backbone to the crest of the Blue Ridge, arriving at the backyard of an old wooden church where the view still astounds. Farms, country roads, and a blanket of green pave the way to Pilot Mountain in the distance.

Our vista differs, though, from that of Bartram and his early-nineteenth-century successors on the road. The farms sprawled below take part in an efficient, highly mechanized economic sector. We also see different vegetation. The massive chestnut trees that once dominated the canopy on the slopes and the plateau disappeared in the early twentieth century under the assault of a fungus brought from Asia. The remaining forest has filled in following timber operations that stripped the old growth. Throughout the area, acid rain caused by automobiles and coal-fired midwestern power plants threatens the soil and water. We hear airplanes overhead plying the crowded East Coast corridors and trucks in the distance hauling goods across the mountains on the interstate highway. The air, too, smells different. At times, pollution hangs heavily at the higher elevations.[91] Even when one stands on a historical mountaintop, haze clouds the horizon.

Acknowledgments

I thank Ken Badgett, Walter Beeker, Carlos Blanton, John Boles, David Brown, Andrew Canady, Greg Eow, Michele Gillespie, Becky Hall, Luke Harlow, Ned Irwin, Caleb McDaniel, Greg McGrady, Bill Owens, Mark Smith, Brent Tarter, Tom Williams, and Nancy Zey. I also appreciate the work of archivists and other librarians at Fondren Library, Rice University (especially Francine Arizmendez, Sarah Bentley, Angela Brown, Esther Crawford, Jean Niswonger, Kim Ricker, Anna Shparberg, DeAndrea Smither, and Randy Tibbits); Newman Library, Virginia Tech (especially John Jackson); Wytheville Community College Library (Cathy Reynolds); the Library of Virginia; the West Virginia State Archives (Debra Basham); the Virginia Historical Society; Alexander Library, Rutgers University (especially Ronald Becker); DeLaMare Library, University of Nevada at Reno; Crerar Library and Regenstein Library, University of Chicago; Swem Library, College of William and Mary; and the Small Special Collections Library, University of Virginia. The excellent morning crew at the Starbucks at the intersection of Shepherd and West Gray, the one on the southeast corner, not the northeast corner, provided much of the fuel needed for preparing this work. And for her encouragement in all that I do, I owe the most thanks to my wife, Naomi Hall.

Appendixes on Technology

These appendixes provide anyone interested in technological development with the opportunity to observe, in some detail, change over time in a unified setting. The ever-growing complexity of these industrial operations highlights that this river valley generally moved in tandem with national trends, though regional economic and environmental needs dictated certain differences. Information, technology, management strategies, and personnel moved across all sorts of artificial boundaries, driven by the desire to exploit natural resources for profit.

Appendix A

In the 1790s, Francis Preston described his ironworks lying along Cripple Creek in Wythe County:[1]

> It lies in the County of Wythe about 12 or 18 miles from the Great Kanhawa and about 60 miles from Holston from which there is a tolerably safe navigation to Natchez.
>
> Cripple Creek affords a full supply of water for the forge and furnace, (from the same dam) being fed from remarkably large Springs which never fail. The neighbourhood around the works is wealthy and provision supplies in great abundance, the lands on the Creek being very fertile and the highland strong and well calculated for small grain and heavily covered with timber suitable for Coal.
>
> There is attached to the Ironworks 8 or 900 acres of Land well timbered[,] none of which is beyond three miles, and any quantity of timber may [be] had for cutting within, from two to six miles, so also may lands be purchased within those bounds from one Dollar per acre to eight dollars which is the highest price.

There is between 3 and 400 acres of land attached to the works capable of Cultivation.

The ore bank which appears inexhaustible is within one mile of the Furnace having a road over which a team of five horses may haul from 3 to 4000 lbs. of ore, as also may the ore be taken by water which is now practised, and with the expense of forty dollars may be delivered within ten steps of the furnace.

The furnace has been built within three years and all the other buildings consisting of dwelling houses, kitchens store house and large convenient stables were commenced within the same time and are now finishing and in good order. The furnace runs from 12 to 15 tons per week, the Castings smooth and of a Superior quality.

The forge which is about 150 yds from the furnace will in a few days be completed. It is said to be the best built forge in Virginia, it being out of Choice timber cut in proper Season and executed under the direction of a first rate forge Carpenter from Pen[n]sylvania it has now three fires and calculated for another, two hammers, it is 45 feet wide and fifty five long, well covered with joint shingles &c.

The quality of the iron is acknowledged to be superior to any in this Country and there is no doubt equal to any on the Continent, it is sought for at a great distance, and particularly by leglocks makers, Saddletree platers[,] cutlers &c.

The demand for iron in this Country is at present far beyond what is made and Iron is transported from Adams & [James] Callaways, to Abingdon etc. passing my works and carried into the neighbourhood of Colo[nel] [James] Kings. The demand is also increasing to an astonishing degree, it is selling from one hundred & forty to an hundred and seventy dollars per Ton and but a small supply offered at present. Contracts for almost any quantity of Iron can be procured at a 140 $ a Ton delivered at the works. Proposals are daily making to me from Tennessee and Cumberland[,] the latter in particular for Contracts of 5, 10 & 20 Tons. Mr. King has also mentioned Contracts for 5 or 7 years continuance, for from 50 to an 100 Tons of Iron and from 20 to 30 Tons of Castings annually on a Credit of 12 & 18 months.

There is also an excellent tub mill on the place just completed which not only answers the works but the neighbourhood.

The Subscriber is assured from the numberless proposals and the great and increasing demand for iron, and its superior quality, the sales will be immediate.

Appendix B

In the April 1884 issue, the *Journal of the United States Association of Charcoal Iron Workers* analyzed the furnaces of the New River–Cripple Creek iron region and the supply of ore and charcoal needed to operate them:[2]

Nearly all of the ore workings are "open cuts," but drifts and shafts have in a number of cases been driven to determine the bounds of the deposits. The physical characteristics of the ores vary considerably, and the greater proportion of them require washing, being quite fine. The face of excavations show [*sic*] shades of color, generally a deep brick red, varied by yellow, brown or earthy tints, with lumps scattered through in greater or smaller proportions. These Virginia ores average higher in metallic iron, and lower in phosphorus and manganese than the Pennsylvania limonites, and the proportion of lump ore is less in the former than in the latter State.

The topography of the "Cripple Creek Region" is broken and rugged, and the ore deposits generally lying at a considerable elevation, are dry and require no pumping machinery.

In mining large quantities of these ores, steam excavators could in some of the banks be used advantageously, but to supply the limited amount required by the small furnaces hand labor is solely resorted to. The washers, or "buddles," are seldom located at the ore-banks on account of the absence of water, and the usual practice is to convey the fine "mine" as taken from the banks by wagon or by car on tram-road to a washer located on some water-course. In exceptional cases water is pumped up to the workings. At the Clark ore-bank, in Pulaski county, the washer is supplied from a steam-pump located on the New river, which raises water three quarters of a mile and elevates it 300 or 400 feet to the bank.

Wherever possible the washer is driven by a water-wheel, but in the absence of this power steam-engines are employed.

From two to four cars of "mine" produce one car of washed ore, the average being about three cars of fine ore to one car of washed ore. Where the ore is conveyed to the washer much of the leaner material goes on to the spoil-bank, which would pay to handle to a washer close by.

The form of washer in use is a single wooden shaft, hewn to an octagon section, with iron paddles held in place by shanks fitting in mortices. . . .

Although the charcoal iron industry has long existed in this locality there is a liberal supply of timber available, but the furnaces on the south side of the New river have material advantages over those between the river and the Norfolk and Western Railroad. In the former case stumpage can be had for 12 to 15 cents per cord, in the latter 40 cents to 50 cents, or even more, is demanded. Few of the iron-works own or control large tracts of timber, the supply of charcoal being dependent upon direct purchase of the coal and the purchase of wood-leave.

The wood is chestnut, oak, hickory, pine, etc., and is of good size for coaling. When cut off but little attention is given to reforestation [sic], and many steep knolls which would produce good supplies of timber are either waste or eroded pasture lands.

Forty cents per cord is the present local price for chopping wood. . . .

All the charcoal is made in meilers and is hauled in wagons of 100 or 200 bushels capacity, with two or four horses, to the furnaces. In some instances quite long hauls have been made.

Some charcoal was purchased for the present season, delivered at 6 cents per bushel of 20 pounds, but most of it is made by employés [sic] of the iron works. Although in exceptional cases, contracts are made with colliers per bushel, the general practice is to employ a boss collier by the month, and laborers by the day.

Coal is accounted for by weight, a bushel of 20 pounds being the standard. We believe there is but one exception to this rule, and in that case coal is paid for by the bushel of 2748 cubic inches, (Association standard.) and charged into the furnace at 2688 cubic inches to allow for loss. The long haul over rough roads breaks up the charcoal considerably, and it averages small sizes. A liberal allowance in brands, however, seems to be the rule.

We believe no attempt has been made to introduce the use of kilns or retorts, as it has been considered impractical to get the wood delivered to central points. We, however, feel convinced that a thorough investigation would demonstrate that some of the difficulties are more easily overcome than is anticipated.

We were informed that the average yield was 33⅛ bushels of charcoal per cord, and some managers claimed to obtain 40 bushels of 20 pounds, per cord of wood.

This would represent very good results from meiler charring, but we doubt if careful measurement of wood and exact weighing of resulting charcoal would show the actual yield to average as much as stated.

The large percentage of brands accepted will have a material influence upon the yield obtained per cord, when the charcoal is accounted for by weight. We found upon inquiry that the cost of coaling after the wood had been hauled into pits, was from 1½ to 2 cents per bushel. . . .

While there are several special features about individual plants, a typical blast furnace of this region consists of a stone stack 30 to 40 feet in height, lined to a bosh diameter of 8 to 10 feet placed against a bank of same level as the tunnel-head. The furnace is worked open-top with cold blast, delivered through from one to three tuyeres; the cinder being flushed at intervals, and casts made every eight hours. An overshot or turbine water-wheel, or a steam engine drives a single wooden blowing tub of rectangular cross-section 4 to 5 feet square and 4 feet stroke. These square tubs, when they have closed ends, have a single piston, air being taken in at the heads of the tub and discharged near the ends of the top side. When they have open ends the piston is double, the air receiving valves being in the pistons, and the discharge valves being in the center of the top side of the tub. The pressure of blast is regulated by a weighted float in a circular tub. Blast-g[au]ges are not used.

Coal and ore are charged by *approximate* weight, that is, a buggy filled with charcoal to a specified height is weighed and the number of bushels (20 pounds) is determined. A barrow is gauged for varied numbers of boxes of ore, which are weighed and then it is always filled to about the same height for a given number of boxes; the barrows of ore are not actually weighed, but are rated as so many boxes. We learned that several managers had adopted and were now employing more exact methods in charging. The furnaces make from 5 to 10 tons per day, on a consumption of from 130 to 160 bushels of charcoal per ton of metal.

We were permitted access to some of the blast records, and from the books of one of the furnaces with a nine foot bosh we took the following data, which we believe is [sic] a fair average record:

In five months, 1,090 gross tons of pig iron were made with a consumption of 152,844 bushels of charcoal, 5,200,160 pounds of iron ore raw, and 320,094 pounds of flux. This is equivalent to 140.2 bushels of charcoal, 4,770.7 pounds of ore, and 293.6 pounds limestone per ton of iron made.

The ordinary charge of the furnace was 40 boxes of ore = 800 pounds, one box of limestone = 54 pounds, and 25¾ bushels of charcoal = 512 pounds. The usual practice in this district is to charge with the limestone varying quantities of aluminous clay, as occasion seems to require. Of this no record is kept.

The hearths, crucibles, and boshes are of dressed sandstone, and the in-walls are lined with shale. The crucibles are either square or round, measuring 24 to 30 inches at the bottom, and from 30 to 36 inches at the top, which is 5 feet above the bottom. The boshes are quite flat, the batter being nine inches to one foot, and the in-walls slope regularly from the top of the boshes to the tunnel-head, 30 to 36 inches in diameter, which is partially covered by a loose plate. The tuyeres are placed about 27 inches above the bottom. A dry dam, water-tymp, and coil tuyeres are used.

Several of the furnaces have put in steeper boshes and have substituted fire-brick for the in-wall lining, or for boshes; there are also individual instances of round wooden blowing-tubs, iron blowing-tubs, a rotary blower, (as yet untried,) and a complete blowing-engine.

But one furnace in the district has a hoist, all the others receive their supplies of stock from banks at tunnel-head level.

Steam crushers, to break the ores, are used at some of the plants, and small roasting-kilns, of the Gjers pattern, are connected with two furnaces.

The newest and largest furnace in the district is the Ivanhoe, which has introduced many modern features, and, except being a bank furnace, has very little in common with the older plants. (In our remarks above we have not included this plant.) It is a brick stack, banded and supported on iron columns and mantle. It has a vertical steam blowing-engine, which delivers blast through six tuyeres into a crucible, which is constructed of fire-brick, and provided with water-breasts and tymp and a dry dam. The stack is 42 feet high, and is now lined to 11 feet bosh, fire-brick being used throughout. It is provided with a bell and hopper, and the furnace gases are conveyed by flues to three boilers and one hot-blast stove, located at hearth-level.

A connection is also made to a small roasting-kiln on the tunnel-head bank, in which the lump ore is calcined by burning the furnace gasses, after which it passes through a crusher.

The ore supplies and the limestone are obtained about one half mile from the furnace and are carried in cars over a tram-road to the tunnel head level. The proportion of lump ore appears to be above the average, and this is carefully prepared by roasting with furnace gas and passed through the crushers. Part of the fine ore is washed at the ore bank and a portion of it carried to a washer at the furnace. About 20 tons of pig-iron iron is the daily average, but an out-put of 35 tons per day has been reached. The basis of a charge is 700 pounds of charcoal.

Appendix C

A British engineer, Douglas Galton, attended the Philadelphia Exhibition of 1876 and reported to his peers on the railway innovations he saw there. The Lobdell Car Wheel Company garnered good notices for both its product and its production methods:[3]

> The use of wheels of chilled cast iron is all but universal on American railroads. . . . The peculiarity of the cast-iron wheel is that each forms a single casting with the tire, and is cast in a chill, consisting of a rim of iron turned perfectly true, so that labour in turning is avoided. A peculiar quality and mixture of iron is required to obtain the necessary hardness in the chill. . . .
>
> The most successful exhibitors of cast-iron wheels were Messrs. Lobdell of Wilmington, Delaware, Mr. Whitney of Philadelphia, the Ramapo Wheel Works, the Pennsylvania Railroad Company, and Messrs. Macdougall of Montreal.

A chilling iron contains a percentage, confined within narrow limits, of uncombined carbon or graphite. The process of chilling was thus explained:—If whilst in the melted state the iron is poured against a good conducting agent such as cold iron, copper, &c., the melted iron, upon receiving the shock of sudden cooling, takes up in combination all the carbon it will unite with, and if the free graphite is not in too great an excess it will remelt in white iron, or what is termed chilled iron; the depth of the chill varies according to the percentage of free carbon, and slightly according to the temperature of the melted iron. Whatever may be the chemical combination in the process of chilling, it is found in practice that the lower the temperature the better the chill, within limits; but when poured too cold it sets before the chemical change can take place to any great depth. Silicon, sulphur, and phosphorus are injurious in irons for car wheels.

A brief account of Messrs. Lobdell's mode of manufacture . . . will illustrate the present position of this question.

Messrs. Lobdell consider that a mixture of different kinds of iron produces the best results. In their opinion the ores should be smelted with charcoal and with the blast cold or nearly so, the colder the better. Some ores are injuriously affected by a warm blast, and even thereby rendered useless for chilled wheels. On the other hand, certain hard refractory specular and magnetic ores can be smelted with a warm blast (about 500°), the result being that the character of the iron is rather improved for car wheels. Iron made of ores containing much phosphorus does not produce good railroad wheels. Ores containing sulphur should be thoroughly roasted before being smelted. Those with the least phosphorus or sulphur are the best. . . .

In casting, each ladle holds enough metal for eight or ten wheels. The mould for the wheels is of sand, but it has a rim of ordinary iron turned to a perfect cylinder; the iron is poured into the mould through the centre or hub where the wheel is eventually bored out. The heat at which the iron is run into the moulds has an influence on the chill; if too cold, it may produce chill cracks, but the cooler the iron when it strikes the rim, the deeper the chill. On the other hand, the iron must flow in uniformly, as much depends on the regularity with which the molten metal strikes the chilled circumference of the mould. Iron irregularly poured becomes blistered. With each ladle a test-bar, 1 inch broad, 2 inches deep, and rather more than 4 feet long is cast; and if this specimen should break when supported on two points 4 feet apart under a weight of less than from 2,900 to 3,000 lbs. the castings from that ladle are rejected. The wheels, when cast, remain ten minutes in the mould, and are then removed to a so-called annealing pit, and covered with dry sand to prevent rapid cooling. All parts are allowed to shrink equally, and the wheels are thus relieved from unequal strains; they remain in this pit for at least twenty-four hours. On every wheel a small test-piece is cast, which is broken to ascertain the quality of the metal; every wheel is tested by being struck, as hard as a man can strike, three blows with a 30-lb. hammer. Messrs. Lobdell prefer to cast the wheels with the flange uppermost.

Appendix D

In 1869, mining engineer Frederic Anton Eilers gave this detailed description of the Union Lead Mine Company's property:[4]

These mines are situate in Wythe county, Va., twelve miles south of Max Meadow station, in that large bend of the New River, where this stream, after breaking through the Iron mountains in a northwestern direction, takes a sudden northeast course, and flows thenceforth, for a long distance, parallel to the mountain chain. The mines are very old. Originally discovered by a Mr. Chisel, they have passed for more than one hundred years through all those stages of eternally changing prosperity and apparently utter failure, to which the best mine can be brought by irregular mining, litigation, and indifferent management. Since the last twenty-five years, however, much of this has been done away with, mainly through the untiring energy and good judgment of Mr. William Kohler, the able superintendent. The mines have prospered, paying a heavy yearly dividend to the stockholders; and to-day they are in as good a condition, and offer as flattering prospects for the future, as they did before an ounce of mineral was removed from the deposits. Perhaps a more cautious and provident and less greedy company would not prevent their superintendent from doing more dead work ahead, so as to be always *certain* of a sufficient supply of ore; perhaps such a company would also be able to see and act accordingly, that it is far cheaper to drain a system of mines by means of *one* deep adit, and to transport the ores through it to the dressing works (especially when the completion of such an adit lacks only about fifty yards driving to connect with the principal shaft,) than to hoist both water and ore several hundred feet, and then haul the latter a long way over a rough hill to the tramway, by which it finally reaches the river. But a really good and rich mine can stand a great deal; and the mismanagement on the part of the company, which would break any other lead mine in the United States, serves here only to show more conspicuously the high value of the mineral deposit.

The mode of occurrence of these lead and zinc "veins" is geologically interesting, and the bountiful concentration of so much mineral on one property perhaps unique. It will be remembered, from the preceding article, that in the dolomite near New River, a steep anticlinal occasions the strata to dip first southeast, then northwest. This fold runs through the Union Lead Mining Company's property; and on the crest and both slopes of it the mineral deposits are found. Furthermore, it must be mentioned that, besides the real dip of the strata, there is also a dip of the back of this anticlinal, so that towards the northeast, near New River, it sinks, while towards the southeast it rises rapidly. Between the strata on this anticlinal, and parallel to their dip and strike, occur three distinct layers of lead and zinc ores, making, apparently, six distinct "veins," of which three dip to the southwest and three to the northwest. Five of these have been and are now being worked; the sixth, or extreme northwest one, runs for the most part in the bed of New River, and in the flat bottom adjoining it, and proves only its existence by the outcrop of a short ledge of dolomite filled with lead and zinc ore on the river bank near the ferry. Owing to the gradual sinking of the back of the anticlinal towards the northeast, the mineral layers approach each other laterally in that direction, while towards the southwest they spread fan-like. The solid back of the anticlinal has been reached by a tunnel driven from the foot of the hill, near the company's shore towards the southwest; and the two middle layers have been extensively worked here by upward stopings. Numerous shafts, some of them connected by galleries, have been sunk on the top of the hill on the different layers. None of these, however, connect either with the tunnel above mentioned, or with a main draining tunnel commenced by Mr. Kohler during the war, and driven from the northwest in the neighborhood of the dressing and smelting works, obliquely across the strata to within fifty yards of the main shaft on the hill. Here Mr. Kohler was stopped by the provident directors of the company, who needed all hands to furnish more lead to the Confederate Government. Nothing has since been done to the adit.

The two middle layers are the most important, on account of their thickness as well as the rich quality of the ore. They vary from five to twenty feet in width, and carry galena, carbonate, phosphate and sulphate of lead, and carbonate silicate and sulphuret of zinc, very evenly distributed. The zinc ores occupy the lowest position, (the footwall, one might say, if there were any walls at all) the lead ores the upper; they are rather sharply separated, so that it is an easy matter to mine each kind for itself and do the principal part of the dressing in the mine. To the depth of thirty to sixty, sometimes even a hundred, feet from the surface, the mineral-bearing layers are entirely decomposed, so that hitherto very little blasting has been necessary for the mining of the richest ores. They lie here in a matrix of red calcareous clay, and consist mainly of carbonates of lead, clustering around solid lumps of undecomposed galena, and carbonate and silicate of zinc. The latter have been, up to within a few years, thrown on the dump as useless "rock"; but are now mined and sold to Northern zinc works. In the deeper workings, the sulphurets of lead and zinc occur mainly distributed through solid dolomite, so that these ores have to be crushed and dressed before smelting. The harder portions of the upper workings, where combs and sheets of dolomite filled with lead occur frequently, undergo the same process. Beautiful crystals are often found.

The dressing works of the company are situated at the river, which furnishes plenty of motive power. They consist simply of Cornish crushers, sluice-boxes and jiggers, and are fully sufficient for the kind of ores they are intended to work; since the deads to be got rid of are almost nothing but dolomite, zincblende and very little quartz. Only this circumstance renders it possible to furnish so high a grade of washed lead ore (sixty-five per cent.) as is actually produced, without even sizing the crushed ore by running it through sieves before jigging and washing. The zincblende, which is lost at present, is actually not worth an extra treatment, so long as thousands of tons of silicate and carbonate of zinc can be picked up on the very surface of the property and on all the dumps.

The smelting works consist of a reverberatory roasting furnace, a Scotch hearth and a low slag-furnace. The necessary wind for the two latter is furnished by a wooden and rather poorly constructed cylinder-blast. Most of the lead is shipped in the shape of pigs; a small part of it is converted into shot at the mines. One of the old shafts is used instead of a shot-tower. There is very little silver, only about six ounces to the ton of two thousand pounds, in the lead, and it is therefore not extracted.

The yearly production of the mines is very large. Exact figures are, however, not at my disposal at present. I can only say, that the works employ over one hundred men and boys at very low wages, from $6 to $26 per month, that the charcoal used costs only seven cents per bushel, and that the economical management of an able and competent superintendent has succeeded in securing regular yearly dividends of from $30,000 to $45,000.

The described property is not the only one in this neighborhood on which lead and zinc ores are found. On the contrary, some of these layers can be traced for more than fifteen miles, and the zinc ores especially are very abundant in numerous localities. But nowhere do all the layers occur under such happy combinations, and concentrated on one property, as they do on the one under discussion. I even doubt whether there is a second locality to be found in the United States equally favored in these respects.

In 1886, a representative of the *Baltimore Manufacturers' Record* visited the mines and recorded his impressions, which document the ongoing growth of the Austinville works:[5]

There are 2,600 acres in the tract in which lead, zinc and some iron are found, the zinc predominating, with sulphurets underlaying the carbonates, which proves them inexhaustible. During the "late unpleasantness," seventeen hundred tons of lead from these works alone were moulded into bullets and used by the Confederate army throughout the South. The process of separating the ores is most interesting. Being located on the river, the works are run by water power, probably the finest in Virginia. First the ore is crushed and passed under heavy chilled iron rollers, which renders it as fine as sand. It then passes through a series of washings by patent "jigs," which separate the metals, the lead being the heavier falling first into a trough, in perfectly pure state, ready for melting and moulding into pigs of 62 lbs.; then into another trough drops the zinc, also in its purity, ready for the furnace, while the rock grindings, being the least weighty of all, are carried off into the sluice and are deposited in the river. The finest washings of lead are wasted before placing them in the furnace in order to have them adhere, thus preventing their being blown away in the blast. I saw some 3,000 tons of pure zinc ore in huge piles awaiting the building of the railroad to that point, which will undoubtedly be done in a very short time, as an immense business awaits its arrival. The company proposes to build speltic works just as soon as railroad transportation can be gotten for their product, and it is to be hoped that the N. & W. R. R. [Norfolk and Western Railroad] will not have them wait very long, particularly as so much money has been expended in grading and tunnelling. All along the lines of the Cripple Creek extension, whose proposed terminus is Speedwell Furnace, there are large iron interests awaiting most anxiously the scream of the freight locomotive dragging in its train the much needed cars to bring their products to the main line for shipment. That the N. & W. R. R. is fully alive to the importance of a speedy completion of this extension is not to be doubted. The Wythe Lead & Zinc Company's works have machinery of 100 horse-power propelled by 3 of Jas. Leffel's 52-inch and one 30½ turbine wheels. They manufacture a very superior quality of various sized shot at their mines by means of a shot shaft two hundred and thirty feet in depth to the underground tunnel. The deposit has been pierced by shafts and tunnels for more than fifteen thousand feet, and the bottom of it has not yet been reached, as the mine has been worked so as to be self-draining.

Appendix E

An 1893 description lays out the entire process of mining and smelting the zinc ore from the Bertha Zinc and Mineral Company mines in Wythe County, Virginia:[6]

The spelter of the Bertha Zinc and Mineral Company, of Virginia, which is so famous for its purity, is made at Pulaski from the calamine ores of the Bertha mines, situated in the Cripple Creek Valley, Wythe County, about 20 miles southwest of Pulaski. These mines, which were described fully in a paper by William H. Case at the Chicago meeting of the American Institute of Mining Engineers, an abstract of which was given in the "Engineering and Mining Journal" for September 16th last, page 292, were first opened in 1879, when a small shipment of ore was sent to Providence, R.I., and smelted there. The resulting metal proved to be of such rare purity that attention was at once directed to these ores, and a small smelting plant was built at Pulaski. Thus commenced, the manufacture of high-grade Bertha spelter has grown into an enterprise of much economic importance, furnishing regular employment to about 750 men.

The Bertha ore, which is free from lead and iron (hence its high value), has as its gangue a soft, unctuous clay, or "buckfat," somewhat difficult to dissolve and of a specific gravity approaching that of the ore; calling, consequently, for careful treatment in separation. The ore as mined contains about 26% zinc. The mine yields 12,000 to 15,000 tons of unwashed ore to the acre, and the ground is now being worked over at the rate of 3½ to 4 acres per annum. The output is 200 tons per day, hoisted from 17 shafts, with a working force of about 300 men.

About half a mile from the mine workings, and upon the bluffs overlooking the New River and railroad (North Carolina extension of the Norfolk & Western), are the bins, where the ore, coming in tram-cars from the mine, is dumped. There are two of these dumping, or storage, bins, each provided with a water-carriage system. The bins consist of timbered trestles built out from the hillside and provided with V-shaped floors, down the center of which passes the water-trough. The ore, having been dumped, is fed regularly into the water-trough and is carried by a current of water down to the dressing house, 1,300 ft. below. The troughs or "flumes" are 12 in. wide and 6 in. deep, made of cast iron. The water required is pumped up from the river by heavy Worthington pumps, through a 6-in. column pipe, to a large tank on the hilltop, whence it runs into the flumes. Between the two flumes is an inclined plane, operated by steam-hoist, up which timbers and supplies are taken to the mines.

The dressing-house is a three-story building, equipped with excellent automatic machinery for the concentration of both zinc and iron ore. The zinc ore brought down the flume falls upon a "grizzley," through which the large lumps are broken, and passes into a single, revolving log-washer, which gives it a gentle primary sluicing, and where the adhering clay and "buckfat" are separated and dissolved. The lumps are then crushed by a Blake breaker, and a pair of Cornish rolls, after which the ore is sized by a conical, perforated revolving screen; the large pieces drop upon a steel-plate conveyor, where they are hand-picked, while the smaller pass down to four sets of Parsons jigs, on which they are thoroughly concentrated. The tailings from the above treatment pass through a spitzkasten, or classifier, and thence to two Harz jigs. The slimes are discharged into a slime pond, whence the muddy water is drained off into the river. The capacity of the dressing-house is 80 tons of concentrated zinc ore per day of 10 hours. The yield is approximately one-third of the crude ore treated, and the product gives the following average analysis when dried at 212°: Metallic zinc, 38.08%; oxide of zinc (ZnO), 47.61%; silica (SiO_2), 29.37%; oxides of iron and aluminum (Fe_2O_3) and (Al_2O_3), 9.23%; combined water, 8.23%; calcium carbonate ($CaCO_3$), 4.54%; magnesium carbonate ($MgCO_3$), 2.07%; lead, trace; total, 101.05. For drying the concentrated ore a roasting plant is attached to the dressing-house, containing an 8-ft. Taylor gas producer and cylindrical revolving roaster 30 ft. long. The dried product is then shipped to the smelting works at Pulaski.

The Bertha smelting works were remodeled and enlarged in 1886, and consist of 10 large Welsh–Belgian furnaces, having 140 retorts or pots each. Each furnace consists of a large skeleton combustion chamber with iron pigeon-hole front, into which are set the retorts. The latter are 4 ft. long and have an inside measurement of 8 by 10 in., being elliptical in section. They are luted into the furnace with ordinary clay.

The retorts are made of selected fireclay, which is brought either from St. Louis, Mo., or Perth-Amboy, N.J. Such clay must be capable of making a tenacious paste, which can be formed into the desired shapes without pulling apart and cracking. It must also be absolutely fireproof, so that the retorts will not weaken or break when resting upon their extreme ends in the furnace at a white heat. . . . The cost of one retort, dried and ready for use, is in the neighborhood of $1, about 30 cents of which is transportation on clay.

The ore, having been calcined to expel its combined water and mixed with the proper proportion of anthracite coal, is charged into these retorts, and a short clay condenser is set in the mouth of each and luted with clay. Then the furnace is fired from below, the flames circulating around and between the pots, causing the reduction of the zinc ore by the combination of the carbon of the coal with the oxygen of the ore. At first a bright blue flame burns at the mouth of each condenser, but when the furnace charge reaches a bright-red heat, say 1,900° F., metallic zinc is volatilized and burns at the mouth of the condenser with a brilliant greenish-white flame. Conical iron pipes are then placed over the condensers in order to assist the condensation of the metal, which deposits inside the pipe in the form of metallic zinc. At stated intervals the pipes are removed and the molten metal scraped out of the condensers into ladles, from which it is poured into molds, forming the slabs of commercial spelter. This is continued until the furnace has been worked off and all the metal extracted from the ore, which takes 24 hours, when the pipes and condensers are removed, the residue scraped out of the retorts, and the furnace recharged with ore. Of the metallic contents of the ore 80% is usually obtained, the remaining 20% being lost by volatilization, absorption by the retorts, or left in the residue. The ordinary charge per furnace is 8,500 lbs. of ore and 6,000 lbs. of coal per day of 24 hours, and the average yield of metal is 1,950 to 2,000 lbs.; thus the output of the plant is 300 to 315 tons per month, or, say, 3,700 tons per annum. The fuel used to fire the furnaces is the well known Pocahontas coal, which gives a very long flame, necessary to reach the higher rows of retorts in the furnace. It gives the following analysis: Fixed carbon, 74.27%; volatile matter, 10.52%; ash, 0.94%. For mixture with the ore in the furnace a supply of coal is obtained from the extensive measures owned by the company at Altoona, about 11 miles from the works, and which is carried over the company's railroad from the mines. It is semi-anthracite in character, and has the following composition: Fixed carbon, 62.72%; volatile matter, 10.52%; sulphur, 1.43%; ash, 25.33%. Although so high in ash, the coal serves its purpose admirably. The vein from which this coal is produced is probably one of the thickest on record, being at one place no less than 115 ft. thick from wall to wall, measured at right angles to its dip. Both white and colored labor is used in the smelting works, the latter being found quite advantageous. Five men are required to each furnace, and they work 24-hour shifts.

The cost of smelting a ton of ore is approximately: Furnace labor, $3.52; yard labor, 14 cents; retorts, 85 cents; Pocahontas coal, $2.30; Altoona coal, 88 cents; all other expenses, $1.83; total, $9.52 per ton.

As metallic zinc has a strong affinity for iron, no iron tool or vessel is allowed to come in contact with the zinc in its molten condition. Only one grade of zinc is made in these works, and it carries the brand of "Bertha Pure Spelter."

Commercial spelter increases in value in proportion to its purity. The ordinary grades of spelter contain certain amounts of iron, lead, cadmium, arsenic, and antimony, which are undesirable. In order to possess the high degree of fluidity necessary for the casting of perfect statuary and works of art, and the ductility and tenacity for such fine sheet brass as is used for making cartridge-blanks and for spinning brass, the spelter must be practically free from admixture with all other metals. It is this purity which has made "Bertha" spelter so widely recognized as one of the standard grades of the world. The following is a recent analysis of the metal: Iron, 0.019%; lead, trace; sulphur, trace; zinc, 99.981%.

Appendix F

In 1924, the superintendent of the National Carbide Corporation plant in Ivanhoe described the making of calcium carbide there:[7]

Carbide is a chemical compound, the proper name of which is calcium carbide, and, as that name indicates, is composed of the elements calcium and carbon. The calcium component is derived from limestone (calcium carbonate) and the carbon from coke. In order to save power and increase the output of the furnaces the limestone after being quarried and broken up to "one man rock" is burnt to lime in modern vertical kilns—of which there are five at the carbide plant. The lime as drawn from the kilns is crushed to approximately two inch size and elevated to one side of a large double concrete storage bin which discharges to a scale hopper over the charging floor of the furnace room. Coke, as received from the ovens, ordinarily contains 3 to 10 percent moisture, and for the same reasons the limestone is burnt, the coke is passed through a rotary dryer after first being crushed to about one inch pieces. From the dryer it is passed on to the other side of the storage bin referred to above.

The lime and coke are then weighed out in predetermined proportions, mixed and shoveled around the three electrodes of the 2400 KVA three phase furnaces, where at the temperature of the electric arc the lime combines with the coke to form calcium carbide and carbon monoxide gas. The gas passes up through the charge and burns on the surface, while the carbide accumulates in a molten pool beneath the surface. At uniform intervals the carbide is drawn off into chill cars, by opening up the tap hole with an electric arc formed by bringing in contact with it a small graphite electrode connected to one leg of the three phase system. When all the molten carbide has run out, the t[a]p hole is closed by ram-[m]ing into it a plug made up of carbide fines and pitch and the carbide allowed to accumulate again till the next tapping time.

The carbide in the chill car cools sufficiently to solidify in an hour or two when it is picked off the car bed by a travelling crane equipped with a pair of special tongs and placed on the floor for further cooling. Later it is rough broken with a sledge and fed to a crusher, passing from there to a system of screens, and secondary crushers with their attendant elevators and conveyors to be sorted into the various sizes required by different types of consumers. Each screen discharges into an individual bin that is provided with a packing spout at which the drums are filled and weighed.

The cans are made in a shop adjoining the packing room, elevated to the floor above for painting, and from there are passed through chutes to the packing room. The filled cans are loaded on a small flat-car running on a track either to the loading platforms or to storage.

The story of acetylene as generated by the action of water on carbide is one that has no end, insomuch as the possible derivatives are practically unlimited, and for that reason it is altogether beyond the scope of this magazine. Such things as vinegar, benzene, starch, sugar, alcohol and artificial silk can be made from acetylene. In fact, the number of derivatives is limited only by their economic necessity and the ingenuity of the modern chemist. It is quite conceivable therefore if present sources of food and clothing were to give out entirely, that from limestone and coal everything that is necessary to the preservation of human life could be produced.

Appendix G

In 1928, the superintendent of the New Jersey Zinc plant in Austinville detailed the newly updated mining and concentrating operation:[8]

The new shaft, mill and surface works of the Austinville Plant of The Bertha Mineral Company represent a development from and addition to similar facilities which had been outgrown.

The Van Mater shaft, named in honor of the late General Manager of Mines, is 750 feet deep and has five compartments. Two compartments at one end, served by a double drum steam hoisting engine, handle skips which are automatically loaded with ore at the sixth level and automatically discharged high up in the headframe. Two compartments at the other end, served by a smaller double drum steam hoisting engine, handle cages on which are carried men, supplies and cars of waste rock. The middle compartment is for service purposes and contains ladders, water pipes, compressed air pipes and electrical conductors.

The headframe over the shaft is of all-steel construction, 115 feet high. The two hoisting engines and the boilers which supply them, are contained in a concrete and steel building, lighted through the roof. To one side of this building is the induced-draft fan and stack for the boilers and the steel structure supporting the switches and lightning arresters for the incoming 13,200 volt power lines. On the other side of the hoist house there is a concrete subway and adjoining that a concrete and steel substation which houses the switchboards, the motor-generator set for supplying direct-current electricity, the mine air compressors and a small automatic gasoline engine and electric generator to supply light to certain important places like stairs and switch-boards in case of failure of the main electrical supply.

Adjoining the boiler and hoist house and behind the sub-station is the coal pile and adjoining the sub-station there is a 500,000 gallon water tank which supplies the mill. The mill building, also of steel and concrete construction, stands with its head end in front of the head frame of the shaft and runs down hill into a flat meadow known from old times as "The Stamping Ground." The name was derived from the use of this natural arena for cock-fights and Sunday festivities, nocturnal or otherwise, safeguarded by location from the all too vigilant eye of austere propriety. It was a veritable "Stamping Ground" for the sports of the neighboring countryside.

The concrete subway before referred to is roofed over flush with the yard level and connects the boiler house, the hoist house, the sub-station, the shaft and the water tank and mill. It contains all pipes for water, compressed air, live steam and exhaust steam and all the electric power cables. The yard around the buildings is thus left free of obstacles to the movement of the crane and cars.

Adjoining the head end of the mill there is on one side a steel and concrete change house for the miners and millmen and offices for the foremen and on the other side buildings of similar construction which will house the machine shop in one case and in the other the blacksmith shop, drill sharpening shop and drill repair shop. . . .

The main mill water tank above mentioned is supplied from a pumping plant on the river bank, 2500 feet away and 300 feet lower, through a 24 inch diameter steel pipe which is large enough to supply several additional units.

Besides supplying the mill, by the means already mentioned, with ore, water, electricity and steam, it is necessary to remove from it [the mill] the lead concentrates, zinc concentrates and all tailings, into which the mill separates the ore. The flotation lead concentrates and zinc concentrates are carried away from the mill through wooden pipes, which are visible as thin lines on poles in the side view of the mill. These concentrates are suspended in water and as the pipes slope down at 3% to 5% they flow freely, although the distance from the mill to the collecting tanks at the railroad is 3500 feet. Wooden pipes are used in order to prevent the freezing of these pulps on their long journey, since their volume is small.

The tailing pulp from the flotation machines is carried away through an 18 inch pipe which runs at a slight down grade for 3500 feet. Where it [the pipe] passes over ravines it is a spiral-rivetted steel pipe on bents. Where it can be placed in the ground it is made of terra-cotta. The volume of pulp is so great that there is no danger of freezing. The tailing pulp is discharged behind a series of dams built across the valley of a small stream, the stream being carried under the tailings pond through a large concrete pipe, thus avoiding contact with the impounded tailings.

In the mine there are cross-cuts or passage-ways connecting the workings with the Van Mater shaft on the second, third, fourth, fifth and sixth levels. These levels are about 100 feet apart in elevation and the second level is about 200 feet below the surface. In each cross-cut there are tracks over which storage-battery electric locomotives haul trains of cars from the working places or stopes to car dumpers which are pneumatically operated machines which take two cars at a time and roll them over to dump the ore. These car dumpers discharge into a single inclined raise or "ore-pass" which runs from the second to the fifth level. At the latter level there is a large control gate consisting of great steel fingers operated by air cylinders by means of which an operator starts or stops the flow of coarse ore. Below the finger gates there is a rough screen or "grizzly" which deflects the large pieces of ore into a jaw crusher which is driven through gears by an electric motor. The crushed ore from the crusher joins that which passes the grizzly and falls into a 500-ton ore pocket from which it feeds by gravity into the automatic skip-loading gates which load the skips mentioned in the second paragraph. It is the crushing of the ore in the mine which makes possible the subsequent automatic loading of the skips. One man feeds the crusher from the finger gates. One man operates the skip hoisting engine. Aside from a daily inspection and oiling, no other men are required between the point where the car dumpers operate in the cross-cuts and the point where the skips deliver the ore to the skip-bin in the head-frame, to which point we now move in our description.

The skips come up the shaft and alternately discharge their crushed ore into a small bin high up in the head frame. From this bin the ore is continuously removed by an apron feeder and delivered to a large belt conveyor which runs through an inclined runway to the top of the rock-house. The stream of ore passes over a powerful magnetic head-pulley which removes scrap iron and then either drops into the first mill storage bin or onto a cross conveyor and into the second mill storage bin.

The concentrating mill is arranged in 500 ton units which can be separately operated if desired. The total floor area of this building is over half an acre, there are dozens of machines all of which must function perfectly or the whole process stops, but so well do these machines coordinate that but few men on each shift actually operate the controls and a small crew altogether on each shift are [sic] required.

Notes

Introduction

The epigraph is from S. F. C., "A Ramble in Southwestern Virginia," *Cultivator,* new ser., 6 (February 1849): 46–48 (quotation on 47).

1. Thomas Jefferson to George Washington, March 15, 1784, in Thomas Jefferson, *Writings,* ed. Merrill D. Peterson (New York: Library of America, 1984), 786–89 (quotations on 787).
2. Ibid.
3. Jefferson, *Writings,* 152.
4. For the many facets of meaning in the word *landscape,* see Mart A. Stewart, *"What Nature Suffers to Groe": Life, Labor, and Landscape on the Georgia Coast, 1680–1920* (Athens: University of Georgia Press, 1996). For examples of using a river valley to discuss environmental and industrial history, see Mark Cioc, *The Rhine: An Eco-Biography, 1815–2000* (Seattle: University of Washington Press, 2002); and Richard White, *The Organic Machine* (New York: Hill and Wang, 1995). To compare with long-term developments in a northern setting, see David Stradling, *Making Mountains: New York City and the Catskills* (Seattle: University of Washington Press, 2007).
5. On America's economic rise, see Gavin Wright, "The Origins of American Industrial Success, 1879–1940," *American Economic Review* 80 (September 1990): 651–68, esp. 661; and Paul A. David and Gavin Wright, "Increasing Returns and the Genesis of American Resource Abundance," *Industrial and Corporate Change* 6, no. 2 (1997): 203–45. For the qualitative and still-rewarding classic on these themes, see David M. Potter, *People of Plenty: Economic Abundance and the American Character* (Chicago: University of Chicago Press, 1954).
6. David Brown, *Southern Outcast: Hinton Rowan Helper and the Impending Crisis of the South* (Baton Rouge: Louisiana State University Press, 2006); Victoria E. Bynum, *The Long Shadow of the Civil War: Southern Dissent and Its Legacies*

(Chapel Hill: University of North Carolina Press, 2010); David Stricklin, *A Genealogy of Dissent: Southern Baptist Protest in the Twentieth Century* (Lexington: University Press of Kentucky, 1999).

7. Arguments placing the South in the Atlantic context have been handily summarized in Jack P. Greene, "Early Modern Southeastern North America and the Broader Atlantic and American Worlds," *Journal of Southern History* 73 (August 2007): 525–38; and Anthony E. Kaye, "The Second Slavery: Modernity in the Nineteenth-Century South and the Atlantic World," *Journal of Southern History* 75 (August 2009): 627–50. On the late twentieth century, see Matthew D. Lassiter and Joseph Crespino, eds., *The Myth of Southern Exceptionalism* (New York: Oxford University Press, 2010). Questioning southern exceptionalism is not a new game. For instance, the contributors to Michele K. Gillespie and Randal L. Hall, eds., *Thomas Dixon Jr. and the Birth of Modern America* (Baton Rouge: Louisiana State University Press, 2006), show that the infamous racist, usually associated with the South, lived much of his life in the North and found a sympathetic audience there.

8. At the level of first principles, I obviously disagree with historians who define the term *capitalism* narrowly as applying only to production based solely on free labor. Joyce Appleby, in *The Relentless Revolution: A History of Capitalism* (New York: W. W. Norton, 2010), provides an accessible introduction to the idea that capitalism does not equate solely to industrialization.

9. Lorena S. Walsh, *Motives of Honor, Pleasure, and Profit: Plantation Management in the Colonial Chesapeake, 1607–1763* (Chapel Hill: University of North Carolina Press, 2010); Walter Johnson, *Soul by Soul: Life inside the Antebellum Slave Market* (Cambridge, Mass.: Harvard University Press, 1999); William Kauffman Scarborough, *Masters of the Big House: Elite Slaveholders of the Mid-Nineteenth-Century South* (Baton Rouge: Louisiana State University Press, 2003), chaps. 4, 6, 11; Peter A. Coclanis, *The Shadow of a Dream: Economic Life and Death in the South Carolina Low Country, 1670–1920* (New York: Oxford University Press, 1989). The argument is not new, though. Louis Hartz, for instance, described John Taylor in *The Liberal Tradition in America: An Interpretation of American Political Thought since the Revolution* (New York: Harcourt, Brace, 1955), 149: "He was a plantation capitalist, and in the Southwest, for all of its stratified social life, he was a very new, very raw, very fierce plantation capitalist." (Of course, one cannot quote Hartz without obligatory caveats. See James T. Kloppenberg, "In Retrospect: Louis Hartz's *The Liberal Tradition in America*," *Reviews in American History* 29 [September 2001]: 460–78.) Note, too, Anthony Kaye's recent observation: "The long debate about whether the Old South was an anachronistic, seignorial society or a variant on modern capitalism is approaching a consensus around the latter" ("Second Slavery," 628). Be sure also to read Laurence Shore's too-often-neglected *Southern Capitalists: The Ideological Leadership of an Elite, 1832–1885*

(Chapel Hill: University of North Carolina Press, 1986); and Thomas P. Govan, "Americans below the Potomac," in Charles Grier Sellers Jr., ed., *The Southerner as American* (Chapel Hill: University of North Carolina Press, 1960), 19–39. For a stellar exposition of generations of prior scholarship, see Mark M. Smith, *Debating Slavery: Economy and Society in the Antebellum American South* (Cambridge, U.K.: Cambridge University Press, 1998). Also see the summary in David Brown and Clive Webb, *Race in the American South: From Slavery to Civil Rights* (Edinburgh: Edinburgh University Press, 2007), 132–35. For a telling snapshot of changes in prevailing interpretations, compare the dissertation-derived monographs of two Jack P. Greene advisees: Joyce E. Chaplin, *An Anxious Pursuit: Agricultural Innovation and Modernity in the Lower South, 1730–1815* (Chapel Hill: University of North Carolina Press, 1993); and S. Max Edelson, *Plantation Enterprise in Colonial South Carolina* (Cambridge, Mass.: Harvard University Press, 2006). For the larger context of Anglo-American settler colonies, see James Belich, *Replenishing the Earth: The Settler Revolution and the Rise of the Anglo-World, 1783–1939* (New York: Oxford University Press, 2009), pt. I.

10. For the older approach, see enduring works such as Robert S. Starobin, *Industrial Slavery in the Old South* (New York: Oxford University Press, 1970); Ronald L. Lewis, *Coal, Iron, and Slaves: Industrial Slavery in Maryland and Virginia, 1715–1865* (Westport, Conn.: Greenwood Press, 1979); and Charles B. Dew, *Bond of Iron: Master and Slave at Buffalo Forge* (New York: W. W. Norton, 1994). Insightful recent work includes Bess Beatty, *Alamance: The Holt Family and Industrialization in a North Carolina County, 1837–1900* (Baton Rouge: Louisiana State University Press, 1999); Susanna Delfino and Michele Gillespie, eds., *Global Perspectives on Industrial Transformation in the American South* (Columbia: University of Missouri Press, 2005); Tom Downey, *Planting a Capitalist South: Masters, Merchants, and Manufacturers in the Southern Interior, 1790–1860* (Baton Rouge: Louisiana State University Press, 2006); Laura Croghan Kamoie, *Irons in the Fire: The Business History of the Tayloe Family and Virginia's Gentry, 1700–1860* (Charlottesville: University of Virginia Press, 2007); Susanna Delfino and Michele Gillespie, eds., *Technology, Innovation, and Southern Industrialization: From the Antebellum Era to the Computer Age* (Columbia: University of Missouri Press, 2008); and Aaron W. Marrs, *Railroads in the Old South: Pursuing Progress in a Slave Society* (Baltimore: Johns Hopkins University Press, 2009). Though a few years older, John C. Inscoe's *Mountain Masters: Slavery and the Sectional Crisis in Western North Carolina* (Knoxville: University of Tennessee Press, 1989) and Kenneth W. Noe's *Southwest Virginia's Railroad: Modernization and the Sectional Crisis* (Urbana: University of Illinois Press, 1994) also effectively stress the importance of infrastructure and the market.

11. Though I use the term *South* "for convenience of presentation," it obscures variations and imposes unity, functioning as what one might call, following liter-

ary critics, an "order-word." On order-words, see Gilles Deleuze and Félix Guattari, *A Thousand Plateaus: Capitalism and Schizophrenia,* trans. Brian Massumi (London: Athlone Press, 1988), 75–110 (quotations on 103).

12. Attentive to both regional particulars and larger patterns, southern environmental history has sprung to life in the past two decades, from pioneering works such as Timothy Silver, *A New Face on the Countryside: Indians, Colonists, and Slaves in South Atlantic Forests, 1500–1800* (Cambridge, U.K.: Cambridge University Press, 1990), and Stewart, *"What Nature Suffers to Groe"* to rich recent books such as the eclectic, sometimes dewy-eyed Jack Temple Kirby, *Mockingbird Song: Ecological Landscapes of the South* (Chapel Hill: University of North Carolina Press, 2006); Lynn A. Nelson, *Pharsalia: An Environmental Biography of a Southern Plantation, 1780–1880* (Athens: University of Georgia Press, 2007); and Paul S. Sutter and Christopher J. Manganiello, eds., *Environmental History and the American South: A Reader* (Athens: University of Georgia Press, 2009). For particularly good historiographical surveys, see Christopher Morris, "A More Southern Environmental History," *Journal of Southern History* 75 (August 2009): 581–98; and, on the colonial era, Timothy Silver, "Learning to Live with Nature: Colonial Historians and the Southern Environment," *Journal of Southern History* 73 (August 2007): 539–52. The environmental history of the southern highlands has attracted the attention of several good scholars. Work on the history of parks is most developed. See Margaret Lynn Brown, *The Wild East: A Biography of the Great Smoky Mountains* (Gainesville: University Press of Florida, 2000); Donald Edward Davis, *Where There Are Mountains: An Environmental History of the Southern Appalachians* (Athens: University of Georgia Press, 2000); Daniel S. Pierce, *The Great Smokies: From Natural Habitat to National Park* (Knoxville: University of Tennessee Press, 2000); Timothy Silver, *Mount Mitchell and the Black Mountains: An Environmental History of the Highest Peaks in Eastern America* (Chapel Hill: University of North Carolina Press, 2003); and Sara M. Gregg, *Managing the Mountains: Land Use Planning, the New Deal, and the Creation of a Federal Landscape in Appalachia* (New Haven, Conn.: Yale University Press, 2010). Silver's *Mount Mitchell and the Black Mountains* provides a particularly good balance of ecological change and human activity. Davis's *Where There Are Mountains* does a good job surveying the environmental effects of antebellum industrial development. And despite the raw political immediacy of the issue of coal mining via mountaintop removal, scholars are beginning to bring perspective on the most environmentally destructive example of extractive industry. See Shirley Stewart Burns, *Bringing Down the Mountains: The Impact of Mountaintop Removal Surface Coal Mining on Southern West Virginia Communities, 1970–2004* (Morgantown: West Virginia University Press, 2007). Paul S. Sutter's detailed analysis of Benton MacKaye's thought provides crucial insight on Appalachian environmental history. See Paul S. Sutter, *Driven Wild: How the Fight Against Automobiles Launched the*

Modern Wilderness Movement (Seattle: University of Washington Press, 2002), 142–93.

13. John Majewski, *Modernizing a Slave Economy: The Economic Vision of the Confederate Nation* (Chapel Hill: University of North Carolina Press, 2009); John Majewski, *A House Dividing: Economic Development in Pennsylvania and Virginia before the Civil War* (Cambridge, U.K.: Cambridge University Press, 2000).

14. John Bezís-Selfa, *Forging America: Ironworkers, Adventurers, and the Industrious Revolution* (Ithaca, N.Y.: Cornell University Press, 2004); Thomas M. Doerflinger, "Rural Capitalism in Iron Country: Staffing a Forest Factory, 1808–1815," *William and Mary Quarterly,* 3rd ser., 59 (January 2002): 3–38.

15. Albert H. Tillson Jr., *Gentry and Common Folk: Political Culture on a Virginia Frontier, 1740–1789* (Lexington: University Press of Kentucky, 1991); Michael A. McDonnell and Woody Holton, "Patriot vs. Patriot: Social Conflict in Virginia and the Origins of the American Revolution," *Journal of American Studies* 34 (August 2000): 231–56; Michael A. McDonnell, "Class War? Class Struggles during the American Revolution in Virginia," *William and Mary Quarterly,* 3rd ser., 63 (April 2006): 305–44.

16. Seth Rockman, *Scraping By: Wage Labor, Slavery, and Survival in Early Baltimore* (Baltimore: Johns Hopkins University Press, 2009); Seth Rockman, "The Unfree Origins of American Capitalism," in Cathy Matson, ed., *The Economy of Early America: Historical Perspectives and New Directions* (University Park: Pennsylvania University Press, 2006), 335–61. On workers' perspectives, see also Bezís-Selfa, *Forging America;* Michele Gillespie, *Free Labor in an Unfree World: White Artisans in Slaveholding Georgia, 1789–1860* (Athens: University of Georgia Press, 2000); and Watson W. Jennison, *Cultivating Race: The Expansion of Slavery in Georgia, 1750–1860* (Lexington: University Press of Kentucky, 2012), chap. 7.

17. Sean Patrick Adams, "Different Charters, Different Paths: Corporations and Coal in Antebellum Pennsylvania and Virginia," *Business and Economic History* 27 (Fall 1998): 78–90; Sean Patrick Adams, *Old Dominion, Industrial Commonwealth: Coal, Politics, and Economy in Antebellum America* (Baltimore: Johns Hopkins University Press, 2004), esp. chap. 5. For the northern context, see Daniel Walker Howe, *What Hath God Wrought: The Transformation of America, 1815–1848* (New York: Oxford University Press, 2007), chaps. 14–15.

18. John Lauritz Larson, *Internal Improvement: National Public Works and the Promise of Popular Government in the Early United States* (Chapel Hill: University of North Carolina Press, 2001); Majewski, *House Dividing;* Majewski, *Modernizing a Slave Economy.* Larson's work has almost no coverage of the South during the late antebellum period. The tone of Howe's *What Hath God Wrought,* like Larson's book, treats the wisdom of centrally planned infrastructure as self-evident.

19. Majewski, *Modernizing a Slave Economy;* Chad Morgan, *Planter's Progress: Modernizing Confederate Georgia* (Gainesville: University Press of Florida, 2005).

Also see Mary A. DeCredico, *Patriotism for Profit: Georgia's Urban Entrepreneurs and the Confederate War Effort* (Chapel Hill: University of North Carolina Press, 1990).

20. Jonathan Daniel Wells, *The Origins of the Southern Middle Class, 1800–1861* (Chapel Hill: University of North Carolina Press, 2004); Peter S. Carmichael, *The Last Generation: Young Virginians in Peace, War, and Reunion* (Chapel Hill: University of North Carolina Press, 2005); Bruce W. Eelman, *Entrepreneurs in the Southern Upcountry: Commercial Culture in Spartanburg, South Carolina, 1845–1880* (Athens: University of Georgia Press, 2008); William A. Link, *Roots of Secession: Slavery and Politics in Antebellum Virginia* (Chapel Hill: University of North Carolina Press, 2003). Lacy Ford has prepared perhaps the most sophisticated analysis of southern splintering in the antebellum period with his subtle rendering of the upper South and lower South before 1840 as they grew apart in their views on slavery. Lacy Ford, "Reconfiguring the Old South: 'Solving' the Problem of Slavery, 1787–1838," *Journal of American History* 95 (June 2008): 95–122. Yet even within the upper South states such as Virginia, considerable variety and conflict marked the time. The New River valley elite's unalloyed support for slavery apparently throughout the antebellum period tempers Ford's distinction (which he acknowledges does not apply rigidly to all locales).

21. Some insightful studies hobbled somewhat by their choice of starting date include Ronald D Eller, *Miners, Millhands, and Mountaineers: Industrialization of the Appalachian South, 1880–1930* (Knoxville: University of Tennessee Press, 1982); James C. Cobb, *Industrialization and Southern Society, 1877–1984* (Lexington: University Press of Kentucky, 1984); and Ronald L. Lewis, *Transforming the Appalachian Countryside: Railroads, Deforestation, and Social Change in West Virginia, 1880–1920* (Chapel Hill: University of North Carolina Press, 1998). For an example of how broadening the time frame can produce excellent results, see Robert S. Weise, *Grasping at Independence: Debt, Male Authority, and Mineral Rights in Appalachian Kentucky, 1850–1915* (Knoxville: University of Tennessee Press, 2001). For the classic work on the period, see C. Vann Woodward, *Origins of the New South, 1877–1913* (Baton Rouge: Louisiana State University Press, 1951).

22. Woodward, *Origins of the New South*, chap. 11; Paul M. Gaston, *The New South Creed: A Study in Southern Mythmaking* (New York: Knopf, 1970); Beth English, "Beginnings of the Global Economy: Capital Mobility and the 1890s U.S. Textile Industry," in Delfino and Gillespie, eds., *Global Perspectives on Industrial Transformation in the American South*, 175–98; and David L. Carlton and Peter Coclanis, "Southern Textiles in Global Context," in Delfino and Gillespie, eds., *Global Perspectives on Industrial Transformation in the American South*, 151–74.

23. Jennifer Klein, *For All These Rights: Business, Labor, and the Shaping of America's Public-Private Welfare State* (Princeton, N.J.: Princeton University Press, 2003); Beth Stevens, "Labor Unions, Employee Benefits, and the Privatization of

the American Welfare State," *Journal of Policy History* 2, no. 3 (1990): 233–60; Marie Gottschalk, "The Elusive Goal of Universal Health Care in the U.S.: Organized Labor and the Institutional Straightjacket of the Private Welfare State," *Journal of Policy History* 11, no. 4 (1999): 367–98; Alan Derickson, "Health Security for All? Social Unionism and Universal Health Insurance, 1935–1958," *Journal of American History* 80 (March 1994): 1333–56. On welfare capitalism, see, for example, Brian Kelly, *Race, Class, and Power in the Alabama Coalfields, 1908–21* (Urbana: University of Illinois Press, 2001), chap. 2; John C. Hennen, *The Americanization of West Virginia: Creating a Modern Industrial State, 1916–1925* (Lexington: University Press of Kentucky, 1996), chap. 6; and David Alan Corbin, *Life, Work, and Rebellion in the Coal Fields: The Southern West Virginia Miners, 1880–1922* (Urbana: University of Illinois Press, 1981), chap. 5.

    24. Michael Dennis, *The New Economy and the Modern South* (Gainesville: University Press of Florida, 2009); Timothy J. Minchin, "'It Knocked This City to Its Knees': The Closure of Pillowtex Mills in Kannapolis, North Carolina, and the Decline of the U.S. Textile Industry," *Labor History* 50 (August 2009): 287–311. David L. Carlton touches on the portions of the South experiencing deindustrialization in his essay "Smokestack-Chasing and Its Discontents: Southern Development Strategy in the Twentieth Century," in Craig S. Pascoe, Karen Trahan Leathem, and Andy Ambrose, eds., *The American South in the Twentieth Century* (Athens: University of Georgia Press, 2005), 106–26. Rick Bragg uses the creative nonfiction genre to cover some of this same ground in *The Most They Ever Had* (San Francisco: MacAdam/Cage, 2009). He discusses deindustrialization in Jacksonville, Alabama. Also see John Gaventa, "From the Mountains to the *Maquiladoras:* A Case Study of Capital Flight and Its Impact on Workers," in John Gaventa, Barbara Ellen Smith, and Alex Willingham, eds., *Communities in Economic Crisis: Appalachia and the South* (Philadelphia: Temple University Press, 1990), 85–95; Steve May and Laura Morrison, "Making Sense of Restructuring: Narratives of Accommodation among Downsized Workers," in Jefferson Cowie and Joseph Heathcott, eds., *Beyond the Ruins: The Meanings of Deindustrialization* (Ithaca, N.Y.: Cornell University Press, 2003), 259–83; and Joy L. Hart and Tracy E. K'Meyer, "Worker Memory and Narrative: Personal Stories of Deindustrialization in Louisville, Kentucky," in Cowie and Heathcott, eds., *Beyond the Ruins,* 284–304. We must also remember that globalization at times has enlarged rather than superseded industrial activity in certain spots in the South. For instance, see Marko Maunula, *Guten Tag, Y'all: Globalization and the South Carolina Piedmont, 1950–2000* (Athens: University of Georgia Press, 2009). Also see James C. Cobb, "Cavaliers and Capitalists: The Transatlantic South from Mercantilism to Mercedes," in Richard Gray and Waldemar Zacharasiewicz, eds., *Transatlantic Exchanges: The American South in Europe—Europe in the American South* (Vienna: Verlag der Österreichischen Akademie der Wissenschaften, 2007), 439–54.

25. Anne Mitchell Whisnant, *Super-Scenic Motorway: A Blue Ridge Parkway History* (Chapel Hill: University of North Carolina Press, 2006).

26. Thomas D. Clark, *The Greening of the South: The Recovery of Land and Forest* (Lexington: University Press of Kentucky, 1984); William Boyd, "The Forest Is the Future? Industrial Forestry and the Southern Pulp and Paper Complex," in Philip Scranton, ed., *The Second Wave: Southern Industrialization from the 1940s to the 1970s* (Athens: University of Georgia Press, 2001), 168–218. Clark's pro-industry antipathy toward fire should be countered by reading Albert G. Way, "Burned to Be Wild: Herbert Stoddard and the Roots of Ecological Conservation in the Southern Longleaf Pine Forest," *Environmental History* 11 (July 2006): 500–526. On the ironies of environmental recovery, see Paul S. Sutter, "What Gullies Mean: Georgia's 'Little Grand Canyon' and Southern Environmental History," *Journal of Southern History* 76 (August 2010): 579–616. See also Justin Reich, "Re-Creating the Wilderness: Shaping Narratives and Landscapes in Shenandoah National Park," *Environmental History* 6 (January 2001): 95–117.

27. Deservedly influential in this regard has been William Cronon, *Nature's Metropolis: Chicago and the Great West* (New York: W. W. Norton, 1991).

1. Industrial Inroads and Pragmatic Patriots

1. John Bartram to Moses and William Bartram, November 9, 1762, in Edmund Berkeley and Dorothy Smith Berkeley, eds., *The Correspondence of John Bartram, 1734–1777* (Gainesville: University Press of Florida, 1992), 574 (first, fourth, and fifth quotations); Bartram to Peter Collinson, [January 13, 1763], in Berkeley and Berkeley, eds., *The Correspondence of John Bartram*, 585 (second and third quotations); John Perry Alderman, *Carroll, 1765–1815: The Settlements; a History of the First Fifty Years of Carroll County, Virginia* (Roanoke, Va.: Alderman Books, 1985), 16–17. On Peter Collinson's support of specimen-gathering trips in North America, see Andrea Wulf, *The Brother Gardeners: Botany, Empire, and the Birth of an Obsession* (New York: Alfred A. Knopf, 2009); Alan W. Armstrong, "John Bartram and Peter Collinson: A Correspondence of Science and Friendship," in Nancy E. Hoffman and John C. Van Horne, eds., *America's Curious Botanist: A Tercentennial Reappraisal of John Bartram, 1699–1777* (Philadelphia: American Philosophical Society, 2004), 23–42; and Kathleen S. Murphy, "Portals of Nature: Networks of Natural History in Eighteenth-Century British Plantation Societies," Ph.D. diss., Johns Hopkins University, 2007, chap. 3. Among Collinson's other natural-history correspondents was William Byrd II. See Murphy, "Portals of Nature," 148. Flower Gap was sometimes known as "Flour Gap," probably owing to the hauling of flour from mills in North Carolina. John Perry Alderman estimates that the Flower Gap road descended twelve hundred feet in less than two miles. Alderman, *Carroll, 1765–1815*, 17.

2. William Hendy Shephard, "Colonel John Chiswell, Chiswell's Lead

Mines, Fort Chiswell," M.A. thesis, University of Virginia, 1936, 1–12; Carl Bridenbaugh, "Violence and Virtue in Virginia, 1766; or, The Importance of the Trivial," in *Proceedings of the Massachusetts Historical Society,* vol. 76, *January–December 1964* (Boston: Massachusetts Historical Society, 1965), 3–29, esp. 10; John G. Deal, "Chiswell, John," in Sara B. Bearss et al., eds., *Dictionary of Virginia Biography,* 3 vols. to date (Richmond: Library of Virginia, 1998–), 3:20–22; William Byrd, "A Progress to the Mines," in *The Writings of "Colonel William Byrd of Westover in Virginia, Esqr.,"* ed. John Spencer Bassett (New York: Doubleday, Page, 1901), 333–86 (quotation on 343). For mention of Charles Chiswell as the agent of the Royal African Company, see Walsh, *Motives of Honor, Pleasure, and Profit,* 464. On his slave trading, also see Stephanie E. Smallwood, *Saltwater Slavery: A Middle Passage from Africa to American Diaspora* (Cambridge, Mass.: Harvard University Press, 2007), 166. On Chiswell's accumulation of landholdings through grants, see Nell Marion Nugent, comp., *Cavaliers and Pioneers: Abstracts of Virginia Land Patents and Grants,* vol. 3, *1695–1732* (Richmond: Virginia State Library, 1979), 191, 337, 350, 364, 401. The randy cavalier Byrd once rained kisses on Charles Chiswell's wife in Chiswell's absence, upsetting her and Mrs. Byrd. See the entry for November 2, 1709, in Louis B. Wright and Marion Tinling, eds., *The Secret Diary of William Byrd of Westover, 1709–1712* (Richmond, Va.: Dietz Press, 1941), 101. On the early iron-making operations, see also Robert A. Rutland, "Men and Iron in the Making of Virginia, Part I, 1619–1860," *The Iron Worker* 40 (Summer 1976): 2–17. The Lynchburg Foundry published *The Iron Worker.*

  3. Shephard, "Colonel John Chiswell," 13–24; Bridenbaugh, "Violence and Virtue in Virginia," 10; Alderman, *Carroll, 1765–1815,* 14; Richard Charles Osborn, "William Preston of Virginia, 1727–1783: The Making of a Frontier Elite," Ph.D. diss., University of Maryland, 1990, 15; Deal, "Chiswell, John," 220–22. On Indians' history in the region, see Will Sarvis, *A History of the Jefferson National Forest* (Eugene, Ore.: Lushan Press, 1990), 22–49; Will Sarvis, "Prehistoric Southwest Virginia: Aboriginal Occupation, Land Use, and Environmental Worldview," *Smithfield Review* 4 (2000): 125–51; Jay F. Custer, Dennis C. Curry, and Joseph M. McNamara, "Prehistoric Settlement-Subsistence Systems in Grayson County, Virginia," *Quarterly Bulletin, Archaeological Society of Virginia* 41 (September 1986): 113–41, esp. 126–27; Howard A. MacCord Sr., "The Intermontane Culture: A Middle Appalachian Late Woodland Manifestation," *Archaeology of Eastern North America* 17 (1989): 89–108; and Keith T. Egloff, "The Late Woodland Period in Southwestern Virginia," in Theodore R. Reinhart and Mary Ellen N. Hodges, eds., *Middle and Late Woodland Research in Virginia: A Synthesis* (Richmond: Archaeological Society of Virginia, 1992), 187–223. The lack of Indian dwellers in Virginia west of the Blue Ridge likely resulted from earlier Iroquois military victories. An Iroquois chief negotiating the 1744 Treaty of Lancaster orated, "All the World knows we conquered the several Nations living

. . . on the Back of the Great Mountains in *Virginia*. . . . [A]s to what lies beyond the Mountains, we conquered the Nations residing there, and that Land, if the *Virginians* ever get a good Right to it, it must be by us." Among the nations he listed as conquered was the Coch-now-was-roonan, thought by scholars to be a tribe that may have lived along the Kanawha River and given its name to it. See *A Treaty, Held at the Town of Lancaster, in Pennsylvania, by the Honourable Lieutenant-Governor of the Province, and the Honourable the Commissioners for the Provinces of Virginia and Maryland, with the Indians of the Six Nations, in June 1744* (Philadelphia: B. Franklin, 1744), 16. Virginia's commissioners replied to the Iroquois claims, "If the Six Nations have made any Conquest over *Indians* that may at any Time have lived on the West-side of the Great Mountains of *Virginia*, yet they never possessed any Lands there that we have ever heard of. That Part was altogether deserted, and free for any People to enter upon, as the People of *Virginia* have done, by Order of the Great King, very justly." *A Treaty,* 20. Also see Matthew L. Rhoades, *Long Knives and the Longhouse: Anglo-Iroquois Politics and the Expansion of Colonial Virginia* (Madison, N.J.: Fairleigh Dickinson University Press, 2011), chap. 3. The 1744 deal was still being discussed even in the early nineteenth century as conflicting land claims came before the state legislature. See *Speeches Delivered by Alexander Smyth, in the House of Delegates, and at the Bar* (Richmond, Va.: Samuel Pleasants, 1811), 3–17.

4. *The Official Records of Robert Dinwiddie. . . . ,* 2 vols. (Richmond: Virginia Historical Society, 1883–1884), 1:387; Andrew Burnaby, *Travels Through the Middle Settlements in North-America, in the Years 1759 and 1760. . . .* (London: T. Payne, 1775), 9.

5. H. R. McIlwaine et al., eds., *Executive Journals of the Council of Colonial Virginia,* 6 vols. (Richmond: Virginia State Library, 1925–1966), 6:157–58.

6. William Byrd to Jeffery [*sic*] Amherst, July 1, 1761, in Edith Mays, ed., *Amherst Papers, 1756–1763: The Southern Sector* (Bowie, Md.: Heritage Books, 1999), 274–75 (first quotation on 274); C. Daniel Crews and Richard W. Starbuck, eds., *Records of the Moravians among the Cherokees: Early Contact and the Establishment of the First Mission, 1752–1802,* vol. 1 (Tahlequah, Okla.: Cherokee National Press, 2010), 16–17 (second quotation); entry for June 10, 1761, in McIlwaine et al., eds., *Executive Journals of the Council of Colonial Virginia,* 6:189 (third quotation); Francis Fauquier, "To the Commissioners to the Cherokees," [ca. April 13, 1761], in George Reese, ed., *The Official Papers of Francis Fauquier, Lieutenant Governor of Virginia, 1758–1768,* vol. 2, *1761–1763* (Charlottesville: University Press of Virginia, 1981), 507–9; Fred Anderson, *Crucible of War: The Seven Years' War and the Fate of Empire in British North America, 1754–1766* (New York: Alfred A. Knopf, 2000), 467; David K. Hazzard and Martha W. McCartney, *Interim Report: Archaeological Excavations at Fort Chiswell, Wythe County, Virginia, August–September 1976* (Williamsburg: Virginia Research Center for Archaeology,

[1976]), 4–15. For details of Indian conflicts and diplomacy in the 1750s through the American Revolution, see Osborn, "William Preston of Virginia," chaps. 4–7. On Fort Chiswell, see also Arthur Hecht, "Lead Production in Virginia during the Seventeenth and Eighteenth Centuries," *West Virginia History* 25 (April 1964), 178 n. 23; and John Alexander Williams, *Appalachia: A History* (Chapel Hill: University of North Carolina Press, 2002), 6. For changes among Cherokees at this time, see Tyler Boulware, "The Effect of the Seven Years' War on the Cherokee Nation," *Early American Studies* 5 (Fall 2007): 395–426. The Wilderness Road and other roads used by early settlers as well as the turnpikes developed later in the area largely followed older Indian paths. See William E. Myer, "Indian Trails of the Southeast," in *Forty-Second Annual Report of the Bureau of American Ethnology to the Secretary of the Smithsonian Institution, 1924–1925* (Washington, D.C.: Government Printing Office, 1928), 727–857, esp. 749–65. The best source of general information on Byrd, along with his letters, is Marion Tinling, ed., *The Correspondence of the Three William Byrds of Westover, Virginia, 1684–1776*, 2 vols. (Charlottesville: University Press of Virginia, 1977), 2:603–821.

7. Shephard, "Colonel John Chiswell," 29, 32, 37; Bridenbaugh, "Violence and Virtue in Virginia," 13; Mary Kegley and Jay Lininger, "Moses Austin and the Founding of the Virginia-Missouri Lead Industry. Part One: The Virginia Years," *Matrix* 7 (Summer 1999): 78–92, esp. 79; Deal, "Chiswell, John," 220–22; Tinling, ed., *Correspondence of the Three William Byrds*, 2:629 n. 3. For a sense of the cold economic worldview held by William Byrd and those around him, see Peter Randolph to William Byrd, September 20, 1757, in Tinling, ed., *Correspondence of the Three William Byrds*, 627–29. Randolph, Byrd's friend and business associate, advised Byrd not to sell land to meet some pressing debts. Randolph had an alternative in mind: "I therefore shall at all events give my opinion against the sale of them [tracts of land]. And if you approve of it, am rather inclinable to sell the young Negroes, for it will by no means answer to sell the workers. The only objection to this scheme is, that it will be cruel to part them from their parents, but what can be done. They alone can be sold without great loss to you, and at present they are a charge."

8. Walsh, *Motives of Honor, Pleasure, and Profit;* Chris Evans and Göran Rydén, *Baltic Iron in the Atlantic World in the Eighteenth Century* (Leiden: Brill, 2007); James D. Rice, *Nature and History in the Potomac Country: From Hunter-Gatherers to the Age of Jefferson* (Baltimore: Johns Hopkins University Press, 2009).

9. Fauquier, "Enclosure: Report on the Colony," [January 30, 1763], in Reese, ed., *Official Papers of Francis Fauquier*, 2:1015.

10. Kegley and Lininger, "Moses Austin," 80; Bridenbaugh, "Violence and Virtue in Virginia," 13–14; Shephard, "Colonel John Chiswell," 38; Hecht, "Lead Production in Virginia," 173–83, esp. 174; Mary B. Kegley, *Wythe County, Virginia: A Bicentennial History* (Wytheville, Va.: Wythe County Board of Supervi-

sors, 1989), 327–28; Deal, "Chiswell, John," 220–22; Mary B. Kegley, "Captain William Herbert," *Wythe County Historical Review,* no. 13 (January 1978): 3–11. On interactions between the lead mines and the Moravians' Wachovia settlements from 1762 to 1765, see Adelaide L. Fries, ed., *Records of the Moravians in North Carolina,* vol. 1, *1752–1771* (Raleigh, N.C.: Edwards and Broughton, 1922), 249, 276, 288, 302, 304, 307, 311–13. On Farell & Jones and other Bristol merchants, see Kenneth Morgan, *Bristol and the Atlantic Trade in the Eighteenth Century* (Cambridge, U.K.: Cambridge University Press, 1993), chap. 6. The name "Farell" is often spelled "Farrell."

11. Complaint of William Herbert and complaint of David Herbert the elder and David Herbert the younger in *Herbert vs. Farrell,* Box 32 (1825–1828), Wythe County Circuit Court Clerk's Office, Wytheville, Va. Working for Chiswell likely was not an easy task. In 1764, David Robinson wrote from Fort Preston about an encounter of some sort with Chiswell: "Our great Colo Chiswell has descended so far as to be ang[r]y with me tho; Im conscious I never did any Thing which merits his Displeasure." David Robinson to William Fleming, October 22, 1764, in William Fleming Papers, Collection 009, Special Collections, James Graham Leyburn Library, Washington and Lee University, Lexington, Va. I thank archivist C. Vaughan Stanley for providing me with a transcription of this letter.

12. William P. Cumming, *The Southeast in Early Maps,* 3rd ed., revised and enlarged by Louis De Vorsey Jr. (Chapel Hill: University of North Carolina Press, 1998), plate 59F and pp. 293–94; Roger E. Sappington, *The Brethren in Virginia: The History of the Church of the Brethren in Virginia* (Harrisonburg: Committee for Brethren History in Virginia, 1973), 9–14; Williams, *Appalachia,* 40. The 1745 date probably reflects the 1744 Treaty of Lancaster. Even before 1745, though, William (perhaps Wilhelm) Mack and others had settled slightly north of Fort Chiswell at what became the community of Max Meadows. Williams, *Appalachia,* 3. Dunkard's Bottom now lies at the bottom of Claytor Lake, an Appalachian Power Company hydroelectric project completed in the late 1930s on the New River.

13. William Herbert to William Byrd III, March 6, 1764, in Tinling, ed., *Correspondence of the Three William Byrds,* 2:768–69.

14. Entries for July 16, 1765, July 29, 1765, June 20, 1768, July 29, 1768, September 17, 1768, October 19, 1768, in *Executive Journals of the Council of Colonial Virginia,* 6:275–77, 297–300; Crews and Starbuck, eds., *Records of the Moravians among the Cherokees,* 1:22. On the Cherokee diplomat Attakullakulla, see James C. Kelly, "Notable Persons in Cherokee History: Attakullakulla," *Journal of Cherokee Studies* 3 (Winter 1978): 2–34. Also see Matthew Lawson Rhoades, "Assarigoa's Line: Anglo–Iroquois Origins of the Virginia Frontier, 1675–1774," Ph.D. diss., Syracuse University, 2000, chap. 3.

15. John Stuart to President Blair, October 17, 1768, in "Virginia and the

Cherokees, &c.: The Treaties of 1768 and 1770," *Virginia Magazine of History and Biography* 13 (July 1905): 20–23; Louis De Vorsey Jr., *The Indian Boundary in the Southern Colonies, 1763–1775* (Chapel Hill: University of North Carolina Press, 1966), 64–65; Archibald Henderson, *The Conquest of the Old Southwest: The Romantic Story of the Early Pioneers into Virginia, the Carolinas, Tennessee, and Kentucky, 1740–1790* (New York: Century Company, 1920), 111–12.

16. Shephard, "Colonel John Chiswell," 33–36, 39; Kegley and Lininger, "Moses Austin," 80–81; Hecht, "Lead Production in Virginia," 174; Bridenbaugh, "Violence and Virtue in Virginia"; J. A. Leo Lemay, "Robert Bolling and the Bailment of Colonel Chiswell," *Early American Literature* 6 (Fall 1971): 99–142; William E. White, "Charlatans, Embezzlers, and Murderers: Revolution Comes to Virginia, 1765–1775," Ph.D. diss., College of William and Mary, 1998, esp. chap. 7; Kegley, *Wythe County, Virginia*, 329–30; Deal, "Chiswell, John," 220–22. On the sale of the slaves to Byrd, see David John Mays, *Edmund Pendleton, 1721–1803: A Biography*, 2 vols. (Cambridge, Mass.: Harvard University Press, 1952), 1:203. The *Maryland Gazette*, October 30, 1766, 156, said Chiswell's doctor blamed Chiswell's death on "Anxiety of Mind." On Robinson, see also Joseph Albert Ernst, "The Robinson Scandal Redivivus: Money, Debts, and Politics in Revolutionary Virginia," *Virginia Magazine of History and Biography* 77 (April 1969): 146–73.

17. Reply of William Byrd, October 12, 1772, in *Herbert vs. Farrell,* Box 32 (1825–1828), Wythe County Circuit Court Clerk's Office; Edmund Pendleton to William Preston, February 6, 1768, in David John Mays, ed., *The Letters and Papers of Edmund Pendleton, 1734–1803,* 2 vols. (Charlottesville: University Press of Virginia, 1967), 1:37.

18. Edmund Pendleton to unknown recipient, February 23, 1776, in Mays, ed., *Letters and Papers of Edmund Pendleton,* 1:154. On Buchanan, see Donald W. Gunter, "Buchanan, John," in Bearss et al., eds., *Dictionary of Virginia Biography,* 2:367–68.

19. Osborn, "William Preston of Virginia," esp. 161–62, 236–37, 261, 292.

20. Gail S. Terry, "Family Empires: A Frontier Elite in Virginia and Kentucky, 1740–1815," Ph.D. diss., College of William and Mary, 1992, chap. 1; Turk McCleskey, "Rich Land, Poor Prospects: Real Estate and the Formation of a Social Elite in Augusta County, Virginia, 1738–1770," *Virginia Magazine of History and Biography* 98 (July 1990): 449–86; Turk McCleskey, "The Price of Conformity: Class, Ethnicity, and Local Authority on the Colonial Virginia Frontier," in Michael J. Puglisi, ed., *Diversity and Accommodation: Essays on the Cultural Composition of the Virginia Frontier* (Knoxville: University of Tennessee Press, 1997), 213–26.

21. Quoted in Shephard, "Colonel John Chiswell," 40.

22. *Virginia Gazette* (Purdie), August 16, 1776, 3 (quotation); Shephard,

"Colonel John Chiswell," 40–44; Kegley, *Wythe County, Virginia,* 330–31. For more on Harry Innes's subsequent career as a distinguished jurist in Kentucky as well as his treasonous flirtations there with the Spanish in 1794, see Mary K. Bonsteel Tachau, *Federal Courts in the Early Republic: Kentucky, 1789–1816* (Princeton, N.J.: Princeton University Press, 1978), chap. 2; and Arthur Preston Whitaker, "Harry Innes and the Spanish Intrigue: 1794–1795," *Mississippi Valley Historical Review* 15 (September 1928): 236–48. On the date by which Callaway began managing the mines, see Edmund Pendleton to unknown recipient, February 23, 1776, in Mays, ed., *Letters and Papers of Edmund Pendleton,* 1:154.

23. Jefferson to Patrick Henry, July 16, 1776, in Paul Leicester Ford, ed., *The Writings of Thomas Jefferson,* vol. 2, *1776–1781* (New York: G. P. Putnam's Sons, 1893), 67.

24. Entry for July 13, 1776, in H. R. McIlwaine, ed., *Journals of the Council of the State of Virginia,* 5 vols. (Richmond: Virginia State Library, 1931–1982), 1:70–71.

25. Entry for October 11, 1776, in McIlwaine, ed., *Journals of the Council of the State of Virginia,* 1:193.

26. John Page to John Hancock, July 27, 1776, in Peter Force, comp., *American Archives: Fifth Series. Containing a Documentary History of the United States of America . . . ,* vol. 1 (Washington, D.C.: M. St. Clair Clarke and Peter Force, 1848), 611.

27. Charles Lynch to the Virginia Delegates to Congress, November 20, 1775, in Julian P. Boyd et al., eds., *The Papers of Thomas Jefferson,* 38 vols. to date (Princeton, N.J.: Princeton University Press, 1950–), 1:262–64 (quotation on 263); Donald E. Reynolds, "Ammunition Supply in Revolutionary Virginia," *Virginia Magazine of History and Biography* 73 (January 1965): 56–77; Robert L. Scribner and Brent Tarter, eds., *Revolutionary Virginia: The Road to Independence,* 7 vols. (Charlottesville: University Press of Virginia, 1973–1983), 6:67, 72 n. 2. The best look at the life of Lynch (1736–1796) is Brent Tarter's entry on him in *American National Biography,* available at http://www.anb.com.

28. Scribner and Tarter, eds., *Revolutionary Virginia,* 7:150 (first quotation), 179–80 (second quotation).

29. Petition of Charles Lynch to the Virginia House of Delegates, November 9, 1778, PAR 11677801, Series 1, Legislative Petitions, Race and Slavery Petitions Project, University of North Carolina at Greensboro, microfilm, reel 16.

30. Thomas Jefferson to Virginia's delegates in Congress, April 6, 1781, in Boyd et al., eds., *Papers of Thomas Jefferson,* 5:367 (quotation); David Ross to Thomas Jefferson, May 4, 1781, in Boyd et al., *Papers of Thomas Jefferson,* 5:600; Shephard, "Colonel John Chiswell," 44–48; Hecht, "Lead Production in Virginia," 177–81; Kegley, *Wythe County, Virginia,* 331; H. R. McIlwaine, ed., *Official Letters of the Governors of the State of Virginia,* vol. 1, *The Letters of Patrick Henry*

(Richmond, Va.: David Bottom, 1926), 163; entries for October 18, 1777, and December 5, 1777, in McIlwaine, ed., *Journals of the Council of the State of Virginia,* 2:12, 42; Patrick Henry to Virginia's delegates in Congress, October 10, 1776, in Peter Force, comp., *American Archives: Fifth Series. Containing a Documentary History of the United States of America . . . ,* vol. 2 (Washington, D.C.: M. St. Clair Clarke and Peter Force, 1851), 986. On the new furnace, see William Preston to William Campbell, April 13, 1778, in Reuben Gold Thwaites and Louise Phelps Kellogg, eds., *Frontier Defense on the Upper Ohio, 1777–1778: Compiled from the Draper Manuscripts. . . .* (Madison: Wisconsin Historical Society, 1912), 265–68. The superintendent's salary of £100 per year had been set on March 20, 1777. See the entry for that day in McIlwaine, ed., *Journals of the Council of the State of Virginia,* 1:372. James Callaway subsequently took up iron manufacturing.

31. Petition of Charles Sayer to the Virginia House of Delegates, June 3, 1777, PAR 11677702, Series 1, Legislative Petitions, Race and Slavery Petitions Project, microfilm, reel 16.

32. Petition of George Daniel, Maurice Smith, and Philip Montague to the Virginia House of Delegates, May 1780, Accession 11678005, Series 1, Legislative Petitions, Race and Slavery Petitions Project, microfilm, reel 16.

33. For William Montague's story, see resolution dated June 10, 1779, in Lead Mines Accounts and Receipts, Entry 661, Box 1791, Auditor of Public Accounts, Record Group 48, Library of Virginia, Richmond; and Randolph W. Church, comp., *Virginia Legislative Petitions: Bibliography, Calendar, and Abstracts from Original Sources, 6 May 1776–21 June 1782* (Richmond: Virginia State Library, 1984), 235. For other petitions relating to slaves employed at the mines, see Church, comp., *Virginia Legislative Petitions,* 7, 41, 53, 63, 66, 83, 98, 101, 102, 110–11, 118, 129–30, 218, 228, 362–63, 365–66, 481. The Council of the State of Virginia began approving payments for the hire of these slaves by the end of November 1776. See entries for November 30, 1776, and December 21, 1776, in McIlwaine, ed., *Journals of the Council of the State of Virginia,* 1:257, 295.

34. Petition of Moss Armistead to the Virginia House of Delegates, June 1784, PAR 11678404, Series 1, Legislative Petitions, Race and Slavery Petitions Project, microfilm, reel 16.

35. Entry for August 29, 1777, in McIlwaine, ed., *Journals of the Council of the State of Virginia,* 1:477.

36. Board of War to George Washington, October 18, 1777, in Paul H. Smith et al., eds., *Letters of Delegates to Congress, 1774–1789,* 26 vols. (Washington, D.C.: Library of Congress, 1976–2000), 8:135–36.

37. Entries for October 25, November 5, November 8, December 8, 1777, and November 11, 1788, in McIlwaine, ed., *Journals of the Council of the State of Virginia,* 2:16–17, 22, 25, 43, 214.

38. "A List of Articles of Cloathing," September 27, 1779, Lead Mines Accounts and Receipts, Auditor of Public Accounts.

39. Governor Benjamin Harrison to William Hay (the state commercial agent), May 23, 1782, in H. R. McIlwaine, ed., *Official Letters of the Governors of the State of Virginia*, vol. 3, *The Letters of Thomas Nelson and Benjamin Harrison* (Richmond: Virginia State Library, 1929), 234.

40. William Rose to Governor Benjamin Harrison, November 26, 1782, reproduced online by the Library of Virginia at http://image.lva.virginia.gov/GLR/04084. On the convict John Dean, also see Edmund Randolph to Thomas Jefferson, February 23, 1781, reproduced online by the Library of Virginia at http://image.lva.virginia.gov/GLR/00818.

41. Jefferson, *Writings,* 150–51. The road Jefferson described cut through a rugged area of what is now the northeastern corner of Carroll County, near Greasy Creek, and proceeded through the less challenging terrain of present Floyd County. Its path allowed lead to be carried to central Virginia with only a single crossing of the New River. Alderman, *Carroll, 1765–1815,* 15–18.

42. Osborn, "William Preston of Virginia," 274–75, 277–78, 312–55; Shephard, "Colonel John Chiswell," 43; Albert H. Tillson Jr., "The Localist Roots of Backcountry Loyalism: An Examination of Popular Political Culture in Virginia's New River Valley," *Journal of Southern History* 54 (August 1988): 387–404; Emory G. Evans, "Trouble in the Backcountry: Disaffection in Southwest Virginia during the American Revolution," in Ronald Hoffman, Thad W. Tate, and Peter J. Albert, eds., *An Uncivil War: The Southern Backcountry during the American Revolution* (Charlottesville: University Press of Virginia, 1985), 179–212, esp. 199–200; entry for July 26, 1776, in McIlwaine, ed., *Journals of the Council of the State of Virginia,* 1:95 (first quotation); Thomas Jefferson to William Preston, March 21, 1780, in Boyd et al., eds., *Papers of Thomas Jefferson,* 3:325 (third quotation); William Preston to Thomas Jefferson, August 8, 1780, in Boyd et al., eds., *Papers of Thomas Jefferson,* 3:533 (fourth quotation); Church, comp., *Virginia Legislative Petitions,* 116; Benjamin Price receipt dated December 20, 1779, Lead Mines Accounts and Receipts, Auditor of Public Accounts (second quotation). The spies' report in 1779 is mentioned in William Preston to William Campbell and Walter Crockett, July 18, 1779, in Craig L. Heath, ed., *The Virginia Papers,* vol. 3, *Volume 3ZZ of the Draper Manuscript Collection* (Westminster, Md.: Heritage Books, 2005), document 3ZZ19. Two hundred Loyalists had supposedly come together in June 1780 at the Glades, which is on the upper reaches of Chestnut Creek in present Grayson County. Evans, "Trouble in the Backcountry," 196; Alderman, *Carroll, 1765–1815,* 23. On James McGavock's ownership of the Fort Chiswell site and his success as a merchant, see Hazzard and McCartney, *Interim Report,* 15–18. For security, lead continued to be stored at McGavock's Fort Chiswell property; see Hazzard and McCartney, *Interim Report,* 18–19. For

broader context on conflict in revolutionary-era Virginia, see McDonnell, "Class War?"

43. Montgomery Order Book 3, September 8, 1779, 64, as quoted and cited in Tillson, "Localist Roots of Backcountry Loyalism," 398. Writing from Fort Chiswell, militia leader Walter Crockett also singled out precisely this area as home to many Loyalists at the height of the crisis in the summer of 1780. He suggested dispatching a contingent of troops: "I should think it very necessary to send a party to Greasey Creek, and Towards the flower Gap." Walter Crockett to William Preston, August 6, 1780, Preston Papers, Draper Manuscript Collection 5QQ48, State Historical Society of Wisconsin, Madison, microfilm. Also see Walter Crockett to William Preston, June 24, 1780, in "The Preston Papers (Continued)," *Virginia Magazine of History and Biography* 27 (January 1919), 49; and "The Preston Papers: Relating to Western Virginia," *Virginia Magazine of History and Biography* 26 (October 1918): 363–79. Michael A. McDonnell is among the latest historians to look at the discord in revolutionary Virginia. See McDonnell, "Class War?"

44. Thomas Jefferson to Samuel Huntington, November 7, 1780, in Boyd et al., eds., *Papers of Thomas Jefferson,* 4:98. The Loyalists in the Flower Gap region continued to endure the rough conditions that John Bartram had described when he passed through the area in 1762. The roughness of the landscape and the weather struck a Moravian traveler in December 1783: "[W]e set out together and toward noon reached the home of Dan. Carlin, at Flower Gap, at the foot of the Blue Ridge. Here we must dismount, and it took us an hour and a half to climb the mile and a quarter to the top. Although we had snow beneath and above us we were soon covered with perspiration. On top of the mountain we tried to refresh ourselves at the home of a Mr. Absolom Burton, but could not get even a drink of water without waiting until snow could be melted. On both sides of this mountain there are such deep gorges that often we could scarcely see the bottom. From here we took the left hand way, which was said to be the better, and had to descend almost as steep a road." The next day they proceeded toward New River: "Our course all day was directly north; the country became constantly more broken, and the woods so thick that often one could not see forty paces through them. One little river we crossed nine times; it was not very deep. Yet I think this way, if there is not too much ice, is better than the road which turns right at Burton's, which on my return journey I found to be still rougher and more difficult." In Crews and Starbuck, eds., *Records of the Moravians among the Cherokees,* 1:45.

45. Tillson, "Localist Roots of Backcountry Loyalism."

46. Charles Lynch to William Preston, August 17, 1780, in Louise Phelps Kellogg, ed., *Frontier Retreat on the Upper Ohio, 1779–1781* (Madison: State Historical Society of Wisconsin, 1917), 250–52 (quotation on 250); Evans, "Trouble in the Backcountry," 201–3. Lynch's actions may have been the origin of the term

lynch law. See "Lynch law," q.v., *Oxford English Dictionary.* Walter Crockett, too, committed atrocities against Loyalists but was indemnified by the Virginia legislature in 1779. In 1782, the legislature also indemnified Lynch, Preston, James Callaway, and others for measures taken in the summer of 1780. Evans, "Trouble in the Backcountry," 194, 203.

47. Charles Lynch to David Ross, May 11, 1782 (quotations), attached to William Hay to the Governor, June 10, 1782, reproduced online by the Library of Virginia at http://image.lva.virginia.gov/GLR/03438. Also see William P. Palmer, ed., *Calendar of Virginia State Papers. . . . ,* 11 vols. (Richmond, Va.: R. F. Walker [and others], 1875–1893), 3:189–90; and Tillson, "Localist Roots of Backcountry Loyalism," 392, 394–95, 401. Some documents spell "Jenkins" as "Jinkins." On December 20, 1778, John Jinkins received "one hundred Pounds together with the work of a Negro for my services at the Lead Mines for the year 1778." Receipt of John Jinkins, December 20, 1778, Lead Mines Accounts and Receipts, Auditor of Public Accounts. He signed with a mark, indicating an inability to write in spite of his skills.

48. Charles Lynch to William Preston, August 17, 1780, in Kellogg, ed., *Frontier Retreat on the Upper Ohio,* 250–52 (quotation on 251).

49. Nancy Devereaux to William Preston, August 1780, in Kellogg, ed., *Frontier Retreat on the Upper Ohio,* 252.

50. William Preston to Thomas Jefferson, April 13, 1781, in Palmer, ed., *Calendar of Virginia State Papers,* 2:34–36 (quotation on 36).

51. Charles Lynch to David Ross, May 11, 1782 (quotations), attached to William Hay to the Governor, June 10, 1782, reproduced online by the Library of Virginia at http://image.lva.virginia.gov/GLR/03438 (quotations). David Ross's Oxford ironworks had earlier supplied iron for the lead mines. See Ross's receipt for Charles Lynch's payment of £100 for a thousand pounds of iron, May 20, 1778, Lead Mines Accounts and Receipts, Auditor of Public Accounts.

52. Scribner and Tarter, eds., *Revolutionary Virginia,* 6:69, 305, 485; 7:60, 62, 284, 550. On Ross, owner of the Oxford Iron Works among many enterprises, see Charles B. Dew, "David Ross and the Oxford Iron Works: A Study of Industrial Slavery in the Early Nineteenth-Century South," *William and Mary Quarterly,* 3rd ser., 31 (April 1974): 189–224.

53. *Virginia Gazette* (Dixon), July 24, 1779, 3 (second quotation); receipt of Samuel Ewing, April 11, 1778 (first quotation); receipt of William Thorp, July 30, 1778; receipt of John Hall, December 20, 1778; and affidavit of Robert Elam, November 2, 1779: all three in Lead Mines Accounts and Receipts, Auditor of Public Accounts.

54. Pension application of John Vest (S15692), Revolutionary War Pension and Bounty-Land-Warrant Application Files, NAMS M805, reel 826, downloaded from HeritageQuest Online database at http://www.heritagequestonline.com. A transcription of this document can be found in the Ancestry.com database.

55. Petition of Margaret Goodrich to the General Assembly, October 1778, PAR 11677802, Series 1, Legislative Petitions, Race and Slavery Petitions Project, microfilm, reel 16. "Goodrich" is spelled "Goodridge" sometimes. On the Goodrich family, also see Lyon Gardiner Tyler, ed., *Encyclopedia of Virginia Biography*, vol. 2 (New York: Lewis Historical Publishing, 1915), 356; and Adele Hast, *Loyalism in Revolutionary Virginia: The Norfolk Area and the Eastern Shore* (Ann Arbor, Mich.: UMI Research Press, 1982), 48–50, 74–76, 128–30.

56. Petition of Aberdeen, November 5, 1783, Legislative Petitions, Folder 12, Box 171, Library of Virginia, microfilm, reel 131. The petition is labeled "Aberdeens petn. November 5th, 1783. to lie on the table." That date is likely the date the House acted rather than the date that the slave named Aberdeen filed the petition because the act of emancipation is dated October in Hening's compilation of statutes (see note 57).

57. William Waller Hening, comp., *The Statutes at Large; Being a Collection of All the Laws of Virginia, from the First Session of the Legislature in the Year 1619*, 13 vols. (Richmond, Va.: Samuel Pleasants, 1809–1823), 11:308–9.

58. Virginia House of Delegates resolution, December 6, 1782, agreed to by the Senate, December 10, 1782, reproduced online by the Library of Virginia at http://image.lva.virginia.gov/GLR/04129. See also Governor Benjamin Harrison to Thomas Madison, December 12, 1782, in McIlwaine, ed., *Official Letters of the Governors of the State of Virginia*, 3:399, which states as follows: "I am ready to receive proposals from the proprietors of the lead mines for delivering up the said Mines to them, and hiring the public Negroes provided they [the proprietors] will furnish the State with one Hundred Tuns of lead delivered at the point of fork on such Terms as will be agreeable to the Executive."

59. Thomas Madison to Governor Benjamin Harrison, December 12, 1782, Letters Received, Virginia Governor's Office, Library of Virginia.

60. Henry Young to Governor Benjamin Harrison, January 27, 1783, reproduced online by the Library of Virginia at http://image.lva.virginia.gov/GLR/04306.

61. Henry Young to Governor Benjamin Harrison, with attachments, January 31, 1783, Letters Received, Virginia Governor's Office, Library of Virginia; "Dr. Johann David Schoepf, Surgeon to the Hessian Troops, 1783," in A. J. Morrison, ed., *Travels in Virginia in Revolutionary Times* (Lynchburg, Va.: J. P. Bell, 1922), 55. Jacob Rubsamen died in Philadelphia in 1792. John Frederick Dornan, ed., *Adventurers of Purse and Person: Virginia, 1607–1624/25*, 3 vols. (Baltimore: Genealogical Publishing, 2004–2007), 1:333. Also see Herbert T. Ezekiel and Gaston Lichtenstein, *The History of the Jews of Richmond from 1769 to 1917* (Richmond, Va.: Herbert T. Ezekiel, 1917), 336–42.

62. Petition of James Parberry, October 27, 1781, Folder 20, Box 290, Legislative Petitions, Library of Virginia, reel 231 (quotations); copy of a decree from March 16, 1796, in *Herbert vs. Farrell*, Box 32 (1825–1828), Wythe County Circuit Court Clerk's Office.

63. Henry Young to Governor Benjamin Harrison, with attachments, January 31, 1783, Letters Received, Virginia Governor's Office, Library of Virginia.

64. Starobin, *Industrial Slavery in the Old South,* chap. 6.

65. John Peyton to Thomas Meriwether, February 20, 1785, in Palmer, ed., *Calendar of Virginia State Papers,* 4:11. The escaped slave Fielding may have been caught by November 1786. In a letter from John Peyton to Thomas Meriwether, November 2, 1786, there is a discussion of a trip from Point of Fork to the lead mines "for," in the document cataloger's summary, "the purpose of bartering off Feilding [*sic*] for Beef and Horses." See Palmer, ed., *Calendar of Virginia State Papers,* 4:181.

66. Opinion of the Attorney General, July 17, 1785, in Palmer, ed., *Calendar of Virginia State Papers,* 4:42.

67. Edmund Pendleton and Peter Lyons to Governor Edmund Randolph and the Council of Virginia, November 7, 1788, in Mays, ed., *Letters and Papers of Edmund Pendleton,* 2:550–51.

68. Edmund Pendleton to Thomas Walker, March 13, 1790, in Mays, ed., *Letters and Papers of Edmund Pendleton,* 2:564 (quotation); Decree of High Court of Chancery, May 30, 1789, Lead Mines Accounts and Receipts, Auditor of Public Accounts. According to the decree, Edmund Pendleton and Peter Lyons, executors of the estate of John Robinson, were suing a long list of people with a stake in the mines: Mary Byrd, Charles Carter of Shirly, John Byrd, Robert and Susanna Nelson, Polly Robinson, Patrick Henry, Charles Lynch, Charles and Elizabeth Carter of Stafford, William and Susanna Griffin, William and Lucy Nelson, an unnamed heir of Mary Lewis, and John Carter Littlepage.

69. Mays, ed., *Letters and Papers of Edmund Pendleton,* 1:203–5.

70. On the Austins at the mines, the most important work is David B. Gracy II, *Moses Austin: His Life* (San Antonio, Tex.: Trinity University Press, 1987), chaps. 3–6. On the work at the mines, also see Kegley, *Wythe County, Virginia,* 331–36; Hecht, "Lead Production in Virginia," 181; Kegley and Lininger, "Moses Austin," 81–88; Beverley Randolph to Thomas Jefferson, July 10, 1790, in Boyd et al., eds., *Papers of Thomas Jefferson,* 17:23–24; and Gregg Cantrell, *Stephen F. Austin: Empresario of Texas* (New Haven, Conn.: Yale University Press, 1999), 20–23.

71. Gracy, *Moses Austin,* 21–39; James Wood to James McGavock, May 24, 1794, Folder 1, McGavock Papers, Special Collections, Swem Library, College of William and Mary, Williamsburg, Va.

72. Gracy, *Moses Austin,* 38–39 (first quotation on 38); William H. Michael and Pitman Pulsifer, comps., *Tariff Acts Passed by the Congress of the United States from 1789 to 1895. . . .* (Washington, D.C.: Government Printing Office, 1896), 9–14 (second quotation on 12; third quotation on 14).

73. Gilbert Imlay, *A Topographical Description of the Western Territory of North America. . . .* (London: J. Debrett, 1792), 121.

74. Gracy, *Moses Austin*, 39–43; Arthur Campbell, R. Sayers, and William Migomry to Beverley Randolph, June 23, 1790, in Executive Papers of Governor Beverley Randolph, 1788–1791, Library of Virginia (quotation). The trio's assessment made its way into the newspapers by a letter from "A Friend to American Productions and Manufactures" that supported the Austins' desire for a tariff on lead. See a letter to the *Virginia Chronicle* that was reprinted in the Hartford, Conn., *American Mercury*, August 2, 1790, 1–2. Visitors in 1799 described the old furnace: "The bellows for the melting-furnace are worked by water, which comes from a spring not two hundred feet away on a hillside; the ore is washed immediately below the spring." Crews and Starbuck, eds., *Records of the Moravians among the Cherokees*, 1:103–4.

75. Land grant, May 27, 1791, reproduced online by the Library of Virginia at http://image.lva.virginia.gov/LONN/LO-4/090/090_0163.tif (first quotation); "Account of Doct. Walker with Loyal Company," in Virginia Documents, Mss. 11313, Small Special Collections Library, University of Virginia, Charlottesville (second quotation); Gracy, *Moses Austin*, 39–43; Kegley, *Wythe County, Virginia*, 333. Walker's ledger in 1778 oddly includes an entry for more than £1,794, explained as "By cash of John Robinson Esqr. May 15, 1764, for Lead Mines."

76. Gracy, *Moses Austin*, 46–47, 52; "Militia Commission," in Eugene C. Barker, ed., *Annual Report of the American Historical Association for the Year 1919*, vol. 2, *The Austin Papers*, pt. 1 (Washington, D.C.: Government Printing Office, 1924) (hereafter cited as Barker, ed., *Austin Papers*), 28.

77. In Crews and Starbuck, eds., *Records of the Moravians among the Cherokees*, 1:103.

78. Gracy, *Moses Austin*, 47.

79. Thomas Ruston to Moses Austin, September 23, 1794, and Ruston to Joseph Burr, November 2, 1794, in Barker, ed., *Austin Papers*, 11–12. Ruston also had investments in South Carolina as an associate of two other notorious 1790s speculators, Philadelphians Robert Morris and John Nicholson. Rachel N. Klein, *Unification of a Slave State: The Rise of the Planter Class in the South Carolina Backcountry, 1760–1868* (Chapel Hill: University of North Carolina Press, 1990), 189 n. 25.

80. See various land contracts and related documents in Barker, ed., *Austin Papers*, 13–21, 25–28.

81. Gracy, *Moses Austin*, 47–52, 68; James Wood to James McGavock, May 24, 1794, Folder 1, McGavock Papers; Michael and Pulsifer, comps., *Tariff Acts Passed by the Congress of the United States*, 475.

82. Gracy, *Moses Austin*, chaps. 4–6; "Statement of Stephen Austin," in Barker, ed., *Austin Papers*, 65 (quotation); Kegley, *Wythe County, Virginia*, 336; Mary B. Kegley, *Early Adventurers in the Town of Evansham, the County Seat of Wythe County, Virginia, 1790–1839* (Wytheville, Va.: Kegley Books, 1998), 286–87;

"The Lead Mines," *Richmond Virginia Argus,* June 30, 1802, 4; "To Be Sold by Auction," *Richmond Enquirer,* February 4, 1806, 4. Of course, when the mines in Missouri did not bring stability and lasting prosperity, Moses Austin made plans for beginning an Anglo-American colony in Spanish Texas. He died in June 1821, but Stephen Austin crossed the Sabine River in December 1821 to start the new venture. See Cantrell, *Stephen F. Austin,* chap. 4. In contrast to Austinville, Wythe County's seat, later known as Wytheville, was described by a traveler on April 22, 1797, as only "a village of ten or twelve houses," though with a "handsome house and a fine inn for the region." See Louis-Philippe, King of France, *Diary of My Travels in America,* trans. Stephen Becker (New York: Delacorte Press, 1977), 52. On the rise of Daniel Sheffey, a one-time shoemaker, see Harry K. Smith, "Daniel Sheffey," *John P. Branch Historical Papers of Randolph-Macon College* 4 (June 1916): 364–71.

83. Charles Austin to Moses Austin, December 8, 1800; "Inventory of Virginia Property," [January 10, 1801?]; Charles Austin to Moses Austin, January 10, 1801; "Statement of Stephen Austin": all in Barker, ed., *Austin Papers,* 57–59, 60–61, 61–62, and 63–64 (quotation on 64).

84. Alderman, *Carroll, 1765–1815,* 3, 305–7; Richard O. Currey, *A Geological Visit to the Virginia Copper Region* (Knoxville, Tenn.: Beckett, Haws, 1859), 24–26; James M. Swank, *History of the Manufacture of Iron in All Ages. . . .* (Philadelphia: James M. Swank, 1884), 204; Kegley, *Wythe County, Virginia,* 345. See also Indenture Between Joseph and Rebekah Jackson and Alexander Smyth, February 23, 1803, Land Records, Folder 7, Blair-Howard Papers, Mss. 2009.2, Special Collections, Wytheville Community College Library, Wytheville, Va.; Indenture Between Alexander Smyth and Thomas Wistar and John Cooke, September 27, 1814, Land Records, Folder 8, Blair-Howard Papers; Indenture Between Thomas Blair and John Blair, June 30, 1804, Land Records, Folder 7, Blair-Howard Papers. On John Blair's long service in the legislature, see Earl G. Swem and John W. Williams, *A Register of the General Assembly of Virginia, 1776–1918* (Richmond, Va.: Davis Bottom, 1918), 348. Matthew Dickey represented Grayson County in the Virginia legislature for two sessions, from 1802 to 1804. Swem and Williams, *Register of the General Assembly of Virginia,* 281. The obituary of Richardson Owen (1744–1822) is reproduced in Thomas M. Owen, comp., *Revolutionary Soldiers in Alabama. . . .* (Montgomery, Ala.: Brown Printing, 1911), 92.

85. William M. Fontaine, "Notes on the Geology and Mineral Resources of the Floyd, Va., Plateau," *Virginias* 5 (January 1884): 8–12 (quotation on 10); Seventh Census of the United States, 1850: Industry, Nonpopulation Census Schedules for Virginia, National Archives Microfilm Publication T1132, Washington, D.C., reel 4. On Fontaine's geological career, see Joseph K. Roberts, *Annotated Geological Bibliography of Virginia* (Charlottesville, Va.: Alderman Library, 1942), 45–50. The periodical *The Virginias: A Mining, Industrial, and Scientific Journal*

Devoted to the Development of Virginia and West Virginia began with the January 1880 issue and was published in Staunton, Virginia, by Jedediah Hotchkiss (1828–1899), a New York–born engineer, Confederate cartographer, friend of William Barton Rogers, and major booster of the region's postbellum extractive industries, particularly related to coal. See Jerry B. Thomas, "Jedediah Hotchkiss, Gilded-Age Propagandist of Industrialism," *Virginia Magazine of History and Biography* 84 (April 1976): 189–202.

86. Blair Ledger, 1795–1797, Mss. MsV Afu3, Special Collections, Swem Library, College of William and Mary.

87. Alderman, *Carroll, 1765–1815,* 15–21; Benjamin Floyd Nuckolls, *Pioneer Settlers of Grayson County, Virginia* (1914; reprint, Baltimore: Genealogical Publishing, 1975), 3, 5–6 (quotation on 6); D[aniel] Hewitt, *The American Traveller; or, National Directory, Containing an Account of All the Great Post Roads. . . .* (Washington, D.C.: Davis and Force, 1825), 330.

88. James R. Rogers, *The Cane Ridge Meeting-House: To Which Is Appended the Autobiography of B. W. Stone. . . . ,* 2nd ed. (Cincinnati: Standard Publishing, 1910), 133 (first and second quotations); Lorenzo Dow, *History of the Cosmopolite; or the Writings of Rev. Lorenzo Dow. . . . ,* 8th ed. (Cincinnati: Alexander S. Robertson, 1850), 186; Joseph Thomas, *The Life of the Pilgrim, Joseph Thomas, Containing an Accurate Account of His Trials, Travels, and Gospel Labours Up to the Present Date* (Winchester, Va.: J. Foster, 1817), 9–10, 48–51 (third quotation on 49), 245, 282 (fourth quotation). When Quaker Joshua Evans visited Grayson County in April 1797, he found an acquisitive mind-set even among his like-minded faithful: "We passed on to a place called Chesnut creek on the Blue Ridge, where were a few Friends, with whom we had a comfortable meeting next day. My condition was the feeling of a heavy heart; for the general cry of the people seems to be for more land, but content with little religion. Thus, among Friends in the mountains of the upper part of Virginia, I fear it is a low time, and too little attention paid to the nature and ground-work of true religion. We then had meetings at Big Reedy Island and Little Reedy Island, also one near the top of the Blue Ridge at a private house not far from Ward's Gap, which was comfortable to me. Coming down this high mountain, at this gap, we got along safely with the help of two young men who bore us company." Joshua Evans, *A Journal of the Life, Travels, Religious Exercises, and Labours in the Work of the Ministry, of Joshua Evans, Late of Newton Township, Gloucester County, New Jersey* (Byberry, Pa.: John and Isaac Comly, 1837), 160–61.

89. Agreement dated [January?] 20, 1786, Folder 22, McGavock Papers.

90. Kegley, *Wythe County, Virginia,* 345.

91. Ibid., 345, 354–55; Crews and Starbuck, eds., *Records of the Moravians among the Cherokees,* 1:103 (quotation).

92. "Description of Francis Preston Ironworks on Cripple Creek," James

Breckinridge Papers, in *Slavery in Ante-Bellum Southern Industries. Series D: Selections from the University of Virginia Library. Part 1: Mining and Smelting Industries,* 37 microfilm reels (Bethesda, Md.: University Publications of America, 1999), reel 2, frames 179–81. James King operated an iron furnace in eastern Tennessee about twenty-five miles outside what became Kingsport. Lewis Preston Summers, *History of Southwest Virginia, 1746–1786, Washington County, 1777–1870* (Richmond, Va.: J. L. Hill Printing, 1903), 751–52. James Callaway, who had supervised the lead mines early in the revolutionary conflict, operated an iron furnace in Rocky Mount in Franklin County. John S. Salmon and Emily J. Salmon, "Callaway, James," in Bearss et al., eds., *Dictionary of Virginia Biography,* 2:517–18; John S. Salmon, *The Washington Iron Works of Franklin County, Virginia, 1773–1850* (Richmond: Virginia State Library, 1986), chaps. 2–4. I have yet to identify the person named "Adams" to whom Preston refers.

93. Indenture Between Thomas Blair and John Blair, June 30, 1804, Folder 7, Blair-Howard Papers; Blair Ledger, Swem Library; Lewis, *Coal, Iron, and Slaves,* 26–27, 119.

94. Francis Preston to John Preston, December 25, 1795, as quoted in Bezís-Selfa, *Forging America,* 156.

95. John Preston to Francis Preston, December 19, 1802, in "Letters of John Preston," *William and Mary Quarterly,* 2nd ser., 2 (July 1922), 191.

96. "Autobiography of Rev. Robertson Gannaway," *Virginia Magazine of History and Biography* 37 (October 1929): 316–22 (quotation on 318).

97. Kegley, *Wythe County, Virginia,* 345–46, 350; J. A. Whitman, *The Iron Industry of Wythe County from 1792* (1935; revised ed., Wytheville, Va.: Southwest Virginia Enterprise, 1942), 7–8. On Preston and the saltworks, see Will Sarvis, *The Salt Trade of Nineteenth Century Saltville, Virginia* (Columbia, Mo.: Will Sarvis, 1998), esp. 19–22, 27, 54–55; Thomas L. Preston, *Historical Sketches and Reminiscences of an Octogenarian* (Richmond, Va.: B. F. Johnson, 1900), 54–63; Robert C. Whisonant, "Geology and the Civil War in Southwestern Virginia: The Smyth County Salt Works," *Virginia Minerals* 42 (August 1996): 21–30, esp. 25; and Goodridge Wilson, *Smyth County History and Traditions* (Kingsport, Tenn.: Kingsport Press, 1932), 193–94. Saltville was in the portion of Washington County that became part of Smyth County when the latter was formed in the 1830s. A visitor in 1848 also noted Thomas L. Preston's enterprising mining of the gypsum banks near his saltworks in Rich Valley in Smyth County but lamented that poor transportation prevented even more sales of the mineral. See S. F. C., "A Ramble in Southwestern Virginia," *Cultivator,* new ser., 6 (February 1849): 46–48, esp. 47. On gypsum in the area, see William Barton Rogers, *A Reprint of Annual Reports and Other Papers, on the Geology of the Virginias* (New York: D. Appleton, 1884), 140–41.

98. Gail S. Terry, "An Old Family Confronts the New Politics: The Preston–Trigg Congressional Contests of the 1790s," in Puglisi, ed., *Diversity and Accom-*

modation, 227–48; Alexander Smyth, *A Letter from Alex. Smyth to Francis Preston* ([Richmond, Va.]: n.p., 1795); Francis Preston, *Address to the People of the Congressional District Composed of the Counties of Wythe, Washington, Montgomery, Greenbriar, Kanhawa, Grayson, Russell, and Lee* (Philadelphia: n.p., 1796); Alexander Smyth, *The Third and Last Letter from Alexander Smyth to Francis Preston* ([Richmond, Va.]: n.p., 1796).

99. William C. Preston, *The Reminiscences of William C. Preston,* ed. Minnie Clare Yarborough (Chapel Hill: University of North Carolina Press, 1933), 2.

100. On change and continuity in late-eighteenth-century U.S. politics, see Peter S. Onuf, "Thomas Jefferson and American Democracy," in John B. Boles and Randal L. Hall, eds., *Seeing Jefferson Anew: In His Time and Ours* (Charlottesville: University of Virginia Press, 2010), 13–39; Eva Sheppard Wolf, "Natural Politics: Jefferson, Elections, and the People," in Boles and Hall, eds., *Seeing Jefferson Anew,* 40–65; and especially Michal Jan Rozbicki, *Culture and Liberty in the Age of the American Revolution* (Charlottesville: University of Virginia Press, 2011), 163–222.

2. Turnpikes to Ore and More

1. I borrow the term *great divergence* from the rich literature that has grown from debates about the origins of the Industrial Revolution and the rising economic power of Great Britain, other northern European countries, and the United States. For a synthetic but thesis-driven introduction to this flourishing literature, see Robert C. Allen, *The British Industrial Revolution in Global Perspective* (New York: Cambridge University Press, 2009). Also see Appleby, *The Relentless Revolution.*

2. Thomas, *Life of the Pilgrim, Joseph Thomas,* 48–49. What Thomas called "Arrarat" is now called "Pilot Mountain," rising within Pilot Mountain State Park. In the late eighteenth century, passing through Flower Gap continued to make strong impressions on travelers. In the late 1780s, the Reverend Thomas Ware traveled southward with Methodist bishop Francis Asbury through the gap: "Bishop Asbury visited my circuit, and took me with him to North Carolina. From New River to the 'Flower Gap,' a distance not exactly remembered, we gradually ascended till we reached the summit of the Blue Ridge, on the border of North Carolina. When we arrived here, I was enchanted, and should have spent hours in surveying the scene below, had I been alone; but it was all familiar to Bishop Asbury, who immediately dismounted and began to descend the mountain. I, of course, must follow him, which I did with a sublimity of feeling that I cannot describe. From this lofty eminence you see the world spread out below you, extended in one continued grove, excepting here and there a spot, until vision is lost in the blue expanse which limits its powers." See Thomas Ware, *Sketches of the Life and Travels of Rev. Thomas Ware. . . .* (New York: T. Mason and O. Lane for the Methodist Episcopal Church, 1840), 160. On Sunday, May 18, 1788, Asbury recorded in his journal, "A twenty miles' ride through the mountains brought us to

our lodgings for the night at K———'s, near the Flower Gap." The following day
he wrote simply, "We rode about fifty miles to S———'s: the weather was warm
in the extreme." Reverend Francis Asbury, *The Journal of the Rev. Francis Asbury.
. . . ,* vol. 2, *From July 15, 1786, to November 6, 1800* (New York: N. Bangs and
T. Mason for the Methodist Episcopal Church, 1821), 32. The Reverend Paul
Henkel, a Lutheran itinerant, also visited Wythe County many times beginning in
the late 1780s. He preached in both German and English and ministered along
Reedy Creek and Cripple Creek. Reverend Paul Henkel, *The Autobiography and
Chronological Life of Reverend Paul Henkel (1754–1825). . . . ,* ed. Melvin L. Miller
et al., trans. William J. Finck (Harrisonburg, Va.: Reverend Anthony Jacob Henkel Family National Association, 2002), 45, 64, 66, 93–95, 267. Quaker Levi
Coffin traveled in the area in the winter of 1823–1824: "I crossed the Blue Ridge
at Good Spur Gap, and spent about two weeks traveling over portions of Grayson,
Wythe, and Montgomery Counties, Virginia. Snow lay on the ground, and the
weather was extremely cold. I frequently encountered heavy snow-storms, and this
exposure gave me a severe cold." Levi Coffin, *Reminiscences of Levi Coffin, the Re-
puted President of the Underground Railroad. . . . ,* 2nd ed. (Cincinnati: Robert
Clarke, 1880), 101. Moravians crossed into the Blue Ridge slightly farther east at
Wards Gap in 1799, and, like Thomas, they saw the marks of settlement: "Wards
Gap was recommended to us as the best way, since it is kept in good repair. For a
good mile we had a steep, rocky road. The forest was largely of beech trees. The
higher we climbed the more beautiful became the country and the growth of the
trees. From a cliff at the side of the road we looked over what had once been a field,
judging by the scattered cherry trees, and had a wide view toward the Sauratown
Mountains, the Pilot, and a broad stretch of land." See Crews and Starbuck, eds.,
Records of the Moravians among the Cherokees, 1:103.

3. "Journal of a Visit to the Blue Ridge, in Patrick and Grayson Counties,
Virginia, in the Month of June, 1841," *United Brethren's Missionary Intelligencer,
and Religious Miscellany* 7 (1st Quarter, 1842): 427–37 (first quotation on 434;
second quotation on 437). Another Moravian missionary, Edwin Senseman, described a similar trip in October 1842: "I left immediately after breakfast, and
soon came to the Flower Gap, which I descended on foot, leading my horse. The
road down the mountain is very winding, there being alternately a precipice and
deep valley on the right and left. Occasionally the woods were sufficiently open to
present the most charming views of mountain scenery." See "Journal of a Visit to
the Blue Ridge, in Patrick and Carroll Counties, Virginia, in October, 1842, by
the Brn. V. Zevely and Ed. Senseman, of Salem, N. Carolina," *United Brethren's
Missionary Intelligencer, and Religious Miscellany* 8 (2nd Quarter, 1843): 90–103
(quotation on 102). Van Neman Zevely had already ascended Flower Gap at least
once during his evangelical tours. In May 1836, he was struck by the cold on the
mountaintop: "[J]e gravis la montagne pour me diriger vers Flower-Gap. Sur le

sommet, l'air était si froid qu'il me fallut envelopper dans mon manteau." See "Rapport du frère Van Neman Zevely, sur ses Visites dans les Montagnes Bleues de la Virginie, au mois de mai 1836," *Journal de l'Unité des Frères* 4 (October 1839): 334–42 (quotation on 341).

4. Skitt [Hardin Taliaferro], *Fisher's River (North Carolina) Scenes and Characters* (New York: Harper and Brothers, 1859), 15–16. Taliaferro writes about hunting deer around "Flour Gap" (63). At the eastern edge of Carroll County, the view from Wards Gap inspired a painter named Meinung to paint *Evening— Ward's Gap, Blue Ridge, Southwest of Virginia,* which was for sale at the 1860 annual exhibition of the Pennsylvania Academy of Fine Arts. See *Catalogue of the Thirty-Seventh Annual Exhibition of the Pennsylvania Academy of the Fine Arts, Chestnut Street above Tenth, 1860* (Philadelphia: Collins, Printer, [1860]), 23. The view near Fancy Gap more recently resulted in Suzanne Caporael's landscape painting *554 (Fancy Gap, Virginia),* which is reproduced in the exhibition catalog *Suzanne Caporael: Roadwork. October 11–November 10, 2007* (New York: Greenberg Van Doren Gallery, 2007), 23.

5. On how stereotypes of southern mountaineers came about, see Anthony Harkins, *Hillbilly: A Cultural History of an American Icon* (New York: Oxford University Press, 2004). Also see Ann Pancake, "'Similar Outcroppings from the Same Strata': The Synonymous 'Development' Imagery of Appalachian Natives and Natural Resources," *Journal of Appalachian Studies* 6 (Spring–Fall 2000): 100–108. Much later, another Surry County native, Andy Griffith, would join Taliaferro on the list of people fashioning the national image of southern upcountry dwellers.

6. James Mease, *A Geological Account of the United States, Comprehending a Short Description of Their Animal, Vegetable, and Mineral Productions, Antiquities, and Curiosities* (Philadelphia: Birch and Small, 1807), 419–21. For more on Mease, see William Snow Miller, "James Mease," *Annals of Medical History* 7 (Spring 1925): 6–30. Mease had ties to the South. He married the daughter of a South Carolina senator, and their son inherited a plantation in Georgia and married Fanny Kemble. Moravian visitors in 1799 had also identified drainage as a major issue for the mine: "The best parts, however, are full of water, and no method has yet been found to get it out." See Crews and Starbuck, eds., *Records of the Moravians among the Cherokees,* 1:22.

7. Kegley and Lininger, "Moses Austin," 87. The tower still stands and in 1981 was named a National Historic Mechanical Engineering Landmark.

8. Quoted in Kegley, *Wythe County, Virginia,* 337.

9. See John Camp to James McGavock, October 13, 1810, and numerous other letters and receipts, all in Folder 7, McGavock Papers.

10. Henry Thompson to Thomas Jackson, June 24, 1818; Henry Thompson to David Peirce, June 24, 1818; Charles M. Mitchell to Thomas Jackson, November

20, 1818; Henry Thompson to Thomas Jackson, January 19, 1822; J. H. Fulton to Andrew S. Fulton, January 6, 1831; Henry Thompson & Son to Peirce & Miller, August 10, 1837 (first quotation); Henry Thompson & Son to Peirce & Miller, January 10, 1838 (second quotation): all in Larry I. Vass Case Replevin Records, Box 4, Local Government Records Replevin Collection, Library of Virginia, Richmond. In 1848, Alexander Peirce sold lead through Harry Carson & Co. of Baltimore. See Harry Carson & Co. to Alexander Peirce, December 19, 1848, Vass Case Replevin Records, Box 4.

11. Mary B. Kegley, comp., *Free People of Colour: Free Negroes, Indians, Portuguese, and Freed Slaves* (Wytheville, Va.: Kegley Books, 2003), 36 (quotations), 80–81.

12. Historical Census Browser, University of Virginia, Geospatial and Statistical Data Center, at http://fisher.lib.virginia.edu/collections/stats/histcensus/.

13. *Peirce v. Jackson,* Wythe County Chancery 1815-25-SC, Wythe County Circuit Court Clerk's Office. I found this case by seeing it mentioned in Kegley, comp., *Free People of Colour,* 76–77. The court dismissed the case on May 20, 1815. For context on slaves and "fits" in Virginia, see Dea H. Boster, "An 'Epeleptick' Bondswoman: Fits, Slavery, and Power in the Antebellum South," *Bulletin of the History of Medicine* 83 (Summer 2009): 271–301.

14. [William Kohler], "Description, History, and Recollections of the Lead Mines," forty-nine-page typed transcription of a handwritten document from around the late 1860s, Special Collections, Wytheville Community College Library, Wytheville, Va.; Kegley, *Wythe County, Virginia,* 336–40; C. E. Taylor, "Early History of the Austinville Mine," *Zinc* 2 (May 1917): 115–17; *Graham et al. v. Pierce* [sic], 60 Va. 28 (1869). On James White, see Mary Verhoeff, *The Kentucky River Navigation* (Louisville, Ky.: John P. Morton, 1917), 152–54. On December 6, 1811, Sheffey, Jackson, and Peirce agreed that Sheffey would have full access with up to fifty hands to work the mines and wash and smelt the ore until January 1, 1813, but would leave the business thereafter in return for $20,000. See the court order in *Daniel Sheffey v. David Peirce and Thomas Jackson,* March 28, 1812, in Vass Case Replevin Records. On White's purchase of John, Michael, Thomas, and Robert Jackson's interest on October 5, 1827, see "Articles of Agreement," in Preston Davie Papers, Virginia Historical Society, Richmond, microfilm. On the fight among Jackson's heirs owing to the fact that his brother John and his sister Ann had never become naturalized citizens, see *Jacksons v. Sanders and Wife and Others,* 29 Va. 109 (1830). On David Graham's partial ownership of the lead mines, see also "The Last Empire Builder: A Life of George L. Carter, 1857–1936," 46, a full-length but yet unpublished biography of George L. Carter written by Ned Irwin, who kindly shared chapter 2 of the manuscript with me.

15. William Phillips, *An Elementary Introduction to the Knowledge of Mineralogy . . . with Notes and Additions on American Articles, by Samuel L. Mitchill* (New

York: Collins, 1818), 215; Samuel L. Mitchill to Parker Cleaveland, February 13, 1820, as quoted in John C. Greene and John G. Burke, "The Science of Minerals in the Age of Jefferson," *Transactions of the American Philosophical Society*, new ser., 68, no. 4 (1978), 92; Parker Cleaveland, *An Elementary Treatise on Mineralogy and Geology. . . .*, 2nd ed. (Boston: Cummings and Hilliard, 1822), 637 (quotations).

16. [Kohler], "Description, History, and Recollections of the Lead Mines"; Kegley, *Wythe County, Virginia*, 336–40; *Graham et al. v. Pierce* [sic], 60 Va. 28 (1869); "An Act Incorporating the Austinville Lead Mining Company" (February 18, 1856), in *Acts of the General Assembly of Virginia, Passed in 1855–6, in the Eightieth Year of the Commonwealth* (Richmond, Va.: William F. Ritchie, 1856), 268–69 (quotation).

17. See the full case record of *Mary Peirce et al. v. James White et al.*, including original briefs, in Folder 82, Box 3, Virginia Court of Appeals, Lewisburg, Records, MS 79–83, West Virginia State Archives Manuscript Collections, West Virginia Division of Culture and History, Charleston.

18. Ibid.

19. Ibid.

20. See table Ba4253–4267 in Susan B. Carter et al., eds., *Historical Statistics of the United States: Earliest Times to the Present*, millennial ed., 5 vols. (New York: Cambridge University Press, 2006), 2:262.

21. Howe, *What Hath God Wrought*, 538–50.

22. *Mary Peirce et al. v. James White et al.*, Folder 82, Box 3, Virginia Court of Appeals, Lewisburg, Records, MS 79–83.

23. Ibid. Slave owners often made such stipulations regarding clothes, board, and taxes when hiring slaves to mines. See Starobin, *Industrial Slavery in the Old South*, 132–33.

24. *Mary Peirce et al. v. James White et al.*, Folder 82, Box 3, Virginia Court of Appeals, Lewisburg, Records, MS 79–83.

25. Ibid.

26. *Walton v. Hale*, 50 Va. 194 (1852). The case in Wythe's circuit court was *Raper v. Anderson*. Anderson filed an appeal with the Virginia Supreme Court of Appeals, but no published decision can be found. Based on later events, it seems the Wythe court's decision was upheld. Nuckolls, *Pioneer Settlers of Grayson County*, 118–23. Original briefs can be found in Virginia Court of Appeals, Lewisburg, Records, for *Walton v. Hale*, Case 777, Folder 86, Box 6; and Case 1028, Folder 62, Box 8, and for *Raper v. Anderson*, also known as *Anderson v. Allison* and *Allison v. Anderson*, Case 1452, Folder 34, Box 12; Case 1518, Folder 6, Box 13; and Case 1305, Folder 76, Box 10. The deed that David Graham, Robert Raper, and Francis Allison Sr. received in 1857 from the Grayson County commissioner of delinquent and forfeited lands is recorded in Deed Book 6, pp. 236–38, Carroll County Clerk's Office, Hillsville, Va. See also *Rakes et al. v. Rustin Land, Mining*

& Manufacturing Co., 22 S.E. 498 (1895). For one of the laws from the mid- to late 1830s that helped bring the Ruston land into the market and caused much of the litigation, see "An Act to amend an act, entitled, 'an act to amend and explain the laws concerning western land titles, and for other purposes,'" March 15, 1838, in *Acts of the General Assembly of Virginia, Passed at the Session of 1838, Commencing 1st January, 1838, and Ending 9th April, 1838, in the Sixty-Second Year of the Commonwealth* (Richmond, Va.: Thomas Ritchie, 1838), 16–22. For guidance on how those laws were applied, see *Virginia Reports, Jefferson–33 Grattan, 1730–1880. Annotated under the Supervision of Thomas Johnson Michie. Volumes 1, 2 and 3 Randolph* (Charlottesville, Va.: Michie, 1904), 652–67. In 1858, the Virginia Supreme Court explained what the legislature had in mind with the 1830s legislation: "[I]t was to remove the obstacles to the settlement and improvement of the country growing out of the ownership of 'large tracts of land' by absentee proprietors who paid no taxes upon them, and took no measures to settle and improve them or to bring them into market." See *Hale v. Marshall,* 55 Va. 489 (1858), at 496. Grayson County, before Carroll was split from it, had earlier faced difficulties caused by large land grants in the pre-revolutionary era. The Virginia Council had granted "one hundred thousand acres of land on the western waters" to "Peter Jefferson and company." Thomas Walker, "an agent for the company," surveyed the land, which "now lies in the county of Grayson." The Virginia General Assembly acted in 1794 to confirm uncertain land titles held by settlers on the grant. See "An Act for the Relief of the People of Grayson County, and Appointing Commissioners to Give Them Settlement and Pre-emption Rights," December 24, 1794, in *The Revised Code of the Laws of Virginia. . . . ,* vol. 1 (Richmond, Va.: Thomas Ritchie, 1819), 460. Walker and the other members of the Loyal Land Company claimed large portions of this region after 1750. See Paula Hathaway Anderson-Green, "The New River Frontier Settlement on the Virginia–North Carolina Border, 1760–1820," *Virginia Magazine of History and Biography* 86 (October 1978): 413–31. Graham had long worried about the Ruston Survey and the land claims of the heirs of Moses Austin and George Lauman and their possible implications for his own forge and iron lands. See a letter fragment dated August 14, 1831; Harold Smyth to James McGavock, January 18, 1833; and Ferguson Jones & Co. to James McGavock, May 14, 1833, all in Folder 2, McGavock Papers; see also David McComas legal opinion, April 12, 1833, Folder 20, McGavock Papers.

27. Deed from Fielden L. Hale to W. Y. C. White and others, February 14, 1866, Deed Book 8, p. 36, Carroll County Clerk's Office; [Kohler], "Description, History, and Recollections of the Lead Mines," 47–49. The public records of the claims made by Jackson and Blanchard's heirs (Isaac W. Blanchard and Lloyd and Emaline Chamberlain) seem deliberately obscure, but the initial agreement regarding the two-sevenths interest seems to be a document dated October 14, 1851,

and the final settlement appears to have been made on August 14, 1860. On this portion of the Ruston Survey saga, see Deed Book 3, pp. 779–86; Deed Book 4, pp. 10–11, 60; and Deed Book 7, p. 431, all in Carroll County Clerk's Office.

28. *Graham et al. v. Pierce* [*sic*], at 33.

29. Seventh Census of the United States, 1850: Industry, Nonpopulation Census Schedules for Virginia, 1850–1880, reel 4; Kegley, *Wythe County, Virginia*, 340.

30. Eighth Census of the United States, 1860: Industry, Nonpopulation Census Schedules for Virginia, 1850–1880, National Archives Microfilm Publication T1132, reel 8.

31. Tench Coxe, comp., *A Statement of the Arts and Manufactures of the United States of America, for the Year 1810* (Philadelphia: A. Cornman, 1814), xvii (quotation, emphasis in original) and 16–17 (first section, "A Series of Tables of the Several Branches of American Manufacturers, Exhibiting Them by States, Territories, and Districts").

32. U.S. Census Office, *Compendium of the Enumeration of the Inhabitants and Statistics of the United States, as Obtained at the Department of State, from the Returns of the Sixth Census. . . .* (Washington, D.C.: Thomas Allen, 1841), 358.

33. Rogers, *Reprint of Annual Reports and Other Papers,* 139–40. On Rogers's background, see A. J. Angulo, *William Barton Rogers and the Idea of MIT* (Baltimore: Johns Hopkins University Press, 2009), chaps. 1–3. Rogers later founded the Massachusetts Institute of Technology.

34. On the significance of the state survey, see Benjamin R. Cohen, *Notes from the Ground: Science, Soil, and Society in the American Countryside* (New Haven, Conn.: Yale University Press, 2009), chap. 5.

35. [Kohler], "Description, History, and Recollections of the Lead Mines," 23–26. The insightful employee from North Carolina likely worked at the Silver Hill Mine in Davidson County. See L. Michael Kaas, "The Silver Hill Mine: First Silver Mine in the United States and Supplier of Lead to the Confederacy," *Mining History Association Journal* 16 (2009): 29–44.

36. "South Western Virginia," *Richmond Daily Dispatch,* June 20, 1855, 1.

37. Rogers, *Reprint of Annual Reports and Other Papers,* 164.

38. Ibid., 350–56; J. P. Lesley, *The Iron Manufacturer's Guide to the Furnaces, Forges, and Rolling Mills of the United States. . . .* (New York: John Wiley, 1859), 74. For a comparative look at the operation of a charcoal-fired blast furnace in New Jersey during the early nineteenth century, see Doerflinger, "Rural Capitalism in Iron Country." Like Doerflinger, I treat iron furnaces as capitalist enterprises embedded in local, regional, and national markets.

39. Lesley, *Iron Manufacturer's Guide,* 73–74, 183–84 (second quotation on 183), 244–45 (first quotation on 245); Kegley, *Wythe County, Virginia,* 356.

40. "An Act Compelling Andrew and James Crockett to Erect a Slope Through

Their Dam over Reed Creek," in Samuel Shepherd, ed., *The Statutes at Large of Virginia*, vol. 3 (Richmond, Va.: Samuel Shepherd, 1836), 174; Kegley, *Wythe County, Virginia*, 356; 1828–1832 Account Book, Graham Family Papers, 1754–1906, in *Slavery in Ante-Bellum Southern Industries. Series D, Part 1*, reel 3, frames 154–55 (hereafter cited as Graham Family Papers, with reel number following); agreement by David Graham to take remainder of William Ross's lease on Crocketts Forge, April 25, 1826, Folder 22, McGavock Papers. A discussion in John Mallory to James McGavock, November 2, 1819, Folder 1, McGavock Papers, may concern the furnace tract. If so, the Crocketts obtained that land from the heirs of William Preston in 1793 for £202. The 363 acres discussed there previously made up part of a grant to James Patton.

41. David Graham to Ephraim McGavock, September 1, 1865, Folder 2, McGavock Papers.

42. Coxe, comp., *Statement of the Arts and Manufactures of the United States of America*, 91, 93; *Compendium of the Enumeration of the Inhabitants and Statistics of the United States, as Obtained at the Department of State, from the Returns of the Sixth Census. . . .* (Washington, D.C.: Thomas Allen, 1841), 166.

43. Seventh Census of the United States, 1850: Industry, Nonpopulation Census Schedules for Virginia, reel 4.

44. Eighth Census of the United States, 1860: Industry, Nonpopulation Census Schedules for Virginia, reel 8.

45. U.S. Census Office, *Statistical View of the United States . . . Being a Compendium of the Seventh Census. . . .* (Washington, D.C.: Beverley Tucker, 1854), 326–31.

46. Kegley, comp., *Free People of Colour,* 80–81.

47. On transportation, see Thomas Graham to David Graham, March 10, 1831, Graham Family Papers, reel 3, frame 292. For mention of the hot-blast method (and some discussion of charcoal versus coke as fuel), see Calvin Graham to David Graham, May 17, August 11, October [?], 1833, Graham Family Papers, reel 3, frames 583, 601, 607. Also see Calvin Graham to David Graham, September 15, 1840, Graham Family Papers, reel 3, frame 805. One way that David Graham and others at the forge stayed abreast of current events was by subscribing to the *Richmond Examiner.* See receipt in Graham Family Papers, reel 4, frame 215. Graham later sent his daughters Elizabeth Ann "Bettie" Graham and Mary Bell Graham to a finishing school in Philadelphia, though he had to bring them home early when the Civil War loomed. Bettie kept a diary during part of her time in Philadelphia. See Anne Ingles, ed., *Journal of Bettie Ann Graham, October 18, 1860–June 21, 1862* (New York: n.p., 1978).

48. Bruce E. Seely, "Blast Furnace Technology in the Mid-19th Century: A Case Study of the Adirondack Iron and Steel Company," *IA, the Journal of the Society for Industrial Archaeology* 7 (April 1981): 27–54, esp. 36; Lesley, *Iron Manufacturer's Guide,* 73–74.

49. For examples of the items Graham sold and cast, see entries in Account Book, September 1845–January 1848, Graham Family Papers, reel 3, frame 870.

50. Regarding the saltworks, see the agreement between Charles H. C. Preston and David Graham, October 17, 1831, and the agreement between James White and David Graham, November 8, 1832, Graham Family Papers, reel 3, frames 424, 565. On the shoe shop, see the account in Graham Family Papers, reel 3, frame 819. For Graham's ties to Greensboro, North Carolina, see W. J. McConnel to David Graham, March 26, 1847, Graham Family Papers, reel 4, frame 15. For a link to Tennessee, see Isaac M. Peirce to David Graham, June 28, 1847, Graham Family Papers, reel 4, frame 21. On gun barrels, see letter from Benjamin Moor at Harpers Ferry, September 22, 1843, Graham Family Papers, reel 3, frame 851. On the Iron Witch Cook Stove, see R. D. Granger to David Graham, September 14, 1847, Graham Family Papers, reel 4, frame 24. The Graham family's enterprising nature is also evident in the choice made by David's son Nicholas Graham to attend the science-oriented Virginia Military Institute rather than a school focusing on classical learning. On the son's conduct at the institute, see David Graham to J. T. L. Preston, November 26, 1858, Graham Family Papers, reel 4, frame 197. On the Virginia Military Institute, see Jennifer R. Green, "Networks of Military Educators: Middle-Class Stability and Professionalization in the Late Antebellum South," *Journal of Southern History* 73 (February 2007): 39–74.

51. "Grayson Sulphur Springs," *Richmond Enquirer,* August 25, 1837, [4] (first quotation); "Summer Travel in the South," *Southern Quarterly Review,* new ser., 2 (September 1850): 24–65 (second quotation on 40); Henry Howe, *Historical Collections of Virginia. . . .* (Charleston, S.C.: Babcock, 1845; reprint, Baltimore: Regional Publishing, 1969), 216; J. J. Moorman, *The Mineral Waters of the United States and Canada. . . .* (Baltimore: Kelly and Piet, 1867), 350–52; W. R. Chitwood, "Grayson Sulphur Springs," *Wythe County Historical Review,* no. 12 (July 1977): 1–10. Alexander Peirce, like Graham, worked as a merchant as well as a mine operator and resort investor. See *Thomson's Mercantile and Professional Directory, for the States of Delaware, Maryland, Virginia, North Carolina, and the District of Columbia . . . for 1851–52* (Baltimore: William Thomson, 1851), 179.

52. *Thirty-Sixth Annual Report of the Board of Public Works to the General Assembly of Virginia, with the Accompanying Documents, 1851* (Richmond: Virginia Board of Public Works, 1851), 110–11, 435, 609–11. For a sense of the early operations of the Board of Public Works, see Robert F. Hunter and Edwin L. Dooley Jr., *Claudius Crozet: French Engineer in America, 1790–1864* (Charlottesville: University Press of Virginia, 1989), chaps. 3, 4, and 6; and Robert F. Hunter, "Turnpike Construction in Antebellum Virginia," *Technology and Culture* 4 (Spring 1963): 177–200. Details of construction of two of the turnpikes are in the Floyd Court House and Hillsville Turnpike Records, 1850–1864, Records of the Virginia Board of Public Works, Library of Virginia, Richmond; and the Tazewell

Courthouse and Fancy Gap Turnpike Records, 1837–1861, Records of the Board of Public Works, Library of Virginia. Also see Robert F. Hunter, "The Turnpike Movement in Virginia, 1816–1860," Ph.D. diss., Columbia University, 1957, and Edward Graham Roberts, "The Roads of Virginia, 1607–1840," Ph.D. diss., University of Virginia, 1950, chaps. 4–5. Ludwell H. Brown (1818–1859), the engineer in charge of the Floyd Court House and Hillsville Turnpike, had previously worked on the James River and Kanawha Canal project and was the son and grandson of state officials. Building the crucial bridge on the turnpike over Big Reed Island Creek was contracted to Robert L. Toncray, owner of a Floyd County iron furnace. Alexander Brown, *The Cabells and Their Kin: A Memorial Volume of History, Biography, and Genealogy* (Boston: Houghton, Mifflin, 1895), 347; "Floyd C. H. and Hillsville Turnpike Road," report by Ludwell H. Brown dated December 5, 1851, in *Thirty-Sixth Annual Report of the Board of Public Works,* 609–11. On Samuel McCamant, see the copy of an order of the Grayson County Court, July 1853, and on Peirce as a director, see an undated list of board members, probably from 1854, both in Wytheville and Grayson Turnpike Company Records, Records of the Virginia Board of Public Works. See also a petition dated December 30, 1853, in the Wytheville and Grayson Turnpike Company Records. It explains, "The Grayson Sulphur Springs have for some years past been resorted to by numbers of persons from North + South Carolina, + the Counties of Patrick, Henry, Franklin, Floyd +c. in Va. and the number of visitors would be greatly increased if the proper and necessary facilities for travel were afforded." On Andrew S. Fulton's service in the legislature in 1840–1841 and 1844–1845, see Swem and Williams, *Register of the General Assembly of Virginia,* 339.

53. On ownership of the Tazewell Courthouse and Fancy Gap Turnpike, see "Report of the Directors of the Tazewell Courthouse and Fancy Gap Turnpike Company," October 4, 1849, Tazewell Courthouse and Fancy Gap Turnpike Records. The quotation is from William H. Cook, John Early, and Ira B. Coltrane to the Virginia Board of Public Works, October 21, 1848, in the related but separately cataloged collection Fancy Gap Turnpike, 1848, Records of the Virginia Board of Public Works. The state also took three-fifths (its standard amount) of the stock of the Wytheville and Grayson Turnpike. See *Acts of the General Assembly of Virginia, Passed in 1855–6,* 138. Coltrane lived until 1894, and in 1884 he was among the group of local men, including iron maker John W. Robinson, incorporated by the General Assembly as the New River and Chambers Valley Railroad Company. The company tried without success to achieve its authorized goal: "to construct, equip, and maintain a railroad . . . from some point on the Norfolk and Western railroad . . . through the county of Carroll, by way of Hillsville, to Mount Airy, in the state of North Carolina." See *Acts and Joint Resolutions Passed by the General Assembly of the State of Virginia during the Session of 1883–84* (Richmond, Va.: R. U. Derr, 1884), 481. On Coltrane, see also Nuckolls, *Pioneer Settlers of*

Grayson County, 123. Carroll County voted to subscribe $100,000 to the New River and Chambers Valley Railroad, evidence of the investors' influence. See *Baltimore Manufacturers' Record* 12 (October 22, 1887), 467.

54. Mary C. Johnson, ed., *The Life of Elijah Coffin; with a Reminiscence, by His Son Charles F. Coffin* ([Cincinnati?]: E. Morgan & Sons, 1863), 225–26.

55. See "Post Office Operations," *Washington Constitution,* June 8, 1860, 3.

56. "Report of the Directors of the Tazewell Courthouse and Fancy Gap Turnpike Company," October 4, 1849. On Fulton and the turnpike, see also *Thirty-Sixth Annual Report of the Board of Public Works,* 110. For a brief biographical sketch of Andrew S. Fulton (1800–1884), see Summers, *History of Southwest Virginia,* 758–59. On the shared membership of Fulton and James Piper (1800–1854) in the Masons, see R. W. Nowlin, *A Funeral Oration in Memory of Col. James H. Piper, Delivered at Speedwell, Wythe Co., Va., Oct. 28th, 1854* (Wytheville, Va.: E. Rider, 1854), 5.

57. Curtis Carroll Davis, "The First Climber of the Natural Bridge: A Minor American Epic," *Journal of Southern History* 16 (August 1950): 277–90; Curtis Carroll Davis, "James Hays Piper, a Sketch," *Tennessee Historical Quarterly* 10 (March 1951): 46–54; Curtis Carroll Davis, "That Daring Young Man," *Virginia Cavalcade* 9 (Summer 1959): 11–15; Whitman, *Iron Industry of Wythe County,* 8–9; *Journal of the Senate of the Commonwealth of Virginia . . . in the Year One Thousand Eight Hundred and Forty-Two* (Richmond, Va.: John Warrock, 1842), 17; William Couper, *Claudius Crozet: Soldier-Scholar-Educator-Engineer (1789–1864)* (Charlottesville, Va.: Historical Publishing, 1936), 74; "Price's Turnpike and Cumberland Gap Road," in *Twenty-Fifth Annual Report of the Board of Public Works, to the General Assembly of Virginia, with the Accompanying Documents, November 9, 1840* (Richmond, Va.: Samuel Shepherd, 1840), 441–42; "Report of James H. Piper," in *Twenty-Fifth Annual Report of the Board of Public Works,* 519–21; "Southwestern Turnpike," in *Thirty-Sixth Annual Report of the Board of Public Works,* 435–41. In 1846, a resident of Speedwell described Piper as "a gentleman of talents and influence and great moral worth." See Alexander S. Mathews to John C. Calhoun, April 5, 1846, in Clyde N. Wilson and Shirley Bright Cook, eds., *The Papers of John C. Calhoun,* vol. 23, *1846* (Columbia: University of South Carolina Press, 1996), 14–15 (quotation on 15). A contemporary remembered Frances Piper in charming terms: "She was a superior woman of fine literary taste, a great reader of good books, a charming conversationalist; deeply pious, cheery, and bright as the sunshine that shone on the blue grass hills about her lovely home. At the camp meeting she entertained with marvelous liberality and grace, always having a pot of hot coffee for the late workers in the altar service. She often shouted in the meeting, as she had a right to do, and her neighbors shouted with her, for they believed in her and loved her." See D[avid] Sullins, *Recollections of an Old Man: Seventy Years in Dixie, 1827–1897,* 2nd ed. (Bristol, Tenn.: King Print-

ing, 1910), 266–67. Her father was Alexander Smyth, a military man, congressman, lawyer, and member of the Virginia Board of Public Works who lived in Wythe County and later Abingdon. See Summers, *History of Southwest Virginia,* 756–57; and Kegley, *Early Adventurers in the Town of Evansham,* 299–308.

58. "An Act to Authorize the Construction of the Wytheville and Grayson Turnpike, and to Make Branches Thereof to the Lead Mines in Wythe County and to Hillsville in Carroll County," in *Acts of the General Assembly of Virginia, Passed in 1852, in the Seventy-Sixth Year of the Commonwealth* (Richmond, Va.: William F. Ritchie, 1852), 143–44 (first and second quotations on 144); Nowlin, *Funeral Oration in Memory of Col. James H. Piper,* 18 (third quotation). Residents had begun using the name "Piper's Gap" for the old Flower Gap area by 1857, when Hardin E. Taliaferro visited the area. See [Taliaferro], *Fisher's River (North Carolina) Scenes and Characters,* 77.

59. "The Abingdon Convention," *Richmond Enquirer,* September 6, 1831, 2, 3.

60. Noe, *Southwest Virginia's Railroad,* chap. 1. Mine owner Samuel McCamant was the railroad's agent selling stock in Grayson County. See "Virginia and Tennessee Railroad Company," in *Thirty-Fifth Annual Report of the Board of Public Works to the General Assembly of Virginia, with the Accompanying Documents, 1850* (Richmond: Virginia Board of Public Works, 1850), 152. William H. Cook of Hillsville had the honor of making a major speech at a celebration of the railroad's having reached its terminus in Bristol in 1856. See "Completion of the Va. and Tenn. Railroad," *Richmond Daily Dispatch,* October 7, 1856, 1. On the railroad, also see Elizabeth Dabney Coleman, "Southwest Virginia's Railroad," *Virginia Cavalcade* 2 (Spring 1953): 20–28.

61. *Biennial Report of the Board of Public Works to the General Assembly of Virginia, 1859–60 & 1860–61* ([Richmond, Va.: Board of Public Works, 1862]), 313.

62. See Graham Family Papers, reel 14, frame 261, for just one example of a receipt to a wagoner for hauling a load of "Rail Road Chairs," in this case to Montgomery County in December 1853.

63. "An Act to Incorporate the New River Navigation Company," in *Acts of the General Assembly of Virginia, Passed in 1855–6,* 116. How much improvement the company managed to make in the coming years has escaped the historical record.

64. J. P. Lesley, "Lesley's Report," in Virginia and Tennessee Railroad Company, *Seventh Annual Report of the President and Directors to the Stockholders . . .* (Richmond, Va.: n.p., 1854), 49–61 (first quotation on 51; second and third quotations on 60). For more on Lesley, see Mary Lesley Ames, ed., *Life and Letters of Peter and Susan Lesley,* 2 vols. (New York: G. P. Putnam's Sons, 1909); and Bradford Willard, "Pioneer Geologic Investigation in Pennsylvania," *Pennsylvania History* 32, no. 3 (1965): 236–53, esp. 251–52. Lesley's visit with Kohler clearly made an impression, for in 1866 Kohler wrote Lesley to confirm a bit of geological speculation that Lesley had made during his earlier visit. See William Kohler to J.

Peter Lesley, June 12, 1866, in "Stated Meeting, September 21, 1866," *Proceedings of the American Philosophical Society* 10 (June 1866), 270.

65. Otis E. Young Jr., "Origins of the American Copper Industry," *Journal of the Early Republic* 3 (Summer 1983): 117–37, esp. 132–33; Collamer M. Abbott, "Copper Mining in the Eastern United States during the Nineteenth Century," *Revue Internationale d'Histoire de la Banque* 4 (1971): 425–48.

66. Jonathan Worth to Sackett, Belcher & Co., May 7, 1853 (first, second, third, and fourth quotations), and Jonathan Worth to G. A. Worth, May 7, 1853 (fifth quotation), both in Jonathan Worth Papers, PC 49.2, North Carolina State Archives, Raleigh. Worth's biographer confirms that Worth invested in the copper mines as part of a larger entrepreneurial pattern. See Richard L. Zuber, *Jonathan Worth: A Biography of a Southern Unionist* (Chapel Hill: University of North Carolina Press, 1965), 88–89.

67. See deed from the Worths and Worth, Earley & Company to John G. Stuart, president of the Meigs County and Virginia Mining Company, dated March 24, 1854, Deed Book 4, p. 350, Carroll County Clerk's Office.

68. Abraham Jobe, *A Mountaineer in Motion: The Memoir of Dr. Abraham Jobe, 1817–1906,* ed. David C. Hsiung (Knoxville: University of Tennessee Press, 2009), 50.

69. "Virginia Copper and Iron," *American Railway Times* (Boston), June 15, 1854, p. [2], reprinting a letter written from Hillsville, Virginia, and printed in the *Dahlonega (Ga.) Mountain Signal.*

70. On the investors' and agents' names and hometowns and the terms of the lease agreements, see the dozens of agreements in Deed Book 4, Carroll County Clerk's Office. On John Rhea and George Bachman, see in particular Deed Book 4, pp. 448–50, Carroll County Clerk's Office. On John Yarnell (d. 1870) and Thomas Roddy (1828–1889), see Robert Partin, "T. H. Roddy: A Nineteenth Century Physician of Old James County, Tennessee," *Tennessee Historical Quarterly* 11 (September 1952): 195–211.

71. Jobe, *Mountaineer in Motion,* 50.

72. See the correspondence in the Blair-Howard Papers.

73. Noe, *Southwest Virginia's Railroad,* 62; Kegley, *Wythe County, Virginia,* 340; [Kohler], "Description, History, and Recollections of the Lead Mines," 26.

74. Currey, *Geological Visit to the Virginia Copper Region,* 51–52; Deed Book 4, Carroll County Clerk's Office. McCamant claimed to have first tried to dig copper at the Peach Bottom Mine in October 1832, using hands from the Wythe lead mines, but to have abandoned the effort as uneconomical until the 1850s boom. On James Kincannon as a physician, see *Thomson's Mercantile and Professional Directory . . . for 1851–52,* p. 179, though his name is misspelled there.

75. See "*Stuart v. Hale and Others,*" *Quarterly Law Journal* 3 (January 1858): 34–42; *Lamar's Ex'or v. Hale and als.,* 79 Va. 147 (1884); company minutes dated

April 14, 1854, in Lillard Family Papers, Tennessee State Library and Archives, Nashville, microfilm, reel 1; "V. K. Stevenson, of Tennessee," *De Bow's Review* 12 [new ser., 5] (February 1852): 212–13; Stewart Lillard, *Meigs County, Tennessee: A Documented Account of Its European Settlement and Growth,* new ed. (Cleveland, Tenn.: Book Shelf, 1982), 191. Fielden Hale, whose first name was misspelled "Fielding" in some documents, was at various times a merchant, land speculator, justice of the peace, county clerk, Carroll County's delegate to the secession convention, and Confederate officer. See Nuckolls, *Pioneer Settlers of Grayson County,* 118–23. The 1860 census lists him as owning $30,000 in real estate and $20,000 in personal estate. The manuscript census data were retrieved from the Heritage-Quest Online digitized database. On Gazaway Bugg Lamar's entrepreneurialism, see Edwin B. Coddington, "The Activities and Attitudes of a Confederate Business Man: Gazaway B. Lamar," *Journal of Southern History* 9 (February 1943): 3–36. On Vernon K. Stevenson, see also the obituary "Vernon K. Stevenson," *New York Times,* October 18, 1884, 5. For land transactions confirming that Aaron Brown and Stevenson made joint investments of their own, see the agreement dated May 9, 1854, and a deed dated May 15, 1854, both in Deed Book 4, pp. 108, 118–20, Carroll County Clerk's Office.

76. See deed from the Worths and Worth, Earley & Company to John G. Stuart, president of the Meigs County and Virginia Mining Company, dated March 24, 1854, Deed Book 4, p. 350, Carroll County Clerk's Office.

77. "Copper in South-Western Virginia," reprinted from the *Hillsville Virginian* in *Mining Magazine* 4 (March 1855): 192–93 (quotations on 193). The Paint Bank operation is linked to George Stuart and Company in "South Western Virginia," *Richmond Daily Dispatch,* June 22, 1855, 1. Locals likely treated work at the mines as a supplement to farming activity. But the local farmers did not always appreciate the influx of laborers, as when a group of Carroll County sheepherders petitioned the legislature in 1858 for the right to destroy copper miners' dogs running at large and endangering the livestock. Link, *Roots of Secession,* 151.

78. Noe, *Southwest Virginia's Railroad,* 73.

79. The story ran on page 1 of the supplement section of *Mining Journal, Railway, and Commercial Gazette* on November 22, 1856, under the title "The Mines and Minerals of America.—No. VII. Virginia: Carrol [*sic*] County."

80. Paul Lucier, "Commercial Interests and Scientific Disinterestedness: Consulting Geologists in Antebellum America," *Isis* 86 (June 1995): 245–67. On geological work in the South in this period, see the various essays in James X. Corgan, ed., *The Geological Sciences in the Antebellum South* (University: University of Alabama Press, 1982). For comparison, see the accounts of the geological investigations leading to copper production's beginning in the mid-1840s in the rich Lake Superior region: David J. Krause, "Testing a Tradition: Douglass Houghton and the Native Copper of Lake Superior," *Isis* 80 (December 1989): 622–39; and David

J. Krause, "Henry Rowe Schoolcraft and the Native Copper of the Keweenaw," *Earth Sciences History* 8, no. 1 (1989): 4–13.

81. Richard Veit, "Mastodons, Mound Builders, and Montroville Wilson Dickeson—Pioneering American Archaeologist," *Expedition* 41, no. 3 (1999): 20–31; Richard Veit, "A Case of Archaeological Amnesia: A Contextual Biography of Montroville Wilson Dickeson (1810–1882), Early American Archaeologist," *Archaeology of Eastern North America* 25 (Fall 1997): 97–123; Montroville W. Dickeson, *Report of a Geological Survey and Examination upon the Lands Owned by the Dickeson Marble and Zinc Mining and Manufacturing Company of Tennessee* (Philadelphia: J. Hufty, 1856). The reports from Carroll County include Montroville W. Dickeson, *Report of a Geological Survey and Examination upon the Lands Owned by the Dalton Mining Company of Virginia* (Philadelphia: Sickels Steam-Power Book and Fancy Job Printer, 1857); Montroville W. Dickeson, *Report of a Geological Survey and Examination upon the Lands Owned by the Tennessee and Virginia Mining Company, of Virginia: Including the Mines Known as the Cranberry, Wild Cat, and Ann Phipps, in Carroll County, Virginia* (Knoxville, Tenn.: John B. G. Kinsloe, 1856); and Montroville W. Dickeson, *Report of a Geological Survey and Examination of the Lands Owned by the Megs County and Virginia Mining Co. of Virginia, Including the Mines Known as the Betty Baker, Anna Mary, Mowlin, Weddle, and Toncrey, in Carroll and Floyd Counties, Virginia* (Philadelphia: Sickels, 1857). Note that the title page of the latter book misspells Tennessee's "Meigs" County as "Megs" County. The report on the properties owned by the Tennessee and Virginia Mining Company was also published in *Mining Magazine* 9 (1857): 226–35. One can find more on that company in *Lamar's Ex'or v. Hale and als.,* 79 Va. 147 (1884), and in company minutes dated April 14, 1854, in Lillard Family Papers, microfilm, reel 1.

82. Young, "Origins of the American Copper Industry," 133–34; Dickeson, *Report of a Geological Survey and Examination upon the Lands Owned by the Tennessee and Virginia Mining Company,* 17; *Exposition of the Baltimore and Cuba Smelting & Mining Company. . . .* (Baltimore: Robert Neilson, 1845). For a detailed description of how the first furnace in Baltimore worked, see "Baltimore and Cuba Copper Smelting Furnace," *Scientific American* 2 (October 31, 1846): 48.

83. "Product of Copper in South Western Virginia," *Mining Magazine* 5 (July 1855): 82. The mining firms listed in this tabulation include John G. Stewart [Stuart] and Company, Meigs' Copper Mining Company, Cranberry Mining Company, Pierce and Company, Dalton Copper Mining Company, Wild Cat Mining Company, Ann Phipps' Mining Company, and Fairmount [Fairmont] Copper Mining Company. On Dickeson's arrival, see Dickeson, *Report of a Geological Survey and Examination upon the Lands Owned by the Dalton Mining Company,* 3.

84. "An Act Incorporating the Dalton Copper Mining Company in the County of Carroll," in *Acts of the General Assembly of Virginia, Passed in 1855–6,*

265–66. For more on the Dalton Copper Mining Company, see the decision in *Kyle v. Early and Others* in *Quarterly Law Journal* 4 (January 1859): 36–44.

85. Dickeson, *Report of a Geological Survey and Examination upon the Lands Owned by the Dalton Mining Company,* 7 (first quotation), 8 (second quotation), 10 (third and fourth quotations). Dickeson uses the spelling "McCammut" for "McCamant" and "Pierce" instead of the proper "Peirce."

86. Dickeson, *Report of a Geological Survey and Examination upon the Lands Owned by the Tennessee and Virginia Mining Company,* 9 (first quotation), 10 (second quotation), 12 (third quotation). Dickeson uses "Earley" instead of the more common spelling "Early." For additional details on the development of the Tennessee and Virginia Mining Company's early operations in the county, see "Copper in Carroll County, Virginia," *Mining Magazine* 5 (October 1855): 338–39. Also see E. P. C. to the editor, April 28, 1856, *Mining Magazine* 5 (May–June 1856): 463. George Bachman's link to the Cranberry Mine appears in "South Western Virginia," *Richmond Daily Dispatch,* June 22, 1855, 1. Other investors in the Tennessee and Virginia Company included Tennesseans A. A. Kyle (a Hawkins County attorney and later a Unionist) and Orville Rice (a Connecticut native, Hawkins County merchant, and marble quarry owner). See *Rice & Kyle vs. Shockley & Wife,* decided in the July term, 1860, by the Virginia Supreme Court of Appeals, in *Quarterly Law Review* 1 (December 1860): 356–61. According to a later report, Rice lost a fortune via his copper investments: "The care and the foresight he had exercised in younger days were not brought into requisition. Without discretion or discrimination, and knowing nothing of their value, he invested in lands said to contain rich copper ore. When his own capital was exhausted he availed himself of the unlimited credit he could always command. Not to stay the hand of oncoming misfortune, he generously indorsed the notes of friends who were buying as unwisely as himself. Eventually, with failure to sell lands or to secure returns, and with creditors clamoring for money lent, and with the approach of the civil war, he was threatened with destitute circumstances. Fortune was swept away, lands were sold, and home was taken from him. . . . The death knell of the Confederacy sounded but a few years before his own." See George F. Mellen, "The Story of 'Marble Hall,'" *Knoxville Sentinel,* February 16, 1907, 13.

87. W. J. March, "A Sketch of the Mines and Copper Region of South-Western Virginia," *Mining Magazine* 9 (September 1857): 217–20 (quotation on 219). According to the U.S. census, each laborer cost the companies from $18 to $20 per month. Eighth Census of the United States, 1860: Industry, Nonpopulation Census Schedules for Virginia, reel 8.

88. Currey, *Geological Visit to the Virginia Copper Region,* 30. On Richard Currey's background and career, see James X. Corgan, "Richard Owen Currey, a Little Known Intellectual Figure of Antebellum Tennessee," *East Tennessee Historical Society's Publications,* no. 50 (1978): 58–68; and James X. Corgan, "Early American Geological Surveys and Gerard Troost's Field Assistants, 1831–1836," in

Corgan, ed., *Geological Sciences in the Antebellum South,* 39–72, esp. 57–60. For more on Gerard Troost, a native of the Netherlands who came to Tennessee via Philadelphia, see Corgan's entry on him in *The Tennessee Encyclopedia of History and Culture,* available at http://tennesseeencyclopedia.net.

89. Currey, *Geological Visit to the Virginia Copper Region,* 29.

90. Ibid., 42 (first quotation), 41 (second quotation).

91. Dickeson, *Report of a Geological Survey and Examination of the Lands Owned by the Megs County and Virginia Mining Co. of Virginia,* 8–9.

92. Currey, *Geological Visit to the Virginia Copper Region,* 39 (quotation), 52. For the terms of the Baltimore and Cuba Smelting Company's land purchase, including the option to buy additional acreage if needed, see the deed dated March 19, 1859, in Deed Book 7, pp. 64–65, Carroll County Clerk's Office.

93. "Alfred Monnier's Process for the Metallurgical Treatment of Sulphuretted Ores," in Julius Silversmith, *A Practical Hand-Book for Miners, Metallurgists, and Assayers. . . . ,* 4th ed. (New York: American Mining Index, 1867), 191; "American Patents," *Journal of the Franklin Institute,* 3rd ser., 35 (January 1858): 49.

3. Wheels and Rails in the New America

1. Andrew M. Schocket, *Founding Corporate Power in Early National Philadelphia* (DeKalb: Northern Illinois University Press, 2007).

2. G. W. Featherstonhaugh, *Excursion Through the Slave States, from Washington on the Potomac to the Frontier of Mexico; with Sketches of Popular Manners and Geological Notices,* 2 vols. (London: John Murray, 1844), 1:119–20, emphasis in original.

3. Quaker Joshua Evans traveled from Tennessee to Wythe County and Grayson County in April 1797. He saw slaves being hauled westward by acquisitive white people: "In travelling along, we saw and met very many people, men, women and children, going towards new settlements. My mind was closely exercised with concern on account of such great numbers, with many slaves in a suffering condition, going to settle on lands lately obtained by force, or against the will of the Indians and native owners. My sympathy was excited towards the poor innocent children thus exposed to hardships, and perhaps going to be brought up in ignorance, and accustomed to cruelty. My concern was increased, on beholding brethren and fellow professors too incautious in respect to such hasty removals to settle on lands thus unrighteously taken from the natives." Evans, *Journal of the Life, Travels, Religious Exercises, and Labours in the Work of the Ministry, of Joshua Evans,* 160. The Quakers in this area largely migrated to Ohio and Indiana in the early nineteenth century. Owen Bowman, *Carroll County, Virginia: The Early Days to 1920* (Virginia Beach, Va.: Donning, 1993), 17–18.

4. See the 1828–1832 Account Book, Graham Family Papers, reel 3, frame 154 (first quotation), frame 157 (second and third quotations).

5. For numbers of slaves, see 1830–1831 Slave Book (Furnace), Graham Fam-

ily Papers, reel 3, frames 273, 282. For David Graham's purchase of a slave on February 14, 1857, see the contract in Graham Family Papers, reel 4, frame 184. In 1857, he was clearly still relying heavily on hired slaves. See his summary of hired slaves' work for the year on December 24, 1857, in Graham Family Papers, reel 4, frame 194.

6. For the hiring of what were probably skilled white forgemen, see Graham's contracts with Edward R. Campbell (September 1829) and with Henry Willis and Jasper Albright (July 1830), in 1828–1832 Account Book, Graham Family Papers, reel 3, frames 167, 176. For the March 1847 ledger, see Graham Family Papers, reel 14, frame 74.

7. For ledger entries regarding the black worker named Trial, see Graham Family Papers, reel 14, frames 247, 277; on Albert, see ledger entries in Graham Family Papers, reel 14, frames 187, 223. On the broader phenomenon of paying skilled slaves for extra work, see Lewis, *Coal, Iron, and Slaves,* esp. 124, and Dew, *Bond of Iron.*

8. See the 1830–1831 Slave Book (Furnace), Graham Family Papers, reel 3, frames 277, 281 (quotations).

9. Quoted in Starobin, *Industrial Slavery in the Old South,* 110, 262 n. 72.

10. For example, in Charles Whitlock to David Graham, May 25, 1847, Graham Family Papers, reel 4, frame 18, Whitlock discusses the hiring of a slave in Surry County, North Carolina. Graham also naturally had to provide for the medical care of his hired and owned slaves. For example, see a summary of charges between 1847 and 1859 in his account book in Graham Family Papers, reel 4, frame 52.

11. David Graham to J. T. L. Preston, November 26, 1858, Graham Family Papers, reel 4, frame 197. On the place of skilled white workers in the antebellum southern social order, see Gillespie, *Free Labor in an Unfree World.* One example of white workers causing trouble is the reported drunken killing of Henry Tutor by Cornelius Worrell in 1854. Both men worked for Graham. "Stop the Murderer," *Richmond Daily Dispatch,* June 27, 1854, 3.

12. On the 1850s in general, see Link, *Roots of Secession.*

13. In 1850, Grayson County had 499 slaves and 36 free colored residents in a total population of 6,677. Census data retrieved from the Historical Census Browser, University of Virginia, Geospatial and Statistical Data Center, at http://fisher.lib.virginia.edu/collections/stats/histcensus/.

14. *Bacon v. the Commonwealth,* 48 Va. 602 (1850), at 603 (quotation); Clement Eaton, *The Freedom-of-Thought Struggle in the Old South,* rev. ed. (New York: Harper & Row, 1964), 133–35; "Rev. J. C. Bacon—John Cornett—False Statement Corrected" [a letter from J. McBride to the editor, May 21, 1852], in *Washington National Era,* June 10, 1852, digital version available at http://www.accessible.com; "Loaning Douglass's Narrative High Felony," *Rochester North*

Star, June 29, 1849, 2. Jarvis Bacon also was charged with and admitted to distributing Frederick Douglass's published narrative and a pamphlet of an antislavery sermon preached in Cincinnati by Edward Smith. The Grayson County jury acquitted him of those charges, however, most likely because he was sharing them with a white person without the necessary intent to incite slave resistance or insurrection. See Grayson County Order Book, 1844–1854, Grayson County Records, Library of Virginia, microfilm reel 15, pp. 355–56 (April 23, 1849), 361–63 (May 29, 1849); and "Rev. Jarvis C. Bacon," *Rochester North Star,* November 9, 1849, 2. Bacon's church had been founded shortly before his arrival with the assistance of fellow Wesleyan Methodist Adam Crooks, who was active in Guilford and Forsyth counties, North Carolina, where he faced his own legal and extralegal harassment. See Roy S. Nicholson, *Wesleyan Methodism in the South: Being the Story of Eighty-Six Years of Reform and Religious Activities in the South as Conducted by the American Wesleyans* (Syracuse, N.Y.: Wesleyan Methodist Publishing House, 1933), chaps. 4–5. On the beliefs and demographics of Wesleyan Methodists, see Chris Padgett, "Hearing the Antislavery Rank-and-File: The Wesleyan Methodist Schism of 1843," *Journal of the Early Republic* 12 (Spring 1992): 63–84. Adam Crooks reported on Bacon's trial in some detail in "Loaning Douglass's Narrative High Felony," *Rochester North Star,* June 29, 1849, 2.

15. Grayson County Order Book, 1844–1854, pp. 581–84 (September 23, 1851) (first quotation on 582; second quotation on 583); "The Grayson County (Va.) Excitement," *Baltimore Sun,* October 6, 1851, [1] (third and fourth quotations); "Fugitive Slaves in Virginia," *Baltimore Sun,* September 19, 1851, [4]; "Executions in Virginia," *Baltimore Sun,* November 27, 1851, [4]; Nuckolls, *Pioneer Settlers of Grayson County,* 12–15; *The Fugitive Slave Bill, and Its Effects,* pp. 14–15 (pamphlet labeled Leeds Anti-Slavery Series, No. 32), in [Wilson Armistead, comp.], *Five Hundred Thousand Strokes for Freedom: A Series of Anti-Slavery Tracts, of Which Half a Million Are Now First Issued by the Friends of the Negro* (London: W. & F. Cash, 1853). Martin Crawford makes brief mention of this incident in *Ashe County's Civil War: Community and Society in the Antebellum South* (Charlottesville: University Press of Virginia, 2001), 64.

16. *Salem People's Press,* October 4, 1851, as quoted in Clement Eaton, "Mob Violence in the Old South," *Mississippi Valley Historical Review* 29 (December 1942): 351–70 (quotation on 364). For more on this incident, see also Harriet Beecher Stowe, *A Key to Uncle Tom's Cabin; Presenting the Original Facts and Documents upon Which the Story Is Founded. . . .* (Boston: John P. Jewett, 1853), 189–90; "Lynch Law," *Washington National Era,* October 2, 1851, available at http://www.accessible.com; "Deal with Them 'above the Law,'" *Washington National Era,* October 16, 1851, available at http://www.accessible.com; "Whipping an Abolitionist," *Columbus Daily Ohio Statesman,* September 27, 1851, [2].

17. See Christopher Waldrep, *The Many Faces of Judge Lynch: Extralegal Vio-*

lence and Punishment in America (New York: Palgrave Macmillan, 2002), chaps. 2–3.

18. "The Grayson County (Va.) Meeting," *Philadelphia Pennsylvania Freeman,* June 3, 1852, [89] (quotations); "The Seat of Justice Dishonored," *Boston Liberator,* July 23, 1852, 118; "A Court Broken Up by a Mob," *Washington National Era,* May 13, 1852, available at http://www.accessible.com; Grayson County Order Book, 1844–1854, p. 662 (June 28, 1852). John Cornutt's name is spelled "Cornett" and "Cornut" in some reports. On William H. Cook, see "Report of the Directors of the Tazewell Courthouse and Fancy Gap Turnpike Company," October 4, 1849, Tazewell Courthouse and Fancy Gap Turnpike Records; and William H. Cook, John Early, and Ira B. Coltrane to the Virginia Board of Public Works, October 21, 1848, in Fancy Gap Turnpike, 1848, Records of the Virginia Board of Public Works. The legacy of dissent did not fade away in Grayson County. The county and surrounding counties maintained a vigorous two-party political system into the twentieth century. For a close look at its functioning in the early twentieth century, see the hundreds of pages of testimony in *Contested Election Case of John M. Parsons vs. Edward W. Saunders from the Fifth Congressional District of Virginia* (Washington, D.C.: Government Printing Office, 1909). A copy of this rare document can be found in the Committee on Elections Committee Papers, 61st Cong., Box 589, HR 61A-F10.1, Records of the House of Representatives, Record Group 233, National Archives, Washington, D.C. Cook and McCamant undoubtedly often encountered each other at the bar. For instance, they were on opposing sides of a case in the Carroll County Circuit Court in August 1857 that settled a dispute among the partners of the Meigs County and Virginia Mining Company. Company president John G. Stuart sued superintendent Fielden L. Hale and others. See *"Stuart v. Hale and Others."* In his rise to prominence, McCamant had served as court clerk from 1833 to 1835. See F. Johnston, comp., *Memorials of Old Virginia Clerks, Arranged Alphabetically by Counties.* . . . (Lynchburg, Va.: J. P. Bell, 1888), 192.

19. *Journal of the House of Delegates of the State of Virginia, for the Extra Session, 1861* (Richmond, Va.: William F. Ritchie, 1861), 122, 149, 215, 264, 265, 293; "An Act to Incorporate the Carroll Mining and Manufacturing Company. Passed April 2, 1861," in *Acts of the General Assembly of the State of Virginia, Passed in 1861, in the Eighty-Fifth Year of the Commonwealth* (Richmond, Va.: William F. Ritchie, 1861), 307–9. In addition to Johns Hopkins, the incorporators of the Carroll Mining and Manufacturing Company included J. Hanson Thomas (a banker and southern sympathizer), William Crichton, Adam Denmead, and Henry R. Wilson. See "An Act to Incorporate the Carroll Mining and Manufacturing Company," 307. McCamant was in the Virginia House of Delegates in 1832–1833, 1859–1860, 1861 (January), 1861–1862, 1862 (April and September), and 1863 (January). Swem and Williams, *Register of the General Assembly of Virginia,* 281.

20. William H. Gaines Jr., *Biographical Register of Members: Virginia State Convention of 1861, First Session* (Richmond: Virginia State Library, 1969), 40, 50–51, 83.

21. See Noe, *Southwest Virginia's Railroad.*

22. Michael A. Morrison, "'New Territory versus No Territory': The Whig Party and the Politics of Western Expansion, 1846–1848," *Western Historical Quarterly* 23 (February 1992): 25–51 (quotation on 51).

23. See "Slavery in Virginia—Rev. J. C. Bacon," *New York Evangelist,* July 19, 1849, 116, which is a reprint of an article from the *Boston Mail;* and "Loaning Douglass's Narrative High Felony," *Rochester North Star,* June 29, 1849, 2.

24. George H. Reese, ed., *Proceedings of the Virginia State Convention of 1861, February 13–May 1,* 4 vols. (Richmond: Virginia State Library, 1965), 1:657–58.

25. Ibid., 1:697–99 and 2:569–71.

26. Ingles, ed., *Journal of Bettie Ann Graham,* 64. The candid young Bettie Ann Graham (1845–1921) also recorded dissension within the family. On May 5, 1861, she wrote, "I pray that none I love may ever know the pangs inflicted by a drunken father & an insane mother" (58).

27. Ralph W. Donnelly, "Confederate Copper," *Civil War History* 1 (December 1955): 355–70; Willard, "Pioneer Geologic Investigation in Pennsylvania," 252; T. Sterry Hunt, "On the Copper Deposits of the Blue Ridge," *Engineering and Mining Journal,* 3rd ser., 16 (August 12, 1873): 106–7 (quotation on 106). On March's Civil War service, see John Perry Alderman, *29th Virginia Infantry* (Lynchburg, Va.: H. E. Howard, 1989), 9, 28, 118.

28. J. R. H[amilton], "Notes from Lower Virginia," *New York Times,* June 9, 1867, 1. In 1870, another traveler concurred that the copper mines "from the depression and demoralization of the war are now unworked." The journalist noted, "Here is a good opportunity for the investment of Northern capital. All through this section the great want is capital, and next to that, enterprise. Good lands and timbers, and inexhaustible mines, all undeveloped." See "Through Virginia," *Port Jervis (N.Y.) Evening Gazette,* November 24, 1870, 1.

29. Kegley, *Wythe County, Virginia,* 356; Robert C. Whisonant, "Geology and History of the Civil War Iron Industry in the New River–Cripple Creek District of Southwestern Virginia," *Virginia Minerals* 44 (November 1998): 25–35. For the ledger entries recording sales to Joseph R. Anderson and Company in Richmond, see Graham Family Papers, reel 16, frames 35, 51, 63.

30. Charles B. Dew, *Ironmaker to the Confederacy: Joseph R. Anderson and the Tredegar Iron Works* (New Haven, Conn.: Yale University Press, 1966), 78, 100–102, 133–36. The quotations are from Anderson & Co. to Graham & Son, November 14, 22, 1861, as quoted in Dew, *Ironmaker to the Confederacy,* 135. Graham's production stopped for a time in August 1861 because "his wheel house has been burned" (134).

31. John Kelly Ross Jr., "Lady Polk Cannon," in John E. Kleber, ed., *The Kentucky Encyclopedia* (Lexington: University Press of Kentucky, 1992), 528; Leonidas Polk to Frances Polk, November 12, 1861, in William M. Polk, *Leonidas Polk: Bishop and General,* 2 vols. (London: Longmans, Green, 1893), 2:44 (quotations).

32. See a receipt for horseshoes and nails dated April 10, 1862, Graham Family Papers, reel 4, frame 260. For wartime sales to the railroad, see ledger entries in Graham Family Papers, reel 16, frames 43, 71. On the sale of salt kettles, see ledger entries in Graham Family Papers, reel 16, frames 64, 67, 75.

33. I. M. St. John to David Graham, December 8, 1863, Graham Family Papers, reel 4, frame 291; Kegley, *Wythe County, Virginia,* 356. For more on the Confederacy's struggle to keep labor in place in the iron industry, see Anne Kelly Knowles, "Labor, Race, and Technology in the Confederate Iron Industry," *Technology and Culture* 42 (January 2001): 1–26.

34. "The Lead and Copper Mines of Wythe," *Richmond Daily Dispatch,* July 10, 1861, 2.

35. Robert C. Whisonant, "Geology and the Civil War in Southwestern Virginia: The Wythe County Lead Mines," *Virginia Minerals* 42 (May 1996): 13–19 (Ordnance Department quoted on 18); Ralph W. Donnelly, "The Confederate Lead Mines of Wythe County, Va.," *Civil War History* 5 (December 1959): 402–14. I consulted the census data on the HeritageQuest Online census database: 1860 Virginia, Series M653, Roll 1397, p. 515. For Graham's 1850 slaveholdings, see Carl Wilson Musser, "Economic and Social Aspects of Negro Slavery in Wythe County, Virginia, 1790–1861," M.A. thesis, George Washington University, 1958, 34. In 1866, an article claimed, "The lead works of Wythe County alone supplied the demands of the whole rebel Confederacy during the latter part of the war." "Affairs in the South," *New York Times,* June 2, 1866, 1.

36. *Journal of the House of Delegates of the State of Virginia, for the Session of 1861–62* (Richmond, Va.: William F. Ritchie, 1861), 32 (quotation), 34, 40, 351, 355.

37. See the New River Navigation Company Records, Records of the Virginia Board of Public Works. Also see *Acts of the General Assembly of the State of Virginia, Passed at Adjourned Session, 1863, in the Eighty-Seventh Year of the Commonwealth* (Richmond, Va.: William F. Ritchie, 1863), 37. At the time of the state takeover, Edwin G. Booth of Nottoway headed the company, leaving unclear whether this business grew from the identically named one incorporating David Graham and others in 1856.

38. John T. Anderson et al. to Jefferson Davis, January 20, 1864, in *The War of the Rebellion: A Compilation of the Official Records of the Union and Confederate Armies,* ser. 1, vol. 33 (Washington, D.C.: Government Printing Office, 1891), 1106–7 (first and second quotations); Captain H. C. Graham to Major J. Stoddard Johnston, December 18, 1864, in *The War of the Rebellion: A Compilation of the*

Official Records of the Union and Confederate Armies, ser. 1, vol. 45, part 1 (Washington, D.C.: Government Printing Office, 1894), 831 (third quotation); "The War News," *Daily Richmond Examiner,* December 27, 1864, 2 (fourth and fifth quotations); Whisonant, "Geology and the Civil War in Southwestern Virginia"; Donnelly, "Confederate Lead Mines of Wythe County." Though born in eastern Tennessee, John C. Vaughn had family ties to Grayson County, Virginia. See Larry Gordon, *The Last Confederate General: John C. Vaughn and His East Tennessee Cavalry* (Minneapolis: Zenith Press, 2009), 8.

39. David Graham to Ephraim McGavock, September 1, 1865, Folder 2, McGavock Papers.

40. Hunt, "On the Copper Deposits of the Blue Ridge," 106–7 (quotations on 106).

41. A. Eilers, "Notes from Southwestern Virginia," *Engineering and Mining Journal,* 3rd ser., 8 (December 7, 1869), 355–56. On Fielden Hale's Civil War wounding, see "A Fight with Deserters," *Abingdon Virginian,* June 19, 1863, [2]. On his Civil War service with the Twenty-Ninth Virginia Infantry as a captain during the first year of the war, see Alderman, *29th Virginia Infantry,* 3, 108. For a photograph of Hale, see Alderman, *29th Virginia Infantry,* 68. For more on his land speculation, see Nuckolls, *Pioneer Settlers of Grayson County,* 120–21. For his service in the 1861 convention, see Swem and Williams, *Register of the General Assembly of Virginia,* 266. Though the southwestern Virginia counties supported secession, it seems possible that Carroll County developed a strong anti-Confederate or Unionist contingent during the war because during Reconstruction newspapers reported five hundred supporters of the pro-Union Red Strings movement parading through Hillsville in support of Republican policies. See "Rebel Recruits for Thad Stevens," *Hartford (Conn.) Weekly Times,* February 16, 1867, 3. For context, see Kenneth W. Noe, "Red String Scare: Civil War Southwest Virginia and the Heroes of America," *North Carolina Historical Review* 59 (July 1992): 301–22; and Rand Dotson, "'The Grave and Scandalous Evil Infected to Your People': The Erosion of Confederate Loyalty in Floyd County, Virginia," *Virginia Magazine of History and Biography* 108, no. 4 (2000): 393–434.

42. On Hale's transaction with Loring P. Hawes, John Howard, Benjamin Gallup, and William Ray, see "Hale Mining Co. Agreement," in Deed Book 8, pp. 440–41, Carroll County Clerk's Office. Hawes, Howard, and Ray signed the document in New York, and Gallup signed locally. Hale moved from Alabama back to Carroll County in 1868 but left Virginia for Volusia County, Florida, in 1884, where he resumed work as a merchant. See *Northern Alabama: Historical and Biographical* (Birmingham, Ala.: Smith and De Land, 1888), 131.

43. Whitelaw Reid, *After the War: A Southern Tour, May 1, 1865, to May 1, 1866* (Cincinnati: Moore, Wilstach & Baldwin, 1866), 340.

44. Eilers, "Notes from Southwestern Virginia" (December 7, 1869), 355–56.

Anton Eilers died in April 1917 at age seventy-eight according to his obituary. "Frederic Anton Eilers," *New York Times,* April 24, 1917, 11. Also see a pamphlet commemorating Eilers after his death: *F. Anton Eilers, 1839–1917* ([New York?]: n.p., 1917). For the detailed Adelberg & Raymond investigation, see the manuscript "Report on the Property Known as the Hale Copper Mine, Carroll Co., Va.," in Geological Reports, 1846–1869, Mss. 835, Small Special Collections Library, University of Virginia, Charlottesville.

45. Eilers, "Notes from Southwestern Virginia" (December 7, 1869), 355–56.

46. A. Eilers, "Notes from Southwestern Virginia," *Engineering and Mining Journal,* 3rd ser., 8 (December 14, 1869), 376.

47. Rossiter W. Raymond, "Anton Eilers," *Engineering and Mining Journal* 103 (April 28, 1917): 762–64.

48. Deed from Ira B. Coltrane, Garland Hale, and Fielden L. Hale to James E. Clayton, October 31, 1871, and deed from John Early to James E. Clayton, Deed Book 10, pp. 486–87 and 488–89 (quotation), Carroll County Clerk's Office. On Coltrane's legislative service, see Swem and Williams, *Register of the General Assembly of Virginia,* 266.

49. Hunt, "On the Copper Deposits of the Blue Ridge," 106–7 (quotation on 106). In 1873, James E. Clayton and his brother Samuel S. Clayton also restarted copper production at the antebellum Ore Knob Mine in nearby Ashe County, North Carolina. See T. Sterry Hunt, "The Ore Knob Copper Mine and Some Related Deposits," *Transactions of the American Institute of Mining Engineers* 2 (May 1873–February 1874): 123–31; Eben E. Olcott, "The Ore Knob Copper Mine and Reduction Works, Ashe County, N.C.," *Transactions of the American Institute of Mining Engineers* 3 (May 1874–February 1875): 391–99; Eben E. Olcott, "The Ore Knob Copper Mine and Reduction Works, Ashe County, N.C.," *Engineering and Mining Journal,* 3rd ser., 20 (September 11, 1875): 260–61; James Douglas Jr., "Copper Mining in the Past, and Its Prospects in the Future," *Engineering and Mining Journal,* 3rd ser., 16 (August 26, 1873): 131–32; T. Sterry Hunt, "Ore Knob Mine," *Engineering and Mining Journal,* 3rd ser., 18 (August 1, 1874): 69–70; and C. R. Boyd, *Resources of South-West Virginia: Showing the Mineral Deposits of Iron, Coal, Zinc, Copper and Lead,* 3rd ed. (New York: John Wiley and Sons, 1881), 313–15. In 1875, James Clayton was supervising the works. He reported to a visiting government engineer that the copper produced had to be hauled by wagon forty-four miles to the Marion, Virginia, depot on the Atlantic, Mississippi, and Ohio Railroad. See "Examination of New River, from the Lead Mines in Wythe County, to the 'Mouth of Wilson,' in Grayson County Virginia," in U.S. House of Representatives, *Report of the Secretary of War; Being Part of the Messages and Documents Communicated to the Two Houses of Congress at the Beginning of the First Session of the Forty-Fourth Congress,* vol. 2, part 2, Executive Documents, 44th Cong., 1st sess., No. 1, Part 2 (Washington, D.C.: Government

Printing Office, 1875), 133–39, esp. 136. The mines closed in the 1880s but re-opened in the 1930s and then closed again at the end of 1962. Arthur L. Fletcher, *Ashe County: A History* (Jefferson, N.C.: Ashe County Research Association, 1963), 223–27. For another, less successful late-nineteenth-century copper mine in Ashe County, see Susan Sokol Blosser, "Calvin J. Cowles's Gap Creek Mine: A Case Study of Mine Speculation in the Gilded Age," *North Carolina Historical Review* 51 (October 1974): 379–400. Tailings and runoff from the Ore Knob mine caused extensive environmental damage that is still problematic. See Linda Burchette, "Ore Knob Dam Draws EPA Attention," *Jefferson (N.C.) Post,* November 18, 2008, A1, A5.

50. On the Claytons' various land deals in the 1870s and early 1880s, see the deed from Samuel S. Clayton and others to New York and Virginia Mineral Company, July 29, 1889, Deed Book 18, pp. 484–85, Carroll County Clerk's Office. The Claytons joined James A. Walker, Albert Fairfax, John S. Draper, and William F. Hart in winning incorporation of the Virginia Mineral Railway Company to run through Pulaski, Wythe, Carroll, and Grayson counties "for the purpose of mining, transporting and manufacturing iron and other ores and minerals." See "An Act to Incorporate the Virginia Mineral Railway Company," March 6, 1880, in *Acts and Joint Resolutions Passed by the General Assembly of the State of Virginia during the Session of 1879–80* (Richmond, Va.: R. F. Walker, 1880), 206–7 (quotation on 206).

51. Frederick Genth's report and information on the company's formation are found in *Wistar Copper Mining Company: Incorporated under the General Laws of the State of Virginia* (Williamsport, Pa.: Gazette and Bulletin Printing House, 1876). Also see Boyd, *Resources of South-West Virginia,* 274, 279–84. Genth's full German name was "Friedrich August Ludwig Karl Wilhelm Genth." He had studied at the University of Giessen under the pioneering chemist Justus von Liebig, among others, and later worked at a mine in Davidson County, North Carolina, and assisted J. Peter Lesley in the 1870s on the second geological survey in Pennsylvania. On Genth, see George F. Barker, "Frederick Augustus Genth," *Proceedings of the American Philosophical Society* 40 (December 1901): x–xxii; and W. M. Myers and S. Zerfoss, *Frederick Augustus Genth, 1820–1893: Chemist—Mineralogist—Collector* (State College, Pa.: School of Mineral Industries, Pennsylvania State College, 1946). On Charles Rufus Boyd's background, see Roberts, *Annotated Geological Bibliography of Virginia,* 50–52; and Germaine M. Reed, *David French Boyd: Founder of Louisiana State University* (Baton Rouge: Louisiana State University, 1977), chap. 1. Pennock Huey, who was promoted to the rank of brevet brigadier-general by war's end, defended his Civil War record in Pennock Huey, *A True History of the Charge of Eighth Pennsylvania Cavalry at Chancellorsville* (Philadelphia: Porter and Coates, 1883).

52. See Charles Rufus Boyd's report to the Virginia and Kentucky Railroad,

circa 1891, p. 8, in Folder 67, Volume 178, Addition, Wilson and Hairston Family Papers #4134, Southern Historical Collection, Wilson Library, University of North Carolina, Chapel Hill.

53. Richard H. Schallenberg, "Evolution, Adaptation, and Survival: The Very Slow Death of the American Charcoal Iron Industry," *Annals of Science* 32 (July 1975): 341–58. Of course, the iron industry evolved slowly in different places depending on local conditions. Anne Kelly Knowles points out that "many American iron companies selectively adopted British technologies and developed hybrid methods that suited their particular region's resource endowment, transport infrastructure, capital resources, and labor supply." Anne Kelly Knowles, "Geography, Timing, and Technology: A GIS-Based Analysis of Pennsylvania's Iron Industry, 1825–1875," *Journal of Economic History* 66 (September 2006): 608–34 (quotation on 612).

54. A. Eilers, "Notes from Southwestern Virginia," *Engineering and Mining Journal,* 3rd ser., 8 (November 30, 1869): 338. On a similar note, see Frederick B. Goddard, *Where to Emigrate and Why: Homes and Fortunes in the Boundless West and the Sunny South . . . with a Complete History and Description of the Pacific Railroad* (Philadelphia: Peoples Publishing, 1869), 352–53.

55. Schallenberg, "Evolution, Adaptation, and Survival."

56. Eilers, "Notes from Southwestern Virginia" (November 30, 1869), 338.

57. Ninth Census of the United States, 1870: Industry, Nonpopulation Census Schedules for Virginia, 1850–1880, National Archives Microfilm Publication T1132, reel 15; Kegley, *Wythe County, Virginia,* 356. Records do not allow for a detailed examination of the move from slavery to the use of wage labor in the New River industries, but the black residents of Wythe County certainly remained in place and continued to contribute to the iron industry. In 1860, Wythe County encompassed 2,162 slaves and 157 free colored residents. In 1870, the census lists 2,342 colored persons in the county, so it is likely that no exodus of the black workers took place. Data retrieved March 20, 2010, from the Historical Census Browser, University of Virginia, Geospatial and Statistical Data Center, at http://fisher.lib.virginia.edu/collections/stats/histcensus/index.html.

58. Ingles, ed., *Journal of Bettie Ann Graham,* 84–85.

59. Boyd, *Resources of South-West Virginia,* 89–90. For another snapshot of production and ownership, see "The Furnaces and Mines of the Southwestern Plateau of the Valley of Virginia in 1880," *Virginias* 2 (February 1881): 29. Also see Irwin, "Last Empire Builder," 49. Charles P. McWane operated a small foundry specializing in agricultural implements such as plows along with a wagon-making shop in Wytheville in the 1870s and 1880s, but his son Henry Edward McWane found much larger success in the foundry business after moving to Lynchburg in 1887, where he turned an ailing company into a major foundry and pipe works. See Lyon G. Tyler, ed., *Men of Mark in Virginia: Ideals of American Life; a Collec-*

tion of Biographies of the Leading Men in the State, vol. 1 (Washington, D.C.: Men of Mark Publishing, 1906), 1:285–87; and Robert A. Rutland, "Men and Iron in the Making of Virginia, Part 2, 1861–1976," *Iron Worker* 40 (Autumn 1976): 2–17.

60. F. P. Dewey, "The Rich Hill Iron Ores," *Transactions of the American Institute of Mining Engineers* 10 (May 1881–February 1882): 77–80 (quotation on 77).

61. "A Series of Tables of the Several Branches of American Manufactures, Exhibiting Them by States, Territories and Districts . . . ," in Coxe, comp., *Statement of the Arts and Manufactures of the United States of America,* 10.

62. James M. Swank, comp., "Statistics of the Iron and Steel Production of the United States," in U.S. Census Office, *Report on the Manufactures of the United States at the Tenth Census. . . .* (Washington, D.C.: Government Printing Office, 1883), 25, 30–31.

63. For example, see J. D. Imboden, *The Coal and Iron Resources of Virginia: Their Extent, Commercial Value, and Early Development Considered. A Paper Read before a Meeting of Members of the Legislature and Prominent Citizens in the Capitol at Richmond, February 19th, 1872* (Richmond, Va.: Clemmitt and Jones, 1872), and M. F. Maury Jr., *The Resources of the Coal Field of the Upper Kanawha, with a Sketch of the Iron Belt of Virginia, Setting Forth Some of Their Markets and Means of Development* (Baltimore: Sherwood, 1873). The noted Pennsylvania geologist J. Peter Lesley had pointed out even earlier the proximity of the two minerals. See his untitled paper in "Stated Meeting, May 16, 1862," *Proceedings of the American Philosophical Society* 9 (May 1862): 30–38. For a description of an abortive 1882 effort by local notables and outside investors to build a major coke furnace, see Robert Enoch Withers, *Autobiography of an Octogenarian* (Roanoke, Va.: Stone Printing and Manufacturing Company Press, 1907), 420–22. And one should take note that the so-called New South support for development was not entirely new. Young elite Virginians and their supporters in the late antebellum period had vocally advocated a more diversified economy to scotch Virginia's supposed decline. See Carmichael, *The Last Generation,* esp. chaps. 2 and 8.

64. David Kirby, "Canalization of New River," *West Virginia History* 15 (April 1954): 269–91; Leland R. Johnson, *An Illustrated History of the Huntington District, U.S. Army Corps of Engineers, 1754–1974* (Washington, D.C.: Government Printing Office, 1977), 114–16; "Examination and Survey of New River from the Mouth of Greenbrier, West Virginia, to the Lead-Mines in Wythe County, Virginia," in U.S. House of Representatives, *Report of the Secretary of War, Being Part of the Message and Documents Communicated to the Two Houses of Congress at the Beginning of the First Session of the Forty-Third Congress,* vol. 2, Executive Documents, 43rd Cong., 1st sess., No. 1, Part 2 (Washington, D.C.: Government Printing Office, 1873), 842–54 (quotation on 848); *United States v. Appalachian Electric Power Co.,* 23 F. Supp. 83 (1938), at 93. A summary of the work can be found in

U.S. Senate Documents, *Dams or Reservoirs, Cheat and New Rivers, Va. and W.Va.,* 63rd Cong., 1st sess., No. 15 (Washington, D.C.: Government Printing Office, 1913), 16–20. Charles Rufus Boyd served as an assistant engineer on the survey.

65. "The Southwest Va. Blast Furnaces in 1882," *Virginias* 4 (January 1883), 5. For a similar paean, see "A Coming Industrial Center in Southwest Virginia," *Baltimore Manufacturers' Record* 10 (January 8, 1887): 775.

66. On Brazil, see William R. Summerhill, *Order Against Progress: Government, Foreign Investment, and Railroads in Brazil, 1854–1913* (Stanford, Calif.: Stanford University Press, 2003), chap. 3. On the Philippines, see Percival E. Fansler, "New Railways in the Philippine Islands," *Cassier's Magazine* (London ed.) 30 (June 1906): 161–74. Fansler captured the economic dynamic well: "It is natural to expect that the building of any railway will greatly increase the value of the territory served, as well as increase the traffic, both freight and passenger. It is obviously essential, however, that a given territory be developed to a certain stage before financial interests will undertake to build a railway through it. Risks are undoubtedly taken along this line, but it is seldom that conservative financiers will undertake construction of this kind without positive assurances of a fair return" (163).

67. Frederick W. Kimball to John W. Robinson, January 17, 1855, Graham Family Papers, reel 6, frame 794. On much of reels 6, 7, and 8 of the Graham Family Papers, one can read Robinson's detailed lobbying and negotiating with his northern contacts and with Norfolk and Western executives, cajoling them to complete the railroad extension in a timely way useful to his businesses. The executives in turn continually sought assurances that there would be sufficient production in the area to provide business for the new line. The railroad also pressured local furnace owners to buy the railroad's bonds that were funding the construction. See Charles B. Squier to John W. Robinson, January 22, 1885, Graham Family Papers, reel 6, frame 828; and Frederick J. Kimball to John W. Robinson, August 21, 1885, Graham Family Papers, reel 7, frame 728. On the transformative effect of Norfolk and Western's presence in what became the city of Roanoke, see Rand Dotson, *Roanoke, Virginia, 1882–1912: Magic City of the New South* (Knoxville: University of Tennessee Press, 2007), esp. chap. 1. Kimball's background can be found in Dotson, *Roanoke, Virginia,* 246 n. 17, and in the unpaginated portion of George S. Jack and E. B. Jacobs, *History of Roanoke County. . . .* (n.p.: n.p., 1912).

68. Barry Thomas Whittemore, "The Rural to Urban Shift in the Appalachian South: Town Building and Town Persistence in Virginia's Blue Ridge, 1880–1920," Ph.D. diss., Carnegie Mellon University, 1996, 74–75, 82, 131–33, 143, 151–54, 162–63; Senate Documents, *Dams or Reservoirs, Cheat and New Rivers, Va. and W.Va.,* 14–20; *In Re the Application Made to Congress by F. H. Fries and W. C. Ruffin, of the State of North Carolina, for Permission to Erect a Dam across New River, in Grayson County, Virginia* (Roanoke, Va.: Stone Printing and Manufacturing, [1900]). Information on Francis H. Fries is from Clement Manly, "Fran-

cis Henry Fries," in Samuel A. Ashe, ed., *Biographical History of North Carolina: From Colonial Times to the Present* (Greensboro, N.C.: Charles L. Van Noppen, 1905), 3:142–51. A local historian reported in 1914 that the grounds of the new textile mill in Fries included the very spot where the battle between escaped slaves and local white men took place in 1851. See Nuckolls, *Pioneer Settlers of Grayson County*, 12. Francis H. Fries's father and grandfather had helped pioneer the textile business in Salem, North Carolina, and their commitment to market values and slavery contributed substantially to the ending of congregational control of that town. See Michael Shirley, "The Market and Community Culture in Antebellum Salem, North Carolina," *Journal of the Early Republic* 11 (Summer 1991): 219–48. The Fries family of Salem can be compared with the Holt textile family a few dozen miles farther east, in Alamance County, North Carolina. On the Holts, see Beatty, *Alamance*. The town of Fries was incorporated December 21, 1901. See "An Act to Incorporate the Town of Fries, in Grayson county, Virginia" (December 21, 1901), in *Acts and Joint Resolutions Passed by the General Assembly of the State of Virginia, during the Session of 1901–2* (Richmond, Va.: J. H. O'Bannon, 1902), 39–41. The act named R. M. Caldwell, R. R. Hooker, George B. Bourne, S. A. Dorsett, S. S. Scott, and J. Ring as councilmen and W. F. Shaffner as mayor of Fries. See "An Act to Incorporate the Town of Fries," 41. The Norfolk and Western Railroad was reorganized as the Norfolk and Western Railway during a brief bankruptcy in 1893.

69. *Norfolk and Western Railway Company v. Board of Supervisors of Carroll County*, 65 S.E. 531 (1909); *An Act to Incorporate the New River Plateau Railway Company, Approved March 2d, 1888* (n.p.: n.p., n.d.), a four-page pamphlet in the author's possession. On Evans R. Dick, see *The History of American Yachts and Yachtsmen* (New York: Spirit of the Times, 1901), 117, and *Directory to the Iron and Steel Works of the United States. . . . ,* 10th ed. (Philadelphia: American Iron and Steel Association, 1890), 36. This attempt to bring a railroad through Carroll County was not Robinson and Bolen's first. On March 10, 1884, only a week after the Virginia General Assembly originally chartered the Virginia and Kentucky Railroad, the legislators passed the Act to Incorporate the New River and Chambers Valley Railroad Company to build a railroad "from some point on the Norfolk and Western railroad, between New river bridge, in Montgomery county, and Wytheville, in Wythe county, or from some point on the Norfolk and Western extension route between New river bridge and Van Lieu's Furnace, in Wythe county, through the county of Carroll, by way of Hillsville, to Mount Airy, in the state of North Carolina." Those involved in this effort included Robinson, Bolen, Carroll County leaders I. B. Coltrane and J. L. Early, and Maryland copper investor James E. Clayton. See *Acts and Joint Resolutions Passed by the General Assembly of the State of Virginia during the Session of 1883–84*, 481–82. The project did not come to fruition.

70. In the Wilson and Hairston Family Papers, see "Supplement to Virginia & Kentucky Ry. Report," Folder 47, Addition (quotation); Alfred Varley Sims to Hicks Brothers, April 13, 1892, Folder 60; and Alfred Varley Sims to B. Newcass, April 26, 1892, Folder 60. See also "An Act to Amend and Re Enact an Act to Incorporate the Virginia and Kentucky Railroad Company, Approved March 3, 1884, as Amended by an Act Approved November 22, 1884, and an Act Approved May 12, 1887. Approved February 16, 1892," in *Acts and Joint Resolutions Passed by the General Assembly of the State of Virginia, during the Session of 1891–92* (Richmond, Va.: J. H. O'Bannon, 1892), 444–47; "Inventory of the Wilson and Hairston Family Papers, 1751–1928, Collection Number 4134," Southern Historical Collection, available at http://www.lib.unc.edu/mss/inv/w/Wilson_and_Hairston _Family.html. For records of the surveying, see level books and transit books (signed G. W. Cantrell, "Transitman") in Folders 586, 587, 592, 598–602, Wilson and Hairston Family Papers. Also see Boyd's report to the Virginia and Kentucky Railroad, circa 1891, p. 8, in Folder 67, Addition, Wilson and Hairston Family Papers. For Alfred Sims's obituary, see *Transactions of the American Society of Civil Engineers* 112 (1947): 1520–23. Sims gained some recompense for his labor. While working on the project, he met Ruth Hairston and in 1891 married into the Hairston family, who were wealthy planters, merchants, and industrialists in the western piedmont of Virginia and North Carolina. After the railroad's demise, Sims moved on to a teaching position at the University of Iowa, though he later returned to railroad work in Cuba and elsewhere.

71. Whittemore, "The Rural to Urban Shift in the Appalachian South," chap. 5; Boyd, *Resources of South-West Virginia*, 78 (third quotation), 291 (second quotation), 306 (first quotation); see also Thomas Fetters, *Logging Railroads of the Blue Ridge and Smoky Mountains,* vol. 1, *Cold Mountain, Black Mountain, and White Top* (Hillsboro, Ore.: TimberTimes, 2007), chap. 2, esp. 23–56.

72. Leonidas Chalmers Glenn, *Denudation and Erosion in the Southern Appalachian Basin and the Monongahela Basin* (Washington, D.C.: Government Printing Office, 1911), 116 (first quotation); Virginia Department of Agriculture and Immigration, *A Handbook of Virginia,* rev. ed. (Richmond, Va.: Everett Waddey, 1910), 149 (second quotation). For more on Galax's early industrial development, see "When Industry Takes the Lead," *Virginia and the Virginia County* 4 (July 1950): 28–31.

73. See Andrew S. McCreath and E. V. d'Invilliers, *The New River–Cripple Creek Mineral Region of Virginia* (Harrisburg, Pa.: Harrisburg Publishing, 1887); Andrew S. McCreath, *The Mineral Wealth of Virginia Tributary to the Lines of the Norfolk and Western and Shenandoah Valley Railroad Companies* (Harrisburg, Pa.: Lane S. Hart, 1884); Dotson, *Roanoke, Virginia,* 62; Willard, "Pioneer Geologic Investigation in Pennsylvania," 252; G. W. Atkinson, "The Coal and Iron Fields of the South," *Engineering and Mining Journal,* 3rd ser., 11 (May 30, 1871): 346. McCreath and d'Invilliers also published an explicitly comparative article: "Com-

parison of Some Southern Cokes and Iron-Ores," *Transactions of the American Institute of Mining Engineers* 15 (May 1886–February 1887): 734–56. On the ties among Henry Rogers, Lesley, McCreath, and d'Invilliers, see George P. Merrill, *The First One Hundred Years of American Geology* (New Haven, Conn.: Yale University Press, 1924), 495.

74. From the Graham Family Papers: Andrew S. McCreath to John W. Robinson, February 18, 1887, reel 8, frame 801; John C. Raper to John W. Robinson, March 4, 1887, reel 8, frame 898; J. H. Shuff to John W. Robinson, March 7, 1887, reel 8, frame 923.

75. *Directory to the Iron and Steel Works of the United States . . . Corrected to July 25, 1882* (Philadelphia: American Iron and Steel Association, 1882), 44–47, 153; Helen M. Lewis and Suzanna O'Donnell, eds. and comps., *Ivanhoe, Virginia*, vol. 1, *Remembering Our Past, Building Our Future* (Ivanhoe, Va.: Ivanhoe Civic League, 1990), 1:39; *Directory to the Iron and Steel Works of the United States. . . . ,* 12th ed. (Philadelphia: American Iron and Steel Association, 1894), 35. John W. Robinson also had prominent roles at Crockett and Company's Beverly Furnace, Eagle Furnace, Raven Cliff Furnace, and Speedwell Furnace; Crockett, Oglesby, and Company's Wythe Furnace; the New River Iron Company's Foster Falls Furnace; and the Reed Island Iron Company's new (1881) Reed Island Furnace (or Tipton, later Boom) on Little Reed Island Creek at the edge of Pulaski County. Robinson had capitalized well on his wife's inheritance. On J. Williamson McGavock, see Irwin, "Last Empire Builder," 49. On Richard Curzon Hoffman, see Bernard C. Steiner, *Men of Mark in Maryland: Biographies of Leading Men in the State*, vol. 1 (Washington, D.C.: Johnson-Wynne, 1907), 188–91. On the Lobdell Car Wheel Company's business practices, see Harold C. Livesay, "The Lobdell Car Wheel Co., 1830–1867," *Business History Review* 42 (Summer 1968): 171–94. William W. Lobdell served as secretary of the Association of Manufacturers of Chilled Car Wheels for a time. See *Cast Iron Chilled Car Wheels: Mode of Manufacture and Relations They Bear to Economy in Railway Practice* (New York: Association of Manufacturers of Chilled Car Wheels, 1895), 4. The Lobdell car wheels had a positive international reputation. A British engineer explained in 1877, "Much ingenuity has been expended in designing car wheels. . . . Wheels made of American chilled iron are, however, perhaps the best for the purpose. . . . Of the American, the waved-plate wheels, manufactured by the Lobdell Car Wheel Company, give great satisfaction." Robinson Souttar, "Street Tramways," *Minutes of Proceedings of the Institution of Civil Engineers* 50, pt. 4 (1876–1877), 21. For another brief explanation of how wheels are produced, see "Casting Chilled Car Wheels," *Scientific American Supplement* 19, no. 483 (April 4, 1885): 7712. For a more technical explanation, see Simpson Bolland, *"The Iron Founder" Supplement: A Complete Illustrated Exposition of the Art of Casting in Iron. . . .* (New York: John Wiley and Sons, 1893), 307–21.

76. *Speech of Sen. J. Hoge Tyler, of Pulaski, Delivered in the Senate of Virginia,*

on Friday, February 1st, 1878 (pamphlet) (Richmond, Va.: J. W. Fergusson and Son, 1878), 2 and 4–5 (quotations). On Hinton Rowan Helper, see Brown, *Southern Outcast,* 95–96.

77. From Graham Family Papers: R. C. Hoffman to John W. Robinson, December 4, 1882, reel 6, frame 580; Richard D. Wood to John W. Robinson, October 22, 1882, reel 6, frame 409; C. S. Van Liew to John W. Robinson, March 3, 1885, reel 6, frame 900.

78. *Peirce v. Graham,* 85 Va. 227 (1888). Despite the suit, at least one member of the aggrieved Peirce family retained confidence in John W. Robinson. Isaac Peirce wrote to Robinson, his guardian, while studying in Philadelphia, telling Robinson, "I have always believed you to be my friend and I want to say that I hope nothing will develop from the matter to change my feelings toward you and I also hope that such will be the case with you." Isaac Peirce to John W. Robinson, January 18, 1887, Graham Family Papers, reel 8, frames 635–36.

79. From Graham Family Papers: R. W. Goodell to John W. Robinson, October 9, 1882, reel 6, frame 376; R. W. Goodell to John W. Robinson, October 23, 1882, reel 6, frame 414; James S. Crockett to John W. Robinson, December 17, 1882, reel 6, frames 626–27 (quotations on frame 626).

80. James S. Crockett to John W. Robinson, November 8, 1882, Graham Family Papers, reel 6, frames 464–65.

81. W. R. Gallimore to Messrs. Graham and Robinson, July 27, 1885, Graham Family Papers, reel 7, frame 628.

82. From Graham Family Papers: M. B. Tate to John W. Robinson, July [?], 1877, reel 4, frame 645; Edward Ely and E. P. Williams to John W. Robinson, October 10, 1877, reel 4, frame 753; Edward Ely and E. P. Williams to John W. Robinson, November 22, 1877, reel 4, frame 764; Charles H. Brown to John W. Robinson, August 16, 1882, reel 6, frame 173; R. C. Hoffman to John W. Robinson, December 23, 1885, reel 8, frame 344.

83. R. C. Hoffman & Co. to John W. Robinson, December 18, 1896, Box 11, Graham Family Papers, Mss. 38–106, Small Special Collections Library, University of Virginia, Charlottesville, hereafter cited as Graham Family Papers (UVA).

84. William H. Wren to John W. Robinson, April 11, 1885, Graham Family Papers, reel 7, frames 73–74; Frederick J. Kimball to John W. Robinson, February 19, 1885, Graham Family Papers, reel 8, frames 475–76; J. H. Hillman & Co. to John W. Robinson, December 20, 1896, Box 11, Graham Family Papers (UVA). On the tensions in 1885 between Russia and Great Britain, see Peter Hopkirk, *The Great Game: The Struggle for Empire in Central Asia* (New York: Kodansha International, 1992), chap. 31. Samuel A. Crozier headed investors who built the extensive Crozier Steel & Iron Company in Roanoke and used ore from Wythe and Pulaski, so the railroad sometimes carried ore out of the New River valley rather than carrying coke into the valley. On Crozier, see *Baltimore Manufacturers' Record*

9 (May 22, 1886): 506; 10 (October 16, 1886): 334; and 11 (February 19, 1887): 50. Crozier supplied metal to the Roanoke Machine Works, which built railroad engines and cars. Dotson, *Roanoke, Virginia,* 13.

85. Kegley, *Wythe County, Virginia,* 355–56. The Reed Island Furnace stopped operating in 1908. See "Iron Industry Was First Started in Section Close to Allisonia," *Pulaski (Va.) Southwest Times,* August 13, 1939, sec. 1, p. 2. The Reed Island Furnace was the second charcoal furnace in Pulaski County. In 1870, the Radford Iron Company had begun a furnace on Max Creek. "Pulaski County's Development Follows Colorful Events," *Pulaski Southwest Times,* August 13, 1939, sec. 9, p. 3.

86. John Birkinbine, "The United States Iron Industry from 1871 to 1910," *Bulletin of the American Institute of Mining Engineers,* no. 56 (August 1911): 603–16 (first and second quotations on 607; third quotation on 613).

87. P. H. Griffin, "The Future of the Chilled Car Wheel," *Bulletin of the American Institute of Mining Engineers,* no. 82 (October 1913): 2593–2604 (first quotation on 2597; second quotation on 2601).

88. *Directory to the Iron and Steel Works of the United States,* 12th ed., 31; Kegley, *Wythe County, Virginia,* 357; Lewis and O'Donnell, eds. and comps., *Ivanhoe, Virginia,* 1:44, 48. James P. Witherow of Pittsburgh won the contract to change the Ivanhoe Furnace from a charcoal to a coke furnace. See *Baltimore Manufacturers' Record* 12 (September 3, 1887): 152. In the 1890s, the Pennsylvania Zinc and Iron Company also had active operations in Ivanhoe. The Trenton Iron Company built for that operation an elevated 580-foot wire tramway to move ore across the New River to be processed. See *Wire Rope Transportation in All Its Branches. . . .* (Trenton, N.J.: Trenton Iron Co., 1896), 38.

89. Rufus Johnston Wysor, *Boyhood Days in Southwest Virginia* (New York: Vantage Press, 1961), 87–88.

90. A. L. Parrish Life History, interview by Maude R. Chandler, Virginia Writers' Project, Library of Virginia, available at http://image.lva.virginia.gov/WPL/00971/.

91. "Striking Negroes," *Knoxville Journal,* April 15, 1896, 8.

92. See "Riot!" *Wytheville Dispatch,* April 17, 1896, as cited and transcribed in John M. Johnson, "Negro Riot at the Max Meadows 'Annie Lee' Furnace," *Wythe County Historical Review,* no. 67 (Winter 2005): 10–12 (quotations on 11).

93. Census data retrieved from the Historical Census Browser, Geospatial and Statistical Data Center, University of Virginia, at http://fisher.lib.virginia.edu/collections/stats/histcensus/.

94. In Helen M. Lewis and Suzanna O'Donnell, eds. and comps., *Ivanhoe, Virginia,* vol. 2, *Telling Our Stories, Sharing Our Lives* (Ivanhoe, Va.: Ivanhoe Civic League, 1990), 2:35–36. Black people in the community also remembered this event. In 1989, Catherine Grubb looked back, "They lynched a man one time

over near Austinville. And they took him way on out past where Lucille Washington lived, and they buried him. They couldn't find the body, and it had rained a long time, and then they finally found him. My dad was one of the ones that helped. It was to do with a woman. And they said that, you know, he was praying." In Lewis and O'Donnell, eds. and comps., *Ivanhoe, Virginia*, 2:179.

95. Paul G. Beers, "The Wythe County Lynching of Raymond Bird: Progressivism vs. Mob Violence in the '20s," *Appalachian Journal* 22 (Fall 1994): 34–59. The *Chicago Defender* reported that mob members doused Bird with gasoline and set him on fire in his cell before he died: "By beating down the flames with straw brooms now and then the mob kept their human torch from blazing up too fast. 'We want him to scorch first, then cook slow,' a white-hooded leader explained to one of the guards. As he spoke he chopped at Bird's foot with a blunted axe." "Klan Burns Man in Jail Cell," *Chicago Defender*, August 21, 1926, 1. For Bird's descendants' continuing interest in his killing, see Ryan Scott Ottney, "In Search of Geraldine," *Portsmouth Daily Times*, available at http://www.portsmouth-daily times.com/pages/full_story/push?article-In+Search+Of+Geraldine%20&id=6789 146 &instance=secondary_news_left_column.

96. Irwin, "Last Empire Builder," chap. 2.

97. Ibid. Both Mills and Robinson had been among the men who incorporated the New River Plateau Railway Company, which was taken over by Norfolk and Western. See *An Act to Incorporate the New River Plateau Railway Company*.

98. George L. Carter to John W. Robinson, November 2, 1897, Box 11, Graham Family Papers (UVA).

99. Irwin, "Last Empire Builder," chap. 2; Willie Nelms, "George Lafayette Carter: Empire Builder," *Virginia Cavalcade* 30 (Summer 1980): 12–21; Alex P. Schust and David R. Goad, *Coalwood: A History of the West Virginia Mining Communities of Coalwood, Caretta, and Six* (Harwood, Md.: Two Mule Publishing, 2006), 2–10; Lyon G. Tyler, ed., *Men of Mark in Virginia: Ideals of American Life; a Collection of Biographies of the Leading Men in the State*, vol. 2 (Washington, D.C.: Men of Mark Publishing, 1907), 64–67; James A. Goforth, *Building the Clinchfield: A Construction History of America's Most Unusual Railroad*, 2nd ed. (Erwin, Tenn.: Gem, 1989); Lewis and O'Donnell, eds. and comps., *Ivanhoe, Virginia*, 1:54; "Buying Vast Properties: Syndicate Acquires Southwest Virginia Iron Industries," *Washington Post*, February 25, 1899, 3; *The Manual of Statistics: Stock Exchange Hand-Book, 1903. . . .* (New York: Manual of Statistics Company, 1903), 778–79 (quotation on 778). On Carter's home in Hillsville, Virginia, see page 6 of the National Register of Historic Places registration form for the "Carter Hydraulic Rams," the water system for the home, available at http://www.dhr.virginia.gov/ registers/Counties/Carroll/237–5003_Carter_Hydraulic_RAMS_2002_Final_ Nomination.pdf. On the demolition, see "Dora Furnace Stack Falls," *Pulaski Southwest Times*, September 22, 1936, 1. On Carter's death, see "Geo. L. Carter Assisted Town," *Pulaski Southwest Times*, December 31, 1936, 1.

4. Corporate Peaks in the Valley

1. Edgar C. Moxham, "The 'Great Gossan Lead' of Virginia," *Transactions of the American Institute of Mining Engineers* 21 (February 1892–February 1893): 133–38 (first and second quotations on 135; fourth quotation on 136); Charles B. Squier to John W. Robinson, September 30, 1889, Box 8, Graham Family Papers (UVA) (third quotation). For corroboration of the excitement among Virginia mining engineers that the opening of the Carroll County gossan deposits caused, see Edmund C. Pechin, "The Iron-Ores of Virginia and Their Development," *Transactions of the American Institute of Mining Engineers* 19 (May 1890–February 1891): 1016–35, esp. 1032. It seems that in 1893 Moxham himself tried to reopen the old Cranberry Mine. See Walter Harvey Weed, *Copper Deposits of the Appalachian States* (Washington, D.C.: Government Printing Office, 1911), 123. In 1905 in neighboring Floyd County, the old Toncrae (sometimes spelled "Toncrey" or "Toncray") Mine, which had been exploited for copper in the 1850s, also reopened. It operated until 1908 and then off and on again from 1935 to 1947. See Gilbert H. Espenshade, *Geology of Some Copper Deposits in North Carolina, Virginia, and Alabama* (Washington, D.C.: Government Printing Office, 1963), 137.

2. Thomas Leonard Watson et al., *Mineral Resources of Virginia* (Lynchburg, Va.: J. P. Bell, 1907), 208. The geologist T. Sterry Hunt had identified the Carroll County ores as a potentially valuable source of sulfur in 1873. T. Sterry Hunt, "On the Copper Deposits of the Blue Ridge," *American Journal of Science and Arts,* 3rd ser., 6 (October 1873): 305–8, esp. 308. Also see mentions of Carroll County and sulfuric acid possibilities in W. H. Adams, "The Pyrites Deposits of Louisa County, Virginia," *Virginias* 5 (May 1884): 74, 80–81; and C. R. Boyd, "The Utilization of the Iron and Copper Sulphides of Virginia, North Carolina, and Tennessee," *Transactions of the American Institute of Mining Engineers* 14 (June 1885–May 1886): 81–84.

3. Edward Rondthaler, *The Memorabilia of Fifty Years, 1877 to 1927* (Raleigh, N.C.: Edwards and Broughton, 1928), 103 (quotation); Gilbert Thomas Stephenson, *The Life Story of a Trust Man: Being That of Francis Henry Fries, President of the Wachovia Bank and Trust Company, Winston-Salem, North Carolina, since February 16, 1893* (New York: F. S. Crofts, 1930), 94–102; Tom E. Terrill, "Fries, Francis Henry," in William S. Powell, ed., *Dictionary of North Carolina Biography,* 6 vols. (Chapel Hill: University of North Carolina Press, 1979–1996), 2:243; *Deed: Norfolk, Roanoke, and Southern Railroad Company to the Norfolk and Western Railway Company of the Railroad Formerly of the Roanoke and Southern Railway Company. Dated December 2d, 1896* (Philadelphia: Allen, Lane and Scott, [1897?]). On the use of convict labor, see minutes on pages 23 (July 19, 1888, directors meeting), 49 (March 1, 1889, directors meeting), and 66–67 (June 18, 1889, stockholders meeting) of the Virginia and North Carolina Construction Company Record Book #5030-z, Southern Historical Collection, Wilson Library, University

of North Carolina, Chapel Hill. Fries, Reynolds, and their partners paid sixty cents per day for each convict and then subleased the convicts for a dollar per day to the contractors doing the actual construction work. As of June 18, 1889, the Virginia and North Carolina Construction Company had made a profit of $15,000 in this way. See the Virginia and North Carolina Construction Company Record Book #5030-z, p. 67. Just as slaves aided industrial development even in the colonial era, this variety of unfree labor had broad importance to industrial development in the post–Civil War South. See Alex Lichtenstein, *Twice the Work of Free Labor: The Political Economy of Convict Labor in the New South* (London: Verso, 1996).

4. On poor soils and the use of chemical fertilizer in the South, see Douglas Helms, "Soil and Southern History," *Agricultural History* 74 (Autumn 2000): 723–58; and Richard C. Sheridan, "Chemical Fertilizers in Southern Agriculture," *Agricultural History* 53 (January 1979): 308–18. For a very readable large-scale synthesis on long-term soil erosion and soil fertility issues, with many examples from the U.S. South, see David R. Montgomery, *Dirt: The Erosion of Civilizations* (Berkeley and Los Angeles: University of California Press, 2007).

5. T. Sterry Hunt, "On the Copper Deposits of the Blue Ridge," *Engineering and Mining Journal,* 3rd ser., 16 (August 12, 1873): 106 (first quotation); T. Sterry Hunt, "The Copper and Sulphur Resources of the South," *Engineering and Mining Journal,* 3rd ser., 16 (October 7, 1873): 234 (second quotation). On the phosphate industry in South Carolina, see Tom W. Shick and Don H. Doyle, "The South Carolina Phosphate Boom and the Stillbirth of the New South, 1867–1920," *South Carolina Historical Magazine* 86 (January 1985): 1–31. Also see Richard A. Wines, *Fertilizer in America: From Waste Recycling to Resource Exploitation* (Philadelphia: Temple University Press, 1985), chap. 8, which shows that among southern locations, not only South Carolina but also Maryland, especially Baltimore, had a major role in the fertilizer industry of post–Civil War America. In 1881, Charles Rufus Boyd echoed T. Sterry Hunt's belief that a railroad would allow Carroll County ore to be tapped by the fertilizer industry: "Thus, when the great West shall have exhausted the virgin strength of its soil, and becomes a much larger purchaser than now of good fertilizers, these heavily sulphureted ores will have been brought into easy communication with other valuable constituents—both those of South Carolina and of Carroll's sister counties—and will become, in the time of the country's greatest demand, one of the heaviest manufacturers of cheap and efficient fertilizers, perhaps, in the world." Boyd, *Resources of South-West Virginia,* 268.

6. Rondthaler, *Memorabilia of Fifty Years,* 164; George F. Swain, J. A. Holmes, and E. W. Myers, *Papers on the Waterpower in North Carolina* (Raleigh: North Carolina Geological Survey, 1899), 349–50 and plate 16. For mention of the formation of the Southern Chemical Company, see "Industrial Notes," *Engineering*

and Mining Journal, 3rd ser., 64 (October 30, 1897): 522. Francis Fries's brother Henry E. Fries managed the Fries Manufacturing and Power Company.

7. Shick and Doyle, "South Carolina Phosphate Boom"; Shepherd W. McKinley, "The Origins of 'King' Phosphate in the New South: Workers, Managers, and Entrepreneurs in South Carolina's Phosphate and Fertilizer Industries, 1865–1884," Ph.D. diss., University of Delaware, 2003.

8. On Southern Chemical's changing hands, see W. Conard Gass, "Battle, Herbert Bemerton," in Powell, ed., *Dictionary of North Carolina Biography,* 1:111.

9. Deed from Samuel S. Clayton and others to New York and Virginia Mineral Company, July 29, 1889, Deed Book 18, pp. 484–85, Carroll County Clerk's Office; deed from New York and Virginia Mineral Company to New York and Virginia Mineral and Mining Company, June 10, 1890, Deed Book 19, p. 508, Carroll County Clerk's Office.

10. F. H. McDowell, "Stripping Ore-Deposits," *Transactions of the American Institute of Mining Engineers* 18 (May 1889–February 1890): 627–39, esp. 634; Williams Haynes, ed., *American Chemical Industry,* vol. 6, *The Chemical Companies* (New York: D. Van Nostrand, 1949), 179–83; *The General Chemical Company after Twenty Years, 1899–1919 March 1st* ([New York: General Chemical Company, 1919]), 20 (first quotation), 31 (second quotation).

11. Annual report of the General Chemical Company, January 31, 1903 (first quotation), Mudd Library, Yale University, New Haven, Conn. (the library holds a run of these annual reports from 1901 to 1919, inclusive); *General Chemical Company after Twenty Years,* 64 (second quotation); *The Mineral Industry during 1904,* vol. 13 (New York: Engineering and Mining Journal, 1905), 389–90; Philip S. Smith, "Sulphur, Pyrites, and Sulphuric Acid," in U.S. Geological Survey, *Mineral Resources of the United States, 1917. Part II—Nonmetals* (Washington, D.C.: Government Printing Office, 1920), 19–62, esp. 52; R. M. Coiner and J. Richard Lucas, "The Largest Undeveloped Sulfide Ore-Body in the Eastern United States," *Mineral Industries Journal* 8 (December 1961): 1–6, esp. 2. In 1935, the Virginia Iron, Coal, and Coke Company controlled the Betty Baker and Cranberry properties, and the Virginia Mining Company, a subsidiary of the General Chemical Company, controlled the Monorat operation. See Clarence S. Ross, *Origin of the Copper Deposits of the Ducktown Type in the Southern Appalachian Region* (Washington, D.C.: Government Printing Office, 1935), 78–83. Government-sponsored geologists again carefully evaluated the economic possibilities of the area's minerals; see Anna J. Stose and George W. Stose, *Geology and Mineral Resources of the Gossan Lead District and Adjacent Areas in Virginia* (Charlottesville: Virginia Division of Mineral Resources, 1957).

12. The General Chemical Company's success and growth can be traced in its annual reports, held by the Mudd Library at Yale University.

13. House of Representatives, *War Expenditures: Hearings before Subcommittee*

No. 5 (Ordnance) of the Select Committee on Expenditures in the War Department, Serial 6, Part 50, 66th Cong., 2nd sess. (Washington, D.C.: U.S. Government Printing, 1920), 2688. On the necessity of sulfuric acid in munitions manufacturing, see also T. J. Sullivan, "The Use of Sulphuric Acid in Smokeless Powder Manufacture," *Zinc* 5 (February 1920): 58. Nearby Saltville, with its alkali plant, gained more from the war. In 1918, the War Department built a $2.5 million plant to produce sodium cyanide; the facility was apparently just completed when the war ended, and only limited production of this chemical weapon ever took place there.

14. Haynes, ed., *American Chemical Industry,* 6:9–11, 180 (quotation); "Senator Capper Assails the Big Profiteers," *Current Opinion,* August 1920, 255.

15. Donald K. Henry, James R. Craig, and M. Charles Gilbert, "Ore Mineralogy of the Great Gossan Lead, Virginia," *Economic Geology* 74 (May 1979): 645–56, esp. 646–47; Bowman, *Carroll County, Virginia,* 83–84; Clarence O. Babcock and Betty I. Stanley, "Sulfur and Pyrites," in *Minerals Yearbook 1962,* vol. 1, *Metals and Minerals (Except Fuels)* (Washington, D.C.: Government Printing Office, 1963), 1169; *Total Maximum Daily Load Development for Chestnut Creek . . . Prepared for Virginia Department of Environmental Quality* (Wytheville and Blacksburg, Va.: n.p., 2006), chap. 6, p. 23, available at http://www.deq.virginia.gov/tmdl/apptmdls/newrvr/chestnut.pdf; James L. Poole, "Iron Sulfide Mines in Virginia," *Virginia Minerals* 19 (August 1973): 29–33; entry for Virginia Mining Company, in Walter Harvey Weed, *The Mines Handbook, an Enlargement of the Copper Handbook. . . . ,* vol. 14 (New York: W. H. Weed, 1920), 1474; Jacob E. Gair and John F. Slack, "Deformation, Geochemistry, and Origin of Massive Sulfide Deposits, Gossan Lead District, Virginia," *Economic Geology* 79 (November 1984): 1483–520, esp. 1484.

16. Many documents related to the Allied-Pulaski site can be found by searching the U.S. EPA Web site at http://www.epa.gov/reg3hwmd/super/sites/VAD980551915/index.htm. Most useful there is a lengthy compendium of information and documents titled *Removal Enforcement Support, Allied Chemical Corporation. Prepared for: U.S. Environmental Protection Agency, Region III, Enforcement Support Services, Hazardous Site Cleanup Division* (Wayne, Pa.: DASTON Corporation, 2001).

17. U.S. Environmental Protection Agency (EPA), *Decision Rationale for the Chestnut Creek Benthic and Bacteriological TMDLs Carroll and Grayson Counties, Virginia* (Philadelphia: U.S. EPA, 2006), available at http://www.epa.gov/reg3wapd/tmdl/VA_TMDLs/ChestnutCreek/ChestnutCreekDR.pdf; Gair and Slack, "Deformation, Geochemistry, and Origin of Massive Sulfide Deposits," 1484; *Total Maximum Daily Load Development for Chestnut Creek,* chap. 6, pp. 24–25.

18. Eilers, "Notes from Southwestern Virginia" (November 30, 1869), 338.

19. Ibid.

20. Johann David Schoepf, *Travels in the Confederation [1783–1784]*, trans. and ed. Alfred J. Morrison (Philadelphia: William J. Campbell, 1911), 67.

21. Donnelly, "Confederate Lead Mines," 408, 414; [Kohler], "Description, History, and Recollections of the Lead Mines," 46 (first quotation); "Iron Making in Southwest Va.," *Baltimore Manufacturers' Record* 5 (May 17, 1884): 385 (second quotation); Ninth Census of the United States, 1870: Industry, Nonpopulation Census Schedules for Virginia, 1850–1880, reel 15; "An Act to Change the Name of the Union Lead-Mine Company and Reincorporate the Same under the Name and Style of the Wythe Lead and Zinc-Mine Company. Approved March 13, 1874," in *Acts and Joint Resolutions Passed by the General Assembly of the State of Virginia, at the Session of 1874* (Richmond, Va.: R. F. Walker, 1874), 85–87. The new corporate charter lists all of the company's stockholders.

22. Edwin Higgins Jr., "Zinc Mining and Smelting in Southwestern Virginia," *Engineering and Mining Journal* 79 (March 30, 1905): 608–10, esp. 610; [Kohler], "Description, History, and Recollections of the Lead Mines," 46. In 1869, David Graham worked with representatives of the Lehigh Zinc Company to explore (apparently fruitlessly) for zinc on Graham's iron properties. See B. C. Webster to David Graham, December 1, 1869, Graham Family Papers, reel 4, frame 563.

23. George C. Stone, "The Development of Zinc Smelting in the United States," in *Transactions of the International Engineering Congress, 1915,* vol. 9, *Metallurgy. . . .* (San Francisco: Neal Publishing, 1916), 416–22 (quotation on 422); "To Enlarge Zinc Works," *Baltimore Manufacturers' Record* 11 (May 21, 1887): 584. Furnaces for making zinc oxide, a less complicated process than refining pure spelter, were built in Austinville in 1905. An engineer explained, "An oxide plant, consisting of 12 furnaces, has just been completed. Low-grade ore and tailing, running from 15 to 20% zinc, are treated here. The zinc oxide from these furnaces, after passing through a 3-ft. iron pipe 600 ft. long, loses nearly all of its heat in the journey, and is caught in bags. The oxide is either smelted or used in the manufacture of zinc white." Edwin Higgins Jr., "Zinc Mining and Smelting in Southwestern Virginia—II," *Engineering and Mining Journal* 79 (April 6, 1905): 658–59 (quotation on 658).

24. William H. Case, "The Bertha Zinc-Mines at Bertha, Va.," *Transactions of the American Institute of Mining Engineers* 22 (1894): 511–36; L. W. Currier, *Zinc and Lead Region of Southwestern Virginia. . . .* (University: Virginia Geological Survey, 1935), 6–7, 97–106; Kegley, *Wythe County, Virginia,* 339. David Forney reportedly identified the ores while engaging "in the amateur pursuit of mineralogical and geological investigations, suggested by the favorable appearance of the region to which he came from Pennsylvania to pursue his profession of landscape-artist." Case, "Bertha Zinc-Mines," 536. Forney painted portraits of mine and furnace owner David Peirce Graham and his children. See the online Art Invento-

ries Catalog of the Smithsonian American Art Museum at http://siris-artinventories .si.edu/ipac20/ipac.jsp?profile=.

25. Edgar C. Moxham, "Zinc Smelting at the Bertha Works, Virginia," *Engineering and Mining Journal* 56 (November 25, 1893): 544; "Zinc," *Virginias* 1 (January 1880): 15; Adison A. Christian, "Pulaski, Virginia," in *South-west Virginia and the Valley: Historical and Biographical* (Roanoke, Va.: A. D. Smith, 1892), 311; C. Kirchoff Jr., "Zinc," in *Mineral Resources of the United States: Calendar Year 1886,* 50th Cong., 1st sess., House of Representatives Miscellaneous Document No. 42 (Washington, D.C.: Government Printing Office, 1887), 155; P[eter] W[enrick] Sheafer, *Report on the Altoona Coal and Iron Co.* (n.p.: n.p., 1880); "An Act to Authorize the Altoona Coal and Iron Company to Make or Carry Out Contracts with the Bertha Zinc and Mineral Company," February 10, 1894, in *Acts and Joint Resolutions Passed by the General Assembly of the State of Virginia during the Session of 1893–94* (Richmond, Va.: J. H. O'Bannon, 1894), 201. On Altoona coal, also see L. S. Randolph, "Virginia Anthracite Coal," *Cassier's Magazine* (London ed.) 27 (February 1905): 328–36.

26. Moxham, "Zinc Smelting at the Bertha Works, Virginia," 544.

27. "Zinc," *Virginias,* 15 (quotation); "Recent Sales of Mineral Properties in the Virginias," *Virginias* 1 (April 1880): 53; William T. Davis, *Plymouth Memories of an Octogenarian* (Plymouth, Mass.: Memorial Press, 1906), 282–83. Also see "An Act to Incorporate the Virginia and North Carolina Mining and Transportation Company," in *Acts and Joint Resolutions Passed by the General Assembly of the State of Virginia during the Session of 1879–80* (Richmond, Va.: R. F. Walker, 1880), 18–19. George W. Palmer had also taken an interest in the Altoona Coal and Iron Company, which supplied some coal to the Bertha smelter. See *A Hand-Book of Virginia. By the Commissioner of Agriculture,* 2nd ed. (Richmond, Va.: R. E. Frayser, 1879), 163–64.

28. Christian, "Pulaski, Virginia," 310.

29. "Testimony of Robert D. Layton, Immigration Inspector," in *Report of the Select Committee on Immigration and Naturalization, and Testimony Taken by the Committee on Immigration of the Senate and the Select Committee on Immigration and Naturalization of the House of Representatives under Concurrent Resolution of March 12, 1890,* 51st Cong., 2nd sess., House of Representatives Report No. 3472 (Washington, D.C.: Government Printing Office, 1891), 343.

30. T. V. Powderly, *Thirty Years of Labor, 1859 to 1889. . . .* (Columbus, Ohio: Excelsior Publishing House, 1889), 645–46; Frederic Meyers, "The Knights of Labor in the South," *Southern Economic Journal* 6 (April 1940): 479–87, esp. 486.

31. "Testimony of Robert D. Layton, Immigration Inspector," 343–44; J. K. Warden, Jas. H. Douthat, and Geo. W. Jones to T. V. Powderly, January 19, 1889, in Terence Vincent Powderly Papers, 94 reels of microfilm (Glen Rock, N.J.: Microfilming Corporation of America, 1974), reel 29. I found the letter to Powderly

by following the mention of it in Melton Alonza McLaurin, *The Knights of Labor in the South* (Westport, Conn.: Greenwood Press, 1978), 58–59, 198 n. 22. I consulted the 1900 manuscript census using the HeritageQuest Online subscription database.

32. Francis E. Weston to John W. Robinson, October 21, 1889, Box 8, Graham Family Papers (UVA).

33. Corbin, *Life, Work, and Rebellion in the Coal Fields.*

34. "Pulaski, Va., March 29, 1888," in U.S. Senate, *Testimony Taken by the Subcommittee on the Tariff of the Senate Committee on Finance in Connection with the Bill H. R. 9051, to Reduce Taxation and Simplify the Laws in Relation to the Collection of the Revenue,* part 1, 50th Cong., 1st sess. (Washington, D.C.: Government Printing Office, 1888), 632.

35. Case, "Bertha Zinc-Mines at Bertha, Va.," 523–35 (quotation on 523).

36. Ibid., 519 (first quotation), 531 (second quotation).

37. Higgins, "Zinc Mining and Smelting in Southwestern Virginia" (March 30, 1905), 608.

38. A. H. Horton, M. R. Hall, and R. H. Bolster, *Surface Water Supply of the United States, 1909. Part III. Ohio River Basin* (Washington, D.C.: Government Printing Office, 1911), 74. For context, see Randall E. Rohe, "Hydraulicking in the American West: The Development and Diffusion of a Mining Technique," *Montana: The Magazine of Western History* 35 (Spring 1985): 18–35.

39. Stone, "Development of Zinc Smelting," 422; Higgins, "Zinc Mining and Smelting in Southwestern Virginia" (March 30, 1905), 608. The Pulaski Iron Company had been incorporated on March 17, 1884, by John W. Robinson, David P. Graham, and others and later became part of George Carter's syndicate. See "An Act to Incorporate the Pulaski Iron Company," in *Acts and Joint Resolutions Passed by the General Assembly of the State of Virginia during the Session of 1883–84,* 655–57. See also *Baltimore Manufacturers' Record* 5 (May 10, 1884): 350. The company may have taken in northern investors in 1886. The *Baltimore Manufacturers' Record* reported in December 1886, "The Pulaski Iron Co., recently reported as being formed at Pulaski Station, Va., have [*sic*] organized, with A. J. Dull, of Harrisburg, Pa., as president, and J. J. Doran, of Philadelphia, secretary and treasurer." *Baltimore Manufacturers' Record* 10 (December 4, 1886), 587. At times, Doran and Dull served together on the Norfolk and Western's board of directors. See *The Manual of Statistics, 1895: Stock Exchange Hand-Book. . . .* (New York: Charles H. Nicoll, 1895), 174. In November 1889, the Pulaski Iron Company's letterhead listed Philadelphia as the location of the headquarters, Dull as president, E. P. Borden as vice president, Abraham S. Patterson as secretary and treasurer, and John W. Eckman as general manager in Pulaski. See John W. Eckman to John W. Robinson, November 21, 1889, Box 8, Graham Family Papers (UVA).

40. Sarvis, *Salt Trade of Nineteenth Century Saltville, Virginia,* 61, 69 n. 5; Wilson, *Smyth County History and Traditions,* 195; "Death of Mr. Geo. W. Palmer," *Richmond Times-Dispatch,* November 19, 1903, 2; "Mrs. Geo. W. Palmer Dead," *Richmond Times-Dispatch,* June 20, 1902, 5. George Palmer and William A. Stuart also had agricultural interests. Wilson reported, "In addition to developing the salt and plaster properties, Palmer and Stuart operated a tremendous farm through which they built up a large cattle business. During the eighties they owned what was then said to be the most valuable herd of registered shorthorn cattle in the world and many of their animals were bought and sold for fabulous prices." Wilson, *Smyth County History and Traditions,* 196. For a detailed description of the progressive approach used at the farm, see "Smythe County Farmers' Club—an Account of Mr. Palmer's Estate at Saltville," *Southern Planter and Farmer,* June 1876, 430. Palmer served as president of the Virginia State Agricultural Society. See "Va. State Agricultural Society," *Southern Planter and Farmer,* November 1880, 415, and "The Great Virginia Salt Works," *Baltimore Manufacturers' Record* 9 (July 24, 1886): 845. Palmer raised and sold tobacco at times, for he faced a lawsuit after selling to R. J. Reynolds some tobacco in 1882 that Reynolds claimed had defects. See Nannie M. Tilley, *The R. J. Reynolds Tobacco Company* (Chapel Hill: University of North Carolina Press, 1985), 40; and *Reynolds v. Palmer,* 21 F. 433 (1884).

41. See George W. Palmer to John W. Robinson, August 26, 1882, and November 22, 1882, Graham Family Papers, reel 6, frames 219 and 526.

42. Case, "Bertha Zinc-Mines at Bertha, Va.," 531 (second quotation); *Bertha Zinc & Mineral Co. v. Carico et al.,* 61 F. 132 (1893), at 133 (first quotation); *Baltimore Manufacturers' Record* 10 (November 27, 1886): 551; *Baltimore Manufacturers' Record* 10 (December 4, 1886): 587; *Baltimore Manufacturers' Record* 10 (January 29, 1887): 891. On George Meade Holstein, see "Membership," *Bulletin of the American Institute of Mining Engineers,* no. 136 (April 1918): liv; and "George Holstein Pioneer Citizen," *Pulaski Southwest Times,* August 13, 1939, sec. 6, p. 1. For a detailed early look at the alkali operation, see Walter Edward Harris, "Saltville and Its Enterprise," *Richmond Times-Dispatch,* July 25, 1905, 4.

43. Daniel E. Sutherland, *The Confederate Carpetbaggers* (Baton Rouge: Louisiana State University Press, 1988), 124–26, 160–65, 290–91; Tammy Harden Galloway, *The Inman Family: An Atlanta Family from Reconstruction to World War I* (Macon, Ga.: Mercer University Press, 2002), chap. 1.

44. See the obituaries on Charles B. Squier (1850–1904) in "Biographical Notices of 1904," *Bi-Monthly Bulletin of the American Institute of Mining Engineers,* no. 4 (July 1905): 783–84, and William Crane Squier (1812–1906), also a Rahway native, in "Necrology," *Proceedings of the New Jersey Historical Society,* 3rd ser., 6 (July 1909): 103. On Manning and Squier's property at Barren Springs, see McCreath and d'Invilliers, *New River–Cripple Creek Mineral Region,* 54–55; and

Kegley, *Wythe County, Virginia,* 355. The other partner in Manning and Squier was Richard H. Manning (d. 1887), and the firm was formed around 1852. The obituary also indicates that early in life, prior to 1852, William Squier had lived and worked as a businessman in Columbia, South Carolina, and New Orleans, making southern-directed business activities also a multigenerational affair. Also see George C. Stone, "History of the N.J. Zinc Co.," *Zinc* 1 (June 1916): 99, and "The Passaic Zinc Company," *Zinc* 7 (May 1922): 139–47, esp. 143–44. When Charles B. Squier died prematurely in 1904, his brother Edwin M. Squier (1852–1926) succeeded him on the board of the New Jersey Zinc Company. See "Edwin M. Squier," *Zinc* 11 (December 1926): 342–43; and "Edwin M. Squier," *Zinc* 4 (January 1919): 4.

45. "New Jersey Zinc and Franklinite," *Hunt's Merchants' Magazine* 28 (March 1853): 315–25, esp. 317; Daniel Hodas, *The Business Career of Moses Taylor: Merchant, Finance Capitalist, and Industrialist* (New York: New York University Press, 1976), 265–67; *The First Hundred Years of the New Jersey Zinc Company: A History of the Founding and Development of a Company and an Industry, 1848–1948* (New York: New Jersey Zinc Company, 1948), 7–32; James D. Tate to John W. Robinson, August 13, 1902 (first quotation), and George L. Carter to John W. Robinson, August 21, 1902 (second quotation), both in Box 12, Graham Family Papers (UVA). For the first few years after the New Jersey Zinc Company's founding, it was known as the Sussex Zinc and Copper Mining and Manufacturing Company. *First Hundred Years of the New Jersey Zinc Company,* 11. For more detail on the series of mergers in the late 1890s, see Pete J. Dunn, *Mine Hill in Franklin and Sterling Hill in Ogdensburg, Sussex County, New Jersey: Mining History, 1765–1900,* pt. 1, vol. 6 (Alexandria, Va.: Pete J. Dunn, 2004). In 1901, the New Jersey Zinc Company and the General Chemical Company seriously considered merging, which would have further consolidated control of the resources along the New River. However, the merger was not completed. See [*Merger Agreement Between the Stockholders of the New Jersey Zinc Company and the General Chemical Company*] ([New York: Farmers' Loan and Trust Company, 1901]), microfilm, Columbia University Libraries, New York.

46. Lewis and O'Donnell, eds. and comps., *Ivanhoe, Virginia,* 1:48–54, 79–90, 164–68; Bowman, *Carroll County, Virginia,* 85–88. Addison Dally, the son of a Pittsburgh-area rolling mill superintendent, was an associate of oilman Michael L. Benedum. Dally died in 1957 at the age of ninety-five. On Dally, see his obituary, "Addison Dally," *New York Times,* May 9, 1957, 31; and "Reminiscences of A. D. Dally Jr.," June 16, 1951, in the Oral History Collection of Columbia University. On Benedum and his association with Dally, see Sam T. Mallison, *The Great Wildcatter* (Charleston: Education Foundation of West Virginia, 1953), chap. 13.

47. *Hydroelectric Power in the South West Virginias* (Bluefield, W.Va.: Appalachian Power Co., 1913), esp. 8, 14, 18–20, 22; Senate Documents, *Dams or Reser-*

voirs, Cheat and New Rivers, Va. and W.Va., 31–32. For technical details of the dams, see also Warren O. Rogers, "Appalachian Hydro-Electric Development," *Power* 37 (March 25, 1913): 402–8. For a biographical sketch and a portrait of Henry M. Byllesby, see Frederick Converse Beach and George Edwin Rines, eds., *The Americana: A Universal Reference Library . . . Biographies* (New York: Americana, 1911), 92. Also see *Power in Southwestern Virginia: A Great Mountain Empire Served by the Appalachian Power Co.* (Wytheville: Southwestern Virginia, [1920?]). On the latter years of the Grayson Sulphur Springs resort, see Munsey W. Webb, *Norfolk and Western Railway Company: North Carolina Branch,* 3rd ed. (Radford, Va.: Commonwealth Press, 2004), 70.

48. *Hydroelectric Power in the South West Virginias,* 5.

49. For context on hydroelectric development, see, for example, Henry Hale, "Great Water Power Sites," *Cassier's Magazine* (London ed.) 40 (September 1911): 387–409; H. Lester Hamilton, "American Hydro-Electric Construction Work Abroad," *Cassier's Magazine* 35 (January 1909): 416–25; John George Leigh, "The White Coal of Sweden," *Cassier's Magazine* (February 1909): 455–79; and Jessica B. Teisch, "Great Western Power, 'White Coal,' and Industrial Capitalism in the West," *Pacific Historical Review* 70 (May 2001): 221–53.

50. See Christopher John Manganiello, "Dam Crazy with Wild Consequences: Artificial Lakes and Natural Rivers in the American South, 1845–1990," Ph.D. diss., University of Georgia, 2010, chap. 2; W. David Lewis, *Sloss Furnaces and the Rise of the Birmingham District: An Industrial Epic* (Tuscaloosa: University of Alabama Press, 1994), chap. 17; Erin Elizabeth Clune, "From Light Copper to the Blackest and Lowest Type: Daniel Tompkins and the Racial Order of the Global New South," *Journal of Southern History* 76 (May 2010): 275–314; and Jessica B. Teisch, *Engineering Nature: Water, Development, and the Global Spread of American Environmental Expertise* (Chapel Hill: University of North Carolina Press, 2011).

51. "Visit of Officers to Appalachian Power Company District," *Electrical Review and Western Electrician* 60 (February 17, 1912): 320; "Special Train to New River Hydroelectric Developments," *Electrical Review and Western Electrician* 61 (July 6, 1912): 4; "Progress in the Development on New River," *Electrical Review and Western Electrician* 61 (July 6, 1912): 6; Bowman, *Carroll County, Virginia,* 86–87. On Arthur S. Huey, see Beach and Rines, eds., *The Americana . . . Biographies,* 32. On Harold Winthrop Buck, see J. McKeen Cattell, ed., *American Men of Science: A Biographical Directory,* 2nd ed. (New York: Science Press, 1910), 64. On the board of directors for Appalachian Power Company, see *Appendix to Eleventh Annual Report of the State Corporation of Virginia for the Year Ending December 31, 1913: Reports and Statistics of Canals, Railroads, Electric Railways and Other Corporate Companies Are for Fiscal Year Ending June 30, 1913* (Richmond, Va.: Davis Bottom, 1914), 1002. Also see Hale, "Great Water Power Sites," 398–400.

52. "National Carbide Corp.," in *Standard Corporation Service, Daily Revised: May–August, 1917* (New York: Standard Statistics Company, 1917), 269; *Appalachian Power Company v. Commonwealth of Virginia, at the Relation of the National Carbide Corporation,* 132 Va. 1 (1922); "Edward James Kearns," *Bulletin of the American Institute of Mining and Metallurgical Engineers,* no. 152 (August 1919): xlvii; Albert H. Buck, *The Bucks of Wethersfield, Connecticut, and the Families with Which They Are Connected by Marriage: A Biographical and Genealogical Sketch* (Roanoke, Va.: Stone Printing and Manufacturing, 1909), 87–90. For more on John J. Lincoln (1865–1948), a native of Lancaster County, Pennsylvania, and a onetime engineer with the U.S. Coast and Geodetic Survey, see W. P. Tams Jr., *The Smokeless Coal Fields of West Virginia: A Brief History* (Morgantown: West Virginia University Press, 1963), 91.

53. Lewis and O'Donnell, eds. and comps., *Ivanhoe, Virginia,* 1:48–54. On the Huddle family and Charles Ross Huddle's long-suffering relationship with A. B. Dally Jr. of Pittsburgh, who controlled the Ivanhoe iron and zinc lands, see the unprocessed Huddle Family Papers, Special Collections, Newman Library, Virginia Tech, Blacksburg. At Dally's request, Huddle constantly did research for and formulated new plans to restart major operations in Ivanhoe, but these plans never came to fruition. By the early 1950s, Dally also owed Huddle years of back pay, causing extreme frustration. Biographical details on Huddle's career can also be found in *Bulletin of the American Institute of Mining Engineers,* no. 110 (February 1916): xxvii; in his obituary in *Mining Engineering* 22 (June 1970): 101; and in the relevant entry in *Virginia: Rebirth of the Old Dominion,* 5 vols. (Chicago: Lewis Publishing, 1929), 4:512–13. Evidence of his father's position at the Cranberry Iron and Coal Company comes from letterhead information on documents dated 1902 in Box 1, Huddle Family Papers. For an example of planning for development at Ivanhoe, see Charles Huddle to A. B. Dally Jr., July 30, 1940, unnumbered box, Huddle Family Papers. On the Cranberry Furnace and mining operation in Mitchell County, North Carolina, see Henry E. Colton, *The East Tennessee, Virginia, and Georgia Railway System: Mineral Wealth, Agricultural and Timber Resources of the Main Line and Branches . . . Embracing the Steel Ore Region of the South* (n.p.: n.p., 1890), 75–85.

54. "Stuart M. Buck," *Transactions of the American Institute of Mining and Metallurgical Engineers* 66 (1922): 841–42; "Acquires National Carbide Corporation," *Gas Age* 47 (May 10, 1921): 386.

55. Haynes, ed., *American Chemical Industry,* 6:5–9; "Acquires National Carbide Corporation." For a celebratory but nonetheless interesting snapshot of the company's founding and growth, see *Air Reduction: A Quarter Century of Progress* (New York: Air Reduction Company, 1941).

56. Haynes, ed., *American Chemical Industry,* 6:5–9; "Air Reduction Combines Units," *New York Times,* December 2, 1960, 45; Bowman, *Carroll County,*

Virginia, 87–88; William L. Woodford to All Employees, November 16, 1960, Box 3, Huddle Family Papers.

57. See the documents collected regarding Superfund and Airco on the EPA Web site at http://www.epa.gov/reg3hwmd/super/sites/VAD988166146/index .htm. Also see Lewis and O'Donnell, eds. and comps., *Ivanhoe, Virginia,* 1:194–95; and "Once-Proud Industrial Plant to Come Down," *Wytheville Southwest Virginia Enterprise,* April 26, 1979, A1, A9.

58. See *United States v. Appalachian Electric Power Co.,* 311 U.S. 377 (1940); *United States v. Appalachian Electric Power Co.,* 107 F.2d 769 (1939) (quotation at 779); *United States v. Appalachian Electric Power Co.,* 23 F. Supp. 83 (1938); and Robert P. Kneeland and Stark Ritchie, "Federal Power Act: Jurisdiction and Functions of the Federal Power Commission—Constitutional Limitations," *Michigan Law Review* 39 (April 1941): 976–1002. The Fondren Library at Rice University holds a bound volume of several of the early printed briefs and other documents in this case. It is cataloged as United States, Complainant-Appellant, *The United States of America, Appellant v. Appalachian Electric Power Company, a Corporation, Appellee. . . .* (n.p.: n.p., [1939?]). Within it, particularly useful for historical perspective, is the pamphlet titled *Supplemental Appendix to Plaintiff's Brief,* by Harry W. Blair and others. Also bound with the volume is a useful map by the Federal Power Commission titled *New River and Connecting Waterways, West Virginia, Virginia, and North Carolina* ([Washington, D.C.: Federal Power Commission], n.d.). The reservoir created by the dam (now Claytor Dam) is called Claytor Lake, which, like the Buck and Byllesby projects, was named in honor of a power company executive.

59. Ashley M. Neville and Debra A. McClane, *The World War II Ordnance Department's Government-Owned Contractor-Operated (GOCO) Industrial Facilities: Radford Ordnance Works Historic Investigation* (Plano, Tex.: Geo-Marine, 1996), 11, 15 (quotation); Davis Dyer and David B. Sicilia, *Labors of a Modern Hercules: The Evolution of a Chemical Company* (Boston: Harvard Business School Press, 1990), 227–29; Vincent B. Smith, "Ten-Month Time Limit Spurs 21,000 Construction Workers on $41,000,000 Powder Plant," *Construction Methods* 23 (April 1941): 42–56. For an insightful overview of the defense-driven southern boomtowns, see Charles D. Chamberlain, *Victory at Home: Manpower and Race in the American South during World War II* (Athens: University of Georgia Press, 2003), chap. 1.

60. John J. Accordino, *Captives of the Cold War Economy: The Struggle for Defense Conversion in American Communities* (Westport, Conn.: Praeger, 2000), 102. I have not been able to discern whether the Radford plant drew on Carroll County ores for its sulfuric acid production. However, on the production of sulfuric acid at the plant and the acid's importance to ordnance manufacture, see Kimberly L. Kane, *Historic Context for the World War II Ordnance Department's Government-*

Owned Contractor-Operated (GOCO) Industrial Facilities, 1939–1945 (Plano, Tex.: Geo-Marine, 1995), 129–31, 156, 184. For a social history of the arsenal, see Mary B. LaLone, Peg Wimmer, and Amanda Hartle, eds., *The Radford Arsenal: Impacts and Cultural Change in an Appalachian Region* (Radford, Va.: Brightside Press, 2003).

61. M. H. Kline and T. J. Ballard, *Investigation of the Great Gossan Lead, Carroll County, Va.,* Bureau of Mines Report of Investigations 4532 (Washington, D.C.: U.S. Department of the Interior, 1949), 1 (first quotation), 4 (second quotation).

62. "Sulfur Shortage Continues," *Science News-Letter* 61 (January 19, 1952): 47 (quotation); M. P. Corriveau, *Mineral Dressing Studies on the Great Gossan Lead Ore from Carroll County, Virginia* (Blacksburg: Virginia Polytechnic Institute, Engineering Experiment Station, 1956); G. W. Josephson and F. M. Barsigian, "Sulfur and Pyrites," in Paul W. McGann, ed., *Minerals Yearbook 1951* (Washington, D.C.: Government Printing Office, 1954), 1227; "Virginia Iron Sells Land," *New York Times,* July 13, 1951, 29. A great deal of information about the Freeport Sulphur Company and the industry at large can found in Williams Haynes, *Brimstone: The Stone That Burns* (Princeton, N.J.: D. Van Nostrand, 1959). Freeport Sulphur may have bought more acreage than initially reported; a trade journal in September 1952 reported that the company was surveying its nine thousand acres in Carroll County. "Sulfur," *Chemical Week* 71 (September 13, 1952): 16. On the sulfur shortage, see the comments by a Freeport Sulphur executive in "South to Meet Sulphur Demands, Leppert Predicts," *Journal of Southern Research* 4 (July–August 1952): 7; and Donald W. Davis, *Washed Away? The Invisible Peoples of Louisiana's Wetlands* (Lafayette: University of Louisiana at Lafayette Press, 2010), chap. 8, esp. 424.

63. Coiner and Lucas, "Largest Undeveloped Sulfide Ore-Body in the Eastern United States"; Arthur R. Kinkel Jr., *The Ore Knob Copper Deposit, North Carolina, and Other Massive Sulfide Deposits of the Appalachians* (Washington, D.C.: Government Printing Office, 1967), 40–41; Stose and Stose, *Geology and Mineral Resources of the Gossan Lead District;* James L. Poole, "Iron Sulfide Mines in Virginia," *Virginia Minerals* 19 (August 1973): 29–33.

64. W. O. Borcherdt, "Underground Sanitation at Mines," *Zinc* 2 (March 1917): 59–63; C. E. Taylor, "Raising at the Austinville Mine," *Zinc* 2 (March 1917): 74; "Fire Protection System at Austinville," *Zinc* 5 (November 1920): 362–63. Walter O. Borcherdt (b. 1883) grew up in Chicago and received his engineering education at the Stevens Institute of Technology in New Jersey. See *Bulletin of the American Institute of Mining Engineers,* no. 83 (November 1913): xvii.

65. "Zinc Notes," *Zinc* 5 (August 1920): 273–74. For the date of the store building's construction, see R. R. Burger and F. B. Campbell, "Store and Office Departments," *Zinc* 15 (May 1930): 150.

66. "Around the Plants," *Zinc* 5 (December 1920): 405.

67. "Austinville," *Zinc* 18 (Summer 1939): 98.

68. "Around the Plants," *Zinc* 7 (April 1922): 120; "Whisperings from the Plants," *Zinc* 7 (December 1922): 378; "Whisperings from the Plants," *Zinc* 8 (March 1923): 90.

69. W. O. Borcherdt, "The New Austinville Shaft and Mill," *Zinc* 13 (January 1928): 6–11. On Joseph A. Van Mater, see his obituary, "J. A. Van Mater," *Zinc* 9 (April 1924): 98. The sale of agricultural limestone began at Austinville in 1925 and grew quite quickly once the new mill opened. A. D. Beers, "Limestone," *Zinc* 13 (October 1928): 292–95. On the use of Austinville limestone, see also R. R. Burger, "Agricultural Limestone," *Zinc* 15 (May 1930): 154; H. Kilborn, "The Farmer Buys Austinville Limestone," *Zinc* 17 (June 1938): 104–9; "Austinville Limestone Proves Useful to Nearby Farmers," *Zinc* 25 (January 1948): 72; "From Mine to Farm: Austinville Limestone Helps Southern Farmers," *Zinc* 31 (September 1953): 8–9; and "A Mining Record," *Zinc* 34 (August 1956): 10. While excavating for the new plant in 1926, workers dug an antebellum pig of lead from an old road, where it had evidently been lost from a wagon many years earlier. C. E. Taylor, "Antiques," *Zinc* 15 (May 1930): 156.

70. U.S. Bureau of Mines, *Minerals Yearbook, 1941* (Washington, D.C.: Government Printing Office, 1943), 330. On government officials visiting the area, see Charles Huddle to A. B. Dally Jr., August 17, 1943, Box 5, Huddle Family Papers.

71. *First Hundred Years of the New Jersey Zinc Company*, 35–37.

72. Ibid., 40–41, 49 (quotation).

73. "Austinville . . . Today," *Zinc* 26 (June 1948): 4–6; "New Construction at Austinville," *Zinc* 26 (November 1948): 12–14; "Austinville Rebuilds Its Flotation Mill for Greater Operating Efficiency," *Zinc* 31 (February 1953): 1–2 (quotation on 1). For highly technical details on some of the improvements made at Austinville at this time, see Boxes 83 and 84, New Jersey Zinc Company Records MC 672 (Annex), Special Collections and University Archives, Anderson Library, Rutgers University, New Brunswick, N.J.

74. "Austinville Improves Fire, Sewage, and Water Facilities: Construction Program Also Includes New Tailings Dam and Remodeled Staff Homes," *Zinc* 26 (January 1949): 1–4; "Our Company Builds New Water Plant at Austinville," *Zinc* 27 (June 1949): 16–17.

75. "Modernized Mill Awaits New Ore," *Zinc* 32 (March 1954): 10. On this period, see also Claire Nichols, "Austinville's Mines," *Virginia County* 8 (December 1954): 28–30.

76. New Jersey Zinc Company, *Annual Report 1951* (New York: New Jersey Zinc, 1952), 2–3 (quotation on 2). The most complete collection of these annual reports can be found in the Regenstein Library, University of Chicago.

77. "Our Company's Expansion and Construction Program—What It Means

to You," *Zinc* 27 (September 1949): 9; "More Ore for Austinville: Sinking of New Flatwoods Shaft Gets Underway," *Zinc* 29 (August 1951): 16; "Work on the Development of the New Ivanhoe Mine Gets Underway," *Zinc* 30 (March 1952): 4–5; "A New Zinc Mine in the Making," *Zinc* 31 (June 1953): 10 (quotation); "Ivanhoe Mine, Va.," *Zinc* 33 (April 1955): 6; "A Mining Record," *Zinc* 34 (August 1956): 10. Charles Ross Huddle had long found the frugal Dally difficult to deal with, as did New Jersey Zinc during negotiations for the option and the property. On the negotiations and sale, see, in the Huddle Family Papers, Charles Huddle to Richard Huddle, October 2, 1946, unnumbered box; Charles Huddle to Richard Huddle, February 22, 1947, unnumbered box; A. B. Dally Jr. to Charles Huddle, October 28, 1950, unnumbered box; and Charles Huddle to A. B. Dally Jr., August 14, 1951, Box 5.

78. "A New Zinc Mine in the Making"; "Ivanhoe Headframe Goes Up," *Zinc* 31 (December 1953): 10; "Progress at Ivanhoe," *Zinc* 32 (June 1954): 12–13; "Work on the Development of the New Ivanhoe Mine Gets Underway"; "Austinville, Va.," *Zinc* 33 (April 1955): 8; Lewis and O'Donnell, eds. and comps., *Ivanhoe, Virginia,* 1:159–68; Kegley, *Wythe County, Virginia,* 341; New Jersey Zinc Company, *Annual Report 1955* (New York: New Jersey Zinc, 1956), 6; New Jersey Zinc Company, *Annual Report 1957* (New York: New Jersey Zinc, 1958), 7. The Dally family's Ivanhoe Mining and Smelting Corporation had produced and sold some zinc ore from Ivanhoe earlier in the century, but the exploitation had been on a very minor, exploratory scale. See Currier, *Zinc and Lead Region of Southwestern Virginia,* 103.

79. "Austinville . . . Today," *Zinc* 26 (June 1948): 4–6.

80. Lewis and O'Donnell, eds. and comps., *Ivanhoe, Virginia,* 1:159–68; Kegley, *Wythe County, Virginia,* 341. For more on the New Jersey Zinc operation's complexity by the 1960s, see W. Horatio Brown and Edgar L. Weinberg, "Geology of the Austinville-Ivanhoe District," in John D. Ridge, ed., *Ore Deposits of the United States, 1933–1967: The Graton-Sales Volume,* vol. 1 (New York: American Institute of Mining, Metallurgical, and Petroleum Engineers, 1968), 169–86, esp. 171, 183. When Brown and Weinberg wrote their article, about 2,600 tons of ore were produced each day (171).

81. New Jersey Zinc Company, *1958 Annual Report* (New York: New Jersey Zinc, 1959), 9; New Jersey Zinc Company, *1959 Annual Report* (New York: New Jersey Zinc, 1960), 7; New Jersey Zinc Company, *1960 Annual Report* (New York: New Jersey Zinc, 1961), 6; New Jersey Zinc Company, *1961 Annual Report* (New York: New Jersey Zinc, 1962), 8; New Jersey Zinc Company, *1964 Annual Report* (New York: New Jersey Zinc, 1965), 7 (quotation). Water control had long been a problem in the underground shafts. For a technical look at the issue in the 1940s, see H. William Ahrenholz Jr., "Austinville Mine Hydrologic Problem," Engineer of Mines thesis, Lehigh University, 1949.

82. Lewis and O'Donnell, eds. and comps., *Ivanhoe, Virginia,* 1:168–72; Nora K. Foley, "A Geoenvironmental Lifecycle Model: The Austinville Platform Carbonate Deposit, Virginia," in Robert R. Seal II and Nora K. Foley, eds., *Progress on Geoenvironmental Models for Selected Mineral Deposit Types* (Reston, Va.: U.S. Geological Survey, 2002), 101–7, available at http://pubs.usgs.gov/of/2002/of02-195.

83. "G&W Agrees to Sell Some of the Assets of New Jersey Zinc," *Wall Street Journal,* July 29, 1981, 46.

84. "A G. & W. Group to Sell Zinc Unit," *New York Times,* July 30, 1981, D4; Lydia Chavez, "A Rocky Start at Jersey Zinc," *New York Times,* October 17, 1981, 29.

85. Lewis and O'Donnell, eds. and comps., *Ivanhoe, Virginia,* 1:168–72; Foley, "Geoenvironmental Lifecycle Model"; Webb, *Norfolk and Western Railway Company,* 54.

86. "Zinc," in Walter L. Emery et al., eds., *1984 Commodity Year Book* (Jersey City, N.J.: Commodity Research Bureau, 1984), 380.

87. Paul Dellinger, "Out of Zinc: Mine Closings Threaten an Area's Way of Life," *Roanoke Times and World News,* December 6, 1981, D1, D3; Joe Heldreth, "Austinville . . . after New Jersey Zinc," *Wytheville Southwest Virginia Enterprise,* May 27, 1982, A1, A16; Paul Dellinger, "Austinville Residents Take Initiative to Keep Their Town Intact," undated clipping in Box 2, Huddle Family Papers; Palmer C. Sweet, "Mining and Processing By-Product Resources in Virginia," *Virginia Minerals* 44 (May 1998): 1; Austinville Limestone Company Web site at http://www.avlime.com. On January 21, 1982, the *Wytheville Southwest Virginia Enterprise* published a special sixteen-page section to mark the mines' closure and to chronicle their history.

88. Lois Caliri, "Power Plant Opponents Take Case to Richmond: Water from Lead Mine Would Cool Plant," *Roanoke Times,* June 27, 2002, B1; Michael Biesecker, "Power Struggle: Duke Energy Hoping to Push a Gas Pipeline across Virginia: Property Owners Mobilize, Promise a Relentless Challenge," *Winston-Salem Journal,* November 17, 2002, A1.

89. Webb, *Norfolk and Western Railway Company,* 98, 111.

5. Left Behind

1. On the long-term globalization of trade and finance, see Jeffry A. Frieden, *Global Capitalism: Its Fall and Rise in the Twentieth Century* (New York: W. W. Norton, 2006); and Nitsan Chorev, *Remaking U.S. Trade Policy: From Protectionism to Globalization* (Ithaca, N.Y.: Cornell University Press, 2007).

2. *General Chemical Company after Twenty Years,* 34–35, 75 (quotation). Few surviving documents allow for a look at workers' lives, but information on one foreman's horrific accident while loading a railcar with acid can be found in *Pulaski Mining Co. v. Hagan,* 196 F. 724 (1912). At the time of the accident on August 26, 1909, the employee was earning $107 per month.

3. "Fabric of a Mill Town," *Roanoke Times and World News,* June 22, 1986, 3 (quotation); Avery Bond and Martha Nichols, comps. and eds., *A History of the Town of Fries* (Collinsville, Va.: Collinsville Printing, [1977]).

4. Thomas T. Read, "The Basis of Welfare Work," *Zinc* 1 (November 1916): 269–71 (quotations on 269).

5. *Zinc* 2 (April 1917): 105–6; 2 (September 1917): 252–53; 3 (March 1918): 82; 3 (April 1918): 113–14; 3 (July 1918): 219–20; 5 (February 1920): 65; 7 (January 1922): 24–27; 7 (March 1922): 91–92; 7 (June 1922): 188; 8 (January 1923): 21; 8 (July 1923): 217–18; 9 (January 1924): 20–21; 12 (March 1927): 54; 12 (April–May 1927): 78–80, 87; 19 (Winter 1940): 55. For a comparative look at the development of work and community life in Palmerton, Pennsylvania, another New Jersey Zinc Company town, see Nathan G. Wagner, "The New Jersey Zinc Company (of Pennsylvania) and Its Founder," M.A. thesis, Lehigh University, 1948. On so-called womanless weddings, see Craig Thompson Friend, "The Womanless Wedding: Masculinity, Cross-Dressing, and Gender Inversions in the Modern South," in Craig Thompson Friend, ed., *Southern Masculinity: Perspectives on Manhood in the South since Reconstruction* (Athens: University of Georgia Press, 2009), 219–45. For an understanding of the importance of early radio in rural communities and small towns, see Randal L. Hall, *Lum and Abner: Rural America and the Golden Age of Radio* (Lexington: University Press of Kentucky, 2007).

6. New Jersey Zinc reported at the close of 1949, "We provide houses for: 90 employees or 18% of all wage earners, . . . 8 pensioners, 4 drillers, 1 Postmaster—TOTAL 103." In addition, "We provide houses for 32 or 47% of our 68 salaried employees." "Personnel Department—Monthly Report, December, 1949," Box 14, New Jersey Zinc Company Records, Special Collections, Newman Library, Virginia Tech, Blacksburg.

7. William L. Woodford to Murray Poller, February 28, 1964, with attached report, Box 2, Huddle Family Papers; Lewis and O'Donnell, eds. and comps., *Ivanhoe, Virginia,* 2:177.

8. *Zinc* 4 (January 1919): 4; *Zinc* 14 (December 1929): 387 (quotation); Carrie Papa, *A Mile Deep and Black as Pitch: An Oral History of the Franklin and Sterling Hill Mines* (Blacksburg, Va.: McDonald and Woodward, 2004), 168 n. 6. The company also prepared an obituary on Thomas Hundley Sr.: "Thomas Hundley died at Austinville, October 27, 1930, at the age of 78 years. 'Uncle Tom,' as he was locally known, was employed by the old Wythe Lead & Zinc Company in 1862, or at the age of 10 years, and worked continuously for the old and present Company to 1921, when he was retired on pension. He had acquired twelve service stars. He worked at various occupations and at the time of his retirement was employed in the old mill department. He leaves a second wife a widow. Ten children survive him, as well as twenty-six grandchildren and thirteen great grandchildren." *Zinc* 16 (February 1931): 63. Papa's *Mile Deep and Black as Pitch* is the fruit of an

oral history project following the closing of two longtime New Jersey Zinc mines in Sussex County, New Jersey. In many ways, the history of the mines and workers there mirrors events in Austinville, with the exception of greater ethnic diversity among the miners in New Jersey.

9. *Zinc* 4 (April 1919): 14.

10. *Zinc* 4 (February 1919): 46.

11. *Agreement Between the New Jersey Zinc Co., Austinville, Virginia, and United Steelworkers of America . . . September 19, 1969* (n.p.: n.p., n.d.).

12. Heldreth, "Austinville . . . after New Jersey Zinc." For a feature on three generations of a single family and their work with New Jersey Zinc, written as the mines closed, see Paul Dellinger, "Out of Zinc: Mine Closings Threaten an Area's Way of Life," *Roanoke Times and World News,* December 6, 1981, D1, D3.

13. "Ivanhoe Worker Honored for Service," *Wytheville Southwest Virginia Enterprise,* December 23, 1965, 1. When the plant closed at the end of 1966, the number of employees was down to eleven hourly workers and seven salaried employees. See "Hourly Employees Contributory Retirement Plan by Length of Continuous Service Groups as of 12/31/66" and "Salary Employees Contributory Retirement Plan by Length of Continuous Service Groups as of 12/31/66," Box 2, Huddle Family Papers.

14. Lewis and O'Donnell, eds. and comps., *Ivanhoe, Virginia,* 2:108 (first quotation), 175 (second quotation).

15. Much has been written on U.S. labor relations during the late 1930s and the 1940s. Some of the works not yet cited that I have found particularly useful include Andrew E. Kersten, *Labor's Home Front: The American Federation of Labor during World War II* (New York: New York University Press, 2006); Nelson Lichtenstein, *Labor's War at Home: The CIO in World War II* (Cambridge, U.K.: Cambridge University Press, 1982); Howell John Harris, *The Right to Manage: Industrial Relations Policies of American Business in the 1940s* (Madison: University of Wisconsin Press, 1982); and Barbara S. Griffith, *The Crisis of American Labor: Operation Dixie and the Defeat of the CIO* (Philadelphia: Temple University Press, 1988).

16. Agreement between Ivanhoe, Virginia, Plant of National Carbide Corporation and Federal Workers Union, Local #22–257, an affiliate of the American Federation of Labor, June 1, 1940, Folder 22257, Strikes and Agreements File, Part I, American Federation of Labor Records, State Historical Society of Wisconsin, Madison.

17. Tom Cairns to William Green, July 2, 1941, Folder 22257, American Federation of Labor Records.

18. In the Matter of National Carbide Corporation and International Association of Machinists, International Chemical Workers Union, A.F. of L., Case No. 5-R-2192, Decided April 25, 1946, 67 NLRB, No. 96; In the Matter of National

Carbide Corporation and United Gas, Coke, and Chemical Workers of America, C.I.O., Case No. 5-R-1628, Decided October 27, 1944, 58 NLRB, No. 261; *Agreement Between National Carbide Co. . . . and International Chemical Workers' Union Local 382, November 2, 1965* (n.p.: n.p., n.d.), copy in Box 2, Huddle Family Papers; handwritten notes, September 29, 1952, and "Certification of Representation," Case 5-RC-1177, January 19, 1953, Operation Dixie: The C.I.O. Organizing Committee Papers, Microfilming Corp. of America, Sanford, N.C., Series 4:216, reel 59, frames 1001 and 1019; H. A. Bradley, "The Chemical Workers," *American Federationist* 58 (January 1951): 23–25 (quotation on 24).

19. Charles Huddle to A. B. Dally Jr., February 18, 1943, Box 5, Huddle Family Papers. In 1997, sixty-four-year-old Harry Donald Shepherd looked back: Hercules, the plant operator, "brought 'em in here by buses and train loads, people from everywhere. . . . [P]eople would rent any little old building you had. Just anything big enough they could sleep in. And [they'd] come out of West Virginia and I guess the Carolinas, all up back west of here. And Roanoke, Lynchburg— and had special trains that would haul people in because when they started construction work over there it was going around the clock. I mean they never stopped, seven days a week. And you could work seven days a week if you wanted to work. So, there was trains goin', buses goin', hauling people, taking 'em to and from work around the clock." *Coal Mining Lives: An Oral History Sequel to "Appalachian Coal Mining Memories"* (Radford, Va.: Department of Sociology and Anthropology, Radford University, 1998), 111.

20. In the matter of General Chemical Company and International Association of Machinists, A.F. of L., Case No. 5-R-1573, Decided October 12, 1944, 58 NLRB, No. 179; *Agreement Between Pulaski Works, General Chemical Division, Allied Chemical Corporation and International Chemical Workers Union, Local No. 119, A.F. of L.-C.I.O., June 21, 1961* (n.p.: n.p., n.d.), copy in Box 2, Huddle Family Papers; *Agreement Between Hercules Powder Company and United Gas, Coke, and Chemical Workers of America, CIO, at Radford Arsenal* (n.p.: n.p., [1952]), copy in Box 2, Huddle Family Papers. On the abortive unionization effort at the Pulaski foundry, see various documents and letters in Operation Dixie: The C.I.O. Organizing Committee Papers, Series 4:262, reel 61, frames 356–67.

21. See agreements between the New Jersey Zinc Company and the unions in the pamphlet holdings, Mary B. Kegley Collection, Special Collections, Wytheville Community College Library, Wythville, Va.; and Paul Gooch to William Green, November 28, 1941, Folder 22363, American Federation of Labor Records.

22. William Green to Robert F. Surratt, June 18, 1945, Folder 22363, American Federation of Labor Records.

23. Kenneth Scott to William Green, May 15, 1946, Folder 22363, American Federation of Labor Records.

24. James J. Lorence, *The Suppression of "Salt of the Earth": How Hollywood,*

Big Labor, and Politicians Blacklisted a Movie in Cold War America (Albuquerque: University of New Mexico Press, 1999), chap. 2.

25. Paul J. Smith to William Green, March 13, 1951, Folder 22363, American Federation of Labor Records; "Workers Return after Lengthy Labor Dispute," *Pulaski Southwest Times,* December 3, 1950, 6.

26. William Green to Fred D. Riggins, April 23, 1951, Folder 22363, American Federation of Labor Records; Paul J. Smith to Harry O'Reiley, June 1, 1951, American Federation of Labor Records (quotation); Paul J. Shupe and Fred Riggins to William Green, June 30, 1951, American Federation of Labor Records; "New Jersey Zinc Struck," *Pulaski Southwest Times,* April 2, 1951, 6.

27. Fred D. Riggins to William Green, September 25, 1951, Folder 22363, American Federation of Labor Records.

28. "Report of Work of Employee Relations Department, 1950," March 12, 1951, Box 10, New Jersey Zinc Company Records (Virginia Tech); John M. Kuhlman, "Right-to-Work Laws: The Virginia Experience," *Labor Law Journal* 6 (1955): 453–61; J. S. Smith and I. C. Welsted, "Labor in Old Virginia," *American Federationist* 59 (July 1952): 20–21.

29. U.S. Bureau of Mines, *Minerals Yearbook 1950* (Washington, D.C.: Government Printing Office, 1953), 1284; U.S. Bureau of Mines, *Minerals Yearbook 1951* (Washington, D.C.: Government Printing Office, 1954), 1503; "Report on Work of Employee Relations Department, 1951," February 26, 1952, Box 10, New Jersey Zinc Company Records (Virginia Tech) (quotation).

30. "Report on Work of Employee Relations Department, 1951," February 26, 1952.

31. New Jersey Zinc Company, *Annual Report 1950* (New York: New Jersey Zinc, 1951), unpaginated (first quotation); New Jersey Zinc Company, *Annual Report 1955,* 8 (second quotation).

32. For a stimulating interpretation of the economic changes in the 1970s that eroded the U.S. industrial sector, see Judith Stein, *Pivotal Decade: How the United States Traded Factories for Finance in the Seventies* (New Haven, Conn.: Yale University Press, 2010).

33. William L. Woodford to C. G. Morganstein, July 29, 1958; John R. Crowgey to A. M. McGavock, January 23, 1958; memorandum by R. C. Berresford, May 29, 1952: all in Box 10, New Jersey Zinc Company Records (Virginia Tech). See also New Jersey Zinc Company, *1954 Annual Report* (New York: New Jersey Zinc, 1955), 9; New Jersey Zinc Company, *1957 Annual Report* (New York: New Jersey Zinc, 1958), 11; Bureau of Mines, *Minerals Yearbook, 1960,* 3 vols. (Washington, D.C.: Government Printing Office, 1961), 3:1082; "Zinc Strike Settled," *Reading (Pa.) Eagle,* November 26, 1960, 3 (quotation); *Agreement Between the New Jersey Zinc Co., Austinville, Virginia, and United Steelworkers of America for Itself and on Behalf of Local Union 5075, August 1, 1978* (n.p.: n.p., n.d.).

34. Lewis and O'Donnell, eds. and comps., *Ivanhoe, Virginia,* 2:77–78.

35. Bond and Nichols, comps. and eds., *History of the Town of Fries,* 19.

36. Ibid., 32 (first quotation), 20; National Register of Historic Places registration form for the Fries Boarding Houses, site number VDHR #220–5015, available at http://www.dhr.virginia.gov/registers/Counties/Grayson/220–5015_ Fries_Boarding_Houses_2007_NRfinal.pdf (second quotation); Jerry Knight, "The Death of a Company Town: Mill Shutdown Devastates the Tiny Community of Fries, Va.," *Washington Post,* September 19, 1988, Washington Business sec., 34–36; *Davison's Textile "Blue Book" . . . July, 1926, to July, 1927,* office ed. (New York: Davison Publishing, 1926), 408; *Davison's Textile Blue Book . . . July 1937 to July 1938,* office ed. (New York: Davison Publishing, 1937), 318.

37. A. J. McKelway, *Child Labor in Virginia* (New York: National Child Labor Committee, 1912), 6 (quotation); Yukiko Maritani, "Child Labor Reform Movement in Virginia: 1890–1938," M.A. thesis, Old Dominion College, 1969, 46.

38. Bond and Nichols, comps. and eds., *History of the Town of Fries,* 61–62.

39. Wade Gilley, *Before Sister . . . in Hilltown* (Huntington, W.Va.: John Deaver Drinko Academy, 2002), 178. This memoir by a man who grew up adjacent to Fries, although romantic, has many insights into the area. Gilley went on to a career in higher-education administration.

40. Lewis and O'Donnell, eds. and comps., *Ivanhoe, Virginia,* 2:199–200.

41. Knight, "Death of a Company Town"; Paul Dellinger, "Fries' Cotton Mill Not Changed a Bit," *Roanoke Times and World News,* April 21, 1977, C4. Extensive documentation concerning Smith W. Bagley and James Ray Gilley and the bankruptcy rests in the Washington Group, Inc., Records #4605, Southern Historical Collection, Wilson Library, University of North Carolina, Chapel Hill. For historical context on the extent to which leading industrial families had controlled twentieth-century Winston-Salem, see Randal L. Hall and Ken Badgett, eds., "Robinson Newcomb and the Limits of Liberalism at UNC: Two Case Studies of Black Businessmen in the 1920s South," *North Carolina Historical Review* 86 (October 2009): 373–403; and a novel, James M. Shields, *Just Plain Larnin'* (New York: Coward-McCann, 1934).

42. Knight, "Death of a Company Town"; Dellinger, "Fries' Cotton Mill Not Changed a Bit." One can find the various allegations conveniently spelled out in indictments, the SEC complaint, and other documents in Folders 2 and 30, Washington Group Records. See also *Fulk et al. v. Bagley et al.,* 88 F.R.D. 153 (1980), and *Gilbert et al. v. Bagley et al.,* 492 F. Supp. 714 (1980). The quotation in the text comes from page 98 of "Report of Trustee's Investigation Pursuant to Rule 10-208 (a)," filed June 30, 1978, by Richard A. Gilbert, copy in Folder 9, Washington Group Records. Biographical information on Gilley can be found in Folder 34, Washington Group Records. On the settlement with the SEC, see "Bagley Consents to Settlement of SEC's Stock Fraud Suit," *Washington Post,* February 22,

1980, F2; and "Smith W. Bagley, Others Enjoined," *SEC News Digest,* February 20, 1980, 2. On the prosecutors' actions following the acquittal, see Merrill Brown, "U.S. Prosecutors Criticize Judge for Handling of Smith Bagley Trial," *Washington Post,* November 2, 1979, A14, and remarks in the U.S. Senate in the *Congressional Record,* November 2, 1979, pp. 30751–30753. Though Bagley supported the Democratic Party, the Washington Group leaders had access to influential Republicans as well. Gilley took an active part in Republican affairs. And the company's top executives for a time in 1976 and 1977, before the bankruptcy filing, included K. Wayne Smith, a Wake Forest graduate, like Gilley, and a former defense and security analyst in Richard M. Nixon's administration, where he reported at times to Henry A. Kissinger. On Smith's being named executive vice president for finance and chief financial officer in May 1976 and then becoming a director of the Washington Group shortly before resigning in the spring of 1977, see Dwight Sparks, "A House Built on Credit," clipping labeled *Madison (N.C.) Messenger,* February 3, 1982, 25, in Folder 50, Washington Group Records; and "K. Wayne Smith," *Carolina Financial Times* (Chapel Hill), May 31, 1976, 20. On Smith's employment through at least March 1977, see also Smith to C. Edwin Allman, September 12, 1977; Joyce Stone to Smith, September 15, 1977; and Allman to Wesley Bailey, June 12, 1978: all in Folder 30, Washington Group Records. Judge Rufus W. Reynolds oversaw the bankruptcy, retired textile executive Richard A. Gilbert served as trustee, and Winston-Salem attorney C. Edwin Allman Jr. handled much of the legal work for Gilbert.

43. One can find the allegation that the Fries plant was sold for less than its value on page 38 of "Report of Trustee's Investigation Pursuant to Rule 10-208 (a)," filed June 30, 1978, by Richard A. Gilbert, copy in Folder 9, Washington Group Records.

44. "Fabric of a Mill Town" (eight-page special section on Fries), *Roanoke Times and World News,* June 22, 1986, 8; Betty Booker, "Workers Wait for Way of Life to End," *Richmond Times-Dispatch,* November 14, 1988, A1, A6; Knight, "Death of a Company Town"; Dellinger, "Fries' Cotton Mill Not Changed a Bit"; Mary Bishop, "Mill That Built Fries to Close," *Roanoke Times and World News,* July 21, 1988, A1, A4; "Foreign Textiles Force Fries Mill to Close," *Richmond Times-Dispatch,* July 21, 1988, 13; National Register of Historic Places registration form for the Fries Boarding Houses. For the Pamplin family's extraordinarily self-indulgent description of acquiring Mount Vernon Mills, see Robert B. Pamplin Jr. et al., *Heritage* (New York: Master Media, 1994), chap. 13.

45. Bill Barker, *A Life in Textiles, 1949–1999: A Memoir* (Rome, Ga.: Wheredepony Press, 2008), 72.

46. Knight, "Death of a Company Town"; Dellinger, "Fries' Cotton Mill Not Changed a Bit"; Bishop, "Mill That Built Fries to Close"; "Foreign Textiles Force Fries Mill to Close."

47. Booker, "Workers Wait for Way of Life to End."

48. Quoted in "Fabric of a Mill Town," 8.

49. Carolyn L. Jones (mayor of Fries) to Dennis P. Carney (EPA Superfund official), March 26, 1992. This document and many others related to Mount Vernon Mills can be found by consulting the EPA Web site at http://www.epa.gov/reg3hwmd/super/sites/VAD988207957/index.htm.

50. Quoted in "Fabric of a Mill Town," 8.

51. Writer David Huddle describes the road from Ivanhoe to Fries in his youth as "twelve miles of keep-the-hell-out-of-here." See David Huddle, "Mission," *Appalachian Heritage* 39 (Spring 2011): 106–7 (quotation on 107).

52. Booker, "Workers Wait for Way of Life to End" (quotations); Rex Bowman, "Will Fries' Ship Come In?" *Richmond Times-Dispatch,* October 20, 2008, A1.

53. Ben Bomberger, "Fries Hears Mill Site Development Ideas," *Galax Gazette,* March 12, 2009, available at http://www.galaxgazette.com/content/fries-hears-mill-site-development-ideas.

54. I have written about this event in considerable detail in "A Courtroom Massacre: Politics and Public Sentiment in Progressive-Era Virginia," *Journal of Southern History* 70 (May 2004): 249–92, and covered the memory of it in "Constructing Violence: Historical Memory and a 1912 Courtroom Massacre in Virginia's Blue Ridge Mountains," in Richard Jackson, ed., *(Re)Constructing Cultures of Violence and Peace* (Amsterdam: Rodopi, 2004), 31–44.

55. Quoted in Harkins, *Hillbilly,* 35–36. In a similar vein, another periodical commented, "Everybody knows about the mountain people of Virginia and the adjoining States, their isolated communities, feuds, clannishness, and lawlessnesses. The pity of the good judge's death is almost equaled by the pity of his murderers' crime. These mountain people are like children who have run wild, and very like the Highland Scotch as we read of them in Scott's novels. It is an ill task to hunt them down, and a dangerous one, too, but of course there is nothing else to do, and it is being done apparently with proper vigor." "The Recall in the Virginia Mountains," *Harper's Weekly,* March 23, 1912, 4.

56. Archie Green, "Hillbilly Music: Source and Symbol," *Journal of American Folklore* 78 (July–September 1965): 204–28 (quotation on 213); Ivan M. Tribe, *The Stonemans: An Appalachian Family and the Music That Shaped Their Lives* (Urbana: University of Illinois Press, 1993); Norm Cohen, "Henry Whitter: His Life and Music," *JEMF Quarterly* 11 (1975): 57–66; Harkins, *Hillbilly,* chap. 3. Stoneman's career perhaps peaked in 1927 when he and his family were the lead-off performers at recording sessions in Bristol, Virginia, that produced popular new stars, the Carter family and Jimmie Rodgers, with slightly different styles of music. Whitter also played in the Bristol sessions. See Tribe, *The Stonemans,* 56–62. In February 1924, Whitter recorded "Sydney Allen," which was a song well

known in his home region. Released as Okeh 40109, it recorded the story of Floyd Allen's brother, one of the assailants in the 1912 courtroom shooting described earlier. See Cohen, "Henry Whitter," 62. On "Sydney Allen" and related songs, see Peter R. Aceves, "The Hillsville Tragedy in Court Record, Mass Media, and Folk Balladry: A Problem in Historical Documentation," *Keystone Folklore Quarterly* 16 (Spring 1971): 1–38; and Robert M. Remnick, "The Tragedy of the Allen Family of Hillsville, Virginia," *North Carolina Folklore* 7 (December 1959): 1–17. For more on Whitter and the lyrics of his songs, see the pamphlet, probably from the mid-1930s, titled *Familiar Folk Songs as Sung by Henry Whitter* (n.p.: n.p., n.d.).

57. Whitter's "The New River Train," recorded in the February 1924 session, was released as Okeh 40143.

58. Tribe, *The Stonemans,* chap. 7; *Traditional Music from Grayson and Carroll Counties* (Folkways Records FS 3811). On John Lomax's being in the area in 1937, see Thomas A. Adler, "Record Reviews," *Western Folklore* 41 (January 1982): 77–84, esp. 82. Michael Yates's recordings of people such as Carroll fiddler William Marshall are now available as a two-volume, four-CD set titled *Far in the Mountains* (Musical Traditions Records MTCD 321-1 and MTCD 323-4). In 1918, the pioneering British collector Cecil Sharp had earlier noted songs in Meadows of Dan, just beyond Carroll County's eastern border, in Patrick County. Like so many people before him, Sharp was amazed by the climb from the foothills to the top of the Blue Ridge escarpment: "The road wh[ich] is ordinarily a very steep, narrow & dangerous one[,] was far worse than usual on account of some recent thunder storms which had washed it clean, right down to the native rock. Some places the inclination of the car was so great in turning a corner with a sheer fall of 5 or 6 hundred feet over the side, that the driver himself suggested we should get out while he negotiated it—which we did with alacrity! How a car could have been driven up at all I can't imagine. I am sure nothing but a Ford could have done it. And then when we got to the top of the Ridge we found a large plateau of rolling meadows and fertile land occupied by a thoroughly respectable, church-going, school-attending population, making money at a great rate owing to the advance in food-prices and many of them housed in comfortable frame-dwellings and sporting their own motor cars." In Mike Yates, "Introduction: Cecil Sharp's Appalachian Journey," in Mike Yates, Elaine Bradtke, and Malcolm Taylor, eds., *Dear Companion: Appalachian Traditional Songs and Singers from the Cecil Sharp Collection* (London: English Folk Dance and Song Society, 2004), 3–27 (quotation on 20).

59. Herman K. Williams, *The First Forty Years of the Old Fiddlers Convention, Galax, Virginia* (n.p.: n.p., n.d.), 11–12; Chris Goertzen, "Galax, Virginia's 'Old Fiddler's Convention': The Virtues and Flaws of a Giant Fiddle Contest," *World of Music* 45, no. 1 (2003): 133–47. Felts Park is named for Thomas Lafayette Felts, who helped first develop Galax and who co-owned the Baldwin-Felts Detective

Agency in the early twentieth century. With principal offices in Roanoke, Virginia, and Bluefield, West Virginia, the agency provided mercenaries for, among other clients, large mining corporations in West Virginia and Colorado.

60. "When Industry Takes the Lead," 30; Paul Hardin Kapp, "Understanding Business District Revitalization and Design in Small Communities: A Revitalization and Design Study of Galax, Virginia," M.S. thesis, University of Pennsylvania, 1992, 54–67; special rotogravure section of the *Galax Gazette* dated March 1937; special section of the *Galax Post-Herald,* July 5, 1945; "Open House at New Hanes Plant in Galax," *Norfolk and Western Magazine* 39 (May 1961): 216; John E. Moes, *Local Subsidies for Industry* (Chapel Hill: University of North Carolina Press, 1962), 131–32. On Burlington Industries, see Allen Tullos, *Habits of Industry: White Culture and the Transformation of the Carolina Piedmont* (Chapel Hill: University of North Carolina Press, 1989), chap. 3; and Jacquelyn Dowd Hall et al., *Like a Family: The Making of a Southern Cotton Mill World* (Chapel Hill: University of North Carolina Press, 1987), chap. 5. In 1929, a list of Galax's furniture-related plants included Edwards Chair Factory, Vaughan Furniture Company, Vaughan-Bassett Furniture Company, and Webb Furniture Company. R. L. Humbert et al., *Industrial Survey: Carroll County, Virginia* (Blacksburg: Engineering Extension Division, Virginia Polytechnic Institute, 1929), 13. Wytheville in 1929 had the H. and M. Overall Factory, Inspiration Hosiery Mills, and the Wytheville Woolen Mills. R. L. Humbert et al., *Industrial Survey: Wythe County, Virginia* (Blacksburg: Engineering Extension Division, Virginia Polytechnic Institute, 1929), 15. On J. Valentine Webb, who founded the Webb Furniture Company, see *Virginia: Rebirth of the Old Dominion,* 4:500–501.

61. John H. Zammito, *Dynamics of Southern Growth* (Memphis: Morgan, Keegan, 1972), 60 (first quotation), 61 (second quotation). For a theory-heavy look at music-related tourism in the area, in particular Floyd County, see Ryan Chaney, "Signing Sounds of the South: Representing Culture and Performing Heritage in Appalachian Virginia," Ph.D. diss., Columbia University, 2008.

62. U.S. Senate, *Problems of the Domestic Textile Industry: Hearings before a Subcommittee of the Committee on Interstate and Foreign Commerce, United States Senate, Eighty-fifth Congress, Second Session, on a Study of the Textile Industry of the United States Pursuant to S. Res. 287, November 12, 13, and 14, 1958 (Hearings Held in New York City), Part 4* (Washington, D.C.: Government Printing Office, 1959), 1569 (quotations); special section of the *Galax Post-Herald,* July 5, 1945. Thomas J. Wallner also developed the Virginia Maid Hosiery Mills in Pulaski before World War II. On Wallner, see "T. J. Wallner Brings Full Fashioned Hosiery Industry South," *Pulaski Southwest Times,* August 13, 1939, sec. 6, p. 1; and "Industrialist Succumbs," *Pulaski Southwest Times,* August 18, 1942, 1, 6. On Waldemar Wallner, see the relevant entry in *Virginia: Rebirth of the Old Dominion,* 4:343–44. On the participation of local investors in the Carroll Hosiery plant, see

"Hosiery Plant Will Be Built at Hillsville," *Pulaski Southwest Times,* May 5, 1938, 1, 5. Also see "South Carolina Firm Will Erect New Hosiery Mill," *Pulaski Southwest Times,* May 19, 1938, 1. On southern leaders' early use of incentives to attract industry, see James C. Cobb, *The Selling of the South: The Southern Crusade for Industrial Development, 1936–1990,* 2nd ed. (Urbana: University of Illinois Press, 1993), chaps. 1–2.

63. Interviewed by the author, December 29, 2010, Carroll County, Va. On the decline of small farms in this period, see Melissa Walker, *Southern Farmers and Their Stories: Memory and Meaning in Oral History* (Lexington: University Press of Kentucky, 2006); and Paul K. Conkin, *A Revolution Down on the Farm: The Transformation of American Agriculture since 1929* (Lexington: University Press of Kentucky, 2008).

64. Charles and Ida Huddle to William R. and Terry Huddle, June 26, 1967, Box 1, Huddle Family Papers.

65. Ivanhoe Industrial Park brochure, Box 1, Huddle Family Papers.

66. Joe Kennedy, "Ghosts of Fires, Furnaces Tell of Once-Busy Community," *Roanoke Times and World News,* November 4, 1979, E1.

67. David Huddle, "Hamlet in the Hills," *Preservation* 53 (May–June 2001): 22–27 (quotation on 26).

68. For excellent reflections on using oral histories to gain a sense of the diversity of the South, see the introduction to Walker, *Southern Farmers and Their Stories,* and W. Fitzhugh Brundage, "Contentious and Collected: Memory's Future in Southern History," *Journal of Southern History* 75 (August 2009): 751–66.

69. Mary Ann Hinsdale, Helen M. Lewis, and S. Maxine Waller, *It Comes from the People: Community Development and Local Theology* (Philadelphia: Temple University Press, 1995). Also see Helen M. Lewis, "Community History," *OAH Magazine of History* 11 (Spring 1997): 20–22; and Maxine Waller, Helen M. Lewis, Clare McBrien, and Carroll L. Wessinger, "'It Has to Come from the People': Responding to Plant Closings in Ivanhoe, Virginia," in Gaventa, Smith, and Willingham, eds., *Communities in Economic Crisis,* 19–28. For a documentary on the efforts in Ivanhoe, see the film *Rough Side of the Mountain,* directed by Anne Lewis (Whitesburg, Ky.: Appalshop Film and Video, 1997). In June 2009, Carroll County sold its 49.2-acre portion of the carbide plant site. Christopher Brooke, "Ivanhoe Land Sold," *Galax Gazette,* July 1–2, 2009, 1–2. Market forces also brought considerable deindustrialization to the Pocahontas–Flat Top coal region that had been so important to late-nineteenth-century iron makers and railroads in the New River valley. See Mark S. Myers, "Deindustrialization and the Decline of Community in the Coalfields: McDowell County, West Virginia, 1950–2000," Ph.D. diss., West Virginia University, 2008, esp. chaps. 5–6.

70. Hinsdale, Lewis, and Waller, *It Comes from the People;* Lewis and O'Donnell, eds. and comps., *Ivanhoe, Virginia.*

71. Lewis and O'Donnell, eds. and comps., *Ivanhoe, Virginia,* 2:66 (first quotation), 73 (second quotation), 75 (third and fourth quotations), 232 (fifth quotation).

72. Ibid., 2:71 (first quotation), 164–65, 171 (second quotation), 216 (third quotation), 211 (fourth quotation).

73. Rex Bowman, "Man's Life Was the Pits for Days after His Fall Through Outhouse Floor," *Winston-Salem Journal,* August 18, 2000, A1, A6; Tom Knott, "Outhouse Survivor Back on His Feet after Soggy Stint," *Washington Times,* September 7, 2000, C2; Mike Gangloff, "New House Replaces Outhouse: Collapsed Privy Leads to New Digs," *Roanoke Times,* March 12, 2001, C1; Tim Thornton, "Winesett Shared His Love of Music, Fiddle: Coolidge Winesett, 1925–2004," *Roanoke Times,* February 17, 2004, A1.

74. Duncan Adams, "Vaughan Furniture to Close Its Last Factory: The 85-Year-Old Galax Company Will Lay Off 275 People and Become a Distributor and Supplier," *Roanoke Times,* March 19, 2008, C8. Some manufacturing and extraction-related work, such as a Spanish firm's shipping of lumber to Europe, remains in the Galax area, but heavy industrial jobs are more and more rare. In 2004, the Bassett family, longtime manufacturers of furniture in Galax, pushed a successful antidumping case claiming that Chinese furniture manufacturers were putting below-cost items on the U.S. market. But the Bassetts' efforts have not been enough to save the furniture industry in Galax. See "A Tale of Two Furniture Makers," in Pete Engardio, ed., *Chindia: How China and India Are Revolutionizing Global Business* (New York: McGraw-Hill, 2007), 70–73.

75. On Montreal-based Gildan, which owns Kentucky Derby Hosiery, the latter's closing, and Gildan's operations in Honduras, see Cindy Skrzycki, "A Great Debate over the Price of a Pair of Honduran Socks," *Washington Post,* February 5, 2008, D2; and Sherry Youngquist, "Gildan to Close Sock Plant in Hillsville, Cut 180 Jobs," *Winston-Salem Journal,* December 12, 2008, B6.

76. For the Galax Wal-Mart store's opening date, see economist Thomas J. Holmes's database at http://www.econ.umn.edu/~holmes/data/WalMart/store_openings.csv. For a weighing of the benefits and drawbacks of Wal-Mart's growth, see Emek Basker, "The Causes and Consequences of Wal-Mart's Growth," *Journal of Economic Perspectives* 21 (Summer 2007): 177–98.

77. On immigrants in Galax, see John William Knowles III, "Winds of Change: Mexico in a Town in Appalachia," Ph.D. diss., Virginia Polytechnic Institute and State University, 2006.

78. See Dickeson, *Report of a Geological Survey and Examination of the Lands Owned by the Megs County and Virginia Mining Co. of Virginia,* 6 (quotation); the Hoover Color Corporation Web site at http://www.hoovercolor.com/about /history/; the explanation of iron oxide pigments on the Web site of the Virginia Division of Mineral Resources at http://www.dmme.virginia.gov/DMR3/feoxide .shtml; Joan Gaidos, "Earthen Colors: The Art and Science of Transforming Pig-

ment into Crayons," *Richmond Times-Dispatch*, November 8, 2001, C1; Tom Angleberger, "They Get the Colors Just Right," *Roanoke Times*, March 7, 2004, NRV17; and Tom Angleberger, "The Color of Dirt," *Roanoke Times*, March 7, 2004, NRV16. On the move of the American Pigment Corporation from Bedford, Virginia, to Hiwassee, see Webb, *Norfolk and Western Railway Company*, 16.

79. Industrial College of the Armed Forces, National Defense University, *Spring 2009 Industry Study Final Report: Weapons Industry* (Fort McNair, D.C.: Industrial College of the Armed Forces, 2009), 6.

80. Mike Gangloff, "Meth 'Epidemic' Prompts Call for Federal Aid in Galax," *Roanoke Times*, May 3, 2009, A1; Thomas J. Schoenbaum, *The New River Controversy: A New Edition* (Jefferson, N.C.: McFarland, 2007). Christmas trees are an extreme case of the scientific forestry criticized in James C. Scott, *Seeing Like a State: How Certain Schemes to Improve the Human Condition Have Failed* (New Haven, Conn.: Yale University Press, 1998), chap. 1.

81. Gangloff, "Meth 'Epidemic' Prompts Call for Federal Aid in Galax" (quotations); U.S. Department of Justice, National Drug Intelligence Center, *Situation Report: Cities in Which Mexican DTOs Operate within the United States* (Washington, D.C.: U.S. Department of Justice, April 11, 2008), available at http://www.justice.gov/ndic/pubs27/27986/27986p.pdf.

82. The importance of the 1840s turnpike climbing to Fancy Gap had endured. In October 1928, regional booster groups held a festival to mark completion of paving this stretch of road, part of present U.S. Highway 52. They proclaimed, "It is truly an event to celebrate when Virginia and North Carolina are joined at one of the highest points in the majestic mountains by a highway that is a marvel of engineering skill. The opening of this road is the connecting link of hard surfaced roads from Canada to Florida, and America through it is made a stronger union." See the poster titled "Fancy Gap Road Celebration: Road Opening, Friday, Oct. 19, 1928," Virginia Tech Imagebase, Maps0006, at http://spec.lib.vt.edu/imagebase/maps/screen/MAPS0006.jpg. Sponsored by booster groups from both North Carolina and Virginia, the event promised, according to the poster, "Prominent Speakers, Governors and Highway Commissioners," along with floats, bands, "Historic Pageants," and even "College Girls." On the celebration, also see E. Gary Marshall, "October 19, 1928: Hillsville's Highway Hey-Day," *Carroll County Chronicles* 18 (Spring 2000): 11–21. The paving had been eagerly anticipated. In 1924, Elon College professor W. P. Lawrence described a drive up that section of road: "This highway winds up the mountain through picturesque gorges and around precipitous mountain spurs at a comfortable grade of perhaps five percent. Notwithstanding dangerous precipices, often rising abruptly from the ribbon of roadway or descending almost perpendicularly from it for hundreds of feet to the dark depths of a shadow glen, there is a great deal of motor vehicles and other forms of travel on this highway, and there is likely to be

much more in the coming years. The State of Virginia, I am told, is already constructing this into a splendid modern highway." W. P. Lawrence, "Our Work in the Mountains," *Herald of Gospel Liberty* 116 (February 28, 1924): 211–12 (quotation on 212).

83. In 1973, White Motor Corporation of Cleveland, Ohio, announced plans for an assembly plant in Dublin, Pulaski County. Workers began turning out trucks in 1975. In 1978, they voted in the United Auto Workers Union. In 1981, Volvo acquired many assets of the bankrupt White firm, and it (or specifically what is now the Volvo Trucks North America division) has since assembled its heavy trucks in Dublin at the now-expanded plant. White's move represented an early entry in a long list of automotive firms from the Rust Belt and from other countries entering the South to build up-to-date, cost-efficient plants. See Sujit M. CanagaRetna, *The Drive to Move South: The Growing Role of the Automobile Industry in the Southern Legislative Conference Economies* (Atlanta, Ga.: Southern Office, Council of State Governments, 2003), esp. 128; Christopher Calnan, "State Began Grants to Volvo Plant in '94," *Roanoke Times,* January 14, 1999, A6. Though the New River valley plant gets little mention, Rosemary Solovey Hritsko traces White's decline in "The White Motor Story," Ph.D. diss., University of Akron, 1988. A second remnant of heavy industry also survives in Hillsville in the form of a plant that makes components for underground mining conveyor systems. The plant originated as part of Long-Airdox, a company founded in West Virginia, and then was owned by DBT Deutsche Bergbau-Technik GmbH before being acquired by Bucyrus, which Caterpillar subsequently bought. On the early history of Long-Airdox, see Jerry Bruce Thomas, *An Appalachian Reawakening: West Virginia and the Perils of the New Machine Age, 1945–1972* (Morgantown: West Virginia University Press, 2010), 19–20.

84. For a history of the Blue Ridge Parkway, see Whisnant, *Super-Scenic Motorway.* On the Appalachian Trail, see Sarah Mittlefehldt, "The Tangled Roots of the Appalachian Trail: A Social and Environmental History," Ph.D. diss., University of Wisconsin, Madison, 2008, 91–129; and Leonard M. Adkins, *The Appalachian Trail: A Visitor's Companion* (Birmingham, Ala., and Harpers Ferry, W.Va.: Menasha Ridge Press and Appalachian Trail Conference, 1998), 23. The Appalachian Trail entered the area in 1930. That year, Myron H. Avery wrote, "The outstanding achievement in trail development in the Southern Appalachians was the 225-mile trip with a measuring wheel by Roy R. Ozmer. Mr. Ozmer undertook the solution of the Trail Conference's most difficult problem, the location of the route through southern Virginia. Ozmer's route follows the Blue Ridge from the Peaks of Otter at the southern end of the Natural Bridge National Forest to Galax on the New River, near the Virginia–North Carolina boundary line. Here he turned west through the Unaka National Forest to reach the Nolichucky River in Tennessee. Mr. S. [Shirley] L. Cole of Floyd, Virginia, has undertaken the ex-

tension of the Trail from the Peaks of Otter to the Virginia-Tennessee line. Groups of interested trail-cutters have been organized at Roanoke, Floyd, Hillsville and Galax, Virginia. Their enthusiasm and energy promise a completed trail across Virginia in the very immediate future." Myron H. Avery, "The Appalachian Trail: Notes on the Appalachian Trail in the South," *Appalachian Mountain Club Bulletin* 24 (December 1930): 198–99; that issue of the bulletin is simultaneously *Appalachia* 18 (December 1930). The volunteers finished the trail in time for the segment to be described in detail in *Guides to Paths in the Blue Ridge. . . .* (Washington, D.C.: Potomac Appalachian Trail Club, 1931), 87–102. Also see Myron H. Avery, "Southern Virginia: Peaks of Otter to New River," *Appalachia* 19 (June 1932): 161–65; *Supplement (Revised) to Guide to Paths in the Blue Ridge: The Appalachian Trail and Side Trails* (Washington, D.C.: Potomac Appalachian Trail Club, 1937), 186–220; and "Trail Relocation in Southern Virginia," *Potomac Appalachian Trail Club Bulletin* 9 (October 1940): 88–90. Following the parkway's construction, the Appalachian Trail route was changed to run more directly through more U.S. Forest Service properties. Leonard Adkins writes, "Prior to the 1950s, the AT headed eastward from the Mount Rogers area, worked its way to Galax, Virginia, and turned north along the eastern rim of the Blue Ridge Mountains. Many of the highlights of that route—Puckett Cabin, Pinnacles of Dan, Mabry Mill, Rocky Knob, and Smarts View—can still be seen or accessed from the Blue Ridge Parkway. Construction of the scenic highway displaced much of the AT and prompted Tom Campbell, Jim Denton, additional members of the Roanoke Appalachian Trail Club, and others to relocate the trail further west onto lands that had been recently acquired by the Jefferson National Forest." Adkins, *Appalachian Trail,* 23.

85. Sarvis, *History of the Jefferson National Forest;* Will Sarvis, "The Mount Rogers National Recreation Area and the Rise of Public Involvement in Forest Service Planning," *Environmental History Review* 18 (Summer 1994): 40–65; Will Sarvis, "An Appalachian Forest: Creation of the Jefferson National Forest and Its Effects on the Local Community," *Forest and Conservation History* 37 (October 1993): 169–78. Williams, *Appalachia,* 1–8, comments on the pivotal spot occupied by the intersection of Interstates 77 and 81 near the site where Fort Chiswell stood. For a look at the early planning for national-forest lands, including a map that projected purchases in the region under study here, see *Message from the President of the United States, Transmitting a Report of the Secretary of Agriculture in Relation to the Forests, Rivers, and Mountains of the Southern Appalachian Region* (Washington, D.C.: Government Printing Office, 1902), esp. the map facing p. 24; Glenn, *Denudation and Erosion in the Southern Appalachian Basin,* esp. 116–20; Gordon B. Dodds, "The Stream-Flow Controversy: A Conservation Turning Point," *Journal of American History* 56 (June 1969): 59–69; and William E. Shands, "The Lands Nobody Wanted: The Legacy of the Eastern National Forests," in

Harold K. Steen, ed., *Origins of the National Forests: A Centennial Symposium* (Durham, N.C.: Forest History Society, 1992), 19–44. For the broader context, see Gregg, *Managing the Mountains;* and Pierce, *Great Smokies.*

86. Schoenbaum, *New River Controversy;* Stephen William Foster, *The Past Is Another Country: Representation, Historical Consciousness, and Resistance in the Blue Ridge* (Berkeley and Los Angeles: University of California Press, 1988), chap. 3. Phil Hanes died on January 16, 2011. See Richard Craver, "Arts Pulled Hanes Away from Family Company, but Not the Business World," *Winston-Salem Journal,* January 17, 2011, A1. Grayson County is now trying to develop a service industry not related to tourism. The Virginia state prison system has finished a 252,088-square-foot prison near Independence, but as of August 2010 it was expected to sit empty for at least two years. Landmark News Service, "Grayson Prison Stalled," *Galax Gazette,* August 4, 2010, available at http://www.galax gazette.com/content/grayson-prison-stalled-0.

87. On the restoration of the nearly depleted deer population in Virginia's mountains, see John Henry Reeves, "The History and Development of Wildlife Conservation in Virginia: A Critical Review," Ph.D. diss., Virginia Polytechnic Institute, 1960, 189–208.

88. For more on the region's living tradition of string music, which in part justified the placement of the Blue Ridge Music Center, see Kevin Donleavy, *Strings of Life—Conversations with Old-Time Musicians from Virginia and North Carolina* (Blacksburg, Va.: Pocahontas Press, 2004). The GrahamFest organizers can cite a local precedent in hoping that their festival will become a major one. On August 6, 7, and 8, 1976, promoter Hal Abramson put on the three-day festival Stompin 76, marked by sex, drugs, and bluegrass. Reporters estimated that more than a hundred thousand young people from throughout the East Coast crowded a farm in the Pot Rock community of Carroll County near the New River to hear performances by such major acts as Bonnie Raitt, the Nitty Gritty Dirt Band, John Prine, Ry Cooder, and many others. Attendees consumed liberal amounts of drugs and alcohol, and traffic overwhelmed the rural roads for many miles.

89. "Grant Sought for Falls Property," *Galax Gazette,* August 12–13, 2009, 2.

90. The closing clause was adapted from a worker's comment quoted in Heldreth, "Austinville . . . after New Jersey Zinc."

91. On changes in farming, see Conkin, *Revolution Down on the Farm.* On the importance of chestnut trees to this region, see Ralph H. Lutts, "Like Manna from God: The American Chestnut Trade in Southwestern Virginia," *Environmental History* 9 (July 2004): 497–525. On acid rain and air pollution, see U.S. Department of Agriculture (USDA) Forest Service Southern Region, *Final Environmental Impact Statement for the Revised Land and Resource Management Plan, Jefferson National Forest* (Roanoke, Va.: USDA Forest Service, 2004), chap. 2, p. 35, and chap. 3, pp. 20–22, 27.

Appendixes on Technology

1. [Francis Preston], "Description of Francis Preston Ironworks on Cripple Creek," James Breckinridge Papers, reel 2, frames 179–81.

2. "Charcoal Iron Industries in South-Western Virginia," *Journal of the United States Association of Charcoal Iron Workers* 5 (April 1884): 100–109.

3. Douglas Galton, "Notes on Railway Appliances at the Philadelphia Exhibition of 1876," *Minutes of Proceedings of the Institution of Civil Engineers* 53, pt. 3 (1877–1878): 28–97 (quotation on 35–37).

4. Eilers, "Notes from Southwestern Virginia" (November 30, 1869), 338.

5. W. M. P., "Virginia's Garden Spot," *Baltimore Manufacturers' Record* 9 (July 17, 1886): 804–5.

6. Moxham, "Zinc Smelting at the Bertha Works, Virginia," 544. For another good description of the Bertha plant's work routine, see Higgins, "Zinc Mining and Smelting in Southwestern Virginia.—II" (April 6, 1905), 658–59. For a detailed look at the production of both spelter and zinc oxide by the Passaic Zinc Company of Jersey City, N.J., in the 1890s, see "Manufacture of Oxide of Zinc," *Scientific American Supplement* 38, no. 967 (July 14, 1894): 15454. Passaic Zinc at the time used ores from Wythe County as well as from elsewhere.

7. Edward James Kearns, "Canned Power," *Searchlight* 3 (January 1924): 2, 6. The Appalachian Power Company put out this brief newsletter. Box 1 of the Huddle Family Papers holds a copy of this issue.

8. W. O. Borcherdt, "The New Austinville Shaft and Mill," *Zinc* 13 (January 1928): 6–11.

Index

NEW DIRECTIONS IN SOUTHERN HISTORY

SERIES EDITORS
Michele Gillespie, *Wake Forest University*
William A. Link, *University of Florida*

The View from the Ground: Experiences of Civil War Soldiers
edited by Aaron Sheehan-Dean

Reconstructing Appalachia: The Civil War's Aftermath
edited by Andrew L. Slap

Blood in the Hills: A History of Violence in Appalachia
edited by Bruce E. Stewart

*Moonshiners and Prohibitionists: The Battle
over Alcohol in Southern Appalachia*
Bruce E. Stewart

Southern Farmers and Their Stories: Memory and Meaning in Oral History
Melissa Walker

Law and Society in the South: A History of North Carolina Court Cases
John W. Wertheimer